PASCAL AND BEYOND...
DATA ABSTRACTION
AND DATA STRUCTURES
USING TURBO PASCAL

PASCAL AND BEYOND...
DATA ABSTRACTION
AND DATA STRUCTURES
USING TURBO PASCAL

Steve Fisher

Apple Computer, Inc.

Stuart Reges

JOHN WILEY & SONS, INC.

New York   •   Chichester   •   Brisbane   •   Toronto   •   Singapore

Acquisitions Editor   Steven Elliot
Copy Editing Manager   Deborah Herbert
Production Manager   Linda Muriello
Senior Production Supervisor   Savoula Amanatidis
Text Designer   Lee Goldstein
Cover Designer   Karin Kincheloe
Cover Photo   Marjory Dressler
Illustration Coordinator   Sigmund Malinowski
Manufacturing Manager   Lorraine Fumoso

Recognizing the importance of preserving what has been written, it
is a policy of John Wiley & Sons, Inc. to have books of enduring
value published in the United States Printed on acid-free paper, and
we exert our best efforts to that end.

Library of Congress Cataloging in Publication Data:

Fisher, Stephen, 1964–
     Pascal and Beyond — data abstraction and data structures using
     Turbo Pascal / Steve Fisher, Stuart Reges.
          p. cm.
     Includes index.
     ISBN 0-471-50261-8
     1. Pascal (Computer program language) 2. Turbo Pascal (Computer program) I. Reges, Stuart. II. Title.
     QA76.73.P35F58 1992
     005.13'3—dc20   91-31406
                                                                          CIP

Printed in the United States of America

10 9 8 7 6 5 4 3 2 1

From Steve and Stuart
to Kathleen and Jean

FOREWORD

As long-time colleagues and friends of Steve Fisher and Stuart Reges, it gives us great pleasure to write the foreword to their new Computer Science 2 (CS 2) book.

The second course in programming is a critical one. At many schools, it is the gateway to advanced courses on a wide variety of subjects: compilers, databases, data structures, analysis of algorithms, operating systems, and others. Students often decide whether to major in computer science based on their performance in this course. Hence, besides covering the requisite material, this CS 2 course must also serve to encourage those students who would do well in the field.

Steve Fisher and Stuart Reges have written a fine book for this important course. It is organized around the specification, implementation, and use of abstract data types (ADTs). It is one of the few books in which ADTs are used not just as window dressing, but as a unifying framework for discussing many otherwise diverse topics in an integrated manner:

- Specification and documentation.
- Modularity and information hiding.
- Standard data types and data structures that implement them.
- Standard algorithms and programming techniques that implement them.
- Analysis of algorithms (complexity classes in big-O notation).
- Error checking and handling.

To convince students of the utility of ADTs, books must use and reuse them in believable contexts. The ADTs discussed in this book are all implemented as Pascal UNITs, which are consistently presented and analyzed. Each chapter, including the first one, reuses ADTs that were presented earlier, in applications like line buffering; parsing, and backtracking search. This pedagogy gives students a model of how to organize their own programs. The final chapter even includes a critique of ADTs, along with pragmatic tips for improving their run-time efficiency and error-handling. Overall, the breadth of coverage presents a realistic view of intermediate programming in computer science.

This book is also enjoyable to read and to teach from. Both Steve and Stuart are experienced instructors who have repeatedly taught CS 1 and CS 2, honing their approach to these courses and the examples that they have selected to present their approach. Both are top-notch instructors. (Don't take just our word for it; each has won a teaching award for his work in these courses at Stanford.) Individually they possess excellent teaching skills, and it shows collectively in their writing: their book is well organized, the material it covers is well presented, and it employs many good programming examples.

The book employs many interesting analogies and metaphors that often give students a deeper insight into topics than may first be apparent. Our personal favorites include:

- The comparison of the abstraction level of various household appliances in Chapter 1.
- The discussion of misbehavior in the street versus in the privacy of one's own home in Chapter 3.
- The description of the error-handling mechanism of pinball machines in Chapter 8.

Other, more traditional aspects of good pedagogy include a thorough coverage of recursion, moving from easy-to-explain examples to more subtle recursive algorithms, and a presentation that emphasizes the intuition behind analyzing algorithms and solving recurrence relations.

No book is perfect: one of us thinks the book should contain more case studies; the other would prefer it to use Ada as the language of discourse. We both think the authors use the word "tricky" too often. But for teaching a CS 2 course in Pascal, this book gets our highest rating (two thumbs up).

Mike Clancy and Rich Pattis

PREFACE

This book is intended for a second course in computer science. We wrote the book because we were unhappy with the presentation of the material in the books available and because we wanted to move our course in a new direction. It was obvious that data abstraction was of increasing concern both in industry and in academia. It was equally obvious that Pascal was inadequate for teaching the fundamentals of data abstraction. The idea for the book came when Borland announced that starting with version 4.0 their product Turbo Pascal would have a special construct called a "unit" that would have most of the features of what has come to be called a "module" in other languages (i.e., a collection of procedures, functions, and related definitions supporting a separation of specification and implementation[1]). We were further encouraged by the almost simultaneous announcement by Think Technologies that their product LightSpeed Pascal would support the same construct with almost exactly the same syntax.

The use of modules to encapsulate what are known as "abstract data types" or ADTs was well known to instructors teaching students to program in the languages Modula and Ada, but the new unit construct allowed us to apply the same idea to Pascal. We reworked our entire course to include ADTs wherever possible. The results surprised even us. We knew that because most of the course time was spent teaching

---

[1] Don't worry if you don't understand all these terms yet. They will be explained in much greater detail later.

data structures, ADTs would blend well with the material we were covering. We were pleasantly surprised to find that ADTs also simplified both our coverage of recursion and the recursive programming assignments we gave to our students by moving unimportant data structure details into modules. And far from being a burden, the teaching of modules and ADTs gave us a concrete framework for teaching the software engineering techniques that previously had been taught at a theoretical level. Finally, the use of modules allowed us to assign an ambitious group project that would have been impossible to coordinate using Standard Pascal.

The writing style of the book matches a teaching style that we find highly successful. We have written the book in a conversational style and have used humor whenever possible to liven up material that might otherwise seem boring. You will almost certainly deduce from reading the text that one of us is a baseball fan and that the other loves movies, but we think that a personal touch makes the book more enjoyable to read. We also make extensive use of analogies and carefully developed examples to make the material accessible to a wider audience. Most of the students we have taught have not been computer science majors. Our experience suggests that almost anyone can master this material, and we have written a book that we hope will be accessible to most college students and to advanced high school students.

The book is divided into two parts. The "core" material, Chapters 1 to 5, introduces data abstraction, recursion, and two fundamental data structures. The remaining chapters cover more advanced material. The book presents the core material around the unifying theme of abstraction, with each chapter building on the previous chapters. Thus, these chapters are designed to be taught in the given order. Chapters 5 to 8, however, may be used as the instructor sees fit.

The book begins by focusing directly on abstraction. Chapter 1 introduces the concept, first by showing how it applies to real-world examples, and then by discussing the already familiar use of *procedural abstraction* in programming. It concludes by introducing the *Unit* programming construct and by describing how *procedural abstraction* can be taken to a higher level by creating utility modules. It includes a *case study* of the development and use of one such utility module. Chapter 2 then covers *data abstraction* in depth, developing several Abstract Data Types (ADTs), from a simple Fraction type to sophisticated Table ADT.

With the foundation established in the first two chapters, Chapter 3 then embarks on a slightly different tack, focusing on using recursion to solve problems. Chapters 4 and 5 use these recursive techniques while exploring the *linked list* and *binary tree* data structures. Each of these chapters concludes with a different implementation of the Table ADT introduced in Chapter 2, thus showing some of the power of the ADT approach (the ability to change an ADT's implementation without having to change the programs that use the ADT) while demonstrating some of the more advanced uses for linked lists and binary trees.

The remaining chapters comprise the more advanced material. Chapter 6 introduces students to Algorithm Analysis at an intuitive level but also presents a significant mathematical foundation, including using recurrence relations to analyze the running time behavior of recursive algorithms. Chapter 7 first discusses *graphs* on an intuitive level, and then gives them a mathematical representation. The chapter then describes a Graph ADT for storing data in graphs, giving two implementations for this ADT (a simple one and an efficient one). The remainder of the chapter consists of a comprehensive introduction to various graph algorithms (transitive closure, all shortest paths, topological sort, etc.). All of these algorithms are first described abstractly, then by example, and finally through an implementation in Pascal using the Graph ADT. The final chapter presents two topics. It first discusses some more advanced ADT techniques, including when it is appropriate to define an ADT and concludes with a presentation on *loop invariants* and how they can be a very useful technique in both program development and proofs of program correctness.

The book also has three appendices. The first reproduces all the Units implemented throughout the chapters, for easy reference. Appendix B provides solutions to exercises. The book includes three types of exercises: *self check exercises* which appear at strategic points within the chapters, are designed to be relatively straightforward checks on whether the student has understood the new material; *programming exercises*, which appear at the end of every chapter, are small programming problems (typically a single procedure); and *programming projects*, which are designed to take a significant amount of time (1–2 weeks), explore in depth the material in the chapter where they appear and in previous chapters. Appendix B includes solutions for all the self-check exercises and the odd programming exercises. The third appendix describes the programming style used throughout the text.

The course we taught using this book was similar to the CS 2 course described in the Communications of the ACM in August, 1985. The new directions that we took are similar to those outlined in "Computing Curricula 1991" published by the ACM/IEEE-CS Joint Curriculum Task Force. This course, more than almost any other in the curriculum, has a balance of the three fundamental processes identified in the report: theory, abstraction, and design. As noted above, abstraction is the underlying theme of the course. The use of modules allows us to show how the process of abstraction can improve the design of a program or data type or utility module. And the most fundamental corresponding theory is also introduced: the efficiency of programs as described by using big-Oh notation. The report goes on to mention recurring concepts that should be stressed and "knowledge units" that should be covered. Our book is unified by the concept of levels of abstraction, and it also makes significant reference to the concepts of reuse and efficiency. The knowledge units covered by our book include AL1, AL2, AL3, AL4, AL6, SE1, and some of SE5.

Steve Fisher
Stuart Reges

ACKNOWLEDGEMENTS

We received excellent feedback from our reviewers:

Ivan Liss, Radford University
Thomas Mcmillian, Radford University
Jeff Parker, Boston College
Mandayan A. Srinivas, California State University—Pomona
Alan Tharp, Boston College
Charles Williams, Georgia State University

We also received much excellent free advice from Mike Cleron, who worked as a lecturer at Stanford at the same time we did. We would like to acknowledge a group of individuals who, although they might not have directly influenced the contents of this book, have greatly influenced our general thinking about computer science and computer science education: Owen Atrachan (Duke), Doug Cooper, Peter Henderson (SUNY/Stony Brook), and Roy Jones. Finally, we owe special thanks to Rich Pattis (University of Washington) and Mike Clancy (University of California at Berkeley) for serving as reviewers, giving us guidance, encouraging us and, more generally, for being smart people who argued with us just enough to make us carefully think through our approach.

S. F.
S. R.

LIST OF FIGURES

CONTENTS

2 DATA ABSTRACTION   49

3 RECURSION   99

4 LINKED LISTS   153

6 SORTING, SEARCHING, AND ALGORITHM ANALYSIS   262

1

INTRODUCTION TO ABSTRACTION

1.1. INTRODUCTION

This chapter introduces basic terminology and fundamental techniques used throughout the text. It begins with a discussion of *abstraction*. One of the more interesting definitions of the word in *Webster's Ninth Collegiate Dictionary* is

Abstract: difficult to understand: ABSTRUSE **

There is an unfortunate level of truth in this characterization. Abstraction is the most difficult concept you must master to work through this book. It is also the common thread that holds together the course and the most powerful programming technique presented.

It is difficult to explain to a non-computer-scientist the tremendous importance of the concept of abstraction. Computer science is still a relatively young discipline and, as such, it hasn't quite decided what it's all about. But even at this stage, abstraction stands out as the most common unifying element of the discipline. Many computer scientists believe that the use of abstraction is the most significant characteristic that distinguishes them from mathematicians, engineers, physicists, and other technically inclined people, especially the ease with which computer scientists quickly jump levels of abstraction, solving a problem on several levels all at once.

Before you can fully understand what that means, you will need to learn more about what abstraction is and how it is applied to programming. The term is first introduced using an intuitive description. Then, after introducing other basic terminology, this intuitive notion of abstraction is tied more concretely to programming. You will find that you already know a lot about the kind of abstraction associated with actions: *procedural abstraction*. Although you might not have heard the specific term used, it turns out that procedural abstraction was the theme of the course you took prior to this one. The chapter reviews those principles, casting them in terms of abstraction.

This chapter ends by introducing a construct not available in Standard Pascal that provides opportunities for procedural abstraction at a higher level than what you've seen before.

1.2. TERMINOLOGY

1.2.1. Abstraction: The Intuition

Although it wasn't advertised as such, Diane Keaton's film *Baby Boom* included a serious treatment of abstraction as it relates to plumbing. In a dramatic scene where Diane has just learned that the well of her country home is dry and that she can't simply use the garden hose to fill it back up, she pleads, "I just want to turn on the faucet and have water come out. I *don't* want to know where it *comes from*." At this point, Diane screams and faints, underscoring her basic need for abstraction in this domain.

Diane has captured on film an all-too-common emotional experience. A complex problem can often seem overwhelming when it presents too many pieces of information for your brain to simultaneously process. This can be particularly true of significant programming problems where the level of detail can quickly exceed the mental capacity of even the brightest students. *Nobody* is immune to this problem. At some point we all find it necessary to learn new techniques for conquering complexity.

The most powerful technique for handling such details in the realm of programming is *abstraction*. It is impossible to capture in a single sentence the many shades of meaning attributed to this term, but you have to start somewhere, so you might as well start with a somewhat abstract definition of the word.

ABSTRACTION
· ·
Reasoning about the essential properties of an object, ignoring unimportant details.

Thus, the first step in abstraction is to examine an overly complex collection of facts and to distinguish between high-level information and low-level information:

The second step is to pull out the high-level information:

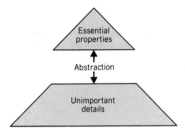

This leaves you a less complex problem to solve on the third step.

If all goes well, the work that you perform at this higher level of abstraction will provide a framework for solving the remaining details.

As an example of abstraction, let's consider four common kitchen devices. A cook must understand the interface of a device before applying it. Consider the extent to which that interface has been abstracted. Abstract devices are those whose interface is understood in terms of inputs and outputs, allowing a cook to ignore the internal details of the device. Cooks can use such devices even if the method they use to accomplish their goal is a complete mystery. Nonabstract devices are those that require a cook to understand all the details of the device's operation.

- *Apple corer.* This is a round metal device that you place on top of an apple and push downward, splitting the apple into its core and several slices. There is no abstraction here. The cook must understand the process to make it work (e.g., to know exactly where to place it).
- *Microwave oven.* The interface is completely abstract: food to be heated and settings for power level and cooking duration are the inputs; hot food is the output.
- *Barbeque.* It would be convenient to use this device with an abstract interface, opening up the grill to pour in the inputs (charcoal, lighter fluid, a lit match, steaks), then switching it on and relaxing until it produces the desired output

(barbequed steaks). Unfortunately, the phrase "slaving over a hot grill" is no exaggeration. To use this device a cook must understand its process in detail.

• *Sink/tap.* This brings us back to Diane Keaton's performance in *Baby Boom*. Most cooks concur that water should simply appear when the tap is turned on. Fortunately modern plumbing provides just such an abstract interface: the cook inputs a desired water flow level (i.e., turns the spigot to adjust the stream of water) and the faucet outputs an appropriate stream of water.

Thus, the apple corer and barbeque are much less abstract than the microwave and sink/tap. It also seems reasonable to classify the apple corer as less abstract than the barbeque because at least the barbeque has some degree of abstraction (e.g., you don't need to know what makes the charcoal burn). Similarly, the sink/tap can't compete with the microwave for highest abstraction classification. This spectrum of abstraction can be expressed as follows:

Increasing Abstraction						
apple corer	$\rightarrow$	barbecue	$\rightarrow$	sink/tap	$\rightarrow$	microwave

Another dimension that can be used to classify devices is the degree of generality.

GENERALITY
· ·
The extent to which a device can be applied to many similar tasks rather than a few specific tasks.

Consider the four kitchen devices from the abstraction example. How do they rate from highest to lowest for generality? This question is not without doubt, but a plausible ranking is as follows.

• *Microwave.* This device can perform cooking tasks like an oven, can boil water like a stove, and is the only device that readily defrosts meat. If this still isn't enough evidence, the microwave's superior generality is certainly demonstrated in the movie *Gremlins* where it even proves useful in exterminating unwanted and downright dangerous household pests.

• *Barbeque.* While this device can be applied only to heating food, that covers quite a lot of the tasks a cook is most interested in. Furthermore, it provides the option to cook food directly on the grill, "smoking" extra flavor into it, or to simply use it as an ordinary heat source (e.g., to boil a pan of water).

• *Sink/tap.* Sinks are another multipurpose device. They can be used not only to fill various cooking devices with water, but also to wash dishes, wash clothes, provide water to wash the floor, and cool hot pots.

- *Apple corer.* This device is not general at all. There are few "coring" and "slicing" tasks in the domain of cooking. Even within those tasks, this device is not general. For example, this device cannot remove artichoke hearts, nor can it slice watermelons.

Thus, placing these four items on a spectrum of generality you get (with one to the far left and three to the far right):

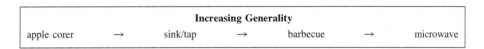

Increasing Generality

apple corer → sink/tap → barbecue → microwave

Combining these two dimensions, you get the following distribution:

1.2.2. Other Basic Terminology

Most engineering problems can be thought of as starting with a *specification* and ending with an *implementation*.

SPECIFICATION

A detailed description of the essential properties of an object. In programming, a complete description of a program unit's *required* behavior.

IMPLEMENTATION

An object built to satisfy a specification. In programming, a program unit written to behave as specified. Not all behavior is specified, which gives the implementor some flexibility in deciding *implementation specific* behavior.

The difference between specification and implementation is really the difference between "what" and "how": what an object does versus how it does it.

As an example, think about the class of objects known as "humidifiers." A concise specification can be found in *Webster's Ninth New Collegiate Dictionary*:

Humidifier: a device for supplying or maintaining humidity

This is the "what" part, the description of the desired behavior. What implementations are possible?

- One approach is to boil water to form steam, which is released as the source of humidity.
- Another approach uses a wheel composed of many thin bristles. This wheel rotates rapidly with the bristles agitating the surface of the water. The result is that tiny drops of moisture are propelled into the air, serving as the source of humidity.

Both approaches satisfy the specification, so both are considered valid implementations. This is the "how" part, an object that uses specific behavior (boiling or agitating) to produce the specified behavior.

You might think that to an engineer, all implementations that meet the specification are created equal. This is partially true. Probably the ultimate expression of such equality is in the creation of what are called *Rube Goldberg machines*.[1] The goal of a Rube Goldberg machine is to perform a simple task in the most complex way possible. For example, here is a Rube Goldberg humidifier:

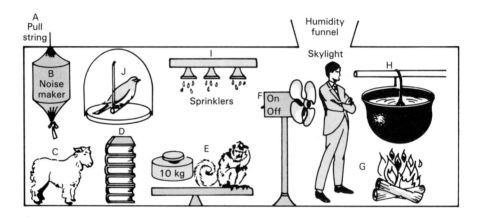

The device works as follows:

A. The string is pulled.
B. The noisemaker goes off, startling the sheep underneath.
C. The sheep leaps forward, knocking over the pile of books.
D. The books land on the balance on the side with the 10 kg weight, tipping that side down.
E. The monkey on the other side of the balance is tipped up, allowing him to reach the fan's on/off switch.

---

[1] Named for an American cartoonist whose drawings popularized the concept.

    F. The monkey switches the fan on, making the space next door colder.

    G. The man doesn't like the cold, so he lights the fire.

    H. The fire heats the soup kettle, generating a delicious steamy aroma.

    I. The soup aroma builds and builds until the entire room is full of steam, causing the sprinklers to activate.

    J. The water from the sprinklers and the steam from the soup fill the room with so much moisture in the air that tweetie, in extreme desperation, escapes from his cage and breaks through the skylight, releasing a rush of humid air.

Even though this device is absurdly complex, it meets the specification. Thus, this constitutes another valid implementation.

By carrying implementation to an absurd extreme, Rube Goldberg machines illustrate several important points. First, any specification can be implemented in an endless variety of ways, all equally "correct." Second, it's not really true that all implementations are created equal. They can obviously differ in complexity, efficiency, cost, number of required live animals, and numerous other dimensions that might be important to consider. Finally, Rube Goldberg machines are a beautiful illustration of the need for *abstraction*. Although it might be fun to trace the pattern of steps in such a machine, it is obvious that to reason about the machine as a whole, you must ignore its inner details and think in terms of its interface, often expressed using the black box model.

INTERFACE

. . . .

The way in which an object interacts with its external environment. In programming, a description of how a programming unit is invoked from its external program environment (e.g., parameter passing conventions) along with a list of any dependencies that exist between the two (e.g., global variables used by the unit).

BLACK BOX MODEL

. . . .

Viewing an object in terms of its interface, ignoring all internal details, pretending that the internal environment is completely hidden inside a black box. In programming, viewing a program element in terms of its interface while ignoring its inner details (e.g., local variables and algorithm).

A black box view of the Rube Goldberg Humidifier should focus on those elements of the machine that are visible to the external world. From the point of view of an outsider, all you know is that a string is pulled, something happens inside the humidifier, and humidity comes out the funnel. Thus, a black box diagram of the device would be drawn as follows:

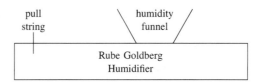

In general, black box diagrams use arrows to indicate the inputs to a device and the resulting outputs. For example, a similar black box diagram can be drawn for the generic humidifier specification, with input in this case being a signal to turn on the device and output being humidity.

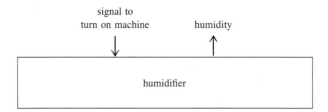

Now consider how specification, implementation, interface, and the black-box model apply to subprograms. For example, consider the following function for calculating x to the nth power.

```
function Power (x, n: integer): integer;
var
  PROD, I: integer;
begin
  PROD := 1;
  for I := 1 to n do begin
    PROD := PROD * x;
  end; (* For *)
  Power := PROD;
end; (* Power *)
```

Which lines make up the "what" part of this function, its specification? Which make up the "how" part, the implementation? Using the black-box approach, you can describe the function as follows:

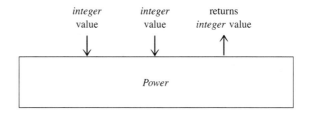

The function has no external dependencies, so this completely describes *Power*'s interface. It is a black box that expects to be fed two integers and it sends back an integer. This interface is part of *Power*'s specification, but it obviously isn't enough. For example, consider the *Max* function that calculates the maximum of two integers:

```
function Max (x, y: integer): integer;
begin
 if x > y then begin
   Max := x;
  end
 else begin
   Max := y;
 end; (* If *)
end; (* Max *)
```

It has the same black box specification as *Power*:

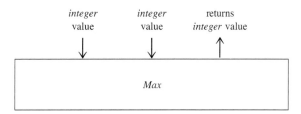

Thus, *Power* and *Max* have the same interface. But they aren't the same function. This is the difference between syntax and semantics. They have the same syntactic behavior in that both are integer functions with two integer arguments. But they have different semantics, different meaning.

Describing the semantics of the subprograms that make up a complete program solution is similar to describing the workers on an assembly line. Charlie Chaplin in *Modern Times* introduced a character that has become almost a comedy archetype by exploring the potential disasters brought on by a worker who doesn't keep up. When one worker fails his task, a domino effect prevents those who follow from performing their tasks. Each worker expects to find the assembly line in a certain *state* when he goes to perform his task (e.g., he expects four bolts loosely screwed onto a device). The worker, in turn, guarantees that the assembly line will be in a new state when he is done (e.g., the four bolts will be tightly screwed onto the device). Such dependencies are usually expressed by *preconditions* and *postconditions*.

PRECONDITIONS OF A SUBPROGRAM

A set of conditions that must be true before a subprogram is invoked. If one or more of the preconditions fail when the subprogram is invoked, it is not guaranteed to perform its intended task.

POSTCONDITIONS OF A SUBPROGRAM
· ·
A set of conditions that will be true when a subprogram terminates provided the subprogram preconditions were true when the subprogram was invoked.

The preconditions describe the initial state expected by the subprogram. Thus, by
adding preconditions to a subprogram you are *simplifying* it by specifying assumptions
it can make. The postconditions describe the extent of the task performed by the
subprogram. Thus, by adding postconditions to a subprogram, you are *complicating* it.

Functions *Power* and *Max* do not have assembly-line kind of dependencies, because they are general utilities. But preconditions are useful not only for expressing
these kind of dependencies, but also in describing any unusual circumstances that
would prevent proper subprogram execution. Because *Power* is an integer-valued function, it cannot return the result obtained from a negative exponent. This introduces
the precondition that the exponent be nonnegative.

Both *Power* and *Max* have the postcondition that they return their function value.
Thus, combining the function headers that specify the syntactic interface and the
pre/postconditions that specify the semantic details, the two functions are specified as
follows:

```
function Power (x, n: integer): integer;
        pre     n >= 0
        post    returns x^n

function Max (x, y: integer): integer;
        post    returns the maximum of x and y
```

This format of subprogram header along with pre/postconditions is used throughout
the book to specify subprograms.

By process of elimination, whatever isn't part of the specification has to be part
of the implementation. Thus, the implementation of function *Power* includes its entire
body along with all its local declarations and its execution part. This is what's inside
the black box, the internal details you would find only if you could open it up.

```
var
  PROD, I: integer;
begin
  PROD := 1;
  for I := 1 to n do begin
    PROD := PROD * x;
  end; (* For *)
  Power := PROD;
end; (* Power *)
```

Similarly, the implementation of function *Max* includes its entire body:

```
begin
  if x > y then begin
    Max := x;
  end
  else begin
    Max := y;
  end; (* If *)
end; (* Max *)
```

Thus, local declarations and details of execution for a subprogram are inside the black box, part of the implementation not available to the outside world.

1.2.3. Software Engineering and the Need for Modules

A new discipline called software engineering has steadily emerged over the last ten years. Most people who call themselves software engineers are particularly interested in the creation and maintenance of very large programs (100,000+ lines of code), and especially sensitive realtime applications where there is no margin for error (e.g., a program to assist air-traffic controllers where even a brief period of poor program performance could cost lives, or a program to control a nuclear missile, where a program bug could start a world war).

Good software engineering is not possible in Standard Pascal. Although Pascal does a good job of supporting the engineering of procedures and functions, it does not provide a similar mechanism for types and it provides no high-level structural units other than a monolithic single program. Think of how frustrating it would be, for example, to make a series of minor changes to a 100,000-line program written in Pascal where you are forced to recompile all 100,000 lines of code even for the most trivial of changes.

Many software engineers are exploring objected-oriented programming languages such as SmallTalk and C++, but for the most part the *lingua franca* of the software engineering community is a programming language called Ada.[2] It was designed in the late 1970s when, in response to what has been called the *software crisis* of rising software maintenance costs, the Department of Defense launched a major initiative to create a language that would facilitate more reliable and more cost-effective software projects. Ada is increasing in popularity, although it has not emerged as the preferred language of any significant group outside the software-engineering community.

If Ada is the language for software engineering, where does that leave Pascal? Pascal and Ada are actually quite similar in philosophy. Although software engineers might try to convince you that Ada is better than Pascal, they will certainly recommend Pascal over Fortran, Cobol, BASIC, and other languages that didn't grow out of the

---

[2] Named after Ada, the Countess of Lovelace, (1815–1851), a British mathematician and contemporary of Charles Babbage, who is the earliest known person to discuss the notion of programming in her work with Babbage's difference and analytic engines.

structured-programming community. The principal differences stem from the fact that
Pascal was designed ten years before Ada and its designer, Niklaus Wirth, set out to
design a language as simple as possible, versus the Ada effort where DOD wanted to
be sure to include everything they might ever want.

Pascal is a good software engineering vehicle for the first course. But you have
reached the point where Pascal runs out of gas. Fortunately, the addition of the following construct to the language extends its usefulness into, and even beyond, this
second course.

MODULE

A separately compiled program unit that can be used to collect related constants,
types, variables, and subprograms in such a way that any program or module can
access module elements that have been designated *public*, while only the source module
can access module elements that have been designated *private*.

Around the same time that Ada was being finalized, Niklaus Wirth, the designer
of Pascal, introduced a new language, which he called Modula-2 because, as he says
in the language specification, "Modules are the most important feature distinguishing
Modula-2 from its ancestor, Pascal." Modula-2 has gained popularity since its introduction, and many software engineers actually prefer it over Ada as a teaching tool
because it has the most important language constructs while remaining a relatively
simple language.

But then modules came to Pascal in the form of a language extension rather
than a complete redesign. In the late 1970s a variant of Pascal known as UCSD
Pascal suddenly gained prominence because it was the most sophisticated programming
language available on the Apple II microcomputer. One of the more impressive features
of UCSD Pascal was a construct called a *unit*, which provides the same functionality
as a module. This construct has appeared in all Pascal variants introduced by Apple
ever since. But it wasn't until Borland International introduced version 4.0 of their
popular Turbo Pascal for MS-DOS machines that the unit construct became common
enough to justify the kind of attention this book gives to it.

This language extension is extremely important. Your authors would not even
have attempted this book if they couldn't use units to explore advanced programming
and new abstraction techniques. Although they are called "units" in Turbo Pascal, this
book more often uses the more commonly used term "modules," and occasionaly the
Ada term "packages."

The syntax and details of the unit construct are not introduced until Section 1.3,
but because this construct is so fundamental to what you'll be studying in this book,
the distinguishing characteristics of modules in general are included below.

> A module is, in many ways, like a program. It can contain any number of
> constants, types, variables, procedures, and functions. But it has no main pro-
> gram specifying actions to be performed. Modules in general (and the Turbo
> implementation of units) allow a begin/end block that appears in the same

place as a main program, but for a module these instructions list initialization steps. Whenever a program includes such a module, the module initialization is performed before the program begins executing.

- Modules are divided into public specification or interface parts and private implementation parts. This separation aids the implementor of the module by allowing sensitive elements to be protected from outside interference. This separation aids users of the module by providing a useful abstraction of the module, allowing them to ignore the uninteresting details of the private part and to instead focus on its interface.

- Modules can be compiled separately. By breaking a large program into smaller modules, a programmer can reduce "dead-time" spent waiting for the system to start executing the program.

- Although it is possible to move procedures and functions from one program to another, the process of physically copying lines of code between files is sufficiently tedious that many programmers don't often take advantage of such reusabilty. With modules you can collect powerful procedures and functions into libraries that are easily accessed by all your programs. This allows you to share code more readily between programs and to keep a single centralized version of each subprogram, which is much easier to modify and maintain than a subprogram whose definition appears in many different program files.

- Like the global variables of a program, the global variables of a module exist for the duration of program execution, unlike local subprogram variables that are allocated and deallocated on each invocation. This ability to store values in an ongoing fashion provides the continuity necessary to solve many complex problems and many problems whose solution is otherwise needlessly awkward.

1.2.4. Other Software Engineering Terminology

This book's focus on basic software engineering principles is exceeded only by the overall theme of data abstraction. As a result, you should review basic software engineering terminology.

There is so much overlap between computer science and software engineering that you shouldn't imagine that each has its own terminology. Abstraction is important in software engineering as well, and the concepts of specification, implementation, interface, and black box diagrams are, in fact, engineering terms more than computer science terms.

While abstraction is the most fundamental concept unifying computer science, the domain of software engineering is unified by the combination of abstraction and decomposition.

DECOMPOSITION
· ·
A separation into discernible parts, each of which is simpler than the whole.

When you divide a program into subprograms, you are applying decomposition. This is the basic technique of structured programming and should be quite familiar to you by now. In this book you will see how decomposition techniques can be applied to divide a program into two or more modules and to divide a complex data structure into two or more types.

Abstraction is a mental process whose subject may or may not be the details of actual code. When abstraction is applied to coding and you create a program unit that embodies the abstraction, you are using a programming technique called information hiding.

INFORMATION HIDING/ENCAPSULATION
. . . .
Embedding the details of a program element *inside* the element in such a way that when it is applied, its inner details do not have to be known. Ideally the inner details are so well hidden that not only are they not needed, they are not even available (usually thought of as "invisible" to the outside).

Thus far we've talked about techniques. Software engineering also has many goals. For example, a software engineer strives for a program that is:

*   **modifiable** when new behavior is desired or when bugs are encountered,
*   **efficient** in its use of program resources (principally memory and execution time),
*   **reliable** in that it behaves as expected and provides reasonable feedback when errors occur.

Modifiability is discussed at length throughout the book; efficiency is the subject of Chapter 6, and reliability is briefly introduced in Chapter 8.

Like other engineers, software engineers think not only in terms of complete systems (i.e., complete programs), but also in terms of *reusable components*. A piece of stereo equipment is called a component only if it can be easily moved from one system to another. For example, if you open up a simple radio, you'll find a loudspeaker inside connected to the radio by wires soldered onto the loudspeaker. Such a device is not easy to disconnect from its system. A component speaker is connected to its system by wires that plug into standard input jacks, allowing it to be easily disconnected from one system and moved to another.

To qualify as a software component, a program unit must be sufficiently encapsulated that it can be easily reused in other programs. For example, a procedure that makes reference to global variables is not well-encapsulated and is not easily "disconnected" from its system. The references to global variables are not unlike the wires soldered onto the loudspeaker in a simple radio. When you try to remove the loudspeaker by tugging on it, you find the cumbersome wires attaching it to the system. When you try to remove the procedure by copying it to another program, you find syntax errors that indicate its cumbersome links to the old program. Conversely, a procedure with parameters can be easily "unplugged" from one program and "plugged back in" to another. Plugging in a procedure with parameters simply involves calling it with an appropriate list of parameters. Just as the component speaker can be plugged into any device using standard stereo jacks, the procedure can be copied to any program and invoked using the appropriate set of parameters.

Subprogram components that are used frequently are called *software utilities*. A module collecting such components is known as a *utility module*.

1.2.5. Abstraction versus Decomposition

Decomposition and abstraction are so closely related that people often confuse them. They both start by dividing up the overall problem:

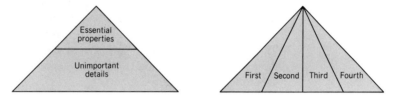

Then they separate the overall problem using this division:

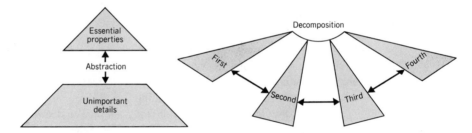

You rarely solve a programming problem using only one of these techniques. Decomposition always involves abstraction, but abstraction is more independent. A person who has the insight to abstract a problem and reason about it at a high level will see a number of possible approaches, simple decomposition being just one such approach.

Thus, in solving a problem, abstraction happens first. As a result of reasoning about the problem at this higher level of abstraction, you will often decompose the overall problem into a series of manageable subproblems. This series of steps is summarized in the following diagram.

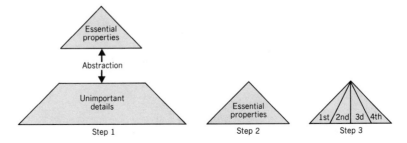

1.2.6. Procedural Abstraction

Procedural abstraction is control- or action-oriented. The only mechanism in Standard Pascal for establishing procedural abstraction is the subprogram (procedures and functions). Abstraction appears in subprograms in several places.

- By naming subprograms, a programmer can assign an abstract description that captures the overall meaning of the subprogram. Using the name instead of writing down the code allows the programmer to apply the action in terms of its high-level description rather than its low-level details.
- Pascal subprograms provide information hiding. Local variables and any other local definitions are encapsulated by the subprogram, actually hiding them to the point where they cannot even be detected from outside the subprogram. Thus, the programmer does not have to worry about potential interference of these local definitions and can use the component without knowing anything about these local details.
- Subprogram parameters, along with the information hiding noted above, allow you to create subprograms that qualify as true software components. Local implementation details can be hidden inside while parameters can be used to establish the desired interface.

Sometimes your abstraction of a subprogram might include parameters (e.g., it's hard to conceive of a sorting procedure that isn't given something to sort), but parameters are more often a good example of establishing generality. Abstraction has much more to do with naming and information hiding.

As an example, consider the following alternative definition of function *Power*. It is not as immediately obvious that this version of the function works. It was written using something called a *loop invariant* explained in Chapter 8. In fact, this version not only returns the same results as the previous one, it does so in much less time (e.g., this version requires only 10 iterations of its loop to calculate 2^{120}, while the previous version requires 120 iterations of its loop).

```
function Power (x, n: integer): integer;
 var
  I,J,K: integer;
begin
 I := 1;
 J := x;
 K := n;
 while K <> 0 do begin
    (* invariant : I * J^K = x^n *)
   if K mod 2 = 0 then begin
    K := K div 2;
    J := J * J;
   end
   else begin
```

```
        K := K - 1;
        I := I * J;
      end; (* If *)
    end; (* While *)
  Power := I;
  end; (* Power *)
```

Both versions of function *Power* have the same interface. Looking inside the black boxes, though, you find several differences. The first version of the function has two local variables whereas the second has three. The first has a *for* loop whereas the second has a *while* loop. And as noted before, the first requires more execution time than the second. Thus, the implementation details of the two functions are quite different.

Power is a good example of a software component and a software utility. It constitutes a component because its definition has been sufficiently abstracted and encapsulated that these two versions of the function can be used interchangeably, with no change necessary to the program using them. It constitutes a utility because programmers often find themselves wanting to raise one integer to another integer power.

1.2.7. SELF CHECK EXERCISES

1. Why are the local variables of a procedure considered to be inside the black box of a procedure or function? What change to Pascal rules would put them outside the black box?

2. Give a specification for the built-in Pascal operation *ln* that returns the natural log of its real-valued argument.

1.3. UTILITY MODULES

You've spent enough time reading about modules. Now it's time for some concrete examples. This section explains the syntax and calling conventions common to all modules, although the specific examples presented are utility modules.

1.3.1. Using a Unit

To make use of a utility module, a program needs to list it in a *uses clause*. The extended syntax of the program is as follows (with the uses clause immediately following the program header and preceding other declarations).

```
program <header>

<uses clause>
```

```
<const, type, and var declarations>

<procedure and function declarations>

begin
    <statement sequence defining main program>
end.
```

The uses clause is either empty or of the form

```
uses <module name>, <module name>, ..., <module name>;
```

As in

```
uses
 Math, Stack;
```

The uses clause has several effects. First, it causes the public definitions from each of the named modules to become accessible to this program. For example, module *Math* includes the functions *Power* and *Max* examined earlier. Thus, a program that includes the clause above can make direct reference to these functions, as in

```
begin
 writeln('Two to the tenth power is ', Power(2, 10));
 ...
end. (* Main *)
```

It is conceivable that one of the module's public elements will have a name that clashes with some other identifier (e.g., you might define a variable called *Power*, or two different modules might declare the identifier *Max*). Every time such a clash occurs, the old definition is wiped out by the new one. Because all your definitions appear after the uses clause, none of the identifiers you introduce will ever be overridden by module variables. But module identifiers can be overridden by you or by other modules.

Even when an identifier is defined multiple times, all the individual elements can be referred to using a *fully qualified identifier*. It has the same syntax as that used to refer to the fields of a record:

```
<unit name> . <identifier>
```

For example, *Math.Power* and *Math.Max* always refer to the *Power* and *Max* functions from module *Math*, even if the simple identifiers *Power* and *Max* are redefined.

Although the syntax of simple identifiers is in many ways more convenient, it soon becomes impractical and even dangerous to use as you start writing very large programs that use many modules. As a result, this book always uses the dot-notation of fully qualified identifiers.

The *uses* clause has a few more subtleties that should be mentioned. First, including the *uses* clause in your main program causes each of the initialization parts (if any) of the named modules to be executed. These are executed in order starting with the first module named after the word *uses*.

A program unit must mention the name of a module in a *uses* clause if and only if it makes use of some element of that module. The "if" part of this statement seems rather obvious: if a program unit is going to use something defined in a module, it should list that module in its *uses* clause. The "only if" part of this statement is less obvious. What happens, for example, if a main program uses module *Big*, and module *Big* uses module *Little?* Does the main program have to mention both *Big* and *Little* in its *uses* clause? As the "only if" part of the statement makes clear, the main program has to mention module *Little* only if it makes a direct reference to an element of the module. Otherwise it simply lists *Big* in its *uses* clause (although *Little* would have to be mentioned in the *uses* clause for *Big* following the same principle).

1.3.2. The Syntax of Units

The syntax for units is as follows:

```
unit <unit name>;

interface

    <uses clause>

    <public constants, types, and variables>

    <headers for public procedures/functions>

implementation

    <uses clause>

    <private constants, types, and variables>

    <private procedures/functions and
    bodies for public procedures/functions>

begin
    <statement sequence for initialization>
end.
```

Notice that the unit is divided into three parts: an interface section where the specifications for publicly available elements appear, an implementation section where implementation details are listed, and an initialization part with a series of statements to be executed before program execution begins so that this module is appropriately initialized. If a unit has no initialization to be performed, the *begin* before the final *end* can be omitted.

Each module can have a *uses* clause to access the public parts of other modules, just like the main program can. Notice that it can have such a clause both in its specification part and in its implementation part. In general, it is best to have this in the implementation part, unless the specification part makes reference to constants or types defined in other modules.

1.3.3. Simple Modules: Math and Chars

The simplest kind of module you can create is one that collects together a group of related utilities. For example, when manipulating characters, it is often useful to capitalize all characters. When capitalizing, sometimes it's more useful to have a procedure with a *var* parameter, and sometimes it's more useful to have a function that returns the capitalized character as its value. It is not uncommon for a utility module to provide two such variations of a single utility. Module *Chars*, specified in Figure 1.1, includes these two character utilities, along with another commonly used character-operation that writes a character to an output file a specified number of times.

Here is module *Chars* in its entirety.

```
unit Chars;

interface

   procedure Capitalize (var Value: char);
      (* post : if Value was initially a small letter,  *)
      (*      : it is now corresponding capital letter; *)
      (*      : Otherwise, Value is unchanged            *)

   function CapOf (Value: char): char;
      (* post : if Value is a small letter, returns *)
      (*      : the corresponding capital letter;    *)
      (*      : otherwise returns Value              *)

   procedure WriteChars (var OutFile: text;
         Number: integer;
         Value: char);
      (* pre  : OutFile is open for writing          *)
      (* post : Given number of occurrences of Value *)
      (*      : written to OutFile                    *)

   implementation

   procedure Capitalize (var Value: char);
   begin
     if Value in ['a'..'z'] then begin
       Value := chr(ord(Value) - ord('a') + ord('A'));
     end; (* If *)
   end; (* Capitalize *)
```

```
function CapOf (Value: char): char;
begin
 Capitalize(Value);
 CapOf := Value;
end; (* CapOf *)

procedure WriteChars (var OutFile: text;
       Number: integer;
       Value: char);
  var
   I: integer;
begin
 for I := 1 to Number do begin
   write(OutFile, Value);
  end; (* For *)
end; (* WriteChars *)

end. (* Chars *)
```

As another example of this kind of collection of useful utilities, consider commonly used mathematical operations, a module we will call *Math*.

Pascal provides no utilities for finding the maximum and minimum of two integers, nor for computing integer exponentiation, so these are all included in the module. Functions *Power* and *Max* have already been discussed, and function *Min* is so similar that it isn't included in Figure 1.2.

OVERVIEW
Character operations; provides two versions of the capitalizing operation and a utility for repeatedly sending the same character to an output file.

```
procedure Capitalize (var Value: char);
       post    if Value was initially a small letter, it is now
               the corresponding capital letter; otherwise,
               Value is unchanged

function CapOf (Value: char): char;
       post    if Value is a small letter, returns the
               corresponding capital letter; otherwise returns
               Value

procedure WriteChars (var OutFile: text; Number: integer;
       Value: char);
       pre     OutFile is open for writing
       post    Given number of occurrences of Value written to
               OutFile
```

FIGURE 1.1. Specification for utility module *Chars*.

```
OVERVIEW
Provides useful arithmetic constants and functions.

const    Pi = 3.14159265358979;
         E  = 2.71828182845904;

function Min (x, y: integer): integer;
        post    returns the minimum of x and y

function Max (x, y: integer): integer;
        post    returns the maximum of x and y

function Power (x, n: integer): integer;
        pre     x >= 0
        post    returns x to the nth power

procedure SwapInt (var X, Y: integer);
        post    The values of X and Y are exchanged

function GCD (X, Y: integer): integer;
        pre     (X <> 0) or (Y <> 0)
        post    returns the Greatest Common Divisor of X and Y

function LCM (X, Y: integer): integer;
        pre     (X <> 0) or (Y <> 0)
        post    returns the Least Common Multiple of X and Y

function Exponent (x, y: real): real;
        pre     x >= 0
        post    returns x to the yth power

function Tan (angle: real): real;
        pre     angle <> k * pi + (pi/2), k = some integer
        post    returns the tangent of angle

function ArcCos (TheCos: real): real;
        pre     -1 <= TheCos <= +1
        post    returns the arccosine of TheCos

function ArcSin (TheSin: real): real;
        pre     -1 <= TheSin <= +1
        post    returns the arcsine of TheSin

function Log (n: real): real;
        pre     n > 0
        post    returns the common log(base 10) of n

function Log2 (n: real): real;
        pre     n > 0
        post    returns the common log to the base 2 of n
```

FIGURE 1.2. Specification for utility module *Math*.

Pascal provides the functions *exp* and *ln*, which operate with base *e*, but it is often useful to work in other bases. The formulas for converting between bases are not difficult, but why memorize them when we can use abstraction and hide the details inside a set of utilities? Similarly, Pascal provides operations for a core of trigonometric functions from which the others can be calculated, but it's easier to work out the details of such calculations once, and then store the results in a utility.

Functions are also included in *Math* to calculate the greatest-common-divisor of a number and the least-common-multiple, along with a procedure for swapping two integer values.

As described in Figure 1.1, module *Math* includes a general real-valued exponentiation function, logarithms for base 2 and base 10, and the trigonometric functions tangent, arccosine and arcsine. These are all very similar in form, so they aren't reproduced here (the module appears in its entirety in Appendix I).

As a representative sample, here is the exponentiation function.

```
function Exponent (x, y: real): real;
(* pre  : y >= 0.                        *)
(* post : returns x to the yth power. *)
begin
 Exponent := exp(ln (x) * y);
end; (* Exponent *)
```

1.3.4. Module Variables

In Section 1.2.3 it was mentioned that modules can have their own variables that exist for the duration of execution, just like programs. These variables are most often accessed in a global manner (i.e., not passed as parameters). This book refers to such variables as *module variables*. Module variables turn out to be very important for modules. They will probably seem "wrong" to you at first because you've been trained to think that global references are not good style.

It's true that global variables are a bad idea in an environment where you are creating a single program file. Let's consider why. As programs get larger, the possibility for interference among procedures grows exponentially. Thus, in an environment like Standard Pascal where there is no high-level grouping mechanism other than a single main program, global variables quickly get out of hand.

Is the same true of a program divided into modules? There's nothing magical about modules that gives them immunity to such problems, which means that in a program and module of equal length, interference is equally likely. But they differ in that a module can always be split into smaller pieces. As long as you keep your module lengths reasonable, you will be able to handle any potential problems the global variables might introduce. This is particularly true if you have chosen a unifying theme for the module. For example, if the module provides subprograms for manipulating a deck of cards, it shouldn't be a problem to have a global variable for the deck of cards that all subprograms refer to.

This is similar to the way you act around family versus acting in public. When you're in public, you obey certain standards of behavior that are necessary to maintain the fabric of society. But you can be much more relaxed around your family, because the family unit is manageable in size, unlike society at large. You know your family members well, so you aren't surprised if your nephew jumps up and down on you while you're napping because he wants to play games with you. The family has a cohesion that holds it together despite the fact that much of the interaction that happens there would lead to trouble if it occurred between strangers.

Similarly, when you write short, thematic modules, you relax the normal rules of style. You can afford to have interaction in such a module. In fact, frequently the module variables are themselves the unifying element, which means there is little danger of unintended interference. If the module grows and starts to become too big to manage, split up the module into smaller modules that can be managed.

This explains why global module variables are not the terrible idea they are in a large Pascal program. Now let's look at the benefit you can gain from them. The answer is simple: abstraction. A module variable is automatically visible to all module subprograms, but it can be hidden from other modules. You will see numerous examples of this technique used in this book.

For example, consider a module that manipulates a deck of cards. While it's conceivable that you might want to manipulate more than one deck for some applications, the fact is that most card-playing tasks involve a single deck. You are used to writing operations like the following:

```
procedure Init (var Deck: DeckType);

procedure Shuffle (var Deck: DeckType);
```

By introducing a module variable for the deck, you can simplify the interface to these and other subprograms:

```
procedure Init;

procedure Shuffle;
```

This allows a programmer using the module to deal with it on a more abstract level. Every operation acts on the same deck of cards, so why force the programmer to declare a variable of the appropriate type and pass it on every call to the module? This way the programmer doesn't have to know that your type is called *DeckType*, doesn't have to declare an extra variable, and can use simpler parameter-passing. The following diagram summarizes this example.

Program Application; uses   Deck; simple interface, no knowledge of deck; Init; Shuffle;

unit Deck; var Deck: DeckType; (private, not available or visible outside) Init accesses Deck globally Shuffle accesses Deck globally

1.3.5. SELF CHECK EXERCISES

1. In writing a module that makes use of another module, when would you put the *uses* clause for the module in the interface part and when would you put it in the implementation part?

2. Suppose that you are writing a utility module that must keep track of a cumulative sum. If the value of the cumulative sum is to be stored in the module variable *TheSum*, would you want to include this declaration in the interface part of the module:

```
var
  TheSum: real; (* current sum *)
```

or would you instead include something like the following in the interface part:

```
function Sum : real;
(* post : returns the current sum *)
```

and then begin your implementation part as follows?

```
implementation

var
  TheSum: real;

function Sum : real;
begin
  Sum := TheSum;
end; (* Sum *)
```

1.4. CASE STUDY: BUFFERED INPUT

Many programming problems are easier to solve if you can "look ahead" in the input stream. For example, if the input is composed of several different kinds of data, you might want to write a separate procedure for each kind of data and use the following overall control structure:

```
if <positioned at first kind of data> then
    <call procedure to process first kind of data>
else if <positioned at second kind of data> then
    <call procedure to process second kind of data>
else if <positioned at third kind of data> then
    <call procedure to process third kind of data>
 . . .
```

You might at first think that this is easy to accomplish without looking ahead as follows:

```
read(NextChar);
if NextChar = <first kind of data> then
    <call procedure to process first kind of data>
else if NextChar = <second kind of data> then
    <call procedure to process second kind of data>
else if NextChar = <third kind of data> then
    <call procedure to process third kind of data>
  . . .
```

There are several problems with this approach. First, it forces the high-level code to perform low-level processing (defining a character variable and reading its value). Second, it complicates the parameter passing, because the value of *NextChar* would have to be passed to each of the procedures. Finally, it requires you to write each of the low-level procedures in a clumsy and nonintuitive way (i.e., assuming that the first character of the data has already been read).

Turbo Pascal provides no mechanism for looking ahead in the input stream. This case study involves the creation of a utility module that provides procedures and functions that allow such lookahead. In creating this utility module, the author used two rather different approaches to buffering the input. As is often the case in real-world programming, many design issues do not become evident until some of the coding and testing has been performed. To preserve some of the evolution of the module, this case study presents both approaches, with a discussion of the design issues that led to each.

1.4.1. Designing Module *CharBuff*

The only way to accomplish lookahead is to *buffer* the input, meaning that you will read ahead in the input stream and keep part of the input in a special place known as a buffer until it is needed. Thus, you look ahead by examining the contents of the buffer.

The biggest design issue for this module is how much of the input stream to buffer. You might imagine that buffering everything would be best, but there are several reasons why this is a bad idea. First, the module would be more complicated in that it needs to define and manipulate a data structure capable of storing the entire contents of a file. Second, it would require storing the entire contents of an input file in main memory all at once, which might not be possible for large input files. Finally, it would be difficult to adapt such a module to interactive input, because it is not possible to obtain all such input at the beginning of program execution (a program wouldn't seem very interactive if it demanded all a user's responses the moment it began executing).

Given the reasons above, it is best for the module to buffer only as much input as it needs to accomplish its task. The smallest amount of input it could buffer would be a single character. This has the appeal of simplicity, which tends to lead to a shorter and more understandable code. It also has the advantage of being closely tied to Pascal, because text files in Pascal are, at their lowest level, considered simple character streams. Because this approach involves buffering a single character of input, the name *CharBuff* seems appropriate for the resulting module.

What, then, would be a minimal set of operations to provide? Obviously there needs to be a way to perform the lookahead. There should also be some way of reading a single character. To "prime the pump" for buffering the input, you will have to write some initialization code, but that can be included in the block for the utility module. Thus, a truly minimal set of operations would be:

```
function Window : char;

procedure ReadChar (var CH: char);
```

This set of operations is too minimal. In particular, Pascal input files provide special state information that cannot be obtained from either of these operations. A Pascal text file is defined to be a sequence of components that are either characters or end-of-line markers. You can find out whether you are currently positioned at an end-of-line marker by testing the value of *eoln*. If this utility module is to duplicate the functionality of Pascal input files, it must also provide such a utility. Standard Pascal also provides a function *eof* that indicates whether or not all input has been processed. The most straightforward approach is to simply include new versions of each function in this module. Remember from the discussion of module syntax that these new versions can be differentiated by using the fully qualified identifiers *CharBuff.eoln* and *CharBuff.eof*.

These four operations constitute a reasonable core. All other reading operations provided by Pascal are built on top of these basic building blocks. We could, therefore, stop right there. This would have the advantage of providing a simple and probably highly reliable utility module. But there is a signficant down-side to such simplicity in this case.

The problem is that a programmer using this module cannot mix standard reading operations with reading operations from this module. The reason is simple. This module keeps the next input character in its buffer, so only it can reliably provide input. For example, if the input stream would normally contain "198.45," when using this utility module, the first character of the stream (the "1") is kept in the utility module's buffer. Thus, a call on Pascal's standard *read* operation to read a real number would return 98.45 instead of 198.45. Thus, a programmer using this utility module would have to perform a series of calls on *ReadChar* and, in essence, construct the real value to which it corresponds.

Reading of numeric values is so common in programs that this utility module isn't very complete without them. Thus, it makes sense to add procedures for reading integers and reals that parallel the character-reading procedure. Similarly, if this module is going to replace calls on built-in reading operations, it should also provide an equivalent of *readln*. The definition for *CharBuff* is shown in Figure 1.3.

1.4.2. Implementing the Core of *CharBuff*

When developing any significant program or unit, it is best to start by writing a small piece first and testing it thoroughly before proceeding. As mentioned in the last section, the most fundamental operations are *Window, ReadChar, Eoln,* and

```
OVERVIEW
Provides reading utilities with one-character lookahead.

function Window : char;
        post     Returns the character that would be read after the
                 next call on ReadChar.

function Eoln : boolean;
        post     Returns true if input cursor is at end-of-line;
                 false otherwise.

function Eof : boolean;
        post     Returns true if input cursor is at end-of-file;
                 false otherwise.

procedure ReadChar (var CH: char);
        post     If Eoln, CH is set to a space; otherwise, CH is
                 set to the value of the character pointed to by
                 the input cursor and the input cursor is advanced
                 to the next character, if any, on the input line.

procedure ReadInt (var num: integer);
        pre      Input cursor positioned at an integer.
        post     Num is set to the value represented by the digit
                 sequence (with a possible leading sign) that
                 follows. If after reading a leading sign character
                 no digit characters are encountered, Num is set
                 to 0.

procedure ReadReal (var Num: real);
        pre      Input cursor positioned at a real.
        post     Like ReadInt, but reading a real instead of an
                 integer.

procedure Readln;
        post     Input cursor is advanced to the first character of
                 the next line, if any.
```

FIGURE 1.3. Specification for utility module *CharBuff.*

Eof. Therefore, it makes sense to develop and test these four before attempting the others.

The basic idea of *CharBuff* is that it reads one character ahead in the input stream. This character needs to be stored somewhere and its value needs to be retained even when procedures and functions of the module are not being executed. Thus, its value should be stored in a module variable. A good first approximation to the implementation part of the module can be obtained by writing just *Window, ReadChar,* and the module initialization, as follows:

```
implementation

var
  Buffer: char;

function Window: char;
begin
  Window := Buffer;
end; (* Window *)

procedure ReadChar (var CH: char);
begin
  CH := Buffer;
  read(Buffer);
end; (* ReadChar *)

begin (* CharBuff *)
  read(Buffer);
end. (* CharBuff *)
```

As a simple test of this program, you can create an external file with some characters to be read by the unit and then write a program that reassigns standard input to this text file and executes the following code segment:

```
begin
  for i := 1 to 5 do begin
    writeln('Window = ', CharBuff.Window);
    CharBuff.ReadChar(CH);
    writeln('Next char = ', CH,);
  end;
end;
```

This should echo the first five characters of the file to the output file, first by using function *Window* to look ahead, and then by using a call on *ReadChar* to actually read the value. If we execute the unit with an input file containing a single line of five characters:

```
12345
```

we obtain the following output.

```
Window = 1
Next char = 1
Window = 2
Next char = 2
Window = 3
Next char = 3
Window = 4
Next char = 4
Window = 5
Next char = 5
```

This is a very good result. It indicates that *Window* is returning the appropriate value (i.e., the value that is about to be read by *ReadChar*) and that the window is properly advancing.

When you try to write the other parts of the module, you run into a problem. Consider how you would implement *Eoln* and *Eof*. The normal versions of these functions can be referenced inside the module as *System.eoln* and *System.eof*. You might think that the following would be a reasonable definition for *Eoln*.

```
function Eoln : boolean;
begin
 Eoln := System.eoln;
end; (* Eoln *)
```

The problem with this definition is that because you are reading one character ahead in the input stream, *System.eoln* becomes true too early. In particular, it becomes true one character too soon because of the buffered input. This is more easily understood by actually executing the program above with a slight variation. Instead of just writing out the value of the window at the beginning of each loop iteration, we will instead execute the following statement so that the value of *Eoln* is also written out.

```
writeln('Window = ', CharBuff.Window, ', Eoln = ',
        CharBuff.Eoln);
```

When we execute this version of the testing program on the input above, we obtain the following output:

```
Window = 1, Eoln = false
Next char = 1
Window = 2, Eoln = false
Next char = 2
Window = 3, Eoln = false
Next char = 3
Window = 4, Eoln = false
Next char = 4
Window = 5, Eoln = true
Next char = 5
```

As you can see in this output, *Eoln* is reported to be true when the window is positioned at the character 5. This is the wrong behavior. *Eoln* is not supposed to be true until the window has advanced *beyond* the last character of the input line.

To solve this problem the module has to keep track not only of the next character to be read, but also of the file *state* for that character. There are three possible states: normal character, end-of-line, and end-of-file. This state information has to be updated every time a new value is read into the buffer.

The introduction of state information complicates the buffer sufficiently that the details associated with it deserve to be encapsulated in a procedure. Let's introduce a procedure called *Advance* that will advance the buffer one position (in terms of Standard Pascal, this would be the equivalent of *Get*). This procedure requires the introduction of a new module variable. The various file states could be stored in several different ways, but an enumerated type seems to make the most sense. Thus, the beginning of the module's implementation part would be written as follows:

```
implementation
 type
  FileState = (normal, EndOfLine, EndOfFile);

 var
  Buffer: char;
  State: FileState;

 procedure Advance;
 begin
  if System.eof then begin
    State := EndOfFile;
   end
  else if System.eoln then begin
    State := EndOfLine;
    Buffer := ' ';
    System.readln;
   end
  else begin
    State := normal;
    read(Buffer);
   end; (* If *)
 end; (* Advance *)


 . . .


 begin (* CharBuff *)
  Advance;
 end. (* CharBuff *)
```

Notice that when *System.eoln* is true, procedure *Advance* uses a call on *System.readln* to read past it and it assigns *Buffer* the value of space. Standard Pascal specifies that files are to behave this way, that advancing one position while at end-of-line should position you to the beginning of the next input line and return a space as the character processed. Turbo Pascal behaves somewhat differently from this, but this gives us a chance to fix Turbo's behavior.

   Once this operation is written, the three lookahead functions can easily be defined.

```
 function Window : char;
 begin
  Window := Buffer;
 end; (* Window *)
```

```
function Eoln : boolean;
begin
 Eoln := (State = EndOfLine) or (State = EndOfFile);
end; (* Eoln *)

function Eof : boolean;
begin
 Eof := (State = EndOfFile);
end; (* Eof *)
```

Once these fundamental operations are written, the other reading operations can all be written in terms of these. As you will see when we go to modify the module, it is highly desirable to keep the low-level details associated with the module variables as localized as possible. Thus, in writing the other module operations, we will no longer make reference to the module variables. Consider, for example, procedure *ReadChar*. We first wrote it as follows:

```
procedure ReadChar (var CH: char);
begin
 CH := Buffer;
 read(Buffer);
end; (*  ReadChar *)
```

To avoid the references to *Buffer*, we can instead use *Window* and *Advance*:

```
procedure ReadChar (var CH: char);
begin
 CH := Window;
 Advance;
end; (* ReadChar *)
```

This allows *ReadChar* to remain simple while also making sure that it behaves properly (e.g., by making sure that file state information is recorded when the window is advanced).

To test these new versions of the operations, we can modify the testing program to report all three values on each iteration of the loop and after the loop terminates. We should also increase the number of iterations to six so that the end-of-line marker is processed by *ReadChar*.

```
begin
 for i := 1 to 6 do begin
   writeln('Window = ', CharBuff.Window, ',  Eof = ',
           CharBuff.Eof);
   CharBuff.ReadChar(CH);
   writeln('Next char = ', CH);
 end;
```

```
        writeln('After loop: Window = ', CharBuff.Window, ',
              Eof = ', CharBuff.Eof);
    end;
```

This program produces the following output:

```
Window = 1, Eoln = false, Eof = false
Next char = 1
Window = 2, Eoln = false, Eof = false
Next char = 2
Window = 3, Eoln = false, Eof = false
Next char = 3
Window = 4, Eoln = false, Eof = false
Next char = 4
Window = 5, Eoln = false, Eof = false
Next char = 5
Window =  , Eoln = true, Eof = false
Next char =
After loop: Window =  , Eoln = true, Eof = true
```

This output is now correct. Notice how *Eoln* does not become true until after the last character of the input line has been read and how the window becomes a space when *Eoln* is true. Also notice that once this end-of-line marker is read as a character, *Eof* becomes true. Standard Pascal does not specify what values the file window and *Eoln* should return when *Eof* is true (in fact, it specifies that it is an error to make such references when *Eof* is true), but it seems reasonable to pretend that *Eoln* is true when *Eof* is true.

1.4.3. The Problem of Terminal Input

While the version of the unit developed in the last section works properly for external input files, it does not have appropriate behavior for terminal input. To understand the nature of the problem, you must first understand the notion of *lazy I/O* (*I/O* stands for *Input/Output*). Consider, for example, the following interactive program that does not make use of unit *CharBuff*.

```
program Sample;

  var
    I: integer;
    CH: char;

begin (* Sample *)
  writeln('This program echos two input lines.');
  writeln;
  for I := 1 to 2 do begin
    write('Input? ');
    while not eoln do begin
```

```
      read(CH);
      write(CH);
     end; (* While *)
    readln;
    writeln;
   end; (* For *)
 end. (* Sample *)
```

When this program is executed, it produces an interaction like the following (where user input is underlined).

```
This program echos two input lines.

Input? some input
some input
Input? some more
some more
```

As you can see, when Turbo Pascal pauses for input from the user, it pauses for an entire line of input. But why does it pause where it does? If you think about it a minute, you'll realize that there are various times during the execution of this program where the input buffer is undefined. When the program first begins executing, for example, the input buffer is empty (because the user hasn't yet typed anything). Think about what would happen, for example, if the following statement were included at the beginning of the main program.

```
writeln('Eoln = ', eoln);
```

What behavior would result? You might at first expect that it would produce this result.

```
Eoln = false
This program echos two input lines.
Input? some input
some input
Input? some more
some more
```

In other words, the only change would be that the program would echo the value of *eoln* before executing the rest. This is not the behavior that results. This would be possible if the computer could somehow predict the future to know that when the first line of input is typed, *eoln* is going to be false (in other words, that the user is going to type at least one character of input before hitting the return key). But the computer can't predict the future. Thus, when this program is executed, the computer pauses and waits for a line of input from the user before it types any of the prompts. That happens because in order to execute the first statement, it needs to know the value of *eoln*, and in order to know the value of *eoln* it needs to obtain input from the user.

But then why did the other program work properly? The answer is that Turbo Pascal uses a convention known as *lazy I/O* (*I/O* stands for *Input/Output*). Procrastinating I/O is probably a more specific description. The idea is that the computer puts off obtaining input until it *needs* to (sort of like a procrastinator putting off doing some work until an actual deadline is looming ahead). Thus, in the first version of the program it can go ahead and execute the initial *writeln* statements and enter the for loop without ever having to obtain any input from the user. But as soon as it hits a reference to the input file (namely, the call on *eoln* in the test of the while loop), it is forced to actually pause and obtain some input.

As noted earlier, when it does pause, it obtains an entire line of input. This input is enough to allow the while loop to execute in its entirety and even provides an end-of-line marker to be processed by the *readln* that follows the while loop. After the call on *readln*, however, the input stream is again undefined. But in the spirit of procrastination, it again delays obtaining input until it needs to. This doesn't occur until it comes back around the for loop and hits the call on *eoln* in the while loop (*after* the second prompt is issued). This produces the desired behavior of issuing prompts before input is expected from the user.

What about the version of *CharBuff* developed in the last section? How does it behave? We can rewrite the original program in terms of *CharBuff*. Because we haven't yet written *Readln*, we use an extra call on *ReadChar* instead to obtain the same result (remember that we tested that in the last section). Thus, the program becomes

```
program Sample;

uses
  CharBuff;

var
  I: integer;
  CH: char;

begin (* Sample *)
  writeln('This program echoes two lines of input to
          output.');
  writeln;
  for I := 1 to 2 do begin
    write('Input? ');
    while not CharBuff.Eoln do begin
      CharBuff.ReadChar(CH);
      write(CH);
     end; (* While *)
    CharBuff.ReadChar(CH);
    writeln;
   end; (* For *)
end. (* Sample *)
```

When this program is executed, it behaves oddly. The answer is rather simple. The module initialization involves reading the first character into the buffer. Remember that the module initialization is executed before the main program. Thus, any program using *CharBuff* will expect to read the first character from input before the program has a chance to execute anything. In particular, if the main program is interactive, the user will be expected to type the first line of input before the program has a chance to explain what it does and to issue a prompt. This kind of behavior would make *CharBuff* useless for interactive programs.

The solution is to apply the notion of lazy *I/O* to *CharBuff*. The idea of lazy I/O is just an extension of the notion of file state. *CharBuff* allows the file to be in any of three states: normal, end-of-line, and end-of-file. Lazy I/O introduces a fourth kind of state: undefined. Naturally, the file can't remain in this state when any of *CharBuff's* operations are to be actually performed (e.g., it can't read a character if it doesn't know what the next character is), but by introducing this state, *CharBuff* can procrastinate by putting off the definition of the file state until the last possible moment. For example, the module initialization can be replaced by the following:

```
begin (* CharBuff *)
  State := undefined;
end. (* CharBuff *)
```

This records the fact that the buffer is undefined without actually reading anything from the input stream. How long can reading be put off? The purpose of reading in the first place is to give a value to the variables *Buffer* and *State* so that they can be examined by the lookahead functions. Thus, reading can be delayed until one of these three functions is actually called. This can be coded as follows:

```
procedure FixBuffer;
begin
  if State = undefined then begin
    Advance;
  end; (* If *)
end; (* FixBuffer *)

function Window : char;
begin
  FixBuffer;
  Window := Buffer;
end; (* Window *)

function Eoln : boolean;
begin
  FixBuffer;
  Eoln := (State = EndOfLine) or (State = EndOfFile);
end; (* Eoln *)

function Eof : boolean;
begin
```

```
            FixBuffer;
            Eof := (State = EndOfFile);
        end;  (* Eof *)
```

This almost completes the modifications necessary to *CharBuff* to enable lazy I/O. There is still one problem to be addressed, however. If you execute the testing program after this modification, you obtain the correct behavior at the beginning of program execution. It executes the *writelns* that explain the program and it produces a prompt before any input is expected from the user. Not until it hits the call on *eoln* inside the for loop does it actually pause for input (because inside *CharBuff* that causes a call on *FixBuffer* that gives a value to the buffer). The problem occurs after that first line of input is entered. Instead of proceeding with execution on that first line of input, the program pauses for a second line of input.

This happens because each iteration of the for loop executes an input line in its entirety. It reads single characters until end-of-line is reached and it executes an extra call on *ReadChar* to process the end-of-line itself. The call on *ReadChar* when it is at the end-of-line causes the module to look ahead to the next character. But the next character is on the next input line. That is why the program pauses for more input, because it is trying to read past the end-of-line for the first line.

The fix is to again apply the notion of allowing the window to be undefined. In this case, the window should become undefined when trying to advance past an end-of-line. Thus, procedure *Advance* should be rewritten to include another branch at the beginning:

```
        procedure Advance;
        begin
         if State = EndOfLine then begin
           State := undefined;
           end
         else if System.eof then begin
           State := EndOfFile;
           end
         else if System.eoln then begin
           State := EndOfLine;
           Buffer := ' ';
           System.readln;
           end
         else begin
           State := normal;
           read(Buffer);
           end;  (* If *)
        end;  (* Advance *)
```

In other words, we are introducing procrastination not only at the beginning of execution, but also every time we cross a line boundary. With this fix, the testing program behaves exactly the same way as its counterpart written with the usual reading operations.

1.4.4. Implementing the Rest of *CharBuff*

As mentioned earlier, once the fundamental operations are implemented, all the others can be written in terms of them. It is desirable to isolate implementation details in this way, so we will purposely make use of the core operations rather than using the module variables when implementing the other operations.

Readln has a simple definition. It should position to the beginning of the next input line, if any. In other words, it should advance the buffer until end-of-line is reached, and then it should advance the buffer once more to position beyond the end-of-line.

```
procedure Readln;
begin
 while not Eoln do begin
   Advance;
  end; (* While *)
 Advance;
end; (* Readln *)
```

ReadInt and *ReadReal* are more complicated because they involve constructing a number from its individual characters. Of the two, *ReadInt* involves fewer details, so let's consider it first. Suppose that the input stream contains the characters 1923. When we read the 1, it looks like the number is just 1. After we read the 9, however, it becomes clear that 1 should become 10 so that we can add 9 to it and get 19. Similarly, when we read 2 it becomes clear that 19 should become 190 so that we can add 2 to it and get 192. Finally, when we read 3 it becomes clear that 192 should become 1920 so that we can add 3 to it and get 1923. Thus, for each new digit character we take the result obtained so far, multiply it by 10, and add the new digit to the result. We stop doing so when there are no more digits to be read. This can be written in Pascal as follows:

```
procedure ReadInt (var Num: integer);
 var
  DIGIT: char;
begin
 Num := 0;
 while (Window in ['0'..'9']) do begin
   ReadChar(DIGIT);
   Num := Num * 10 + (ord(DIGIT) - ord('0'));
  end; (* While *)
end; (* ReadInt *)
```

This version of the procedure works fairly well. But in order to parallel Standard Pascal, the procedure should skip any leading spaces and end-of-line markers and should deal with a leading sign character if it appears. Thus, the procedure should be rewritten to account for these possibilities.

```
procedure ReadInt (var Num: integer);
 var
```

```
      NEGATIVE: boolean;
      DIGIT: char;
   begin
    while Window = ' ' do begin
      Advance;
      end; (* While *)
    Num := 0;
    Negative := (Window = '-');
    if Window in ['+', '-'] then begin
      Advance;
      end; (* If *)
    while (Window in ['0'..'9']) do begin
      ReadChar(DIGIT);
      Num := Num * 10 + (ord(DIGIT) - ord('0'));
      end; (* While *)
    if NEGATIVE then begin
      Num := -Num;
      end; (* If *)
   end; (* ReadInt *)
```

The definition of *ReadReal* is fairly similar. To avoid some redundancy, we can begin the procedure by calling *ReadInt* to read the integer part of the real number. That leaves just the problem of processing any decimal part that follows. For this loop, each successive digit character should be considered one-tenth as large as the previous one (i.e., the first digit character represents tenths, the next represents one-hundredths, the next one-thousandths, and so on). Thus, we need some variable to keep track of what multiplier to use and we will want to divide that multiplier by ten each time through the loop. Thus, the procedure can be written as follows:

```
   procedure ReadReal (var Num: real);
    var
     I: integer;
     MULTIPLIER: real;
     DIGIT: char;
   begin
    ReadInt(I);
    Num := I;
    if Window = '.' then begin
      Advance;
      MULTIPLIER := 1.0;
      while Window in ['0'..'9'] do begin
        ReadChar(DIGIT);
        MULTIPLIER := MULTIPLIER * 0.1;
        if Num < 0 then begin
          Num := Num - MULTIPLIER * (ord(DIGIT)-ord('0'));
          end
        else begin
          Num := Num + MULTIPLIER * (ord(DIGIT)-ord('o'));
          end;
```

```
          end; (* While *)
        end; (* If *)
      end; (* ReadReal *)
```

1.4.5. A Sample Program Using *CharBuff*

To see how *CharBuff* might be used and to provide a good test of its correctness, consider the following problem. Suppose an input file contains lines of the form

<variable> <expression>

as in

```
a 12.4-19.85
b a*a-16.3
a a*b/III
b a + b - 198.8
```

where the variable is always either a or b and the expression is composed of a legal combination of real numbers, Roman numerals, variables, and operators ($+$, $-$, $*$, and $/$). For each input line, the program is to read the variable, evaluate the expression, and assign the variable the given value. The two variables should be initialized to zero. The program should echo the values of both variables after processing each line of input. In evaluating, operators should be applied left-to-right (as if you were using a calculator). For example, for the input file above, the following output should be produced:

```
A =    -7.45, B =      0.00
A =    -7.45, B =     39.20
A =   -97.35, B =     39.20
A =   -97.35, B =   -256.95
```

CharBuff simplifies this program in two significant ways. First, in the reading of Roman numerals, it is easier to process the number if you can look ahead one character. That is because characters appearing in a Roman number sometimes represent something to add to the total and sometimes represent something to subtract. For example, XXI represents $10 + 10 + 1$ or 21 while XIX represents $10 - 1 + 10$ or 19. The rule is that if the following character is greater in value than the current character, then you subtract (as in IX), and otherwise you add.

The program is also simplified by the ability to decide what kind of value is being read. By looking ahead, the program can tell whether the next item on the input line is the name of a variable, a real value, or a Roman number.

The program is written as follows:

```
program EvalExprs;
```

```pascal
uses
 CharBuff;

var
 a, b: real;

function RomanValue (CH: char): integer;
begin
 if not (CH in ['I', 'V', 'X', 'L', 'C', 'D', 'M']) then
 begin
   RomanValue := 0;
  end
 else begin
   case CH of
    'I':
    RomanValue := 1;
    'V':
    RomanValue := 5;
    'X':
    RomanValue := 10;
    'L':
    RomanValue := 50;
    'C':
    RomanValue := 100;
    'D':
    RomanValue := 500;
    'M':
    RomanValue := 1000;
  end; (* Case *)
 end; (* If *)
end; (* RomanValue *)


procedure ReadRoman (var Value: real);
 var
  NEXT: char;
begin
 Value := 0.0;
 while RomanValue(CharBuff.Window) > 0 do begin
   CharBuff.ReadChar(NEXT);
   if RomanValue(NEXT) >= RomanValue(CharBuff.Window) then
   begin
     Value := Value + RomanValue(NEXT);
    end
   else begin
     Value := Value - RomanValue(NEXT);
    end; (* If *)
  end; (* While *)
end; (* ReadRoman *)
```

```
procedure SkipSpaces;
 var
   DUMMY: char;
begin
 while (CharBuff.Window = ' ') and not CharBuff.Eoln do
 begin
   CharBuff.ReadChar(DUMMY);
  end; (* While *)
end; (* SkipSpaces *)

procedure ReadValue (a, b: real;
      var Value: real);
 var
   WHICH: char;
begin
 SkipSpaces;
 if CharBuff.Window in ['a', 'b'] then begin
   CharBuff.ReadChar(WHICH);
   case WHICH of
    'a':
     Value := a;
    'b':
     Value := b;
   end; (* Case *)
   end
 else if CharBuff.Window in ['0'..'9'] then begin
   CharBuff.ReadReal(Value);
   end
else begin
  ReadRoman(Value);
 end; (* If *)
end; (* ReadValue *)

procedure ProcessLine (var a, b: real);
 var
   WHICH, OPER: char;
   RESULT, NEXT: real;
begin
 CharBuff.ReadChar(WHICH);
 ReadValue(a, b, RESULT);
 while not CharBuff.Eoln do begin
   CharBuff.ReadChar(OPER);
   ReadValue(a, b, NEXT);
   case OPER of
    '+':
     RESULT := RESULT + NEXT;
    '-':
     RESULT := RESULT - NEXT;
    '*':
```

```
          RESULT := RESULT * NEXT;
        '/':
          RESULT := RESULT / NEXT;
       end; (* Case *)
      end;
     case WHICH of
      'a':
       a := RESULT;
      'b':
       b := RESULT;
     end; (* Case *)
     CharBuff.Readln;
    end;

   begin
    a := 0.0;
    b := 0.0;
    while not CharBuff.Eof do begin
      ProcessLine(a, b);
      writeln('a = ', a : 8 : 2, ', b = ', b : 8 : 2);
    end; (* While *)
   end. (* Main *)
```

1.4.6. Beyond *CharBuff*: *LineBuff*

CharBuff turns out to be a fairly powerful module, but it does have some limitations. If lookahead in an input file turns out to be fairly important, it is not unlikely that you will want to be reading more than one input file at once in this way. All the programs used to test *CharBuff* used a single source of input. By reassigning standard input, it is possible to make that source of input be either the terminal or an external file. But it is not possible to use *CharBuff* to process two sources of input.

This limitation of *CharBuff* is fairly obvious. It has one set of module variables to keep track of the next character and the file state. To keep track of two buffers and two file states, it would need another set of variables. This is not a simple extension to *CharBuff* because its interface includes no indication of the source of input (it is always assumed to be standard input). Even adding a file identifier as a parameter to all the operations does not solve the problem, because there is no way to compare file variables for equality.

Another limitation of *CharBuff* is that it allows looking ahead only one character in the input stream. For example, suppose that you wanted to write a function *AtNum* that tested to see if you were positioned at a number. You might write it as

```
function AtNum : boolean;
begin
 while CharBuff.window = ' '  do begin
   CharBuff.ReadChar(dummy);
  end; (* While *)
```

```
AtNum := CharBuff.Window in ['0'..'9'];
end; (* AtNum *)
```

One problem with this definition is that it actually advances the window past leading spaces, which might be an undesirable side-effect. Another problem is that the number might have a leading sign. You could change the last line to be

```
AtNum := CharBuff.Window in ['0'..'9', '+', '-'];
```

but then the function will return true when positioned at a sequence of characters such as +garbage. You would need to be able to look ahead two characters instead to be able to write this function.

To address these problems adequately, the basic approach needs to be changed. Instead of buffering a single character of input, we can instead buffer an entire line of input. This allows us to look ahead on the current input line as many characters as we want. It can also solve the multiple file problem. Because this module is buffering an entire line of input instead of a single character, it doesn't seem like an unreasonable burden on the programmer using the unit to call a procedure whenever the buffer should be updated. Let's call the procedure *ReadLine*. By giving *ReadLine* a file variable as parameter, a program can read lines of input from many different sources of input into the buffer one line at a time. Instead of a function like *Window*, we should include a more general *Peek* that takes an integer argument. Some algorithms are easier to write if an input line can be scanned multiple times, so it might also be helpful to provide a utility for resetting to the beginning of the input line. Finally, the operation *AtNum* described above turns out to be generally useful enough that it seems reasonable to include it in the module, but in the form of *AtInt* and *AtReal*, so as to be able to make the distinction.

In addition to these operations, the new module should include most of the operations from *CharBuff*. The only exceptions are *Eof* and *Readln*, because both of these operations now become the responsibility of the programmer using the module rather than the responsibility of the module itself.

Thus, *LineBuff* would be specified as in Figure 1.4.

1.4.7. Implementing *LineBuff*

Most of the difficult work was done in implementing *CharBuff*. We can make use of the work done there to make the implementation of *LineBuff* simpler. Instead of two local variables for storing the next character and the file state, we will need a structure for storing an entire line of input. The following declarations seem reasonable for doing so.

```
const
MaxChars = 200;

type
Linearray = array[1..MaxChars] of char;
```

45

OVERVIEW
Provides reading utilities with one-line lookahead.

---

procedure ReadLine (var InFile: text);
        post   Next line of InFile is read into buffer and input
                cursor is positioned at the first character of the
                line. MUST be called before any other input
                operations are called.

function Peek (Ahead: integer): char;
        pre   Ahead >= 1.
        post   Returns the character that would be read after
                Ahead calls on ReadChar. If Ahead is 1, it returns
                the character pointed to by the input cursor.

function AtNum : boolean;
        post   Returns true if input cursor is positioned at a
                number, false otherwise.

procedure ResetLine;
        post   Input cursor is reset to the beginning of the
                current input line. Note that this does not read
                another line of input. This procedure should be
                used only when you want to process an input line
                more than once.

function Eoln : boolean;
        post   Returns true if input cursor is at end-of-line;
                false otherwise.

procedure ReadChar (var CH: char);
        post   If Eoln, CH is set to a space; otherwise, CH is
                set to the value of the character pointed to by the
                input cursor and the input cursor is advanced to
                the next character, if any, on the input line.

procedure ReadInt (var Num: integer);
        pre   AtNum.
        post   Num is set to the value represented by the digit
                sequence (with a possible leading sign) that
                follows. If after reading a leading sign character
                no digit characters are encountered, Num is set
                to 0.

procedure ReadReal (var Num: real);
        pre   AtNum.
        post   Like ReadInt, but reading a real instead of an
                integer.

FIGURE 1.4. Specification for utility module *LineBuff.*

```
BufType = record
  Chars: Linearray;
  Len: integer;
  Cursor: integer;
  end; (* BufType *)


var
 Buf: BufType;
```

In fact, the most difficult code to write for *LineBuff* is the code that reads characters into this structure. In case the system does not preprocess backspace and delete characters, the module should be careful to process them. *ReadLine* can be written as follows:

```
procedure ProcessChar (var Next: char);
 const
  Backspace = 8;
  Delete = 127;
begin
 if (Next = chr(Backspace)) or (Next = chr(Delete)) then
 begin
   if (Buf.Len > 0) then begin
     Buf.Len := Buf.Len - 1;
     end; (* If *)
   end
 else begin
   Buf.Len := Buf.Len + 1;
   Buf.Chars[Buf.Len] := Next;
   end; (* If *)
end; (* ProcessChar *)

procedure ReadLine (var Infile: text);
 var
  NEXT: char;
begin
 Buf.Len := 0;
 while not System.eoln(Infile) do begin
   read(Infile, NEXT);
   ProcessChar(NEXT);
   end; (* while *)
 readln(Infile);
 Buf.Cursor := 1;
end; (* ReadLine *)
```

The two lookahead operations of the module, then, involve simple manipulations of this structure. The peeking function should be careful not to examine an uninitialized array element in case it is asked to peek beyond the end-of-line marker, but otherwise these operations are fairly straightforward.

```
function Eoln: boolean;
begin
 Eoln := (Buf.Cursor > Buf.Len);
end; (* Eoln *)

function Peek (Ahead: integer): char;
begin
 if Buf.Cursor + ahead - 1 > Buf.Len then begin
   Peek := ' ';
 end
 else begin
   Peek := Buf.Chars[Buf.Cursor + ahead - 1];
 end; (* If *)
end; (* Peek *)
```

Remember that most of module *CharBuff* is written in terms of *Window* and *Advance*. To avoid rewriting those operations, we can give them new definitions appropriate for this implementation of buffering.

```
procedure Advance;
begin
 Buf.Cursor := Buf.Cursor + 1;
end; (* Advance *)

function Window: char;
begin
 Window := Peek(1);
end; (* Window *)
```

Once these two are written, we do not have to rewrite either *ReadChar*, *ReadInt*, or *ReadReal*.

Consider function *AtNum*. As mentioned in the previous section, it would be best if this function looked past leading spaces without actually reading them. Once it has found the next nonspace character, it should look to see that it is a digit, or a sign character followed by a digit. Thus, the function can be written as follows:

```
function AtNum : boolean;
 var
  I: integer;
begin
 I := 1;
 while Peek(I) = ' ' do begin
   I := I + 1;
  end; (* While *)
 if Peek(I) in ['+', '-'] then begin
   AtNum := Peek(I + 1) in ['0'..'9'];
  end
 else begin
```

```
      AtNum := Peek(I) in ['0'..'9'];
   end;  (* If *)
end;  (* AtNum *)
```

This completes the module except for procedure *ResetLine* and the module initialization. It turns out that no module initialization is needed because the module is, in effect, reinitialized everytime *ReadLine* is called. And to reset to the beginning of the line, we need only reset the buffer to position 1:

```
procedure ResetLine;
begin
 Buf.Cursor := 1;
end;  (* ResetLine *)
```

This, then, completes the implementation of this new version of the module.

2

DATA ABSTRACTION

2.1. INTRODUCTION

This chapter introduces a new kind of abstraction that is so powerful that the authors have made it the focus of this book.[1] This new kind of abstraction is associated with objects rather than actions and is known as *data abstraction*. The chapter closes with a significant example of data abstraction, introducing a powerful "table" type.

Given that data abstraction permeates this book more than any other concept and given that the table type is used as a significant programming example in several subsequent chapters, it is very important that you read this chapter carefully and thoroughly.

2.2. DATA ABSTRACTION

Abstraction concepts such as specification, implementation, and black-box diagrams are not intended just for action-oriented constructs like procedures. They apply equally well to object-oriented constructs like types.

---

[1] Your authors, however, are not being capricious. As mentioned in the preface, official curriculum guidelines now reflect the growing consensus that data abstraction *should* be the major topic of study for computer science students at your level.

You saw that the specification for a procedure is its header and pre/postconditions. What constitutes the "what" part for a type? One way a type can be specified is by using an abstract data type.

ABSTRACT DATA TYPE (ADT)
....
A description of the domain of a type and the set of operations that can be performed on objects of that type.

Thus, an ADT is specified by answering two basic questions: what values might potentially be stored by variables of this type (i.e., what is to be kept inside the black box) and what operations are available for manipulating such variables (i.e., what subprograms can be used to manipulate what's inside the box)?

ADTs are a tool of the mind and, therefore, need not have a concrete relationship to the programming language they describe, but modules provide an ideal structure for encapsulating the definition of a type.

The combination of subprograms and parameters is so powerful that learning the many ways to apply this combination dominates the experience of students in the first course. Similarly, it turns out that the combination of ADTs and modules is so powerful that ADT modules will dominate your experience in this course.

It's reasonable to characterize the first course as focusing on *subprograms* as software components whereas the second course focuses on *data types* as software components. Other topics are included in each course, but none comes close to rivaling the central status of these ideas.

The essential idea behind an ADT is that a program's data are organized into high-level packages. This package consists of both the data structure and operations that allow the user to manipulate that structure. Encapsulated in a module, the ADT exports a *type* definition to the ADT's users, thus allowing these programmers to declare variables of that type. The users then manipulate these variables by calling the ADT's operations. Thus, users never need to examine the ADT's low-level implementation details. Instead, they only need to understand the ADT's specification.

To qualify as a software component, an ADT module has to be usable in many different programs. Thus, it is important that you carefully consider its interface to design a powerful set of operations and use abstraction to keep its specification clean and simple.

2.2.1. The ADT Fraction

As a first example, consider an ADT for storing fractions. You could introduce arithmetic operations that would allow you to give commands like

```
Add(A, B, C);
Divide(B, A, D);
Subtract(B, D, C);
Multiply(C, B, A);
```

A more elegant approach is to introduce a single procedure that performs any of the four operations depending upon what character you pass as a parameter. You can even manage to try to make it look like the kind of assignment statements you use for the predefined numeric types. To make it look like

```
C := A + B;
B := A / D;
B := D - C;
C := B * A;
```

you could define *Fraction* to have parameter-passing like this:

```
Assign(C, A, '+', B);
Assign(B, A, '/', D);
Assign(B, D, '-', C);
Assign(C, B, '*', A);
```

The complete specification for ADT Fraction can be found in Figure 2.1. The term "standard operators" is defined in the next section.

The following example shows you how module *Fraction* would be used by a program. Notice that even *Typ* is fully qualified to *Fraction.Typ*, even in procedure headers.

DOMAIN

The set of all numbers a/b where a and b are integers, b is nonzero, and $\gcd(a, b) = 1$.

OPERATIONS

```
procedure Initialize (var Fract: Typ; a, b: integer);
        pre       b <> 0
        post      a/b is reduced appropriately and the result is
                  stored in Fract.

procedure Assign (var Result: Typ; Fractl: Typ; Operator: char;
               Fract2: Typ);
        pre       Fractl and Fract have been initialized;
                  operator in ['+', '-', '*', '/'];
                  not ((operator = '/') and (Fract2 represents 0))
        post      Result is assigned the value obtained by applying
                  the given operator to Fractl/Fract2 (e.g.,
                  Fractl + Fract2).
```

STANDARD OPERATORS
Write

FIGURE 2.1. Specification for ADT *Fraction.*

```
program ShowFractions;

uses
 Fraction;

var
 a, b, c: Fraction.Typ;

procedure ShowAssign (var Result: Fraction.Typ;
        Fractl: Fraction.Typ;
        Operator: char;
        Fract2: Fraction.Typ);

begin
 Fract.Assign(Result, Fractl, Operator, Fract2);
 Fract.Write(output, Fractl);
 write(output, ' ', Operator, ' ');
 Fract.Write(output, Fract2);
 write(output, ' = ');
 Fract.Write(output, Result);
 writeln(output);
end; (* ShowAssign *)

begin (* Main *)
 Fract.Initialize(a, 3, 2);
 Fract.Initialize(b, 8, 3);
 ShowAssign(c, a, '+', b);
 ShowAssign(c, a, '-', b);
 ShowAssign(c, a, '*', b);
 ShowAssign(c, a, '/', b);
end. (* Main *)
```

The output of the program appears below. Notice that the fraction value can be written any one of several different ways depending upon the factors: positive/negative, less than 1/greater than 1, even integer/fractional part.

```
(1 and 1/2) + (2 and 2/3) = (4 and 1/6)
(1 and 1/2) - (2 and 2/3) = -(1 and 1/6)
(1 and 1/2) * (2 and 2/3) = 4
(1 and 1/2) / (2 and 2/3) = 9/16
```

The detailed unit itself appears below. Look closely at how the identifier *Write* is used when defined in the module's implementation part. To distinguish between the normal Pascal *Write* operator and the one defined here, you have to use a fully-qualified identifier for the normal operator, which comes from module *System*, generating references to *System.Write*.

```
unit Fraction;

interface

 type
  Typ = record
    a, b: integer;
    end;

procedure Initialize (var Fract: Typ;
      a, b: integer);
    (* pre  : b <> 0                                          *)
    (* post : a/b is reduced appropriately and the result *)
    (*      : is stored in Fract.                          *)

procedure Assign (var Result: Typ;
      Fractl: Typ;
      Operator: char;
      Fract2: Typ);
    (* pre  : Fractl and Fract have been initialized;       *)
    (*      : Operator in ['+', '-', '*', '/'];             *)
    (*      : not ((Operator = '/') and (Fract2             *)
    (*      : represents 0))                                *)
    (* post : Result is assigned the value obtained by      *)
    (*      : applying the given Operator to Fractl/Fract2 *)
    (*      : (e.g., Fractl+Fract2).                        *)

procedure Write (var OutFile: text;
      var Fract: Typ);
    (* post : value of Fract is written to OutFile. *)

implementation

 uses
  Math;

    (* The fraction is stored as a record with two        *)
    (* integer fields to store a and b.  Procedure         *)
    (* Reduce makes sure that gcd(a,b)=1 and that b > 0. *)
    (* It is called every time a fraction takes on a      *)
    (* new value.                                          *)

  procedure Reduce (var Fract: Typ);
   var
    DIVISOR: integer;
  begin
   if Fract.b < 0 then begin
     DIVISOR := -Math.GCD(Fract.a, Fract.b);
     end
   else begin
```

```
       DIVISOR := Math.GCD(Fract.a, Fract.b);
     end; (* If *)
  Fract.a := Fract.a div DIVISOR;
  Fract.b := Fract.b div DIVISOR;
end; (* Reduce *)

procedure Initialize (var Fract: Typ;
       a, b: integer);
begin
  Fract.a := a;
  Fract.b := b;
  Reduce(Fract);
end; (* Initialize *)

procedure Assign (var Result: Typ;
       Fract1: Typ;
       Operator: char;
       Fract2: Typ);
begin
  case Operator of
   '+' :
    Result.a := Fract1.a * Fract2.b + Fract2.a * Fract1.b;
   '-' :
    Result.a := Fract1.a * Fract2.b - Fract2.a * Fract1.b;
   '*' :
    Result.a := Fract1.a * Fract2.a;
   '/' :
    Result.a := Fract1.a * Fract2.b;
  end; (* Case *)
  if Operator = '/' then begin
    Result.b := Fract1.b * Fract2.a;
   end
  else begin
    Result.b := Fract1.b * Fract2.b;
   end; (* If *)
  Reduce(Result);
end; (* Assign *)

procedure Write (var OutFile: text;
      var Fract: Typ);
   (* Three primary formats to consider:                     *)
   (*    when Fract.b = 1:              simple integer    *)
   (*    when abs(Fract.a) > Fract.b: (int and int/int) *)
   (*    otherwise:                    int/int          *)
   (* Negatives have to be carefully handled in the 2nd *)
   (* and 3d cases                                       *)

begin
  if (Fract.b = 1) then begin
    System.write(OutFile, Fract.a : 1);
```

```
          end
        else if abs(Fract.a) > Fract.b then begin
          if Fract.a < 0 then begin
            System.write('-');
          end; (* If *)
          System.write(OutFile, '(', abs(Fract.a) div Fract.b : 1,
          ' and ', abs(Fract.a) mod Fract.b : 1);
        end
        else begin
          System.write(outFile, Fract.a : 1, '/', Fract.b : 1);
        end; (* If *)
    end; (* Write *)
  end. (* Fraction *)
```

2.2.2. ADT Module Conventions

It is easier to remember how to use many different devices if their interfaces are somewhat standardized. For example, you might not know how an electronic device works, but you're likely to recognize its power cord and power switch, because power cords have a standard shape and power switches are usually labeled with the English words "on/off" or "power," or with the international standard "0/1."

Software components are similarly easier to use if their interfaces follow certain standard conventions. To assist you in studying and applying the ADT modules that dominate this book, your authors have established standards for ADT modules that have been followed throughout.

While the distinction between var and value parameters is useful both as a protection mechanism and as a means of explaining intent, value parameters are problematic for ADT implementations because they can lead to excessive copying for large data structures and because they don't behave quite the way you would expect when you create the kind of data structures described in Chapters 4 and 5. Thus, ADT parameters are generally made var parameters in this book.

Some operations are common to many, if not all, ADT specifications. The identifier used to describe such an operation is standardized in the examples that appear in this book. The following standard subprograms are used. In addition to these standard operations, the identifier *Typ* is used in all ADT modules as the name of the type (as in the headers below).

```
procedure Create (var Data: Typ);
        post    Data is initialized and empty.  MUST be
                called before any other ADT operation is
                applied to Data.

procedure Destroy (var Data: Typ);
        post    Memory allocated for Data is released;
                Data becomes uninitialized

procedure Copy (var Data1, Data2: Typ);
        post    value of Data2 has been copied to Data1
```

```
procedure Write (var OutFile: text; var Data: Typ);
        post    value of Data is written to OutFile

procedure Read (var InFile: text; var Data: Typ);
        post    value of Data has been read from InFile

function Compare (var Data1, Data2: Typ): char;
        post    returns '<' if Data1 < Data2;
                        '=' if Data1 = Data2;
                        '>' if Data1 > Data2

function Empty (var Data: Typ): boolean;
        post    True if Data is empty, False otherwise
```

The operations *Create* and *Destroy* deserve special comment. For a structure like an array or a record, the computer automatically allocates and deallocates an appropriate block of memory when the corresponding variable is created and destroyed. In Chapter 4 you will learn a new kind of data structure where the management of memory is not automatic, where it is performed by the program. To accommodate such implementations, you would either have to accept the fact that the memory being used by your variables is never freed up, or you have to add operations like *Create* and *Destroy* that allow such implementations to allocate and deallocate memory when appropriate. As you will see in the next section, however, some ADTs have such a small number of elements that the advanced data structuring techniques of Chapter 4 are not advantageous, which means it's okay to preclude such implementations by leaving out *Create* and *Destroy*.

When part of the ADT, *Create* and *Destroy* need to be called once for each variable. The simplest way to do this is to follow the convention that in the block that declares the variable, you will include *Create* as the first statement of the block and *Destroy* as the last. For example, suppose your program has the following structure:

```
program Example;

 var
  Str: String.Typ;

procedure OneMore;
 var
  MYSTR: String.Typ;
begin
  . . .
end; (* OneMore *)

begin (* Main *)
 . . .
end. (* Main *)
```

You would introduce calls on *Create* and *Destroy* as follows:

```
program Example;

var
 Str: String.Typ;

procedure OneMore;
 var
  MYSTR: String.Typ;
begin
 String.Create(MYSTR);
 . . .
 String.Destroy(MYSTR);
end; (* OneMore *)

begin (* Main *)
 String.Create(Str);
 . . .
 String.Destroy(Str);
end. (* Main *)
```

2.2.3. The ADT String

As another example, consider an ADT for character strings. The standard operators *Create, Destroy, Copy, Write, Read*, and *Compare* all seem appropriate, so they are included. It's difficult to know how much of the input file to process when *Read* is called. By default, the module reads until end-of-line, but as you'll see, this behavior can be altered.

In addition to the standard operations, you will probably want operations that allow you to access the individual characters in the string. You might want to inspect characters, change characters, or delete characters. Thus, the ADT also includes *Nth*, *ChangeNth*, and *DeleteNth*.

The most common string operation other than these is finding the length of the string, so the ADT also includes *Length*. These operations cover a wide range of string uses, but there is still one area uncovered: initialization. *Create* initializes to an empty string, but more often you want to initialize to a specific string value. Unfortunately, Standard Pascal does not have a construct that would allow you to create a procedure that could be called with varying length string constants, as in

```
Initialize(Str1, 'short');
Initialize(Str2, 'A medium length');
Initialize(Str3, 'A string much longer than the others');
```

Pascal does, however, allow you to pass string constants all the same length. Thus, one approach would be to decide on a standard length for the strings (e.g., 40). Then you could write a procedure *Initialize* that would take arguments such as the following:

```
Initialize(Str1, 'short                                    ');
Initialize(Str2, 'A medium length                          ');
Initialize(Str3, 'A string much longer than the others     ');
```

Counting 40 characters can be tedious, and even this solution won't allow you to initialize to strings of length greater than 40. The ADT instead includes an operation for appending a 10-character constant to the end of a string variable. To use it, you first call *Create* to initialize to an empty string. Then you call *Append10* as many times as necessary, depending on the length of the string constant you are initializing to. You can even make use of indentation and line breaks to underscore the idea that you are actually initializing the string through the *combination* of *Create* and *Append10*. For example, the strings above would be initialized as follows:

```
Create(Str1);Append10(str1, 'short     ');
Create(Str2);Append10(Str2, 'A medium l');
             Append10(Str2, 'ength      ');
Create(Str3);Append10(Str3, 'A string m');
             Append10(Str3, 'uch longer');
             Append10(Str3, 'than the o');
             Append10(Str3, 'thers     ');
```

The details of *String*'s specification appear in Figure 2.2.

2.2.3.1. Customizing the *String* Module

Module *String* has several operations that alter its behavior. The first three are relatively easy to understand whereas the last three can be rather complicated.

You can cause string output to be in fixed-width columns (padded with spaces on the right) rather than the usual free format by calling *FixOutput*. You can cause *Read* to capitalize lowercase letters as they are read in by calling *ConvertToUppercase*. This will produce strings with all capital letters. Procedure *IgnoreCase* offers an alternative where strings retain their mixture of lowercase and uppercase letters, but when compared, case is ignored. Both of the case-controlling procedures have boolean arguments, allowing you to *toggle* the option on and off as many times as you like.

The next three procedures control exactly what characters are read into a string. Before you can understand them, you need to consider the sequence of elements in the input file (the input stream). The input stream can contain any of the following:

- End-of-line markers
- Legal characters (i.e., those that may be stored in the string)
- Illegal characters (i.e., those that may not be stored in the string)

No character is considered both legal and illegal, so you should think of the set of all characters as being divided into two parts: legal and illegal. When the module is initialized, all characters are considered legal and none are illegal. You have two operations for changing this definition, both of which pass as their parameter a set of characters.

DOMAIN

The set of all sequences of characters, including the empty sequence.

OPERATIONS

```
procedure Append10 (var Str: Typ; CharConst: string10);
        post    CharConst is appended to the end of Str

procedure ChangeNth (var Str: Typ; n: integer; Value: char);
        post    Changes nth character of Str to Value

function Length (var Str: Typ): integer;
        post    returns number of characters in Str

procedure DeleteNth (var Str: Typ; n: integer);
        pre     1 <= n <= Length (Str)
        post    character at position n is deleted from Str

function Nth (var Str: Typ; n: integer): char;
        pre     1 <= n <= Length (Str)
        post    returns character at position n of Str
```

STANDARD OPERATORS

Create, Destroy, Copy, Write, Read, and *Compare*

ADDITIONAL DECLARATIONS

```
type string10 = packed array [1..10] of char;
```

FIGURE 2.2. Specification for ADT *String* (see also Figure 2.3).

DefineLegal expects you to include in the set constant that you provide as a parameter *every* character that you want to be legal from this point forward. You are allowed to call the procedure more than once, but remember that each call sets an absolute definition for legal characters. If you call it once saying that letters of the alphabet are legal, and call it a second time saying that digit characters are legal, there is no accumulation. Although the letters of the alphabet are considered legal once the first call is made, the second call makes the digit characters *and only the digit characters* legal. All others are automatically categorized as illegal.

DefineIllegal has behavior that parallels *DefineLegal*, but in this case you define every character that you want to be illegal. As with *DefineLegal*, each call nullifies the effect of any previous call. Furthermore, each call on *DefineIllegal* nullifies the effect of any previous call on *DefineLegal*, and vice versa.

To start back at the beginning with everything legal, you simply call *DefineIllegal* with an empty set:

```
DefineIllegal([]);
```

This explains the classification of characters and the operators for altering it. Now consider what happens when *Read* is actually called. Normally, it will read the longest sequence of legal characters appearing at the beginning of the input stream (e.g., if the next four characters to be read are legal and the fifth is illegal, *Read* will process only the four legal characters). But keep in mind that *Read* follows your instructions strictly. **Thus, if the next character to be read from input is illegal, *Read* does not process the character and, instead, returns an empty string.** Don't make the mistake of writing code like the following:

```
String.DefineLegal(['a'..'z']);
while not eof do begin
  String.Read(input, next);
end;
```

This code generates an infinite loop. For example, if the input stream begins with 'fun! and more fun!', the first time through the loop *String.Read* returns the string 'fun'. It doesn't read any further because the next character is '!'. But a second call on *String.Read* will be no more successful at reading the '!', so it returns an empty string. Then a third call is made, and another empty string is returned, and a fourth call, and another empty string, and so on.

If you are writing incorrect code like the infinite loop above, you are probably trying to get the module to exhibit fairly simple behavior—reading certain input characters into your string, and ignoring the rest. You can request this behavior by calling *SkipJunk* with the value *True*. This causes *Read* to skip all illegal characters appearing at the beginning of the input stream, including end-of-line markers, before it carries out the string reading operation. The only way you can get an empty string returned from a call on *Read* with junk-skipping turned on is when there were nothing but illegal characters left in the input stream (i.e., when you get back an empty string, you'll also find that *eof* is True).

Turning on junk-skipping is sort of like unplugging a graphic equalizer from your stereo because you either don't understand how to use it or don't really care to learn. This example is particularly relevant to one of your authors, because he has never taken the time to learn how to use a graphic equalizer, even though his friends claim that the kind of fine adjustments it allows are truly amazing.

The string module is similar in that you can make extremely fine distinctions about an input file. For example, suppose that you want to know for a given input line how many integers and words appear on the line (where an integer is defined as a sequence of digits and a word is defined as a sequence of letters). You basically need three definitions of legality: one for integers, one for words, and one for everything else (so that you can read past those other characters rather than getting stuck in an infinite loop, as above). You don't know which of these will come first or second or third, so you simply try all three cases each time through the loop. Every character matches one of these three definitions, so eventually you have to reach the end-of-line. Thus, you would code this as follows:

```
procedure CountLine (var Ints, Words: integer);
 var
  NEXT: String.Typ;
begin
 String.Create(NEXT);
 Ints := 0;
 Words := 0;
 while not eoln do begin
    String.DefineLegal(['0'..'9']);
    String.Read(input, NEXT);
    if String.Length(NEXT) > 0 then begin
       Ints := Ints + 1;
     end; (* If *)
    String.DefineLegal(['a'..'z', 'A'..'Z']);
    String.Read(input, NEXT);
    if String.Length(NEXT) > 0 then begin
      Words := Words + 1;
     end; (* If *)
    String.DefineIllegal(['0'..'9', 'a'..'z', 'A'..'Z']);
    String.Read(input, NEXT);
  end; (* While *)
 String.Destroy(NEXT);
end; (* CountLine *)
```

Figure 2.3 summarizes the operations for customizing *String*.

2.2.3.2. One Implementation of Module *String*

One simple implementation for strings is to use a record with an array of characters and a length variable, as in

```
const
 MaxLen = 30;

type
 CharList = array[1..MaxLen] of char;
 Typ = record
    Chars: CharList;
    Length: integer;
  end;
```

To facilitate later modification, this implementation defines a core of operations that are used to define others. Here is the core for this implementation:

```
procedure CoreInit;
begin
    (* nothing *)
end; (* CoreInit *)
```

OPERATIONS

```
procedure FixOutput (Width: integer);
      post    Subsequent calls on Write will output string
              values in a fixed column with the given width
              (padding with spaces after the string value to
              fill up the column).  String values are always
              displayed in their entirety, even if their
              length exceeds the current column width.  Thus,
              calling this procedure with a width of 0 will
              generate standard behavior.

procedure ConvertToUppercase (Value: boolean);
      post    If Value is True, subsequent calls on Read will
              cause lowercase letters to be converted to their
              uppercase equivalents when read.  For example,
              if Read would normally have returned 'what FUN I
              had today!', it will now return 'WHAT FUN I HAD
              TODAY!'.  This has NO effect on the definition of
              legal/illegal characters.  For example, if legal
              characters are defined as ['A'..'Z'] and this
              option is turned on, lowercase letters will still
              be considered illegal characters (even though IF
              they were read in, they would be converted to
              values in the legal range of ['A'..'Z']).  If
              Value is False, subsequent calls on Read do not
              perform any special conversion on lowercase
              letters.
```

FIGURE 2.3. *Customizing module String.*

```
procedure Create (var Str: Typ);
begin
 Str.Length := 0;
end; (* Create *)

function Length (var Str: Typ): integer;
begin
 Length := Str.Length;
end; (* Length *)

procedure FreeCell (var Str: Typ;
       n: integer);
begin
 if n = Length(Str) then begin
    Str.Length := Str.Length - 1;
   end; (* If *)
end; (* FreeCell *)

procedure ChangeNth (var Str: Typ;
       n: integer;
       Value: char)
begin
```

```
procedure IgnoreCase (Value: boolean);
        post    If Value is True, subsequent calls on Compare
                will ignore the case of letters when comparing
                strings (i.e., 'a' and 'A' will be treated the
                same, 'b' and 'B' will be treated the same,
                etc.). Thus, Compare would report that the
                strings 'MICkey' and 'mIcKeY' are equal while
                this option is on.  If Value is False,
                subsequent calls on Compare will resume
                distinguishing on the basis of case.

procedure DefineLegal (NewSet: CharSet);
        post    For subsequent calls on Read, legal characters
                are now defined to be NewSet; those not in NewSet
                are now considered illegal.

procedure DefineIllegal (NewSet: CharSet);
        post    For subsequent calls on Read, illegal characters
                are now defined to be NewSet; those not in NewSet
                are now considered legal.

procedure SkipJunk (Value: boolean);
        post    If Value is True, subsequent calls on Read will
                skip any illegal characters (including
                end-of-line markers) appearing at the front of
                the input stream before the string-reading
                operation is performed.  If Value is False,
                subsequent calls on Read will behave normally
                (i.e., reading only legal characters).
```

ADDITIONAL DECLARATIONS

```
type CharSet = set of char;
```

FIGURE 2.3. *Customizing module* String *(continued)*.

```
if n = Str.Length + 1 then begin
  Str.Length := Str.Length + 1;
 end; (* If *)
Str.Chars [n] := Value;
end; (* ChangeNth *)

function Nth (var Str: Typ;
        n: integer): char;
begin
Nth := Str.Chars [n];
end; (* Nth *)
```

Similarly, many of the other operations can be accomplished in one or two lines of code, as in:

```
procedure Destroy (var Str: Typ);
 var
  I: integer;
begin
 for I := Length(Str) downto 1 do begin
   FreeCell(Str, I);
  end; (* For *)
end; (* Destroy *)

procedure DeleteNth (var Str: Typ; n: integer);
 var
  INDEX: integer;
begin
 for INDEX := n to Length(Str) - 1 do begin
   ChangeNth(Str, INDEX, Nth(Str, INDEX + 1));
  end; (* For *)
 FreeCell(Str, Length(Str));
end; (* DeleteNth *)

procedure Append10 (var Str: Typ; CharConst: string10);
 var
  INDEX: integer;
begin
 for INDEX := 1 to 10 do begin
   ChangeNth (Str, Length(Str) + 1, CharConst [INDEX])
  end; (* For *)
end; (* Append10 *)

procedure Copy (var Str1, Str2 : Typ);
 var
  I: integer;
begin
 for I := 1 to Length(Str2) do begin
   ChangeNth(Str1, I, Nth(Str2,I));
  end; (* For *)
end; (* Copy *)

procedure Write (var OutFile: text; var Str: Typ);
 var
  INDEX: integer;
begin
 for INDEX := 1 to Length(Str) do begin
   write(OutFile, Nth(Str, INDEX));
  end; (* For *)
 Chars.WritChars(OutFile, FieldWidth - Length(Str), ' ');
end; (* Write *)

procedure Read (var InFile: text; var Str: Typ);
      (* This procedure makes use of a function called *)
      (* Window from a unit called Peek defined in     *)
```

```
                    (* Appendix A                                  *)
        var
         NEXT: char;
        begin
         Str.Length := 0;
         while DoSkipJunk and not (Peek.Window(InFile) in
         LegalSet) and not eof(InFile) do begin
            read(InFile, NEXT);
          end; (* While *)
         while not eoln(InFile) and (Peek.Window(InFile) in
         LegalSet) do begin
            read(InFile, NEXT);
            if ConvertCase then begin
              Chars.Capitalize(NEXT);
            end; (* If *)
            ChangeNth(Str, Length(Str) + 1, NEXT);
          end; (* While *)
        end; (* Read *)
```

The only challenging procedure is *Compare*, because there are many special cases to consider. If one string is shorter than the other, then you have to be careful not to end up examining uninitialized array elements. Even if you keep that under control, you have to deal with the fact that some strings are prefixes of others, as in 'Mick' and 'Mickey'. The normal convention for such strings is to consider the shorter one "less."

Almost all of this complexity can be eliminated by the application of a little abstraction. Step back for a minute and think about which parts of this problem are easy and which are difficult. The easiest case to deal with is the one where you find some position where the corresponding characters differ between the two strings. Then you just have to look to see whether that difference implies a less-relation or a greater-relation. It wouldn't be difficult to deal with the other case where you find the strings identical, except for the complexity introduced by strings that differ in length. Thus, to eliminate much of the complexity, you should eliminate the length difference. You don't have to actually modify the strings to accomplish the equivalent of this. You can write your own special version of *Nth* that pads a short string with blanks. This function also provides an excellent opportunity for dealing with case insensitivity by returning the capitalized version of each character when that option has been selected.

```
        function NthAux (var Str: Typ;
               n: integer): char;
        begin
         if n > Length(Str) then begin
           NthAux := ' ';
          end
         else if CaseInsensitive then begin
           NthAux := Chars.CapOf(Nth(Str, n));
          end
```

```
    else begin
      NthAux := Nth(Str, n);
    end; (* If *)
end; (* NthAux *)
```

Using this function, *Compare* becomes relatively simple to implement:

```
function Compare (var Str1, Str2: Typ): char;
var
  I : integer;
begin
  I := 1;
  while (NthAux(Str1, I) = NthAux(Str2, I)) and (I < MaxLen)
  do begin
    I := I + 1;
  end; (* While *)
  if NthAux(Str1, I) = NthAux(Str2, I) then begin
    compare := '=';
  end
  else if NthAux(Str1, I) < NthAux(Str2, I) then begin
    compare := '<';
  end
  else begin
    compare := '>';
  end; (* If *)
end; (* Compare *)
```

The customizing operations are accomplished through module variables. For example, legal characters are stored in a module variable called *LegalSet* that is manipulated as follows:

```
const
  MinChar = 0;
  MaxChar = 127; (* appropriate value for ASCII character*)
                 (* set                                  *)

var
  LegalSet: CharSet;

procedure Init;
begin
  LegalSet := [chr(MinChar)..chr(MaxChar)];
  . . .
end; (* Init *)

procedure DefineLegal (NewSet: CharSet);
begin
  LegalSet := NewSet;
end; (* DefineLegal *)
```

```
procedure DefineIllegal (NewSet: CharSet);
begin
  LegalSet := [chr(MinChar)..chr(MaxChar)] - NewSet;
end; (* DefineIllegal *)
```

2.2.4. The Danger of Redundancy and the Need for Isolation

Despite their similarities, software components differ from their physical counterparts in significant ways. Because they are made from information and not from matter, they are easily duplicated and don't suffer physical deterioration when exposed to the elements.

But software components can suffer their own peculiar kind of deterioration. One factor encouraging decay is the ease with which components are copied. Imagine the fate of a component that has been copied to ten different programs, and each copy has been updated with different improvements. Soon the component turns into a tribe of mutations, all the same in some sense, but with subtle differences.

The goal of abstraction is to allow you to apply such components based on a *simple* specification. As the variations of a component proliferate, it accumulates more and more unnecessary detail, like a snowball getting bigger and bigger as it rolls downhill faster and faster, speeding toward disaster.

Modules provide a reasonable alternative to this fate. By encapsulating a component in a module, any program that wants to use it can link to it through the module. That way a single copy of the component's definition can be maintained, ensuring that all updates are made in the same place and that the component's interface will remain as simple as possible. This also enhances the potential reliability of the component, given that you can concentrate more attention on the testing of a single version of the component than you can on a series of its variations.

This idea of keeping only one copy of a component's definition can be carried even further to the point of complete *isolation* of the component's implementation inside the module that defines it. Procedures and functions in Pascal can be written to have this complete level of isolation. This leaves any high-level code independent of the low-level implementation details. For example, the calls on module *Math*'s function *Power* might number in the thousands, but only the body of the procedure needs to be changed to reimplement it.

2.2.5. Isolation and ADTs

Suppose that you have used module *String* to give a value to string variable *Str*. How would you write its contents in reverse order? You could say

```
for I := Str.Length downto 1 do begin
  write(Str.Chars[I]);
end; (* For *)
```

This turns out to be a very bad approach. To put you in the correct frame of mind, let's pause for an analogy. Suppose that you have just received a shipment of plutonium isotopes for an experiment you want to perform. The easiest thing to do would be to rip open the package and take out the plutonium, but you won't do that because you know that the radiation can kill you. So what do you do? You put the plutonium in a sealed chamber that shields you from radiation and you use either gloves or a robot arm to actually handle the plutonium.

Suppose you use a robot arm. You will probably find this frustrating because you have to give commands to move the robot arm rather than using your own arm, which is bound to be more clumsy. If the robot arm is unable to carry out some essential operation, you will either have to scrap the experiment or unseal the room and do it yourself. Unless you don't care about failed experiments or unless you have a strong death wish, you will probably carefully consider all operations you want the robot arm to perform *before* the experiment begins.

The code fragment above is like the experimenter who opens up the plutonium and manipulates it directly. Instead of using the operations *Length* and *Nth*, it makes direct reference to the fields of the record. Using the "official" subprograms instead, you would get this code:

```
for I := Length(Str) downto 1 do begin
  Write(Nth(Str, I));
  end; (* For *)
```

While these two code fragments look similar, the difference between them is tremendous. ADT String was specified with a specific interface in mind. That interface did *not* include mention of references like *Str.Length* and *Str.Chars[I]*, which rely on the fact that the implementation is a record with fields called *Length* and *Chars*. In fact, the specification made no mention of the underlying structure at all.

Pascal does a good job of protecting procedures and functions, forcing other parts of the program to access them through their intended interface. For example, if you try to call function *Power* using the wrong number of parameters or if you make reference to one of its local variables from the ouside, your program won't even compile. Unfortunately, there is no corresponding enforcement of a data type's interface. You are more than welcome to try to open up the record structure and fiddle around with the insides, as the code at the beginning of this section does.

You might be wondering, what's the big deal? Does it really matter if you use *Str.Length* instead of *Length(Str)?* The answer is yes, and for the same reasons outlined in the last section. When a component's implementation is isolated from high-level manipulations, it can easily be replaced. The implementation of function *Power* can be replaced without making *any* change to high-level manipulations.

What happens if the *String* module is reimplemented in such a way that *Str.Length* is no longer a valid reference to the string's length? The answer is that such code will fail to work. Thus, you not only have to rewrite the implementation details of module *String*, but also any code like the example at the beginning of this section that makes direct reference to the underlying structure.

The implementation details of an ADT need to be isolated from high-level manipulations. Because the language doesn't provide a protection mechanism, you have to police yourself. Just as the researcher didn't permit himself to touch his radioactive isotopes, you can't allow yourself to violate the abstraction and touch the structure directly. This barrier is often referred to as *the wall* that should separate the implementation from the application of an ADT. The best way to stay on your side of the wall is to always adhere to the ADT's interface. The following diagram expresses this idea.

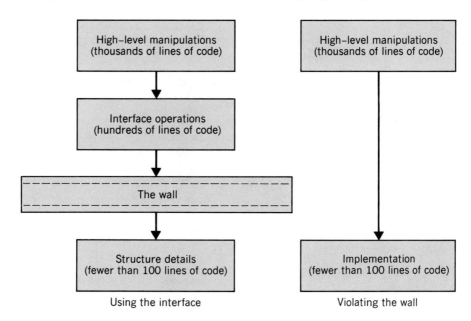

The interface operations cross the wall, but that's okay, because they are part of the module's implementation. If you obey the wall, as in the left-hand side of the diagram, you can change implementations by changing the structure details and the interface operations (on the order of hundreds of lines of code). If, however, you bypass the wall, changing implementations will require changes to high-level manipulations, which could lead to thousands of lines of code to change.

2.2.6. Reimplementing the ADT String

The implementation of strings in Section 2.2.3 can be highly wasteful of space. Each string is allocated an array big enough to hold the largest legal string, even if it only uses a small percentage of those elements. Another approach is to have all strings stored in a very large common array. That way they can be packed more tightly together. For example, instead of using ninety elements to store three short strings:

string1	Length	[1]	[2]	[3]	[4]	[5]	[6]	[7]	[8]	[..]	[30]
	2	'O'	'n'	?	?	?	?	?	?	...	?

string2	Length	[1]	[2]	[3]	[4]	[5]	[6]	[7]	[8]	[..]	[30]
	2	'm'	'y'	?	?	?	?	?	?	...	?

Length	[1]	[2]	[3]	[4]	[5]	[6]	[7]	[8]	[..]	[30]
string3 3	'w'	'a'	'y'	?	?	?	?	?	...	?

You can use 7 array elements and 6 integers:

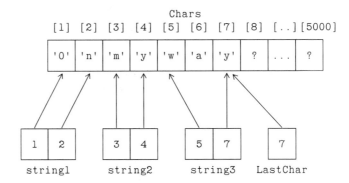

As indicated in the diagram above, a fixed-length character array called *Chars* is used as the common storage area for the strings. Because all the characters are stored here, the strings need only store the two indices that mark the first and last characters of the string. Finally, the variable *LastChar* keeps track of the last element of the common storage area that is being used. This is necessary because you need to know what part of the common block to use when new strings are added.

The type declarations are as follows:

```
const
  MaxLen = 5000;
  MinChar = 0;
  MaxChar = 127;

type
  CharList = array[1..MaxLen] of char;

  Typ = record
    start: integer;
    stop: integer;
  end;

var
  Chars: CharList;
  LastChar: integer;
```

The core would be rewritten as follows for this implementation:

```
procedure NewLastChar (Value: char);
begin
 LastChar := LastChar + 1;
 Chars[LastChar] := Value;
end; (* NewLastChar *)

procedure CoreInit;
begin
 LastChar := 0;
end; (* CoreInit *)

procedure Create (var Str :Typ);
begin
 Str.start := LastChar + 1;
 Str.stop := LastChar;
end; (* Create *)

function Length (var Str: Typ): integer;
begin
 Length := Str.Stop - Str.Start + 1;
end; (* Length *)

procedure FreeCell (var Str: Typ;
        n: integer);
begin
 if (n = Length(Str)) then begin
   if (Str.stop = LastChar) then begin
    LastChar := LastChar - 1;
    end; (* If *)
   Str.stop := Str.stop - 1;
  end; (* If *)
end; (* FreeCell *)

procedure ChangeNth (var Str: Typ;
        n: integer;
        Value: char);
 var
  I: integer;
begin
 if n <= Length(Str) then begin
   Chars[Str.Start + n - 1] := Value;
  end
 else begin
   if (Length(Str) > 0) and (Str.Stop <> LastChar) then begin
     for I := Str.Start to Str.Stop do begin
       NewLastChar(Chars[I]);
       end; (* For *)
```

```
      Str.Start := LastChar - Length(Str) + 1;
      Str.Stop := LastChar;
    end; (* If *)
  NewLastChar(Value);
  if Length(Str) = 0 then begin
    Str.start := LastChar;
    Str.stop := LastChar;
  end
  else begin
    Str.stop := Str.stop + 1;
    end; (* If *)
  end; (* If *)
end; (* ChangeNth *)

function Nth (var Str: Typ;
        n: integer): char;
begin
 Nth := Chars[Str.Start + n - 1];
end; (* Nth *)
```

Notice that in this implementation, functions *Length* and *Nth* have entirely new definitions. Consider again the two code fragments from the last section. The first is not only incorrect, it actually generates compiler error messages because there are no fields called *Length* and *Chars* in *Str*.

```
for I := Str.Length downto 1 do begin
  write(Str.Chars[I]);
end; (* For *)
```

The code that stays on the appropriate side of the wall by adhering to the interface, however, works without modification in this implementation, because the necessary changes all occur in functions *Length* and *Nth*.

```
for I := Length(Str) downto 1 do begin
  Write(Nth(Str, I));
  end; (* For *)
```

The detailed code for this implementation is presented in Appendix A, but let's review a few of the more central operations in this implementation. When strings are created, they are set up pointing to *LastChar*:

```
procedure Create (var Str: Typ);
begin
    Str.start := LastChar + 1;
    Str.stop := LastChar;
end; (* Create *)
```

The tricky operation in this implementation is *ChangeNth*. The easy case is where you're changing a character inside the string. The difficult case is when you change the character at *Length* + 1, in which case you have to find space for the new character. There are two possibilities that would allow you to simply use the character at position *chars[LastChar* + 1] to store this value: if the string is currently empty, or if the end of the string is already pointing to *chars[LastChar]*. The other case is where you are asked to add a character to a nonempty string appearing somewhere in the middle of the space currently being used in *chars*. You have few alternatives in this situation. If you try to take over the array element to the right of the string's current position, it's likely that you will overlap with another string variable. The alternative is to copy the entire string to the end of *chars* (i.e., so that it now starts at *LastChar* + 1). Here is the code that implements this strategy:

```
procedure ChangeNth (var Str: Typ;
         n: integer;
         Value: char);
  var
   I: integer;
begin
 if n <= Length(Str) then begin
   Chars[Str.Start + n - 1] := Value;
   end
 else begin
   if (Length(Str) > 0) and (Str.Stop <> LastChar) then
   begin
     for I := Str.Start to Str.Stop do begin
       NewLastChar(Chars[I]);
       end; (* For *)
     Str.Start := LastChar - Length(Str) + 1;
     Str.Stop := LastChar;
    end; (* If *)
   NewLastChar(Value);
   if Length(Str) = 0 then begin
     Str.Start := LastChar;
     Str.Stop := LastChar;
    end
   else begin
     Str.Stop := Str.Stop + 1;
    end; (* If *)
  end; (* If *)
end; (* ChangeNth *)
```

2.2.7. Generic Structures

When writing subprograms, you often find yourself solving a problem that can be generalized to solve more than just the current problem. Most typically, you recognize a useful pattern of manipulations on a particular variable and you realize that there is nothing special about the current variable you're using; other variables could be manipulated in the same way. Parameters give you a means for expressing your generalization. By using a parameter, you can define the procedure in terms of a generic name used as a placeholder. Then you can call the procedure as many times as you like, supplying a different specific value each time to fill the placeholder.

When you write ADTs you also find a spectrum of generality. For example, if you are creating an ADT for a deck of cards, you will probably find that it's a fairly specific structure that can't be easily reused for another ADT. But if you find yourself creating a powerful ADT whose properties seem to have little to do with the specific kind of data being stored, but rather, seem to be an outgrowth of generic structural principles, then you have found an ADT that can be generalized and used again. For example, if you are creating a structure for storing a sorted list of words, you will soon start recognizing that many of the properties of the structure are the result of the sorting, not the fact that words were being sorted.

Ada provides a mechanism called a *generic type* that does for ADT modules what parameters do for subprograms. You define the ADT module using a generic placeholder for a type. Then you can create different versions of the module by supplying specific types to fill the placeholder.

Pascal doesn't have generic types, so we have to settle for something less. This book presents several structures that are referred to as *structure-ADTs*. A structure-ADT does not mean an ADT with structure. It means an ADT whose structure is generic enough that it can be thought of as representing a family of structures whose ADT modules are virtually identical, differing only in the specific type of data they store.

All of the structure-ADTs presented in this book store an indefinite number of elements all of the same type. Instead of writing the ADT module using a specific type name like *Integer*, you introduce a generic placeholder for the type before you write any code. The standard identifier your authors have chosen for this purpose is *ElementType*. Thus, you write the ADT module using *ElementType* whenever you need to refer to the type of the elements being stored. If you happen to be creating a structure for storing integers, you would then include the following declaration at the beginning of the ADT module:

```
type
  ElementType = integer;
```

This technique is similar to removing magic numbers from a program by introducing program constants. It also suffers from the same limitations. You have to recompile the module everytime you change the definition of *ElementType*. And if you need to simultaneously be able to use this structure with two different kinds of elements, you'll have to create two copies of the module that differ only in their definition of *ElementType*. Thus, the generic type identifier *ElementType* will allow you to generalize the ADT, but without the kind of support Pascal gives to parameters and Ada gives to generic types, this will still prove a somewhat tedious solution.

2.2.8. The ADT Stack

One of the most common techniques we have for managing multiple occurrences of an item is to stack them one on top of the other. We make stacks of books, stacks of papers, stacks of empty pizza boxes, and so on.

The same simple principle proves incredibly useful in programming and leads to a structure known as a *Stack*. Stacks store elements all of the same type, but it is a generic structure because its behavior in no way depends on the items it stores.

The governing structural principle for a Stack is that when elements are removed from the structure, they appear in *Last In First Out*, or *LIFO*, order. If you imagine forming a stack of books on your desk, this is exactly the behavior you would expect. The first book that you put down ends up on the bottom of the stack, which means that you won't remove it until all others have been removed. Conversely, the most recent element added to the stack will always be on top, making it the easiest element to remove.

If you are the kind of person who is the first to arrive at the airport (just like one of the authors) or if you are the kind of person who always arrives with just seconds to spare (like the other author), you've probably noticed that stacks introduce a kind of inherent unfairness in that they reverse the order of things. Thus, the last-minute flyer who often manages to delay the flight is usually the first person to get his luggage at the other end, which only encourages his bad behavior even more.

You will find, however, that in the world of programming, there are a surprising number of applications where reversing a sequence is not only acceptable, it is actually desirable.

The detailed specifications of the structure Stack appear in Figure 2.4.

Its implementation in an array is fairly straightforward. All the manipulations reduce to modifying the value of *S.Top* as the Stack changes and storing or retrieving the value at *S.Elems[S.Top]*.

Here is the detailed code in standard unit syntax. You will notice one minor change from the generic specification. In function *Empty*, the Stack is passed as a *var* parameter in this implementation to avoid the wasteful copying of the Stack structure that would result if it were left as a value parameter.

```
unit Stack;

interface

  const
  MaxStack = 1000;

  type
  ElementType = integer;

  ElementList = array[1..MaxStack] of ElementType;
```

STRUCTURE
Stores a series of elements all of type *ElementType*

Initially empty

Elements removed in LIFO order

OPERATIONS
```
procedure Push (var S: Typ; Item: ElementType);
        post    Item is added to the top of S

procedure Pop (var S: Typ; var Item: ElementType);
        pre     not Empty(S)
        post    S has its top element removed.
                Item holds that element.
```

STANDARD OPERATORS
Create, Destroy, Empty

ADDITIONAL DECLARATIONS
Type *ElementType* (default = *integer*)

FIGURE 2.4. Specification for structure-ADT *Stack.*

```
Typ = record
  Elems: ElementList;
  Top: integer;
  end;

procedure Create (var S: Typ);
   (* post : S is initialized and empty *)

procedure Destroy (var S: Typ);
   (* post : Memory allocated for S is released; *)
   (*        S is uninitialized                  *)

procedure Push (var S: Typ;
     Item: ElementType);
   (* post : Item is added to the top of S *)

procedure Pop (var S: Typ;
     var Item: ElementType);
   (* pre  : not Empty(S).                 *)
   (* post : S has its top element removed. *)
   (*      : Item holds that element.       *)

function Empty (var S: Typ): boolean;
   (* post : True if S is empty, False otherwise *)
```

```
implementation

 procedure Create (var S: Typ);
 begin
  S.Top := 0;
 end; (* Create *)

 procedure Destroy (var S: Typ);
 begin
       (* nothing to do *)
 end; (* Destroy *)

 procedure Push (var S: Typ;
      Item: ElementType);
 begin
  S.Top := S.Top + 1;
  S.Elems[S.Top] := Item;
 end; (* Push *)

 procedure Pop (var S: Typ;
      var Item: ElementType);
 begin
  Item := S.Elems [S.Top];
  S.Top := S.Top - 1;
 end; (* Pop *)

 function Empty (var S: Typ): boolean;
 begin
  Empty := (S.Top = 0);
 end; (* Empty *)

end. (* Stack *)
```

2.2.8.1. A Simple Stack Program: Reversing Numbers

Because Stacks by nature put things in reverse order, it is easy to use them to reverse lists. For example, the following program reads a sequence of integers one per line, as in:

```
100
32000
-20
150
```

and it generates the same sequence of numbers in reverse order:

```
150
-20
32000
100
```

This is easily accomplished by first pushing numbers onto the Stack, and then emptying it by popping them back off again.

```
program Numbers;

uses
 Stack;

var
 S: Stack.Typ;

procedure ReadAndStoreNumbers (var NumberStack: Stack.Typ);
 var
  TEMP: Stack.ElementType;
begin
 while not eof do begin
   readln(TEMP);
   Stack.Push(NumberStack, TEMP);
  end; (* While *)
end; (* ReadAndStoreNumbers *)

procedure PrintNumbers (var NumberStack: Stack.Typ);
 var
  TEMP: Stack.ElementType;
begin
 while not Stack.Empty(NumberStack) do begin
   Stack.Pop(NumberStack, TEMP);
   writeln(TEMP);
  end; (* While *)
end; (* PrintNumbers *)

begin (* Main *)
 Stack.Create(S);
 ReadAndStoreNumbers(S);
 PrintNumbers(S);
 Stack.Destroy(S);
end. (* Main *)
```

2.2.8.2. A Complex Stack Program: An RPN Calculator

Many early calculators did not perform arithmetic the way people normally do. Instead of accepting input like "3 * 9" or "18 * 24 − 3 / 4," these calculators allowed expressions to be entered with each operator appearing *after* its two operands, as in "3 9 *" and "18 24 * 3 4 / −." This is called *Reverse Polish Notation*, or *RPN*.

Many calculators used RPN because it turns out that computing RPN expressions is fairly simple if you have a Stack for auxiliary storage and because it allows the user to avoid using parentheses. Because the operator appears after the operands (e.g., "3 9 *"), when you see numbers, you put them on the Stack for safe keeping while you wait for the operator(s) to appear. When you see operators, you pop two operands off the Stack, evaluate the operator, and put the result back on the Stack in case this is a subexpression of a larger expression. For example, to evaluate "3 9 *," you would

start with an empty Stack, S = ()
read 3, push it on the Stack, S = (3)
read 9, push it on the Stack, S = (9, 3)
read *, pop 9 and 3, push result of 27 onto Stack, S = (27)

To evaluate "18 24 * 3 4 / −," you would

start with an empty Stack, S = ()
read 18, push it on the Stack, S = (18)
read 24, push it on the Stack, S = (24, 18)
read *, pop 24 and 18, push result of 432 onto stack, S = (432)
read 3, push it on the Stack, S = (3, 432)
read 4, push it on the Stack, S = (4, 3, 432)
read /, pop 4 and 3, push result of 0.75 onto Stack, S = (.75, 432)
read −, pop 0.75 and 432, push result of 431.25 onto Stack, S = (431.25)

Consider the task of creating an interactive RPN calculator. It should behave something like this:

```
CALC> 3 9 *
  =  27.000000
CALC> 18 24 * 3 4 / -
  =  431.250000
CALC> 2
  =  2.000000
CALC> 2 ^
  =  4.000000
CALC> 3 ^
  =  64.000000
CALC> 85 *
  =  5440.000000
```

It turns out that the main loop is quite simple to write using the standard Stack operations and using module *LineBuff* to take care of some of the input details. Basically, you prompt the user, and then read a series of tokens from the input line. If you see a number, push it on the Stack. If you see an operator, pop off two operands, evaluate a result, and push it back on the Stack. When you reach the end of the line, report the current top of the Stack to the user (but be sure to put it back on the Stack so that the user can perform the kind of cumulative calculations that appear in the last few requests above). Here is the basic code:

```
program RPN;

uses
 Stack, LineBuff, Chars;

var
 S: Stack.Typ;
 Quit: Boolean;

procedure ReportTopOfStack (var S: Stack.Typ);
 var
  ELEM: Stack.ElementType;
begin
 Stack.Pop(S, ELEM);
 writeln(' = ', ELEM : 1 : 6);
 Stack.Push(S, ELEM);
end; (* ReportTopOfStack *)

procedure ProcessOneToken (var S: Stack.Typ;
      var Quit: boolean);
 var
  NUM1, NUM2: Stack.ElementType;
  OPER: char;
begin
 if LineBuff.AtNum then begin
   LineBuff.ReadReal(NUM1);
   Stack.Push(S, NUM1);
  end
 else begin
   LineBuff.ReadChar(OPER);
   Quit := (Chars.CapOf(OPER) = 'Q');
   if not Quit then begin
     Stack.Pop(S, NUM1);
     Stack.Pop(S, NUM2);
     case OPER of
      '+':
      Stack.Push(S, NUM2 + NUM1);
      '-':
      Stack.Push(S, NUM2 - NUM1);
      '*':
      Stack.Push(S, NUM2 * NUM1);
      '/':
      Stack.Push(S, NUM2 / NUM1);
      '^':
      Stack.Push(S, exponent(NUM2, NUM1));
     end; (* Case *)
    end; (* If *)
  end; (* If *)
end; (* ProcessOneToken *)
```

```
begin (* Main *)
 Stack.Create(S);
 repeat
  write('CALC> ');
  LineBuffReadLine (input);
  while not LineBuff.Eoln do begin
    ProcessOneToken(S, Quit);
   end; (* While *)
   ReportTopOfStack(S);
  until Quit;
  Stack.Destroy(S);
end.
```

One subtlety in this code is the fact that the expressions in the case statement have *Num2* appearing before *Num1*. That is because the Stack reverses their order, so you have to reverse them back again, or you will get incorrect results for operators like / and ˆ where order is significant.

2.2.9. The Stream ADT

One of the most significant limitations of the Stack ADT is that you cannot easily traverse the elements, since the *Pop* operation is the only mechanism for examining the elements of a Stack, and every *Pop* removes an element. Thus, to nondestructively traverse a Stack you must store each popped element in a separate data structure (probably another Stack), and then restore your original Stack upon completing your traversal. The Stream ADT, like the Stack, is a generic structure ADT, but is one that permits simple traversals.

The Stream ADT will probably look very familiar to you, since Pascal's file type is an example of a Stream. The ADT allows you to write data to the Stream and then traverse the Stream repeatedly, starting from its beginning. Just as with Pascal's files, though, you can write only to the end of the Stream, and going from the Reading to the Writing mode erases the contents of the Stream. Even given these limitations, though, the Stream ADT has a number of applications. It is particularly useful when you first generate a set of data, and then want to examine that set nondestructively.

The Stream ADT maintains a position pointer, analogous to Pascal's file window, which indicates the client's current position in the Stream. If the client is in the Reading mode, then the pointer references the next element to be accessed, while if the client is Writing, then the pointer indicates the end of the Stream. The detailed specifications of the structure Stream appear in Figure 2.5. Note that the Stream ADT uses the standard ADT operations Read and Write, but does so to make the relationship between Streams and Pascal files clear, and thus does not use meaning ascribed to them as standard operations.

Implementing the Stream is also fairly straightforward. Below is one implementation that uses an array to store the elements:

STRUCTURE

Stores a series of elements all of type *ElementType*

Initially empty

Inserts elements at end

Accesses elements sequentially

Is either in the Undetermined, Reading, or Writing mode. Switching to the Writing
   mode erases the contents

OPERATIONS

```
procedure Reset (var S: Typ);
        post    S is in the Reading mode.
                Sets the position pointer so that the first
                element in S is the next element returned by
                Read.

procedure Rewrite (var S: Typ);
        post    S is in the Writing mode.
                S is empty.

procedure Read (var S: Typ;
                var Item: ElementType);
        pre     S is in the Reading mode.
        post    Item returns the value of the element at the
                position indicated by the position pointer.
                The position pointer references the next item in
                the Stream.

procedure Write (var S: Typ;
                 Item:ElementType);
        pre     S is in the Writing mode.
        post    Item is appended to the end of S.

function AtEnd (var S: StreamTyp): boolean;
        pre     S in in the Reading mode.
        post    True is S's position pointer is past the last
                element.
```

STANDARD OPERATORS

Create, Destroy

ADDITIONAL DECLARATIONS

Type *ElementType* (default = *integer*)

FIGURE 2.5. Specification for structure-ADT *Stream.*

```
unit Stream;

interface

 const
  MaxStream = 80;

 type
  ModeType = (Undetermined, Reading, Writing);
  ElementTyp = integer;
  StreamArray = array[1..MaxStream] of ElementTyp;
  Typ = record
    Mode: ModeType;
    Data: StreamArray;
    Length: integer;
    CurrPos: integer;
   end; (* Typ *)

 procedure Create (var S: Typ);

 procedure Destroy (var S: Typ);

 procedure Reset (var S: Typ);

 procedure Rewrite (var S: Typ);

 procedure Read (var S: Typ;
      var Item: ElementTyp);

 procedure Write (var S: Typ;
      Item: ElementTyp);

 function AtEnd (var S: Typ): boolean;

implementation

 procedure Create (var S: Typ);
 begin
  S.Mode := Undetermined;
  S.Length := 0;
 end; (* Create *)

 procedure Destroy (var S: Typ);
 begin
      (* nothing to do *)
 end; (* Destroy *)

 procedure Reset (var S: Typ);
 begin
  S.Mode := Reading;
```

```
      S.CurrPos := 0;
    end; (* Reset *)

    procedure Rewrite (var S: Typ);
    begin
      Destroy(S);
      Create(S);
      S.Mode := Writing;
    end; (* Reset *)

    procedure Read (var S: Typ;
          var Item: ElementTyp);
    begin
      S.CurrPos := S.CurrPos + 1;
      Item := S.Data[S.CurrPos];
    end; (* Read *)

    procedure Write (var S: Typ;
          Item: ElementTyp);
    begin
      S.Length := S.Length + 1;
      S.Data[S.Length] := Item;
    end; (* Write *)

    function AtEnd (var S: Typ): boolean;
    begin
      AtEnd := S.CurrPos = S.Length;
    end; (* AtEnd *)

  end. (* Stream *)
```

Note that this code omits any error-checking. This is particularly glaring since the mode is set, but is never examined. Proper error-checking in ADTs, however, is difficult in Pascal, which does not provide a formal exception-handling mechanism, and this discussion is therefore deferred until Chapter 8.

2.2.9.1. A Simple Stream Example: Computing Standard Deviation

Standard deviation is a statistical measure that indicates the amount that a set of numbers deviates from its mean (where the mean is the sum of the numbers divided by the number of numbers). For example, both of the following sets of numbers have a mean of 100:

```
Set 1:  100, 100, 101, 99, 100
Set 2:  50, 200, 0, 150
```

but the standard deviation of the first set is very small (0.71) because all the numbers are close to the mean, while the deviation for the second set is large (91.3). If $\overline{x}$

represents the mean of the set of numbers $\{x_1, \ldots, x_n\}$, then the following formula gives the standard deviation:

$$\text{standard deviation} = \sqrt{\frac{\sum\limits_{i=1}^{n} (x_i - \overline{x})^2}{n - 1}}$$

A Stream is appropriate for storing the numbers because you first gather the numbers (from, say, the keyboard), and then traverse the stream twice, first to compute the mean, and then to compute the standard deviation (which requires the value of the mean):

```
program CompStandardDev;

uses
  Stream;

var
  NumStream: Stream.Typ;

procedure ReadNums (var NumStream: Stream.Typ);
  var
    NUM: integer;
begin
  Stream.Rewrite(NumStream);
  while not eoln do begin
    read(NUM);
    Stream.Write(NumStream, NUM);
  end; (* While *)
  readln;
end; (* ReadNums *)


function ComputeMean (NumStream: Stream.Typ): real;
  var
    COUNT, SUM, NUM: integer;
begin
  Stream.Reset(NumStream);
  COUNT := 0;
  SUM := 0;
  while not Stream.AtEnd(NumStream) do begin
    COUNT := COUNT + 1;
    Stream.Read(NumStream, NUM);
    SUM := SUM + NUM;
  end; (* While *)
  ComputeMean := SUM / COUNT;
end; (* ComputeMean *)
```

```
function ComputeSD (NumStream: Stream.Typ): real;
var
  COUNT, NUM: integer;
  SUM, MEAN: real;
begin
MEAN := ComputeMean(NumStream);
Stream.Reset(NumStream);
COUNT := 0;
while not Stream.AtEnd(NumStream) do begin
  COUNT := COUNT + 1;
  Stream.Read(NumStream, NUM);
  SUM := SUM + sqr(NUM - MEAN);
 end; (* While *)
ComputeSD := sqrt(SUM / (COUNT - 1));
end; (* ComputeSD *)

begin
Stream.Create(NumStream);
ReadNums(NumStream);
writeln('The standard deviation is ',
ComputeSD(NumStream) : 1 : 2, '.');
Stream.Destroy(NumStream);
end. (* Main *)
```

2.2.10. SELF CHECK EXERCISES

1. Why does the program have to call *Create* for a variable? Why can't each module procedure and function check to see if the variable has not yet been created and call *Create* if it hasn't?

2. Why is it necessary to have a procedure *Copy* that copies the value of one variable to another? Why can't you use simple assignment statements such as:

```
data2 := data1;
```

2.3. THE TABLE ADT

You will often want to structure your data by some implicit ordering function. For example, you might want to keep a list of names in alphabetical order, or you might want to keep a list of events in order by date. For such applications, you usually build a list by inserting new elements in their proper place, as defined by the ordering function. This section presents an abstract specification for one such structure called a Table.

Each Table stores several elements, each of the same type *ElementType*. The complete specification for the type appears in Figure 2.6.

STRUCTURE

Stores a series of elements all of type *ElementType*

Initially empty

Stored such that *FindMin* and *InTable* require little execution time

---

OPERATIONS

```
function InTable (var T: Typ; Item: ElementType) : boolean;
        post    True if an element of T equals Item, False
                otherwise

procedure Insert (var T: Typ; Item: ElementType);
        post    Item is added to T such that T remains sorted.

procedure Delete (var T: Typ; Item: ElementType);
        pre     InTable(T, Item)
        post    The first element of T equal to Item is deleted

procedure FindMin (var T: Typ; var Item: ElementType);
        pre     not Empty(T)
        post    Item is set to the first element in T whose value
                is minimal

procedure Extract (var T: Typ; Item: ElementType; var NewT: Typ);
        post    All elements of T equal to Item (if any) are
                transferred to NewT
```

STANDARD OPERATORS

Create, Destroy, Write, Empty

ADDITIONAL DECLARATIONS

Uses module TableElement with definitions for:

Type *ElementType* (default = *integer*)

Function *Compare* (default = simple $<$, $>$, $=$)

Procedure *PrintElement* (default = simple *writeln(entry)*)

FIGURE 2.6. Specification for structure-ADT *Table*.

Sometimes you will want to store simple data like integers, but other applications will require more complex structures. To accommodate this variety, the Table type module uses a module called *TableElement* with definitions that control ordering and printing of individual elements. These are default values for the definitions. You will often tailor the module to behave properly for a specific element type:

```
unit TableElement;

interface
```

```
type
 ElementType = integer;

procedure PrintElement (var Outfile: text;
      var Entry: Typ);

function Compare (var Datal, Data2: Typ): char;

implementation

procedure PrintElement (var Outfile: text;
      var Entry: Typ);
begin
 writeln(entry);
end; (* PrintElement *)

function Compare (var Datal, Data2: Typ): char;
begin
 if x < y then begin
   Compare:= '<';
  end
 else if x = y then begin
   Compare:= '=';
  end
 else begin
   Compare:= '>';
  end;
end; (* Compare *)

end. (* TableElement *)
```

2.3.1. Sorting Integers

The Table type can be used to read a sequence of integers from an input file and produce an output file with the numbers in sorted order and with duplicates removed. For example, if the input is:

```
16
94
8
5
16
90
94
5
```

the output should be

```
     5
     8
    16
    90
    94
```

This is a simple task using the Table type. The default value of an integer table and the simple versions of *Compare* and *PrintElement* work fine, so you need only to write a short main program that reads an external data file called numbers.dat and inserts the elements into a table, checking for duplicates, printing the table to the standard output (i.e., the terminal).

```
program SortNumbers;

uses
  Table;

var
  Numbers: Table.Typ;
  NEXT: integer;
  infile: text;

begin (* Main *)
 assign(infile, 'numbers.dat');
 reset(infile);
 Table.Create(Numbers);
 while not eof(infile) do begin
    readln(infile, NEXT);
    if not Table.InTable(Numbers, NEXT) then begin
      Table.Insert(Numbers, NEXT);
    end; (* If *)
  end; (* While *)
 Table.Write(Numbers);
 Table.Destroy(Numbers);
end. (* Main *)
```

2.3.2. Manipulating Birthdays

Suppose that you have an input file of birthday entries, one per line, each line containing a name terminated by a semicolon followed by three integers that represent the month, day, and year of the birthday, as in

```
Martin, Ruth; 3 19 24
Brent, Charlie; 9 18 70
Martin, Joe; 7 23 26
Chandler, Adam; 3 19 18
```

To use these birthday entries to figure out which people have the same birthday, you must put them in order by month and day, producing output like this:

```
3/19    1918    Chandler, Adam
3/19    1924    Martin, Ruth
7/23    1926    Martin, Joe
9/18    1970    Brent, Charlie
```

This is easily accomplished with the Table type. The String type can be used to store and manipulate the name. This is a structured type, so you can no longer rely on the simple definitions for *Compare* and *PrintElement*. Thus, module *TableElement* is rewritten as follows:

```
unit TableElement;

interface

uses
 String;

 type
  ElementType = record
    Name: String.Typ;
    Month, Day, Year: integer;
   end; (* ElementType *)

 procedure PrintElement (var Outfile: text;
       var Entry: ElementType);

 function Compare (var Data1, Data2: ElementType): char;

implementation

 procedure PrintElement (var Outfile: text;
       var Entry: ElementType);
 begin
  write(Entry.Month : 2, '/', Entry.Day : 2, 19 : 5,
  Entry.Year : 2, ' ' : 4);
  String.Write(Entry.Name);
  writeln;
 end; (* PrintElement *)

 function Compare (var Data1, Data2: ElementType): char;
 (* Compares two dates ignoring the year *)
 begin
  if (x.Month < y.Month) or ((x.Month = y.Month) and
  (x.Day < y.Day)) then begin
    Compare := '<';
   end
```

```
      else if (x.Month = y.Month) and (x.Day = y.Day) then
      begin
        Compare := '=';
       end
      else begin
        Compare := '>';
       end; (* If *)
    end; (* Compare *)

  end. (* TableElement *)
```

Now you can write the main program. The String module can be customized to break on a semicolon character, which makes reading an entry fairly simple. Each entry in the input file should be read into a variable of type *ElementType* and inserted into the Table. When *eof* is reached, the table can be printed. Thus, the program is as follows:

```
program SortBirthdays;

uses
  String, Table;

var
  People: Table.Typ;
  ENTRY: TableElement.ElementType;
  infile: text;

begin (* Main *)
  assign(infile, 'birthdays.dat');
  reset(infile);
  Table.Create(People);
  String.Create(ENTRY.Name);
  String.DefineIllegal([';']);
  while not eof(infile) do begin
    String.Read(infile, ENTRY.Name);
    readln(infile, ENTRY.Month, ENTRY.Day, ENTRY.Year);
    Insert(People, ENTRY);
   end; (* While *)
  Table.Write(People);
  Table.Destroy(People);
  String.Destroy(ENTRY.Name);
end. (* Main *)
```

2.3.3. Solving Anagrams

An anagram is obtained by rearranging the letters of a word. For example, CAT has anagrams: CTA, ACT, ATC, TCA, and TAC. Anagrams are presented as puzzles, requiring you to imagine how the letters might be rearranged to form a legal word.

If you have access to a dictionary-like list of words, you can solve these anagrams easily using a Table.

For example, suppose the anagram you are trying to solve is REAPS. It has many legal anagrams: SPEAR, SPARE, PEARS, REAPS, PARES, etc. You could more easily solve the puzzle if you had a list of all such words from the dictionary. To produce such lists, you need to create a table where all of the anagrams of REAPS are grouped together and can be located using REAPS. The trick is to devise a transformation on words such that all of the anagrams of a given character sequence are transformed into the same sequence. This can be done by putting the characters of the word into sorted order:

```
REAPS  -->  AEPRS
SPEAR  -->  AEPRS
SPARE  -->  AEPRS
PEARS  -->  AEPRS
REAPS  -->  AEPRS
PARES  -->  AEPRS
```

Thus, if the table is sorted by the transformed word, then all of the words above will be grouped together, because they all transform into AEPRS. Of course, you'll want to display the original word, so each element should store both the original word and the transformed word. The String type can again be used to store words. You again must reimplement the type definition and operations *Compare* and *PrintElement* of module *TableElement*. You want to use the transformed word for ordering and the original word for display:

```
unit TableElement;

interface

  uses
  String;

  type
   ElementType = record
     Word: String.Typ;
     Transform: String.Typ;
    end; (* ElementType *)

  procedure PrintElement (var Outfile: text;
       var Entry: ElementType);

  function Compare (var Data1, Data2: ElementType): char;

implementation

  procedure PrintElement (var Outfile: text;
       var Entry: ElementType);
  begin
```

```
      String.Write(Entry.Word);
      writeln;
    end; (* PrintElement *)

    function Compare (var Data1, Data2: ElementType): char;
    begin
      Compare := String.Compare(x.Transform, y.Transform);
    end; (* Compare *)

  end. (* TableElement *)
```

The only difficult part left is figuring out how to transform a word by sorting its characters. This can be accomplished by repeatedly removing the smallest character stored in the word and appending it to the end of a new word:

```
  procedure TransformWord (Word: String.Typ;
          var Transform: String.Typ);
  var
  I, J, SMALL: integer;
  TEMP: String.Typ;

  begin
   String.Create(TEMP);
   String.Copy(TEMP, Word);
   for I := 1 to String.Length(TEMP) do begin
     SMALL := 1;
     for J := 2 to String.Length(TEMP) do begin
       if String.Nth(TEMP, J) < String.Nth(TEMP, SMALL)
       then begin
         SMALL := J;
       end; (* If *)
     end; (* For *)
     String.ChangeNth(Transform, String.Length(Transform) + 1,
                  String.Nth(TEMP, SMALL));
     String.DeleteNth(TEMP, SMALL);
   end; (* For *)
   String.Destroy(TEMP);
  end; (* TransformWord *)
```

Assuming that the dictionary is stored in a file with one word per line, this table type can be used to write an interactive program that shows a user all the legal matches for a given anagram. The user doesn't want to see the whole dictionary, so the *Extract* procedure is called to create a smaller table with just the matching anagrams. This smaller table is printed for the user. The main program is as follows:

```
  program FindAnagrams;

    uses
     Table;
```

```
      var
        Dictionary: text;
        ENTRY: TableElement.ElementType;
        Anagrams, Matches: Table.Typ;

    begin (* Main *)
      assign(dictionary, 'dictionary.dat');
      reset(dictionary);
      Table.Create(Anagrams);
      String.Create(ENTRY.Word);
      String.Create(ENTRY.Transform);
      String.ConvertToUppercase(True);
      while not eof(Dictionary) do begin
        String.Read(Dictionary, ENTRY.Word);
        readln(Dictionary);
        TransformWord(ENTRY.Word, ENTRY.Transform);
        Table.Insert(Anagrams, ENTRY);
       end; (* While *)
      write('What anagram are you trying to solve? ');
      String.Read(input, ENTRY.Word);
      readln;
      TransformWord(ENTRY.Word, ENTRY.Transform);
      Table.Extract(Anagrams, ENTRY, Matches);
      writeln;
      writeln('The legal anagrams are: ');
      Table.Write(Matches);
      Table.Destroy(Anagrams);
      String.Destroy(ENTRY.Word);
      String.Destroy(ENTRY.Transform);
    end. (* Main *)
```

2.3.4. Creating a Cross-Reference Listing

It is often useful to know where certain words appear in a text. If you are working
on a program, you might want to know where variables or procedures are defined and
used. If you are studying a poem, you might want to see which words appear on more
than one line. Both tasks can be solved by a cross-reference listing that shows all the
words from a text and the line numbers on which they appear. For example, if the
input is

```
How much wood
could a woodchuck chuck
if a woodchuck
could chuck
wood?
```

the output should be

```
A                       2   3
CHUCK                   2   4
COULD                   2   4
HOW                     1
IF                      3
MUCH                    1
WOOD                    1   5
WOODCHUCK               2   3
```

This task can be accomplished with a table of word/line entries. By putting them in
alphabetical order, you can group all occurrences of a single word together. The String
type developed is again appropriate for storing the words. To alphabetize the words,
Compare should use the string package's compare function. Printing is a little more
tricky. A good first guess is to have *PrintElement* display the word and line number
stored in each element:

```
A                       2
A                       3
CHUCK                   2
CHUCK                   4
    . . .
```

The repetition of words is not acceptable. As in the sample output, you should produce
a single line of output for each word, providing a list of line numbers when there
are duplicates. As a result, *PrintElement* should print only line numbers. Thus, you
would define module TableElement as follows:

```
unit TableElement;

interface

uses
  String;

  type
   ElementType = record
     Line: integer;
     Word: String.Typ;
   end; (* ElementType *)

 procedure PrintElement (var Outfile: text;
       var Entry: ElementType);

 function Compare (var Data1, Data2: ElementType): char;

implementation

 procedure PrintElement (var Outfile: text;
```

```
                            var Entry: ElementType);
                        begin
                         write(' ', Entry.Line);
                        end; (* PrintElement *)

                        function Compare (var Data1, Data2: ElementType): char;
                        begin
                         Compare := String.Compare(x.Word, y.Word);
                        end; (* Compare *)

                        end. (* TableElement *)
```

Now a call on *Table.Write* produces the following output:

```
    2   3   2   4   2   4   1   3   1   1   5   2   3
```

Thus, *Table.Write* prints just a list of line references. So how are the words printed? The combination of *FindMin* and *Extract* provide a reasonable solution to this problem. To write out the first row of the table, you find the minimum word, write it out, extract all of its occurrences into a separate table, and print its line references using that table. With that value extracted from the overall table, the process can be repeated to write out the next row, and so on. This operation is complex enough that it deserves to be incorporated into its own procedure:

```
                procedure ProduceTable (var Words: Table.Typ);
                  var
                    Duplicates: Table.Typ;
                    ENTRY: TableElement.ElementType;
                begin
                  while not Table.Empty(Words) do begin
                    Table.FindMin(Words, ENTRY);
                    Table.Extract(Words, ENTRY, Duplicates);
                    while Table.InTable(Words, ENTRY) do begin
                      Table.Delete(Words, ENTRY);
                     end; (* While *)
                    String.Write(ENTRY.Word);
                    Table.Write(Duplicates);
                    writeln;
                   end; (* While *)
                end; (* ProduceTable *)
```

The program is now simple to write. The String module should be customized to this application by specifying that only alphabetic characters are to be read, that characters are to be converted to uppercase when read, and that output is to be in fixed columns to make the table line up properly. *String.Read* will not perform any reading when positioned at an illegal character, so the main program needs to include a loop that skips nonalphabetic characters on the current input line. The program ends by displaying the table it produces.

```
program CrossReference;

uses
  String, Table;

var
  Words: Table.Typ;
  ENTRY: TableElement.ElementType;
  infile: text;

begin (* Main *)
 assign(infile, 'text.dat');
 reset(infile);
 Table.Create(Words);
 String.Create(ENTRY.Word);
 String.ConvertToUppercase(True);
 String.DefineLegal(['a'..'z', 'A'..'Z']);
 String.SkipJunk(True);
 String.FixOutput(15);
 ENTRY.Line := 1;
 while not eof(infile) do begin
   if eoln(infile) then begin
     readln(infile);
     ENTRY.Line := ENTRY.Line + 1;
    end·
   else begin
     String.Read(infile, ENTRY.Word);
     Table.Insert(Words, ENTRY);
    end; (* If *)
  end; (* While *)
 ProduceTable(Words);
 Table.Destroy(Words);
 String.Destroy(ENTRY.Word);
end. (* Main *)
```

2.3.5. SELF CHECK EXERCISES

1. Why is it important that *Delete* remove the *first* table element with a given value?

2. What change(s) would you have to make to the birthday program to cause it to list people with the same birthday in alphabetical order?

2.4. SUMMARY OF KEY POINTS

- This book emphasizes the application of abstraction to the creation of data types, a process called data abstraction. An abstract data type (ADT) is used to specify a data type by indicating the domain of the type and the set of legal operations that can be performed on variables of the type.

- This book uses certain standard conventions for the creation and use of modules. Module identifiers are always referred to using fully qualified identifiers (e.g., *Math.Max* to specify the function *Max* from module *Math*). The standard identifier *Typ* is used for the type definition of an ADT and certain standard identifiers are used for operations that tend to appear in many ADTs (e.g., *Read, Write,* and *Compare*).

- The standard procedures *Create* and *Destroy* are included in ADTs to facilitate storage management in case the ADT is implemented using techniques described later in this book where the program dynamically maintains data storage. These procedures *must* be called once for each variable of the given type (the former before any operations are performed on it, the latter after it has served its useful lifetime in a program).

- The concept of information hiding when applied to ADTs leads to the notion of a wall separating the implementation of a type from its use in high-level code. The isolation of implementation details facilitates maintenance and reimplementation of the ADT, so the wall should never be violated in high-level code.

- ADTs for storing Strings, Stacks, Streams, and Tables are developed in this chapter. They are highly reusable structures and will be used in later programs in this book.

3

RECURSION

3.1. INTRODUCTION

So far you have made use of a programming technique known as iteration. In this chapter you will learn a new technique.

RECURSION/RECURSIVE

A kind of problem solving analysis where a program unit is defined in terms of itself (e.g., calling a procedure inside itself and, thus having its name *recur* inside the procedure body). Definitions formulated using this kind of analysis are called *recursive* (as in "a recursive procedure").

The iterative method that you have used up to now involves expressing the solution of a problem as a series of steps to take one after the other. By solving this sequence of subproblems, you get a solution to the overall problem. When one of those steps needs to be performed several times, you generally introduce a loop that repeatedly performs the task until some exit criterion is satisfied.

The recursive method involves a different kind of reduction. Instead of reducing to a sequence of steps, all of which are some small part of the overall task, your primary reduction is to express the problem as one or more subproblems that are in some sense the same as the original problem. These subproblems are solved by calling the original procedure (i.e., recursive calls on the procedure from within the procedure).

Suppose that a procedure is to solve some problem (e.g., writing out a line of *n* stars). Such a procedure usually solves a class of related problems, not just one (draw 0 stars or 1 star or 2 stars, etc.). Using iterative analysis, you would find a sequence of steps that manage to solve any specific problem (a series of steps that together write out all *n* stars). Using the recursive approach, however, you make use of the fact that you are creating a general procedure that solves all problems from the class. Thus, to solve any one specific problem, you can reduce it to a simpler member of the class, and call the procedure you are writing to solve that simpler problem (in the example, reduce the problem of writing *n* stars to some simpler star-writing problem and then call the procedure itself to solve that problem).

Recursion requires a leap of faith that you can call up the solution to your problem in the middle of solving the problem. This approach *does* work as long as you reduce to a simpler problem. In recursion, the subproblems are each *simpler* than the one before, so eventually you reach a point where a subproblem becomes solvable immediately.

To help you ease into this perhaps unfamiliar way of thinking, the chapter begins by solving a simple problem both iteratively and recursively, so that you can compare the solutions. Then the chapter moves on to an example where recursion allows you to create a solution that is not easily mirrored as an iterative procedure. Once this context is established, the chapter revisits the leap of faith issue and some general guidelines for programming recursively. The chapter then provides a number of sample problems, some of them quite large and extensively described, where recursion provides a simpler solution than would be possible using iteration. Two of these examples include a common recursive technique called *backtracking* that proves useful in searching for a right answer from among many possibilities. The chapter ends with some discussion of how to debug recursive definitions and what you might pay in execution time and memory usage for using recursion instead of iteration.

3.2. ITERATION VERSUS RECURSION

3.2.1. Recursive Stair Descent

Suppose you want to program a robot to descend a flight of stairs. Using the iterative method, you would probably see that there are some number of steps to descend (call that number *n*), that descending one step is an easy thing to do, and so your procedure would loop *n* times, each time descending one step, and then step off the staircase. Your code might look something like the following:

```
procedure DescendStairs (N: integer);
  var
    I: integer;
begin
  for I := 1 to N do begin
    GoDownOneStair;
  end; (* For *)
```

```
        StepOffStaircase;
    end; (* DescendStairs *)
```

Recursive solutions involve a different form of analysis. In this example, the process of descending n stairs can be reduced to descending one stair, and then descending $n - 1$ stairs. This sounds trivial, but when using the recursive method you break the problem into simpler versions of the same problem, assume your routine will solve those simpler versions, and then use those solutions to solve your complete problem.

This approach works because your procedure DescendStairs is meant to solve many stair-descending problems (four of which are shown below). The point is that solving one of the problems (e.g., descending four stairs) can be defined in terms of solving another one of these problems (descending three stairs) by calling the procedure you are writing to solve that simpler problem (because the procedure is supposed to solve *all* these problems, not just the specific one you are working on).

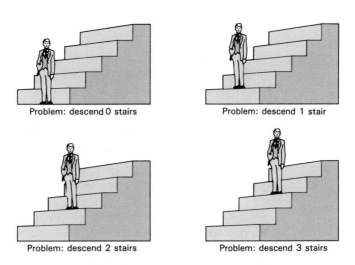

Problem: descend 0 stairs   Problem: descend 1 stair

Problem: descend 2 stairs   Problem: descend 3 stairs

Thus, by breaking up the problem into one of descending one step, followed by descending $n - 1$ steps, you have used the recursive method to solve the problem, since descending one step is easy to do, and descending $n - 1$ steps is a simpler version of the more complex task of descending n steps.

So far you've reduced the problem of descending n steps to one of descending $n - 1$ steps. There comes a point, however, at which you want to stop descending. Once you've descended all the steps, you can't descend any more, so you need to step off the staircase (the "descend 0 stairs" problem above). This is the last step of the recursive method, the complex problem having been reduced to simpler and simpler versions. At this point you finally reach the simplest case, which you solve directly. In this example, once there are no more steps to descend, you step off the staircase.

The following pseudocode demonstrates a recursive solution to the problem of descending stairs:

```
procedure DescendStairs (N: integer);
begin
 if N = 0 then begin
   StepOffStaircase;
  end
 else begin
   GoDownOneStair;
   DescendStairs(N - 1);
  end; (* If *)
end; (* DescendStairs *)
```

This code differs in two significant ways. First, there is no *for* loop in this procedure. In fact, there are no loops at all. Instead, this procedure *calls itself*. This self-reference, or recursive call, generates a series of procedure calls that provide the repetition of going down many steps, rather than using a loop to repeat the operation inside a single procedure call. The recursive approach allows you to think of the problem as a whole, writing its solution in terms of simpler versions of the same overall problem. Rather than thinking of it as a sequence of detailed steps that all need to be solved, you just have to consider what are known as the *recursive* and *simple* cases.

In solving the recursive case you reduce the problem to one or more simpler versions of the same problem, and then, under the *assumption* that the routine will solve these simpler subproblems, you put together their solutions so as to solve the complex version. In the example, the recursive case is solved when you realize that descending n stairs can be accomplished by descending one stair, followed by descending $n - 1$ stairs.

Because the solution to the recursive case involves simplification, you expect to eventually reach one or more simplest cases, known as base cases, which you can solve directly. In the staircase example, you reach the base case of no more steps to descend, where you simply step off the staircase.

3.2.2. And She Told Two Friends, And So On, And So On...

Let's look at one more abstract example before some concrete Pascal programs.

Suppose you're the president of an organization with a large membership and you suddenly realize that you forgot to inform your members about an important meeting the next day. Using the iterative approach, you would probably solve the problem by calling up all the members personally. Because one person (you) has to do all the work, this is a fairly daunting task. If you were to code this in pseudo-Pascal, it might look something like the following:

```
procedure Inform (N: integer;
        Message: MsgType);
 var
  I: integer;
begin
 for I := 1 to N do begin
   Give Message to the Ith person;
  end; (* For *)
end; (* Inform *)
```

With this solution one agent performs all the work. You can approach this problem a different way by using an idea from an old TV commercial in which information about the quality of the product was spread by having each person who used it tell two friends about it.

In fact, that commercial is just an application of recursion. Rather than informing many members about the meeting, you can tell two people about it, and have them pass the word on. Thus, while the complete problem is to inform n people, you can break it up into two subproblems, in which you tell two people, and then have them pass the information on to $(n/2 - 1)$ people each (you subtract one because although the two people must each tell half the people, they don't have to tell themselves because you did so). That's the recursive case. It's important to note that you don't just tell two people about the meeting. You also have them each tell two more people. In that way, you propagate your method of informing people through this network of agents, so that each person has to do little work to accomplish their subtask, but by having everybody fulfill their commitment, the entire mission is accomplished.

Now that you've got the recursive case, you need to come up with your base case. Because in the recursive case you tell two people, you can't perform the recursive case if you have less than two people to tell. Thus, you stop the recursion when you reach the base case of telling either nobody or only one person.

Given the base case and the recursive case, the pseudocode follows quickly.

```
procedure Inform (N: integer;
        Message: MsgType);
begin
 if N = 1 then begin
   Give Message to person;
  end
  else if N > 0 then begin
    choose two people to tell.
    Give Message to first person;
    Inform((N div 2) - 1), Message);
    Give Message to second person;
    Inform((N div 2) - 1, Message);
   end; (* If *)
end; (* Inform *)
```

This pseudocode uses an if/then/else construct to distinguish three cases:

- $N = 1$, in which case the last person is told
- $N > 1$ (obtained by making sure N is not 1 and is greater than 0), in which case you want to apply the recursive case
- $N = 0$, in which case you want to do nothing.

The pseudocode seems to have only two cases, but if you look closely you'll notice that because the second branch tests against $N = 0$, there is an implied empty:

```
else
    (* do nothing *);
```

for the case when N is 0.

This pseudocode has a minor problem in that it doesn't properly deal with telling an odd number of people, but you should be able to see the general idea (and, in fact, dealing with an odd number is a simple fix—see the Self Check Exercises).

3.2.3. The Leap of Faith

Using this method, you, as president, need to tell only two people. The rest of the work all gets taken care of, seemingly by magic. Believing that recursion works is a large obstacle to overcome, requiring a "leap of faith" that solving the base case and the recursive case will solve the complete problem. Because of this, it is often helpful to go step by step through the execution of a recursive program.

3.2.4. SELF CHECK EXERCISES

1. Rewrite procedure Inform from Section 3.2.2 to deal with the case where n is odd.

2. What is the output the following program produces?

```
program GiantsWillWinWorldSeries;

    function XXX (X, Y: integer): integer;
    begin
     writeln(X, Y);
     if (X mod Y) = 0 then
       XXX := Y
     else
       XXX := XXX(Y, X mod Y);
    end; (* XXX *)

    begin
     writeln(XXX(40, 30));
    end. (* Main *)
```

The function *XXX* computes a useful mathematical property of the two parameters. What is that property?

3.3. PROGRAMMING RECURSIVELY

This section contains a number of examples that demonstrate different classes of problems that can be solved recursively on the computer and some commentary on how to understand recursive definitions.

3.3.1. An Iterative Problem Recursively: Writing Stars

To start off, consider a simple iterative Pascal example that can be rewritten using the recursive method. A typical procedure discussed when first learning parameters is *WriteStars*, which prints out a given number of asterisks. The procedure can be coded as follows:

```
procedure WriteStars (Num: integer);
  var
    I: integer;
begin
  for I := 1 to Num do begin
    write('*');
  end; (* For *)
end; (* WriteStars *)
```

To write this routine recursively, you need to take a different approach. Although you would probably not actually write this procedure recursively in practice, since it is so easy to write iteratively, it is a good starting point for developing your understanding of recursion.

3.3.1.1. Writing the Recursive Routine

To write this procedure recursively you need to develop both the base case and the recursive case. You design the recursive case by first looking at the problem as a whole. You then reduce this complex problem to one or more simpler versions of the same problem, assume your procedure will solve these simpler versions, and then use these solutions to solve the entire problem.

This example is similar to the stair-descending example. You can print out *n* stars by first printing out one star, and then printing out *n* − 1 stars. You can directly print out the first star with a simple *write* statement. To print out the *n* − 1 stars you need to take the leap of faith that your procedure will work on this simpler version of the problem. Thus, your recursive case consists of writing out one star directly, followed by a recursive call to write out the remaining stars.

For the base case you have to determine when the recursive case no longer applies, or, in other words, when you want the recursion to stop. Since the recursive case directly writes out one star, you can't perform that case when writing out fewer than one star. Thus, you reach the base case when you try to write out zero stars. You might think that writing a single star should also be a simple case, but in general, you should include the simplest possible case and not worry about things that are "close." This should make intuitive sense, because you want the base case to reflect the simplest possible version of the problem, which you solve directly. Since it is trivial to write out zero stars (in fact, you do nothing), this becomes the base case.

Given the recursive case and the base case, you can write the code recursively:

```
procedure WriteStars (Num: integer);
begin
 if Num > 0 then begin
   write('*');
   WriteStars(Num - 1);
   end; (* If *)
end; (* WriteStars *)
```

Just as in the stair-descending example, there are no loops in this routine. You have only the base case and the recursive case. The base case, however, is coded in a peculiar way. The base case occurred when you wanted to write out no stars, and in that case you wanted to do nothing. Rather than writing something like

```
procedure WriteStars (Num: integer);
begin
 if Num <= 0 then begin
         (* Do Nothing *)
   end
 else begin
   write('*');
   WriteStars(Num - 1);
   end; (* If *)
end; (* WriteStars *)
```

the previous version performs the same action, but is written in a cleaner way.

3.3.1.2. Tracing Through the Recursion

Suppose you want to print out four stars. Thus, somewhere in your program you say:

```
WriteStars(4);
```

Upon invocation of *WriteStars*, *Num* is set to four. Since four is greater than zero, the procedure enters the recursive case, in which it first outputs an asterisk, and then calls a procedure named *WriteStars*, passing in the value three as a parameter. It so happens that the program is in the middle of the *WriteStars* procedure when this call is made, but that is not important as far as the calling procedure is concerned. All it knows is that a procedure is invoked to solve some problem (in fact, a simpler star writing problem), and when that call finishes, the calling procedure will continue executing where it left off, as indicated below.

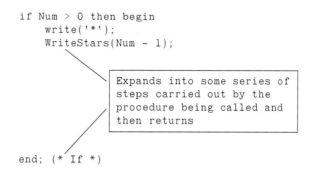

```
if Num > 0 then begin
    write('*');
    WriteStars(Num - 1);
```

Expands into some series of steps carried out by the procedure being called and then returns

```
end; (* If *)
```

This seems like a conflict, because the computer is already executing a version of *WriteStars*. What happens, in effect, is that a second independent version of the procedure is created. The two versions of *WriteStars* can execute simultaneously and independently. In fact, the first version simply remains idle, waiting for the second to finish executing, just as it would if it had called up any other procedure. In this example, because the procedure call is the last statement in the procedure, once the call terminates, the calling procedure will also end.

Thus, at this point, you have one star of output and have suspended executing the procedure call on *WriteStars(4)* to make the procedure call *WriteStars(3)*.

When this new procedure call starts executing, its goal is to write out three stars, and so it enters the recursive case. It again writes out an asterisk, so that you now have two stars of output (one from the previous procedure call), and makes another procedure call. This time it invokes the procedure *WriteStars* and passes it *two* as the parameter, temporarily suspending the execution of the current procedure.

As before, entering the recursive case, it writes out an asterisk, leaving three on the line (two from previous calls), and recursively calls, this time, *WriteStars(1)*. This call again suspends execution of the current procedure, which will continue upon termination of the recursive call.

You once again enter another version of *WriteStars,* whose task this time is to write out one star. Note how each call tries to solve the same general problem (writing out a certain number of asterisks), but on each call the *size* of the problem is reduced. To write out one asterisk, it first outputs a single star, which leaves four stars on the line, and then makes another recursive call to write out zero stars.

Finally, you have reached a call to print out zero stars. Because this is the base case, rather than executing the recursive case, the procedure terminates, at which time execution continues with the calling procedure, as it always does when a procedure call ends. The procedure that called *WriteStars(0)* was the version whose goal was to output one star. When control returns to that procedure, it picks up where it left off. Since it finished the call on *WriteStars(0)*, and since no statements follow that procedure call,

WriteStars(1) also ends, and you're back in the procedure that was printing out two stars. Since the recursive call was also the last statement in that procedure, it ends, putting you back in *WriteStars(3)*, which ends, as does *WriteStars(4)*, and thus all the recursive calls have completed. Moreover, since the procedure did indeed generate the four stars, recursion, at least in this case, seems to have worked.

The following diagram depicts the execution of this recursive procedure in a more compact form:

```
Entering WriteStars, Num = 4
Write out '*'
Calling WriteStars(3)

        Entering WriteStars, Num = 3
        Write out '*'
        Calling WriteStars(2)

                Entering WriteStars, Num = 2
                Write out '*'
                Calling WriteStars(1)

                        Entering WriteStars, Num = 1
                        Write out '*'
                        Calling WriteStars(0)

                                Entering WriteStars, Num = 0
                                Base case, so do nothing
                                Exiting WriteStars, Num = 0

                        Exiting WriteStars, Num = 1

                Exiting WriteStars, Num = 2

        Exiting WriteStars, Num = 3

Exiting WriteStars, Num = 4
```

3.3.1.3. Tail Recursion

Having no statements after the recursive call in procedure *WriteStars* makes everything come out in a reasonably straightforward manner. The remaining examples are more complex in that the procedures won't end with recursive calls. Nevertheless, routines of this form, which have a recursive call at the end, belong to a special class of recursive procedures, and are known as *tail recursive*. It is reasonably easy to transform a procedure that contains a simple loop into a tail recursive procedure. This transformation can always be made, and, more importantly, any tail recursive procedure can be rewritten using a loop. Since recursion has significant overhead associated with it, an iterative approach is usually preferred for efficiency reasons. Efficiency considerations will be explored in more detail at the end of the chapter, but it is worth noting early that while recursion is a helpful problem solving technique, it should be used cautiously.

3.3.2. A Recursive Function: Number of Digits

You can write recursive functions just as you can write recursive procedures. For example, consider the problem of determining whether a number has one digit, two digits, three digits, etc. The following function uses iteration to solve the problem:

```
function NumDigits (Num: integer): integer;
 var
  COUNT: integer;
begin
 COUNT := 1;
 while abs(Num) > 9 do begin
   Num := Num div 10;
    COUNT := COUNT + 1;
   end; (* while *)
end; (* NumDigits *)
```

This example is again like stair descending and writing stars. You can determine the number of digits in a number by adding 1 to the number of digits in that number divided by 10 (using integer division). The base case here is a one-digit number. Thus, the function can be written recursively as follows:

```
function NumDigits (Num: integer): integer;
begin
 if abs(Num) <= 9 then begin
   NumDigits := 1;
  end
 else begin
   NumDigits := 1 + NumDigits (Num div 10);
  end; (* If *)
end; (* NumDigits *)
```

Here is a trace of execution for the value −349:

```
Entering NumDigits, Num = −349
Calling NumDigits (−34)

    Entering NumDigits, Num = −34
    Calling NumDigits (−3)

        Entering NumDigits, Num = −3
        Base case, return 1

    return 2

return 3
```

3.3.3. A "Natural" for Recursion: Reversing a Line

The next step to take is to develop a recursive procedure that is not tail recursive, i.e., that does not end with a recursive call. The problem you are to confront is that of taking a line of text from an input file and writing the same line out, but in reverse order. For example, given the line

```
baseball
```

you would want to output

```
llabesab
```

3.3.3.1. Writing the Recursive Routine

Since you want to write this routine recursively, you need to develop your base case and your recursive case. For the recursive case you try to reduce the complete problem into simpler versions, and then use the solutions to those simpler versions to solve the entire problem. In this example you want to reverse a line of text, where the line has some number of characters. To reduce this line of n characters, you reduce the problem to one of reversing a line of fewer characters, which you assume you can do, and then use that solution to reverse a line of n characters.

What do you know about a line of characters in an input file? All you can easily do is read in characters and write them out. Look again at the sample input file, in which you have 8 characters to reverse:

```
baseball
^
```

where the ^ represents the input cursor, which points to the next character to be read in. You know that this character, the 'b', is the first character in the input line, but should be the *last* character written out. Further, it will be written out *after all the other characters have been written out in reverse order*. Thus, you would like to read in the 'b', wait while the other 7 characters are written out in reverse order, and then write out the 'b' to complete the operation. Hopefully you're beginning to see where this leads. You have reduced the problem of reversing 8 characters to one of reading in one character, reversing 7 characters, and then writing out that one character that was read in. But the problem of reversing 8 characters and the problem of reversing 7 characters are both in the same overall class of problems, and should both be solved by the same procedure. Thus, you have reduced the complex problem to a simpler one, and then used your assumption that you can solve the simpler one by a recursive call. This is the recursive case, and will be coded something like the following:

```
read(CH);
Make a Recursive Call
write(CH);
```

Now you need the base case. Since the recursive case reads in a character, you must not enter that case if there are no characters left to read. Thus, you hit the base case when you want to reverse a line of zero characters. Again, this should make intuitive sense, because the base case should reflect the simplest version of the problem, which is solved directly. Since no line is easier to reverse than an empty line, this should be the base case, and to solve this version of the problem you again do nothing.

Thus, you can combine the base case and the recursive case into a procedure as follows:

```
procedure ReverseLine (var Infile, Outfile: text);
  var
    CH: char;
begin
  if not eoln(Infile) then begin
    read(Infile, CH);
    ReverseLine(Infile, Outfile);
    write(Outfile, CH);
  end; (* If *)
end; (* ReverseLine *)
```

Again, this code has no loops in it, and does not need an array to store the characters. The iterative solution would have both of these. Further, you hit your base case when you *are* at end of line. But you take no action when you hit the base case, so the code simply executes the recursive case when there are characters to reverse, and does nothing in the base case.

3.3.3.2. Tracing Through the Recursion

Getting back to the example, the input file is in the following state when you make the first call on *Rev*:

```
baseball
^
```

On this first call you read in the 'b', and then make a recursive call. This call suspends operation of the currently executing procedure and begins executing the new procedure. When the recursive call terminates, you will continue executing where you left off. Thus, when the recursive call completes, you will execute the write statement and output the 'b', as indicated in the diagram at the top of page 112.

Just before making the first recursive call, you have read in only the 'b', leaving the file in this state:

```
baseball
 ^
```

This second procedure call will read in the 'a', leaving the file in this state:

```
baseball
  ^
```

```
if not eoln(Infile) then begin
    read(Infile, CH);
    ReverseLine(Infile, Outfile);
```

```
                    ┌──────────────────────────────┐
                    │ Expands into some series of  │
                    │ steps carried out by the     │
                    │ procedure being called and   │
                    │ then returns                 │
                    └──────────────────────────────┘
```

```
    write(Outfile, CH);
end; (* If *)
```

and then make a recursive call. Upon termination of that recursive call it will output
the 'a' it read in. This process of reading in the characters from the file continues
until all the characters have been read in and you are at end-of-line. When you finally
do reach end-of-line (the base case), that procedure call terminates without taking
any action. Returning to the previous call, you execute the statement immediately
following its recursive call, which is the *write* statement. In this example, you will
output a 'l', because that is the last character on the line. The following diagram
shows the execution of this procedure on the example line:

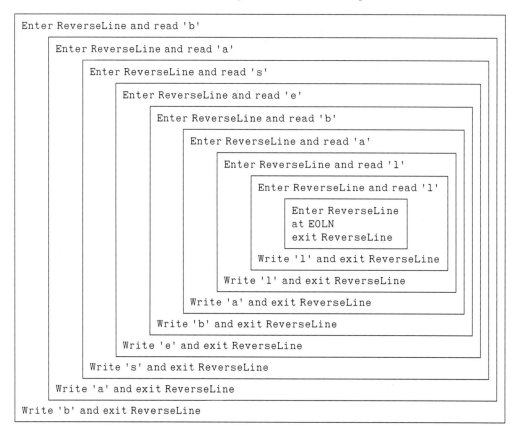

3.3.4. Why This Is Hard to Understand

Now that you have seen *WriteStars*, *NumDigits*, and *ReverseLine* as examples of recursive procedures, you have reached a point where you can appreciate two aspects of recursive programming that make this seem more confusing than it needs to be.

When you write a nonrecursive procedure, you deal with it on two levels:

- *Application Level*. At the level of the *caller* of the procedure, you think of it as a black box that performs some task. You don't care what inner details make it work, you care only what it accomplishes. You don't care that the procedure might call up other procedures to do its work, you care only that it execute in its entirety, performing the specified task, and then returns control to the statement immediately following the call. As caller of the procedure, you know that the execution of the procedure will not somehow interfere with the current execution, it will merely cause control to shift momentarily to another part of the program, but then control will return to the caller to execute whatever comes after the procedure call. Similarly, if the caller has local variables, these are generally protected from interference while the called procedure executes unless they are passed as parameters or, in the more rare case, where the called procedure is nested and makes a global reference.

- *Implementation Level*. At the level of the *implementor* of the procedure, you must determine some algorithm for performing the overall task. You don't know anything about who called the procedure, you know only what work has to be performed before the procedure terminates. To obtain and manipulate variables and values, the procedure should introduce parameters. If local variables are required to carry out the algorithm, these are introduced by the implementor. All these local definitions are free from interference from the caller.

The ability to ignore one level while working at the other is an important separation of detail that makes programs easier to write. The problem with recursive procedures is that you must work at both levels *simultaneously*. You are implementing the procedure, but you are also calling it up to perform some of the work.

You will minimize your confusion if you keep this dual usage in mind and, as noted earlier, the easiest way to handle these two views is to think at the implementation level, but take on faith that this procedure is also available at the application level.

This faith in the procedure at the application level requires believing the second aspect of recursive programming, and that is what makes this difficult to understand. To help you understand this point, consider the flow of control established by the following two procedures:

```
procedure Second;
begin
 writeln('Second');
end;
```

```
procedure First;
begin
 Second;
 writeln('First');
 Second;
end;
```

When *first* is called, you get the following flow of control:

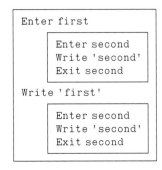

The important and perhaps obvious point is that the inner execution of procedure *Second* cannot change the expected flow of control in the outer procedure *First*. Procedure *First* has three steps to perform, as specified in its definition. It will perform these three steps in order even though control temporarily shifts to procedure *Second* twice when it is invoked.

More generally, each invocation of a procedure is independent of other procedure invocations in that each has its own local definitions and each keeps track of what statement to execute next. This point should be so familiar to you that it hardly seems worth saying for iterative programming, but it takes on new meaning in recursive programming. Consider the inner details of *ReverseLine*:

```
procedure ReverseLine (var Infile, Outfile: text);
  var
    CH: char;
begin
 if not eoln(Infile) then begin
    read(Infile, CH);
    ReverseLine(Infile, Outfile);
    write(Outfile, CH);
  end; (* If *)
end; (* ReverseLine *)
```

This definition says that the procedure has a local variable called *CH* and that if you execute the body of the if/then, you have three steps to carry out. In the example of reading 'baseball' from the input line, the first procedure invocation reads the 'b' (the first of three steps inside the if/then), recursively calls itself to reverse 'aseball' (the second of the three steps), and finally writes out the character 'b' (the third step). The second of these steps invokes a procedure *ReverseLine*. Normally you wouldn't worry about this, but in this case you have to wonder how this new version of *ReverseLine* affects the current version of *ReverseLine*. The answer, as always, is that the invoked procedure is independent of the original procedure. Thus, the new invocation will create a new local variable *CH* that is guaranteed not to interfere with the current *CH*'s value and the new invocation will keep track of what step it is executing without interfering with the current procedure's sense of what step to take next (i.e., since this recursive call was the second step inside the if/then, after it terminates, the computer will execute step three from the if/then next).

If you keep this independence of procedure invocations in mind, you will understand what does and doesn't need to be done when a recursive call is performed. Perhaps it will have the added benefit of helping you to keep the faith when you make your recursive calls. Of course, that leap of faith requires confidence not only in your Pascal system to do the right thing, but also in your own programming skills to have handled the cases properly, but even that level of confidence comes quickly when you have written a few recursive procedures that surprise you by working.

3.3.5. A More Complicated Example: The Towers of Hanoi

The next example goes one step further—a procedure with more than one recursive call. The Towers of Hanoi is a famous puzzle that can be solved handily using recursion. You are given three towers and a number of disks of differing diameters with all disks initially on one tower from widest to thinnest (i.e., a disk can only rest on a disk of greater diameter), as in the following example using four disks.

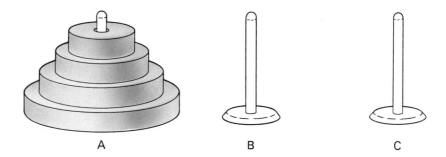

A   B   C

The goal of the puzzle is to move all the disks from the initial tower to one of the other towers (e.g., from A above to B) adhering to the following rules:

1. Only one disk can be moved at a time.
2. Only the disk on top of a tower can be moved.
3. No disk can be put on top of a disk of smaller diameter.

Consider writing a procedure that searches for a solution to the puzzle.

3.3.5.1. Solving the Puzzle

Before you start worrying about how to write a procedure to solve these puzzles, it would probably be a good idea to first look at a few simple cases to get a feel for the problem. The simplest puzzle is zero disks (remember this when base case time rolls around). In this case you don't have to do anything.

How about the case of one disk?

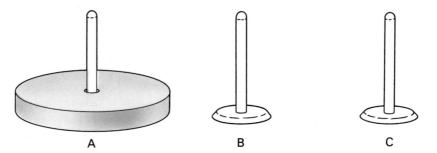

All you need to do is move the disk from A to B and you're done. The two-disk case is slightly more interesting:

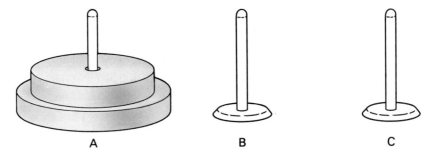

You want to move both disks from A to B. Since you can move only one disk at a time, you need to first move the top disk. You can move it to either B or C. If you move it to B, then you can't move the bottom disk over to B, since it is wider than the disk you just put there. To accomplish your goal, however, you *need* to move the bottom disk to B, where it must also be the bottom disk. If, instead of moving the top disk to B, you move it to C

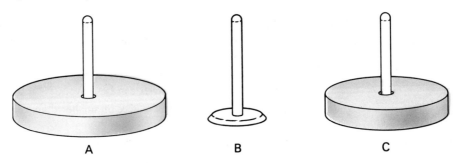

you can then immediately move the bottom disk from A to B, where it belongs.

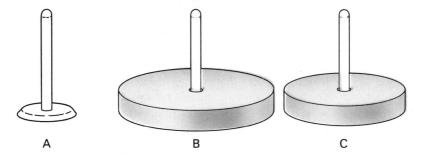

A   B   C

You can now move the smaller disk from C to B and you're done.

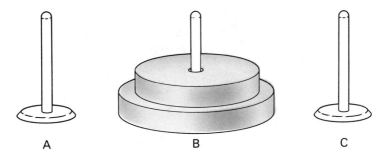

A   B   C

Now, what about the case of three disks? This is where it starts to get tricky.

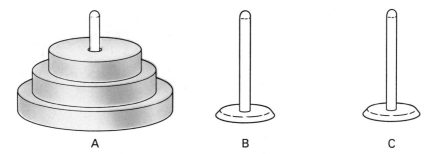

A   B   C

To solve this puzzle you should set up some subgoals. Since you want to move all three disks from A to B, and since no disk can be on top of a smaller disk, you know that the disk that is on the bottom of A will eventually need to be on the bottom of B, and that you can't put either of the two other disks into their correct positions until this bottom disk has been correctly placed. Accordingly, to solve the puzzle you must first move the bottom disk over to B.

Accomplishing this subgoal requires that you move the disks on top of B over to C, so that you can move the bottom disk freely from A to B. This is where things get interesting. You now need to move the top two disks from A to C. This is simply the two disk version of the puzzle you just saw, only instead of moving from A to B, you are moving disks from A to C.

To review, before you can solve the puzzle of moving three disks from A to B, you first need to accomplish the subgoal of moving the bottom disk from A to B. But to do this you need to move the top two disks from A to C. You have therefore reduced one part of solving the puzzle of moving three disks from A to B to one of moving two disks from A to C, which is a simpler version of the same puzzle. Do you see the recursive case lurking about? At this point you should make the leap of faith and assume that your procedure will solve this simpler problem. Since you just saw how to solve the puzzle for two disks, hopefully this assumption makes sense. So you move the two disks from A to C (by using your recursive procedure, since you obviously can't move the two disks directly—that would break the rules).

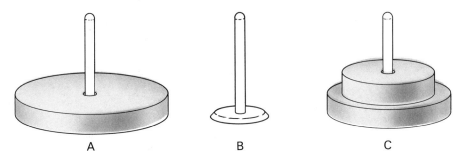

A   B   C

You can then directly move the bottom disk from A to B.

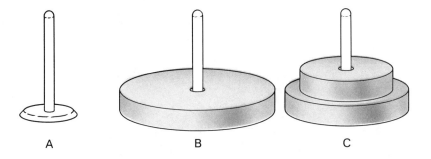

A   B   C

Now you've accomplished the subgoal of moving the bottom disk over to B, but you still need to move the two disks from C to B to complete the solution. In other words, you have reduced another part the problem of moving three disks from A to B to one of moving two disks from C to B, which is another simpler version of the same problem. Again, use your recursive assumption that you can solve simpler versions of the same problem, and by doing so you've solved the entire problem! Amazing.

To summarize, moving three disks from A to B requires the following steps:

* Move the top two disks from tower A to tower C (a simpler problem from the same class) using tower B as temporary storage.
* Now that you have the two top disks from tower A on tower C, move the bottom disk from tower A to tower B. Since there are no disks bigger than this disk on tower B, you can do this directly.

- To finish the job, you need to move the two disks from tower C to tower B, this time with tower A serving as a temporary.

This can be put more succinctly as:

- Move 2 disks from A to C.
- Move 1 disk from A to B.
- Move 2 disks from C to B.

3.3.5.2. Writing the Recursive Routine

To develop the recursive procedure you need to generalize from the specific puzzles you saw above and then develop your base case and your recursive case. To state the problem as generally as possible, you are given some number of disks on a *source* tower and you want to move them to a *destination* tower. You also have access to a *temporary* tower, which you can use to temporarily store any of the disks.

Given n disks on the source tower, your subgoal is to move the bottom disk to the destination tower. You first move $n - 1$ disks from the destination to the temporary tower. Because this is a simpler version of the more complex problem (you only need to move $n - 1$ disks instead of n disks), you can solve this subproblem with a recursive call. You then move the nth disk to the destination tower directly. Finally, you move the $n - 1$ disks now on the temporary tower to the destination tower, another simpler version of the overall problem, which can be solved by a recursive call. The recursive case can therefore be summarized as

- Move the top $n - 1$ disks from the source tower to the temporary tower, using the destination tower as a temporary.
- Move the remaining disk from the source to the destination.
- Move the $n - 1$ disks from the temporary to the destination, using the original source tower as a temporary.

Or more succinctly

- Move $n - 1$ disks from *Source* to *Temp*.
- Move 1 disk from *Source* to *Destination*.
- Move $n - 1$ disks from *Temp* to *Destination*.

The recursive case involves moving at least one disk (in step 2), so you can't enter that case if there are no disks to move. Thus, as was hinted at earlier, you reach the base case when you want to solve the puzzle for zero disks.

Finally, before you can write the code for this procedure, you need to think about the parameters that are needed. The parameters represent the parts of the routine that change from invocation to invocation. According to the summary of the recursive case, each recursive call needs to change both the number of disks to move as well as which towers are the source, destination, and temporary. Thus, you need to pass this information as parameters. Having determined the recursive case, base case, and the parameter list, you can now write the code:

```
procedure MoveDisks (Num: integer;
        Source, Dest, Temp: char);
begin
  if Num <> 0 then begin
    MoveDisks(Num - 1, Source, Temp, Dest);
    writeln('Move disk from ', Source, ' to ', Dest, '.');
    MoveDisks(Num - 1, Temp, Dest, Source);
  end; (* If *)
end; (* MoveDisks *)
```

3.3.5.3. Tracing Through the Recursion

Let's go through the case for three disks. The initial call (from, say, the main program) will look like

```
MoveDisks(3, 'A', 'B', 'C');
```

and you get the following output:

Move disk from A to B.
Move disk from A to C.
Move disk from B to C.
Move disk from A to B.
Move disk from C to A.
Move disk from C to B.
Move disk from A to B.

Hopefully, you can believe this procedure works without having to step through it. If you can, then you're well on your way to writing your own recursive routines, because if you don't *believe* in recursion, you can't use recursion. But, to clear up any lingering doubts, we will go through all the calls from the execution above in the diagram on the following page.

3.3.5.4. Why This Isn't the Most Fun Puzzle Around

In case you're planning to solve different versions of this puzzle in your free time, think about how many calls are made to solve a puzzle of size n. The case of three disks requires solving two two-disk puzzles, each of which requires solving two one-disk puzzles, each of which requires solving two zero-disk puzzles, as indicated below (where *mt* (n) represents an n-disk *MoveDisks* problem to solve and *1dsk* represents moving one disk). This leads to 15 calls on the *MoveDisks*.

Call for 3 disks with Source A, Dest B, and Temp C

> Call for 2 disks with Source A, Dest C, and Temp B
>
> > Call for 1 disks with Source A, Dest B, and Temp C
> >
> > > Call for 0 disks with Source A, Dest C, and Temp B
> > >
> > > > MoveDisks called for zero disks, so do nothing.
> > >
> > > Move disk from A to B.
> > > Call for 0 disks with Source C, Dest B, and Temp A
> > >
> > > > MoveDisks called for zero disks, so do nothing.
> > >
> > > Move disk from A to C.
> >
> > Call for 1 disks with Source B, Dest C, and Temp A
> >
> > > Call for 0 disks with Source B, Dest A, and Temp C
> > >
> > > > MoveDisks called for zero disks, so do nothing.
> > >
> > > Move disk from B to C.
> > > Call for 0 disks with Source A, Dest C, and Temp B
> > >
> > > > MoveDisks called for zero disks, so do nothing.
>
> Move disk from A to B.
> Call for 2 disks with Source C, Dest B, and Temp A
>
> > Call for 1 disks with Source C, Dest A, and Temp B
> >
> > > Call for 0 disks with Source C, Dest B, and Temp A
> > >
> > > > MoveDisks called for zero disks, so do nothing.
> > >
> > > Move disk from C to A.
> > > Call for 0 disks with Source B, Dest A, and Temp C
> > >
> > > > MoveDisks called for zero disks, so do nothing.
> >
> > Move disk from C to B.
> > Call for 1 disks with Source A, Dest B, and Temp C
> >
> > > Call for 0 disks with Source A, Dest C, and Temp B
> > >
> > > > MoveDisks called for zero disks, so do nothing.
> > >
> > > Move disk from A to B.
> > > Call for 0 disks with Source C, Dest B, and Temp A
> > >
> > > > MoveDisks called for zero disks, so do nothing.

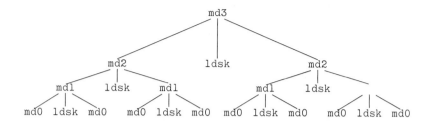

Now, what about the general problem? Every call reduces the problem by using two more calls. Thus, you start with one call, which generates two, which in turn generate four, which generate eight, which generate sixteen, etc. See a pattern?

Procedure Calls Needed to Solve Puzzle

Puzzle	Result	Explanation
0 disks	1 call	it's the base case
1 disk	3 calls	initial plus two calls of size 0
2 disks	7 calls	one of size 2, two of size 1, four of size 0
3 disks	15 calls	as seen above

In general, because you go from n down to zero, with each call generating two more calls, you will generate $2^{n+1} - 1$ calls. Suppose you wanted to solve the problem for, say, 20 disks. That would mean you would need to make $2^{21} - 1$ calls, and since each call but the base case results in an action, you would have to actually move $2^{20} - 1$ disks. That is 1,048,575 moves, which is *a lot* of moves. If each move takes one second, and you work on the puzzle continuously, then you could solve the puzzle in 12 days (plus epsilon). That's *a lot* of work done by such an innocent-looking procedure.

3.3.5.5. More Caveats

The procedure makes many moves because every call generates two more calls, which results in the exponential growth rate. Perhaps there is another solution in which you don't have to make two calls within the procedure.

In writing the procedure, you reduced the problem of moving n disks to two subproblems of moving $n - 1$ disks, and you then assumed you could solve those simpler problems using recursion. Keeping this same assumption, consider the following decomposition (to move a tower of n disks):

1. Move 1 disk from *Source* to *Temp*
2. Move $n - 1$ disks from *Source* to *Destination*
3. Move 1 disk from *Temp* to *Destination*

Since you now make only one recursive call, this should greatly reduce the number of moves. The only problem with this method is that *it won't work*. When making a recursive subdivision of a problem, *it is extremely important to ensure that any subproblems that are to be solved recursively obey exactly the same rules as the original problem*. To see why this solution violates this rule, look at the case of three disks. You first move the top disk to tower C and get the following situation:

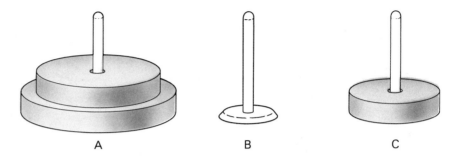

You then make a recursive call to move the two disks from A to B. In the original problem, however, the third tower was a temporary on which you could place disks. In this formulation of the problem, there is already a disk on the temporary, and it is the smallest disk in the puzzle. You therefore can't place any other disks on that tower. Thus, the recursive call requires you to move the two disks from A to B without the benefit of a temporary tower, which is not possible. The lesson is that you must make sure that every recursive call is trying to solve *exactly* the same kind of problem as the original call.

3.3.6. SELF CHECK EXERCISES

1. The following iterative function calculates integer exponentiation (x^n). Rewrite it as a tail-recursive function.

```
function power (X, N: integer): integer;
 var
   PROD, COUNT: integer;
begin
 PROD := 1;
 for COUNT := 1 to N do begin
   PROD := PROD * X;
 end; (* For *)
 power := PROD;
end; (* power *)
```

2. Write another recursive power function, this time making use of the following observations:

when n is 0, the result is 1

when n is odd, the result is $x \times x^{n-1}$

when n is even, the result is $(x^{n/2})^2$

3. What would be the output of the following program, which uses a variation on procedure *ReverseLine* from Section 1.3.3, assuming the input line contains, as in the section, the eight-character string 'baseball'?

```
program Mystery (input, output);

  var
    CH: char;

  procedure ReverseLine (var Infile, Outfile: text);
  begin
   if not eoln(Infile) then begin
     read(Infile, CH);
     ReverseLine(Infile, Outfile);
     write(Outfile, CH);
    end; (* If *)
  end; (* ReverseLine *)

begin
  ReverseLine(input, output);
end. (* Mystery *)
```

4. The Towers of Hanoi puzzle was solved with the following approach:

If $n > 0$ then begin Move $n - 1$ disks from *Source* to *Temp*.

Move 1 disk from *Source* to *Destination*.

Move $n - 1$ disks from *Temp* to *Destination* end.

This pseudocode uses 0 as the one and only base case; everything else is handled by the recursive case. Consider the possibility of identifying two base cases: $n = 0$ and $n = 1$. There is nothing to be done in the first case, and in the second, you have merely to move one disk from its source to its destination. Because your base cases deal with $n = 1$, you can assume that in the recursive case you have at least two disks to move. Thus, you could also improve on the efficiency of the recursive case by moving stacks of 2 and $n - 2$ disks rather than stacks of 1 and $n - 1$ disks. Following this approach, you might write the following pseudocode:

If $n > 1$ then begin Move $n - 2$ disks from *Source* to *Temp*.

Move 2 disks from *Source* to *Destination*.

Move $n - 2$ disks from *Temp* to *Destination* end else.

If $n = 1$ then begin Move disk from *Source* to *Destination* end.

Will this approach work? Why or why not?

3.4. RECURSIVE BACKTRACKING

In this section you will explore an application of recursion that will enable you to solve a large class of problems. You will also apply many of the data abstraction techniques discussed in the last chapter so that you can examine significant problems without getting bogged down in data type implementation issues that would distract from the recursive aspects of your solution.

3.4.1. The Technique of Backtracking

Until now you have used recursion to break down problems in a forward direction, always moving progressively toward a solution. For example, every recursive call in Towers of Hanoi brought you one step closer to solving the puzzle. Many problems, however, have no algorithmic solution of this type.

Rather than proceeding directly toward a solution, you instead look for one among a "space" of possible right answers.

> **SEARCH SPACE**
> ∙
> **A set of possible right answers to be explored.**

You could randomly wander the search space in hopes of finding a right answer, but this section presents a more reliable approach where the problem is defined in terms of *paths* that may eventually lead to solutions. A path that is known to be devoid of right answers is known as a *dead end*.

> **BACKTRACKING**
> ∙
> **A technique whereby the search space is explored by systematically trying each possible path, backing up to try another whenever a dead end is encountered.**

Thus, each path is followed until either a solution is found, or it becomes apparent that the path is a dead end. Once you reach a dead end, you back up one step and try a different path. If this path also leads to a dead end, you back up one step and try another path. In this way you end up searching through all the paths, until you either find a solution or show that all the paths are dead ends.

The interesting thing about recursive backtracking is that procedures never need to actually "back up." Instead, each recursive call represents one step along a given path. Because of this, the procedures stay active until either their paths lead to a solution, or it's discovered that all paths radiating from their position lead to dead ends. Thus, procedures either find a solution along their path, or discover that no such path exists. For any given procedure execution, one of two things happens:

  * It finds a solution, in which case no more work needs to be done and all the procedures that called the successful procedure should terminate without further exploration, passing on the good news.

• It fails, in which case the procedure terminates without any good news and you return automatically to the calling procedure, which represents the previous step along the path. This procedure now knows that one possible direction it could follow is a dead end (since the recursive call ended in failure), and so it can try an alternative direction.

This process continues until all the possible directions have been tried, at which point this procedure also ends in failure, returning control to its caller, which follows the same process. If no solution is ever found, the highest-level procedure returns to the caller who started the search in the first place, reporting that all paths are dead ends.

The sections that follow give you good Pascal examples, but let's first look at a simple non-programming example that will help to explain the terminology while also demonstrating important aspects of successful backtracking.

Many businesses try to speed up their customer throughput by attaching change machines to registers so that cashiers don't have to fumble with coins. The cashier simply rings up the total and the amount paid, and the customer finds his change sliding down an incline and into a metal dish.

How do they work? How do they find the correct collection of coins for making change? Backtracking can be applied once the problem has been expressed in terms of paths. As is often the case in backtracking applications, you can be misled by focusing on the end result, in this case a pile of coins in no particular order. Even though the coins end up as a pile, they are released by the machine one at a time. Thus, the solution involves an ordered sequence of coins. The sequences generated by the machine, then, are the most natural way to define the paths. For example, there are only four sequences of only one coin, generating four paths:

As the arrows above indicate, each possible coin consitutes a path that leads to a specific amount of change (1, 5, 10, or 25 cents). For a sequence of two coins, you might imagine that there are sixteen possibilities, as follows:

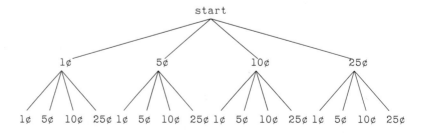

When solving a problem by backtracking, however, you should carefully examine your definition of paths, avoiding redundancy as much as possible so as to minimize the solution space, and you should carefully consider the order in which you will search them so as to maximize efficiency and produce the most desirable results.

For example, the diagram above suffers from redundancy in that the path (1¢, 5¢) generates the same result as (5¢, 1¢). Such duplicates are easily eliminated by restricting the paths to increasing or decreasing sequences.

That addresses redundancy, but what about efficiency in the search and desirability of results? For 50 cents, for example, many solutions exist. Which one is best? It doesn't matter in terms of correctness, but people generally like to receive as few coins as possible in change (i.e., 2 quarters rather than 50 pennies).

To favor short sequences over long sequences, you should restrict sequences to decreasing order and always search from high denominations toward low denominations. You can see cashiers following this same basic algorithm as they place their hands over the container for quarters and move steadily over to dimes and nickels and pennies, always picking up as many coins as possible without going over the amount. They even, if you watch closely, use backtracking sometimes when they accidentally pick up too many of one of the coins, forcing them to back up by putting the coins back in their appropriate container.

With up to two coins you get the four legal sequences of length 1 and 10 new sequences of length 2 (restricting the solution space to decreasing sequences).

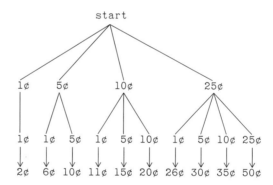

As indicated by the preceding arrows, this solution space has 14 paths in it, each leading to a specific amount of change (although notice that two different paths yield total change of 10 cents: 10¢ by itself, or 5¢ followed by 5¢). Moving up to a possible three coins, the solution space is shown in the diagram on the following page.

Consider how you could use backtracking to explore this solution space. In typical backtracking fashion, you explore all the paths, but as noted previously, all searching proceeds from highest denomination toward lowest denomination so that the path of shortest length will be discovered first.

For example, consider trying to return 21 cents in change. Exploring from highest to lowest, you find an answer in six steps, as follows (where paths are drawn here horizontally rather than vertically):

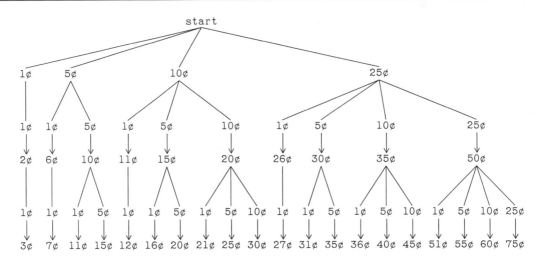

Step	Path	Total	Status	Result
1	start→25¢	25¢	> 21¢	dead end
2	start→10¢	10¢	< 21¢	continue
3	start→10¢→10¢	20¢	< 21¢	continue
4	start→10¢→10¢→10¢	30¢	> 21¢	dead end
5	start→10¢→10¢→5¢	25¢	> 21¢	dead end
6	start→10¢→10¢→1¢	21¢	= 21¢	success

Notice that bad paths are always discovered by accumulating a total higher than the amount, resulting in a backtrack step where the last coin is removed and the next lowest one is considered instead.

For an example that requires more coins, consider searching for a path that produces 63 cents.

Step	Path	Total	Status	Result
1	start→ 25¢	25¢	< 63¢	continue
2	start→ 25¢→ 25¢	50¢	< 63¢	continue
3	start→ 25¢→ 25¢→ 25¢	75¢	> 63¢	dead end
4	start→ 25¢→ 25¢→ 10¢	60¢	< 63¢	continue
5	start→ 25¢→ 25¢→ 10¢→ 10¢	70¢	> 63¢	dead end
6	start→ 25¢→ 25¢→ 10¢→ 5¢	65¢	> 63¢	dead end
7	start→ 25¢→ 25¢→ 10¢→ 1¢	61¢	< 63¢	continue
8	start→ 25¢→ 25¢→ 10¢→ 1¢→ 1¢	62¢	< 63¢	continue
9	start→ 25¢→ 25¢→ 10¢→ 1¢→ 1¢→ 1¢	63¢	= 63¢	success

In the next section you'll apply backtracking to cave adventuring, and then you'll use it to solve the classic Eight Queens chess problem.

3.4.2. The Raiders of the Lost Cave

For a vacation, you decide to go searching the infamous Lost Cave for its legendary Treasure Room, which is rumored to contain most of the wealth of the universe (or something equally silly). Rather than wander haphazardly in the cave, hoping to stumble upon the Treasure Room, you decide to use backtracking to systematically search the cave.

3.4.2.1. Writing the Recursive Routine

Following the backtracking method, you want to write a recursive procedure in which each procedure call represents a single position along a path. From that position you try to move in all possible directions, taking another step in each of these directions by making a recursive call. These calls will either end by finding a path to the Treasure Room, in which case you're done, or by finding dead ends that you know don't lead to treasure. If you can show that all possible directions lead to dead ends, your procedure will terminate having failed.

Assuming that paths go only in the directions North, South, East, and West, from each position you would like to move in each of these directions, trying to find a path to the Treasure Room. So that you don't accidentally start exploring parts of the cave you've already seen, you can bring along a couple of types of markers (just like the bread crumbs used by Hansel and Gretel to record their path through the forest). One you'll use to mark positions along the current path. That way, when you find the Treasure Room, the path from the cave entrance to the room will be clearly specified. Because you expect to find a number of dead ends (positions from which no path leads to the Treasure Room), you'll want to mark those as well, so once you've found a dead end you won't explore it again. By using these markers you ensure that you never reexplore any part of the cave.

Thus, if there is a path going North (and not a wall), and you haven't explored the path to the North, you'll try that first. If that path leads to the Treasure Room, then you're done. Otherwise, you look South. Again, if there is an unexplored path to the South, you try it. Then you try East and West. This continues until either you've found the Treasure Room or you've tried all four directions without success, in which case you mark the current position as a dead end and give up, returning to the previous position.

Backtracking can easily be expressed recursively as follows. You want to search a cave with n positions, each position having paths that radiate from it in four possible directions (but, obviously walls block some possible paths). To solve this problem you move in one of these directions and then try to solve the puzzle, given this move. Since you will never reexplore your original position, you have reduced the size of the problem from one of n positions to one of $n-1$ positions. Thus, you can reduce the problem by dealing with one position and then recursively call your procedure to explore the remaining $n-1$ positions. All you need now is the base case.

Since there are a number of ways in which the recursive case breaks down, there are a couple of ways of reaching the base case. First, if you happen to be in the Treasure Room, then you're done. Not only do you not want to make any more recursive calls, but you want all the previous calls to stop as well. You therefore need to set some sort of flag variable once you find the Treasure Room, so that the recursion can be stopped at the higher levels. In other words, once one procedure ends successfully, all the procedure invocations that preceded it would also end successfully.

On the other hand, what if you explore in all directions and find no solution? In this case you know that your current position is a dead end. You should mark it as such, and then have the procedure end in failure.

Now that you've defined the recursive case and the base cases, you can begin to write your code. The code will look something like the following pseudocode:

```
procedure Explore();
if you're in the Treasure Room then begin
  set flag that you're done
end
else begin
 put down Path marker
 for moves North, South, East, West do begin
   if (move OK) and (Treasure not found) then begin
     make move
     Explore
     move back to current position
   end; (* If *)
  end; (* Loop *)
 if Treasure Room not found then begin
  put down Dead End marker;
  end; (* If *)
end; (* If *)
```

As a clarification, a move is considered "OK" if there is a path in that direction (and not solid rock) and that path has not yet been explored (there are no markers there).

Now you come up against a serious problem. You need to find some way of representing the cave. This is no small problem, however. In fact, there are a number of interesting issues to deal with when designing a "CaveType." Interesting though they may be, however, you are concerned with implementing the recursive aspects of this routine, and not the data aspects. By representing the cave abstractly, however, you can solve this problem. Simply design a unit that encapsulates the significant data details of the program. Your unit should maintain the state of current exploration and should provide sufficient operations for you to manipulate this state. You should not, however, worry about the implementation details of this unit. If you are interested, a sample implementation is provided in Appendix B. For the purposes of this presentation, you need read only the interface section of the "Cave" unit (Figure 3.1).

The code is easy to write using this abstract definition. Now you can take the above pseudocode and almost directly translate it into Pascal. The sole parameter will be the flag telling whether or not you've found the Treasure Room. Here's the code:

OVERVIEW
Provides utilities for exploring a maze.

---

type   MarkerType = (Path, DeadEnd);
            (* Used to specify which kind of marker to place. *)

        MoveType = (North, South, East, West);
            (* Used to specify in which direction to move. *)

---

procedure Write (var Outfile: text);
        pre   Outfile open for writing; cave initialized.
        post   Contents of cave written to OutFile showing
                current path.

function TreasureIsHere : boolean;
        pre   cave initialized; current position is legal.
        post   returns true if treasure is at current position;
                false otherwise.

function MarkerIsHere : boolean;
        pre   cave initialized; current position is legal.
        post   returns true if a marker is at current position;
                false otherwise.

procedure PlaceMarker (Marker: MarkerType);
        pre   cave initialized; current position is legal.
        post   given marker is placed at current position.

function MoveOK (Move: MoveType): boolean;
        pre   cave initialized; current position is legal.
        post   returns true if given move is legal (i.e., not
                into a wall) or off the edge of the grid; false
                otherwise.

function Opposite (Move: MoveType): MoveType;
        post   returns the direction opposite the given direction
                (i.e., South exchanging with North, East with
                West).

procedure DoMove (Move: MoveType);
        pre   cave initialized; current position is legal; move
                is legal.
        post   performs the given move, resetting current
                position.

FIGURE 3.1. Specification for utility module *Cave*.

```
procedure Explore (var Found: boolean);
(* pre  : cave initialized; current position is legal;  *)
(*      : found is initialized to false; previously     *)
(*      : explored positions marked.                    *)
(* post : If a path from current position to treasure   *)
(*      : exists, found is set to true and the path is  *)
(*      : marked; if not, found is unchanged and no     *)
(*      : path is marked.  In both cases, all dead      *)
(*      : ends found by procedure are marked.           *)
var
 MOVE: Cave.MoveType;
begin
 if (Cave.TreasureIsHere) then begin
   Found := true;
  end
 else begin
   Cave.PlaceMarker(Cave.Path);
   for MOVE := Cave.North to Cave.West do begin
     if (Cave.MoveOK(MOVE)) and (not Found) then begin
       Cave.DoMove(MOVE);
       Explore(Found);
       Cave.DoMove(Opposite(MOVE));
      end; (* If *)
    end; (* For *)
   if not Found then begin
     Cave.PlaceMarker(Cave.DeadEnd);
    end; (* If *)
   end; (* If *)
 end; (* Explore *)
```

Now all you need to do in the main program is call this procedure to explore the cave, and then print out the cave, showing the path from the entrance to the Treasure Room. Your complete program could look like the following:

```
program CaveExplorer (output);

 uses
  Cave;

 var
  Found: boolean;

<procedure Explore, as above>

 begin (* Main *)
  Found := false;
  Explore(Found);
  if Found then begin
    writeln('Here is the solution:');
    Cave.Write(output);
   end
```

```
        else begin
          writeln('There is no path to the Treasure Room.');
        end; (* If *)
end. (* Main *)
```

3.4.3. The Eight Queens Problem

The *Eight Queens* problem is another puzzle that can be solved by means of recursive backtracking. For those of you unfamiliar with the game of chess, it is played on an 8×8 grid of squares. Various pieces can be placed on this board, with no more than one piece on a given square. The Queen is the most powerful piece in the game, in that it can travel vertically, horizontally, and diagonally any number of squares on a single turn, provided it does not have to pass through another piece. For example, in the grid below the Queen can move to any of the marked squares:

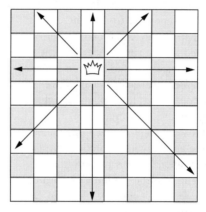

A Queen is said to *threaten* another piece if it can move to the same square as that piece on a single turn. Thus, the above Queen would threaten any piece in a marked square. The object of the Eight Queens problem is to place eight Queens on a chessboard in such a way that no Queen threatens any other Queen. Below is one solution to the Eight Queens problem:

3.4.3.1. Writing the Recursive Routine

Since you are using recursive backtracking, you need to define the paths you will follow when looking for a solution. These paths will either lead to dead ends, in which case your procedure should end in failure, or else you find a path to your goal, and you end successfully.

Think about what constitutes a step along the path. You want to place eight Queens on the board, and so it would make sense that each step would consist of placing another Queen in a legal position. Determining where to search for a legal move, however, is a little tricky. In the cave searching problem, each position had exactly four directions from which paths could radiate. In this problem, however, there are 64 squares upon which each Queen could be placed. If you approach the problem in this way, though, each procedure will need to consider 64 different paths, which means 64 recursive calls! Considering how much searching the cave procedure generated with a mere four calls, having a procedure that could potentially make 64 calls is somewhat frightening.

The search space can be narrowed considerably, however, if the problem is examined from a somewhat different angle. Rather than viewing the board as consisting of 64 squares, it can be seen as being comprised of eight columns, each with eight rows. Because Queens can move any number of squares vertically in a single turn, and because you are placing eight Queens on the board, there must be *exactly* one queen in every column. Thus, rather than having to place eight Queens in 64 squares, you instead want to place one Queen in each of the eight columns. You can obviously derive an equivalent solution by placing Queens in rows, but you have to choose one or the other, so let's use columns.

The positions in the Cave Search problem are therefore equivalent to the columns in the Eight Queens problem. In each column you will place a Queen in one of the eight rows, and then take a step forward along the path by making a recursive call. This call will return having either succeeded in finding a solution, in which case you're done, or having failed, meaning that there is no solution given the current placement of Queens. If the recursive call fails, you move the Queen to another row and try again. You have to be careful, however, not to place a Queen in an illegal row. If a row is threatened by another Queen that has already been placed at a previous point along the path, then you don't want to place your Queen in that row. You want to place Queens only in rows that are not yet threatened.

The recursive case, therefore, consists of picking a safe row in the given column, placing a Queen there, and then making a recursive call to find a solution given that placement. If a solution is found, then you're done. Otherwise, pick another safe row, and repeat.

Now, what about the base case? Just as in the Cave Search problem, there are two parts to the base case, one for success and one for failure. Since each recursive call moves you into another column, and there are only eight columns, you hit one base case when you step into column nine. You don't actually use column nine, but remember how your recursion works. You call the procedure to place a Queen in column n, assuming that Queens have been placed legally in columns 1 through $n - 1$. Thus, if you get a request to place a Queen in column nine, you know that eight Queens have been legally placed, and you will want the exploration to stop. To tell all the previous procedure calls that a solution has been found, you can set a flag and end the procedure, just as in the cave program.

When else does the recursive case break down? It places a Queen in a safe row and makes a recursive call. If that call fails to find a solution, it picks another safe row and makes another recursive call. This continues until all the safe rows have been tried. At that point you know that the path you are on is a dead end, and so the procedure ends unsuccessfully.

Having defined both the recursive case and the base case, you can begin to write the code. A first attempt might look like the following:

```
procedure Solve (Col: integer;
        var Success: boolean);
  var
    ROW: integer;
begin
  if Col >= 9 then begin
    Success := true;
  end
  else begin
    for each row in column Col do begin
      if (Square[ROW, Col] is safe) and (not Success) then
      begin
        Put Queen in Square[ROW, Col]
            Solve(Col + 1, Success);
      if not Success then begin
        Remove Queen From Square[ROW, Col]
      end; (* If *)
    end; (* If *)
    end; (* For *)
  end; (* If *)
end; (* Solve *)
```

Once again, however, you run up against the problem of representing the data, in this case the chessboard, in an appropriate way. While this is an interesting problem, it has nothing to do with recursion, and as such pursuing it would be a serious digression from the topic at hand. If you choose to define the chessboard abstractly, you can go ahead and implement the recursive solution without worrying about the low-level details of building a chessboard data type. You simply need to specify the necessary operations, and your "Queens" unit will do all the work. Since the only required operations are the ability to check to see if a given square is safe, to place a Queen on a square, and to remove a Queen from a square, the following utility module should suffice (Figure 3.2).

This unit will maintain a chessboard object that you manipulate through the specified operations. All the information about how the chessboard is stored, and how the operations are implemented, remains hidden. This offers two advantages. First, as stated above, you don't have to worry about implementing the data type, and can

---

OVERVIEW
Provides utilities for managing a chessboard where multiple Queens
(and only Queens) are to be placed on the board.

```
    const NumRows = 8;
        NumCols    = 8;
```

```
procedure Write (var Outfile: text);
        pre     Outfile open for writing; board initialized.
        post    Contents of board written to OutFile showing
                current placement of pieces.

function Safe (Row, Col: integer): boolean;
        pre     board initialized; 1 <= Row <= NumRows;
                1 <= Col <= NumCols.
        post    returns true if a Queen can be placed at position
                without threatening any Queens in previous rows.

procedure Place (Row, Col: integer);
        pre     board initialized; 1 <= Row <= NumRows;
                1 <= Col <= NumCols.
        post    places a Queen at given position.

procedure Remove (Row, Col: integer);
        pre     board initialized; 1 <= Row <= NumRows;
                1 <= Col <= NumCols.
        post    removes a Queen from given position if present.
```

FIGURE 3.2. *Specification for utility module* Queens.

instead focus on writing the recursive algorithm. Second, if, at a later date, the
implementation of the chessboard should change, your program, which uses this unit,
would not even have to know about the change. Since the program only accesses
the board through the specified operations, any changes in the low-level details of
the chessboard will also remain hidden from the program. For example, if a more
efficient implementation is created, the only reason you'll know about it is that your
program will now run faster. By isolating all the data in a separate unit you make your
program independent of a particular implementation of that data type.

You can now polish off the code for the program. Since you want all searching
to stop once a solution has been found, you should code the loop in the recursive
routine as an indefinite loop, such as a *repeat* loop, rather than as a definite *for* loop.
Other than making this modification, the code flows almost directly from the above
sketch.

```
        procedure Solve (Col: integer;
                var Success: boolean);
        (* pre  : board initialized; 1 <= col <= Queens.NumCols   *)
        (*       : + 1; success initialized to false.              *)
```

```
(* post : sets success to true if a legal placement of    *)
(*       : Queens is possible given the previously placed *)
(*       : Queens; otherwise does nothing.                *)
  var
    ROW: integer;
begin
  if Col > Queens.NumCols then begin
    Success := true;
  end
  else begin
    ROW := 0;
    repeat
     ROW := ROW + 1;
     if Queens.Safe(ROW, Col) then begin
       Queens.Place(ROW, Col);
       Solve(Col + 1, Success);
       if not Success then begin
         Queens.Remove(ROW, Col);
        end; (* If *)
      end; (* If *)
    until (Success) or (ROW = Queens.NumRows);
   end; (* If *)
end; (* Solve *)
```

The rest of the program follows fairly easily. The main program needs to make the initial call on the procedure, and then print out the resulting solution.

```
program ProblemSolver (output);

 uses
  Queens;

 var
  Success: boolean;

<procedure Solve, as above>

begin (* Main *)
 Success := false;
 Solve(1, Success);
 if Success then begin
   writeln('Here is the solution:');
   Queens.Write(output);
  end
 else begin
   writeln('There is no solution.');
  end; (* If *)
end. (* Main *)
```

3.4.3.2. Wrapping Recursive Procedures

Because recursion requires you to identify some problem solving class that matches both the overall problem and its subproblems, recursive procedures often require parameters that exist solely for maintaining an internal state, and have nothing to do with the program outside the recursive procedure. In the Eight Queens example, you wanted a procedure that would simply solve the problem. Instead, you wrote a procedure that solves the puzzle one column at a time, and requires that you initialize a flag variable. You can get the fully self-contained procedure you were after, however, by "wrapping" your procedure inside an outer nonrecursive procedure. The analogy is to a candy wrapper that allows you to store sticky candy by keeping it in a clean, protective wrapper. While your wrapped procedure does most of the dirty work, the rest of the world only sees the clean wrapping on the outside.

Wrapping one procedure inside another is relatively straightforward. Just as constants, types, and variables can be declared local to a procedure, so can other procedures. You simply declare your procedure after the variable declaration block, but before the wrapping procedure's main body. For example, below is the *Solve* procedure wrapped inside a procedure that cleanly handles the entire problem:

```
procedure EightQueens (var Success: boolean);
(* pre  : board initialized to be empty.               *)
(* post : sets success to true if a legal placement of  *)
(*        : Queens is possible and stores their positions *)
(*        : in the board; otherwise does nothing.         *)

  procedure Solve (Col: integer;
        var Success: boolean);
    (* pre  : board initialized; 1 <= col                 *)
    (*        : <= Queens.NumCols + 1; success initialized *)
    (*        : to false.                                  *)
    (* post : sets success to true if a legal placement   *)
    (*        : of Queens is possible given the previously *)
    (*        : placed Queens and stores their positions   *)
    (*        : in the board; otherwise does nothing.      *)

  var
    ROW: integer;

begin
  if Col > Queens.NumCols then begin
    Success := true;
  end
  else begin
    ROW := 0;
    repeat
      ROW := ROW + 1;
      if Queens.Safe(ROW, Col) then begin
        Queens.Place(ROW, Col);
        Solve(Col + 1, Success);
```

```
            if not Success then begin
              Queens.Remove(ROW, Col);
            end; (* If *)
          end; (* If *)
        until (Success) or (ROW = Queens.NumRows);
      end; (* If *)
    end; (* Solve *)

  begin (* EightQueens *)
    Success := false;
    Solve(1, Success);
  end; (* EightQueens *)
```

As the pre/post comments indicated, procedure *EightQueens* is easier to manipulate than procedure *Solve*, as reflected in the updated main program:

```
  begin (* Main *)
    EightQueens(Success);
    if Success then begin
      writeln('Here is the solution:');
      Queens.Write(output);
    end
    else begin
      writeln('There is no solution.');
    end; (* If *)
  end. (* Main *)
```

This technique is useful when any of the following occur:

* When some initialization needs to be performed before the recursion, but either shouldn't or doesn't need to take place for each recursive call (e.g., setting *Found* to false in the cave and Eight Queens searches). In this case, the outer procedure can perform the initialization once, just before starting the recursion.

* When the recursive solution requires peculiar parameter passing that you wouldn't want to force on the rest of your program (e.g., the parameter *Col* passed to the Eight Queens searching procedure). Your outer procedures can call the nonrecursive procedure using the normal parameter passing (in this case, simply a *Found* flag, no reference to column number) and it can call the inner recursive procedure using the unusual parameter passing (giving it an initial column number as well as the found flag).

* You want to make nonlocal but also nonglobal references to data from within your recursive procedure. For example, if you want to refer to a depth variable without passing it as a parameter and without declaring it as a global, you can make depth local to the outer procedure, which limits it to the scope of the outer procedure while still making it visible without parameter passing to the inner procedure. Many recursive procedures can be drastically sped up by simplifying their parameter passing and having them make nonlocal references

to variables local to the outer procedure (e.g., passing a large data structure to the outer procedure, but choosing to make nonlocal references to it from the inner procedure rather than slowing down the recursion with parameter passing overhead).

Some of these programming practices (particularly the last) sound rather dangerous, but the outer procedure insulates the rest of the program from the gooey things happening inside (and sometimes you need to be gooey). You might suspect some hypocrisy in that students are often graded down for such practices, but the explanation comes from the locality of the offense. If you steal your neighbor's TV because yours is broken, you're likely to see a policeman on your doorstep before the show is over, because stealing is a serious offense that society doesn't condone. But if you borrow your daughter's TV for the same reason, you won't be seeing any police, because the police don't interfere in household squabbles unless a crime is being committed. Your daughter might claim that your theft is a crime, but she will be shouting to deaf ears, because we operate under the assumption that it's a good idea to control many things in a friendly local context usually referred to as "home" and save the police for violations of a nonlocal and unfriendly manner.

Similarly, the outer procedure provides a kind of home that limits the extent of damage the gooey code can cause (just as a candy wrapper keeps sticky stuff from oozing all over). Thus, the outer procedure wraps the inner procedure in two ways (one at compile-time and one at run-time): it localizes any bad or unusual coding, protecting the rest of the program; and it provides a single outer procedure execution that can perform one-time initialization and/or set up parameter passing for many inner recursive executions.

Wrapping has further advantages when it comes time to debug recursive procedures, as you will see in the next section.

3.4.4. SELF CHECK EXERCISES

1. Rewrite the Eight Queens program from Section 3.4.3 so that it finds *all* solutions to the problem, instead of just one solution.

3.5. DEBUGGING RECURSIVE PROCEDURES

Because recursive procedures accomplish so much with so little code, they are both simple and difficult to debug. They are simple because the small amount of code isolates errors to a small number of statements. They are difficult to debug because it is extremely hard to mentally trace through a recursive procedure without getting lost. Applying a few simple techniques, however, can make the computer do most of the work, and therefore make the programmer's work much easier.

Rather than tracing through recursive procedure calls, it is usually helpful to have the computer print out its state information as each call is made. In that way, the programmer can easily follow the program's progress without going insane. For example, all the "tracings" for the examples have been generated in this way. After analyzing each procedure in terms of its actions, you can have the procedure print out a message each time an action is taken. In the Eight Queens problem, this means every time a square is examined. As such, assigning a Queen to a square, removing a Queen from a square, and detecting an unsafe square are all reported. Because finding a solution is also a significant event, that is also reported. Here is the version of the *EightQueens* procedure that generates the trace using an auxilliary procedure WriteSquare that reports one square's coordinates.

```
procedure WriteSquare (Row,Col: integer);
begin
 writeln (' (', Row : 1, ', ', Col : 1, ')');
end; (* WriteSquare *)

procedure EightQueens (var Success: boolean);

 procedure Solve (Col: integer;
       var Success: boolean);
  var
   ROW: integer;
 begin
  if Col > Queens.NumCols then begin
    Success := true;
   end
  else begin
    ROW := 0;
    repeat
     ROW := ROW + 1;
     if Queens.Safe(ROW, Col) then begin
       Queens.Place(ROW, Col);
       write ('Placing Queen at');
       WriteSquare(ROW, Col);
       Queens.Write(output);
       Solve(Col + 1, Success);
       if not Success then begin
         Queens.Remove(ROW, Col);
         write ('Removing Queen from');
         WriteSquare(ROW, Col);
         Queens.Write(output);
        end; (* If *)
      end; (* If *)
     else begin
       writeln('Square is not safe:');
       WriteSquare(ROW, Col);
       writeln;
      end; (* If *)

    until (Success) or (ROW = Queens.NumRows);
```

```
      end; (* If *)
    if Success then begin
      writeln('Solution found so stop searching.');
      writeln;
    end; (* If *)
  end; (* Solve *)

begin (* EightQueens *)
  Success := false;
  Solve(1, Success);
end; (* EightQueens *)
```

The primary problem with these *writeln* statements, however, is that they create a state of information overload. As you probably noticed, these procedures do a lot of work, and having to follow a trace that shows every detail can be an intimidating task while debugging. It is often useful to examine only portions of a trace, rather than having to absorb the entire thing. As a first step, it would probably be useful to look at, say, every 20th call, instead of every call. You could introduce a debugging counting variable that you would increment on each call. You would then print out the information only if the number of calls is a multiple of 20.

On the other hand, you may be more concerned with what's happening at a particular depth in the recursion. For example, you may want to look at the first level of calls, debug that level, and then move on. You can keep track of your current depth by having another counting variable that you increment every time you enter a recursive call, and decrement upon every return.

You can get even more sophisticated, combining both of these factors with program-specific information to determine when a state becomes "interesting," and then printing out the significant information at these interesting times. For example, suppose when debugging the Eight Queens problem you decided that you wanted to examine the state of your program every 20 calls, and you also wanted to look at every action you took in the third column. You could come up with the following procedure:

```
procedure EightQueens (var Success: boolean);

var
  Count, Depth: integer;

procedure Solve (Col: integer;
      var Success: boolean);
  var
    ROW: integer;
  begin
    Count := Count + 1;
    Depth := Depth + 1;
    if (Count mod 20 = 0) or (Depth = 3) then begin
```

```
        writeln('Depth = ', Depth : 1, '   Count = ', Count : 1);
        Queens.Write(output);
      end; (* If *)
    if Col > Queens.NumCols then begin
      Success := true;
    end
    else begin
      ROW := 0;
      repeat
       ROW := ROW + 1;
       if Queens.Safe(ROW, Col) then begin
         Queens.Place(ROW, Col);
         Solve(Col + 1, Success);
         if not Success then begin
           Queens.Remove(ROW, Col);
          end; (* If *)
        end; (* If *)
      until (Success) or (ROW = Queens.NumRows);
     end; (* If *)
   Depth := Depth - 1;
  end; (* Solve *)

 begin (* EightQueens *)
  Depth := 0;
  Count := 0;
  Success := false;
  Solve(1, Success);
 end; (* EightQueens *)
```

To change when information is printed out all you need to do is alter what you consider "interesting" by changing the condition of the *if* statement at the beginning of the procedure.

It is also worth noting that the variables *Depth* and *Count* have been defined to be local to the procedure *EightQueens*, but have not been passed as parameters to *Solve*. Although making nonlocal references is usually severely frowned upon, the preceding method is acceptable because you have restricted the nonlocality to the single procedure contained within the wrapping. Returning to the wrapping analogy, inside the wrapper a piece of candy can have lots of different fillings all mixed up, because the outer wrapper protects you from the gooey middle. Similarly, it is OK for your inner procedure to be somewhat messy, so long as the mess is limited and the wrapping is clean.

As a final debugging tip, knowing the depth of a procedure call is also useful in formatting output. For example, for the trace of the "reverse line" procedure, the depth is used to determine how much to indent each line. Thus, the depth is displayed in the way the output is formatted. In case you're curious, here's the code used to generate that trace. Note how the depth is used to determine the indentation by passing it as a parameter to an *Indent* procedure, which outputs the given number of spaces.

```
procedure ReverseLine (var Infile, Outfile: text;
       Depth: integer);

 var
  CH: char;
 begin
  if not eoln(Infile) then begin
    read(Infile, CH);
    Indent(Depth);
    writeln('Enter ReverseLine and read "', CH, '"');
    ReverseLine(Infile, Outfile, Depth + 1);
    Indent(Depth);
    write('Write "');
    write(Outfile, CH);
    writeln('" and exit ReverseLine');
   end
  else begin
    Indent(Depth);
    writeln('Enter ReverseLine');
    Indent(Depth);
    writeln('at EOLN');
    Indent(Depth);
    writeln('exit ReverseLine');
   end; (* If *)
 end; (* ReverseLine *)
```

3.6. THE COST OF RECURSION

While recursive solutions are often elegant, their apparent simplicity often disguises the hidden costs. You have seen how an innocent-looking procedure to solve the Towers of Hanoi problem actually generates many moves. Computing Fibonacci numbers reveals another example of the hidden costs of recursion.

The Fibonacci sequence is defined as follows. The first two numbers are 1. Successive numbers are the sum of the previous two, yielding

   1, 1, 2, 3, 5, 8, 13, 21, 34, 55, 89, 144, ...

It can be defined recursively as

   $\text{Fib}(0) = 1$
   $\text{Fib}(1) = 1$
   $\text{Fib}(n) = \text{Fib}(n - 1) + \text{Fib}(n - 2)$, for $n > 1$.

Because this sequence is defined recursively, translating it into a recursive function that will compute the nth Fibonacci number is both easy and natural. Below is the code:

```
function Fib (Num: integer): integer;
begin
 if Num < 2 then begin
   Fib := 1;
 end
 else begin
   Fib := Fib(Num - 1) + Fib(Num - 2);
 end; (* If *)
end; (* Fib *)
```

Although this function is clear and easy to understand, it is also extremely inefficient, for to compute a Fibonacci number it ends up recomputing previous numbers in the sequence several times. Below is a trace of the work done to compute the sixth number in the sequence (which is *Fib(5)*, since the sequence starts at zero).

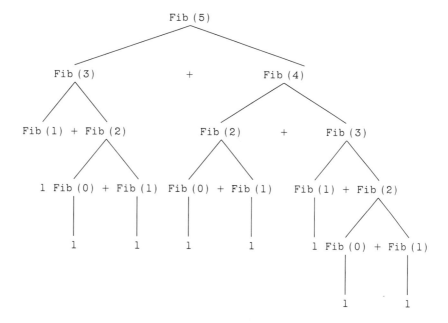

While computing the sixth number you end up computing *Fib(1)* five times! And it gets worse. If you were computing *Fib(30)* by this method, you would in the process recompute *Fib(1)* 514,229 times! Clearly a much better solution would be to start with the first two numbers, which you are given, and then successively compute the next number in the sequence. By this method, you compute each number in the sequence exactly once, and it takes a mere 29 steps to compute *Fib(30)*.

Therefore, although recursion is a powerful technique, and is often entirely appropriate for solving problems, it should be used both wisely and cautiously.

3.6.1. SELF CHECK EXERCISES

1. Write an efficient nonrecursive function to compute the nth Fibonacci number.

2. Write a function *FibCalls*, with the header below, which will return the number of *calls* on *Fib* that are made to compute the nth Fibonacci number. Here is the header:

```
function FibCalls (n: integer): integer;
```

3. The nth Fibonacci number is asymptotically approximated by an expontial sequence (i.e., the nth number is approximately equal to c^n, for some constant c). What is c?

3.7. SUMMARY OF KEY POINTS

- *Iteration* involves solving problems by breaking them up into smaller subproblems, each of which constitutes some different aspect of the overall problem. *Recursion* involves a different kind of analysis whereby problems are reduced to one or more simpler subproblems from the same overall class as the original problem.

- As with most procedures, recursive procedures are meant to solve a class of related problems (e.g., a single calculation, but with variable-length input). In using recursion, you exploit this by including calls on a procedure inside that procedure (known as *recursive calls*). This mechanism often replaces loops that would appear in an iterative counterpart, because recursion works mostly by repeated procedure calls rather than by repeated execution inside a loop.

- Developing a recursive definition requires identifying both the *recursive case* or cases (obtained by reducing the overall problem to a simpler problem from the same class) and the *base case* or cases (the members of the class of problems that can be solved immediately because they are so simple).

- Most recursive definitions have branching if/then/else constructs as their outer level of control, because the outermost context is one of distinguishing various recursive and base cases.

- Recursion requires a certain leap of faith. When dealing with a procedure, you as a programmer are usually either calling a previously written procedure or writing a procedure that others will call. You operate on both levels with recursion, which means you have to have faith while implementing the procedure that it can be trusted to solve part of the overall problem when called recursively. This leap of faith is justified as long as each recursive call is performing a simpler problem than the original and you handle all base cases.

- Recursion is possible because each activation of a procedure is independent of any other procedure activation, even one for the same procedure. Thus, if several versions of a single procedure are executing at one time, each has its own set of local variables and its own execution state that keeps track of what statement to execute next.

- Some programming problems cannot be solved in a systematic first step, second step, third step manner, but instead require searching for a correct answer from a *solution space* of possible answers. Such problems are often easily solved by applying *backtracking*, a technique whereby all possible paths are explored and branches that lead to dead ends are eliminated, causing the search to back up to the decision made just before the dead end was encountered. Backtracking algorithms are most elegantly expressed using recursion.

- When solving a difficult recursive problem, you will be able to more easily concentrate on the recursion if the data details of the problem have been isolated into a separate program unit so that you can manipulate data in an abstract manner in your recursive procedures, leaving the data details for someone else to solve or to solve at a different time.

- Recursive procedures are challenging to debug because they are so terse. You will be able to more easily pinpoint errors if you include debugging *write* and *writeln* statements in your procedures that describe the state of variables as you enter and exit the procedure and as you make critical changes to data in the middle of your procedure's execution. Because of the sheer volume of recursive calls, you might need to specify some criteria for an "interesting" activation worth reporting, perhaps taking into account the total number of activations that have occured and/or the maximum depth the recursion has achieved.

- It is often useful to "wrap" a recursive procedure inside a nonrecursive procedure (literally including the text of the recursive procedure inside the other procedure to create a local procedure, much like a local variable). The outer procedure is called once and it calls the inner recursive procedure, starting the chain of recursive calls. This technique is useful when special one-time initialization is required, the recursive call requires unusual parameter passing, or the recursion is easier to implement by making nonlocal but also nonglobal references to data.

- Although recursion is a powerful technique that allows you to express certain algorithms more easily than you could iteratively, it can also be an expensive way to solve a problem in terms of the time it takes to execute and the amount of computer memory it requires (especially when the recursion calculates values more than once rather than saving partial results).

3.8. PROGRAMMING EXERCISES

1. Write a recursive function, with the header below, which returns the number of digits in the parameter Num. For example, *NumDigits(101)* should return 3.

```
function NumDigits (Num: integer): integer;
```

2. Write a recursive procedure that will take an input file and write that file reversed to an output file. For example, given the following input file

   ```
   Hello
   there!
   ```

   your procedure will output the following:

   ```
   !ereht
   olleH
   ```

3. Binary is the base two number system. In binary, only the digits zero and one are used. The weighting system for binary is very similar to decimal. For example, the number $347_{\text{base } 10} = (3 \times 10^2) + (4 \times 10^1) + (7 \times 10^0) = 300 + 40 + 7 = 347_{\text{base} 10}$. Similarly, the binary number $1101_{\text{base } 2}$, equals $(1 \times 2^3) + (1 \times 2^2) + (0 \times 2^1) + (1 \times 2^0) = 8 + 4 + 0 + 1 = 13_{\text{base } 10}$.

   To convert a number from decimal to binary, you simply divide by two until a quotient of zero is reached, then use the successive remainders in reverse order as the binary representation. For example, to convert $35_{\text{base } 10}$ to binary, you perform the following computation:

   $$35 / 2 = 17 \text{ R } 1$$
   $$17 / 2 = 8 \text{ R } 1$$
   $$8 / 2 = 4 \text{ R } 0$$
   $$4 / 2 = 2 \text{ R } 0$$
   $$2 / 2 = 1 \text{ R } 0$$
   $$1 / 2 = 0 \text{ R } 1$$

   If you examine the remainders from the last division to the first one, writing them down as you go, you will get the following sequence — 100011, and $100011_{\text{base } 2} = 35_{\text{base } 10}$.

   With this in mind, write a recursive procedure that accepts a nonnegative decimal integer as a parameter, and writes out its binary representation.

4. Write a procedure that examines the next line on an input file and determines whether or not the line contains balanced parentheses. For example, the following lines contain balanced parentheses:

   ```
   ( )
   <an empty line>
   ( ) ( ) ( ) ( )   ( )
   ( ( ( ) ) )
   ( ( ) ( ( ) ( ) ) )
   ```

   the following lines do not contain balanced parentheses:

```
( ( ) ( ) ( ) (
( ) )
(
) ) ) ( ( (
```

Your procedure should have the following header:

```
procedure BalancedParens (var Infile: text;
        var IsBalanced: boolean);
```

5. You are to write a procedure that will evaluate arithmetic expressions that are given in "prefix" notation. When using prefix notation, the operator precedes the two operands. For example,

   + 5 3

evaluates to eight. Prefix notation has the nice property that it is unambiguous (unlike standard infix notation). Here are some other examples:

$$* 3 + 2\ 6 = 24$$
$$/ 7\ 3 = 2 \ (note: \ integer \ division)$$
$$+ * - 6\ 3 + 1\ 2\ 5 = 14$$

You can assume that the expression is in an input file and that spaces separate operators and numbers. Here is the procedure header:

```
procedure Eval (var Infile: text; var Answer: integer);
```

3.9. PROGRAMMING PROJECTS

1. Write a function that compares two sequences of characters (known as *strings*). If the strings are equal the function will return *true*. Otherwise it will return *false*. The tricky part is that one of the two strings will be allowed to contain wildcard characters. A wildcard is a character that can match several characters in the other string.

   Here are the wildcard characters that your program should recognize:

Character	—	Matches
'%'	—	Any single character
'#'	—	Any single numeric
'&'	—	Any single alphanumeric
'$'	—	Any single alpha
'*'	—	Nul, or any series of characters
'@'	—	Nul, or any series of spaces

where *alpha* means an upper- or lowercase letter, *numeric* indicates a digit, and *alphanumeric* characters are both letters and digits. Here are some examples that should clarify things.

Wild	*Simple*	
gi*	giants	Match
gi	gi*	No Match { '*' is not interpreted as a wildcard.}
%#*x	y643x	Match
*p*p	ppppep	Match
$$$	hlw	Match
$$$$	hlw	No Match

Suppose you have the following declarations:

```
const
 MaxString = 20;
type
 StrArray = packed array[1..MaxString] of char;
 String = record
   Chars: StrArray;
   Length: 0..MaxString;
  end; (* String *)
```

Your function should have the following header. Note that the parameters are passed as *var* parameters for efficiency reasons.

```
function Match (var Wild, Simple: String): boolean;
```

2. Most of the digits on a telephone are associated with three letters. Thus, you can transform telephone numbers into combinations of words and digits. Write a program that takes in a phone number and outputs all the word/digit combinations that can be derived from the number. For example, the phone number 568-3427 corresponds to LOT-3427, LOVE-4-CS, etc. You will have an external dictionary file, containing one word per line, which will store the legal words.

3. The following is an example of a cryptarithmetic puzzle. Each letter stands for one digit, and different letters stand for different digits (i.e., a digit may be assigned to only one letter). A solution has been found when all the top words add up to the last word.

```
    FORTY
     NINE
       IS
    SEVEN
    -----
   SEVENS
```

In this case, the following is one solution:

$$
\begin{array}{r}
85924 \\
6760 \\
71 \\
10306 \\
\hline
103061
\end{array}
$$

Think carefully about defining the steps along the path. You will probably find it convenient to start in the upper right-hand corner (the first row of the last column) and work your way down the rows and then back through the previous columns. In that way you can find dead ends when you reach the last row of a column (the sum row), assign a number to the letter in that position, and then discover that the puzzle is inconsistent. Remember to consider carrying, and that a carry out of the rightmost column can propagate through the entire puzzle.

4. Consider the problem of expressing integers as the sum of distinct squares. For example, there are three ways of expressing 91 as the sum of perfect squares

$$91 = 1^2 + 2^2 + 3^2 + 4^2 + 5^2 + 6^2$$
$$91 = 1^2 + 4^2 + 5^2 + 7^2$$
$$91 = 1^2 + 3^2 + 9^2$$

Given an integer, you could search for a combination of integers whose squares add up to that integer. More generally, given an integer and an exponent, you could search for a combination of numbers that, when carried to the given exponent, add up to the given integer. This is, in fact, a simple backtracking problem. You are to develop a general-purpose procedure that given an integer and an exponent, writes out the shortest combination of integers (if any) that sum to the given integer using the given exponent.

Using this procedure, you should be able to construct a table showing for all integers between 1 and 1000 the shortest combination of squares, cubes, and fourth-powers, that add up to the integer. For example, there is a sample format for the table showing the correct answers for the numbers 881 through 900 on the following page. The first line of the table, for example, indicates that:

$$881 = 2^2 + 6^2 + 29^2$$
$$881 = 3^3 + 5^3 + 9^3$$
$$881 = 4^4 + 5^4$$

The table will have 1000 lines, so you might want to have just one header. In the solution above the author chose to "box" every 20 lines with a header, so that the output produced would show many of these mini-tables. Another hint that you can derive from the table above is that you should leave room for seven integers for

	exponent = 2	exponent = 3	exponent = 4
881	2, 6,29	3, 5, 9	4, 5
882	1, 2, 6,29	1, 3, 5, 9	1, 4, 5
883	1, 4, 5,29	1, 3, 7, 8	
884	10,28		
885	1,10,28		
886	3, 6,29		
887	1, 3, 6,29		
888	2,10,28	2, 3, 5, 6, 8	
889	1, 2,10,28	2, 3, 5, 9	
890	7,29	1, 2, 3, 5, 9	
891	1, 7,29	1, 2, 3, 7, 8	
892	1, 3, 4, 5,29		
893	4, 6,29		
894	2, 7,29		
895	1, 2, 7,29		
896	1, 2, 3, 4, 5,29		
897	2, 4, 6,29		2, 4, 5
898	1, 2, 4, 6,29		1, 2, 4, 5
899	3, 7,29		
900	30		

each "cell" (i.e., any particular choice of power and number in this range always leads to 7 or fewer numbers in the sum). This will be true only if you manage to find the *shortest* sequence of integers, so if your algorithm performs incorrectly, you might find some solutions that have sequences longer than seven but if you get the right answers, you'll fit.

4

LINKED LISTS

4.1. INTRODUCTION

The amount of information processed by a program is often quite large. Moreover, individual pieces of information often have complex relationships that a programmer will want to represent when designing a structure for maintaining the data. Such data-intensive programs require efficient use of storage space and flexibility in expressing data relationships, neither of which can be accomplished using the simple Pascal data structures you have explored so far.

For example, arrays are a convenient structure for storing large amounts of data, but the size of each array must be declared at compile-time. A programmer must therefore anticipate the data requirements before the program begins executing. Data requirements for most programs vary from one execution to the next, forcing the programmer to declare an array large enough for even the most complex executions. This technique wastes too much space to be acceptable if the data requirements are not well known when the program is written.

Furthermore, while arrays and records provide some ability to express relationships among pieces of data, a programmer often wants more flexibility. Records group related pieces of information, and arrays establish a linear ordering of data elements, but neither could be used to represent multiple groupings or multiple orderings.

This chapter introduces new techniques for allocating variables and designing data structures. By allocating variables at runtime, a program can maximize space efficiency by allocating exactly as many variables as it needs. Variables allocated in this way can be linked together, providing programmers the flexibility to express complex data relationships.

These techniques are explained using examples of one-dimensional or linear data, which lead to a family of similar structures known as *linked lists*. The next chapter will show how these techniques can be applied to nonlinear data. After a general consideration of simple linked lists, the chapter shows how these structures can be used to implement some important ADTs.

4.2. POINTERS AND DYNAMIC DATA

So far your programs have requested storage space for variables at compile time by including *var* declarations in which you name a series of variables and their types. For this reason, you have needed to precisely anticipate the eventual storage requirements for your program. Using *dynamic allocation*, however, the necessary variables can be created as the program is executing.

DYNAMIC ALLOCATION
A process by which variables are created at runtime, allowing the program to request exactly as much space as it needs for the current execution.

Dynamically allocated variables are not named in the program listing, so they are called *anonymous* variables. They are accessed through variables that "point to" them. Using this pointing mechanism the programmer can solve not only the space problem, but also the problem of data relationships, because it can be used to link variables together.

POINTER VARIABLE
A variable that stores a reference or pointer to a dynamically allocated variable. Pointer variables, also called pointers, can be used to establish links between variables.

The concepts of dynamic allocation and pointer variables are, in theory, independent, but not in Pascal. In Pascal, dynamic allocation is always requested using pointer variables and pointer variables can reference only dynamically allocated variables.

4.2.1. Introduction to Linked Lists

To help you understand pointers and the data structures built using them, you will almost always find it helpful to draw pictures. Pointers are generally drawn as arrows.

For example, when you group a character variable with a pointer inside a record structure you get the following:

Look closely at this structure. If you have ever played with Lego, Lincoln Logs, or any other set of interlocking pieces, you'll remember that you could build large structures using many simple pieces all with the same basic structure. Pointers can be used to create such patterns in Pascal. The picture above is one such pattern, the basic building block of a structure called a *linked list*. Each of these units is called a *node* of the list and stores a single data item along with a pointer to the next list element. By linking several together, you can make lists of varying length, as in

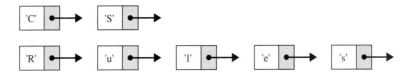

As the arrows indicate, it is possible to traverse the list in one direction (from left to right in the diagram above). Because they are chained together in this fashion, the entire list can be accessed from the first element, because all other elements can be reached by following the appropriate number of links. Thus, linked lists are generally maintained by keeping a pointer to the first element. The last element of a list cannot point randomly into space as the lists above do. Instead, their pointer fields are set to a special value called *nil* that indicates, "this doesn't point to anything." It is denoted by putting a slash through the box from which the arrow normally originates. Thus, the two lists above would normally be maintained using pointer variables and would be terminated by *nil*, as follows:

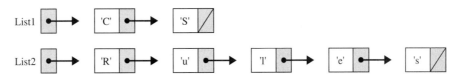

Novices often confuse pointers with the objects they point to. This is like confusing an address book with the people named in the book. Your party will be fairly dull if you just invite your address book. You need to follow the references in the book to get to the actual people you want to invite. Similarly, destroying the address book won't harm the people, it just might make it hard to reach them.

4.2.2. Pointer Details

Pointers are interesting only when used to create linked structures, so that is where you will want to invest significant energy trying to understand what is going on.

This section briefly summarizes several pointer details by defining an uninteresting pointer type and quickly seeing all of the ways it can be manipulated. You should pay attention, because all the important pointer operations are included, but don't expect to have a full understanding until you work through the detailed examples in the sections that follow.

The term *pointer* actually refers to a family of types. Every pointer type has a *base type*, and all variables of this pointer type can reference only variables of that particular base type. Any named type, either predefined or defined within a program, can be a base type. Pointer types are specified by placing the ^ character before the name of the base type. For example, the following declaration specifies that variable *AnInt* of type *IntPtr* points to an integer.

```
type
  IntPtr = ^integer;
var
  AnInt: IntPtr;
```

As with all variables, it is created uninitialized:

$$\text{AnInt} \quad \boxed{?}$$

You can give it an initial value by setting it to *nil*:

```
AnInt := nil;
```

which is represented as follows:

$$\text{AnInt} \quad \boxed{/\!\!/}$$

The value *nil* means "I don't point anywhere." Since an undefined value doesn't point anywhere either, these two states might seem the same. They are, in fact, quite different. As you'll see in later sections, a *nil* pointer is like a person who admits to being ignorant, while an uninitialized pointer is like a person who happens to be ignorant but doesn't realize it. The distinction turns out to be quite important.

You can use this pointer to request dynamic allocation by calling the standard procedure *new*, passing the pointer variable as a parameter. The computer looks up that pointer variable's base type, creates an anonymous variable of that type, and causes the pointer variable to reference it. Thus, the statement

```
new(AnInt);
```

causes the computer to dynamically allocate an integer variable with *AnInt* pointing to it:

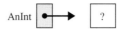

After calling *new*, there are *two* variables: one is a named pointer variable and the other is an anonymous integer variable. The new variable, as always, is created uninitialized. It has no name, so it can only be accessed through *AnInt*. You do so by *dereferencing* the pointer, which basically means following the arrow until you get to the data it points to. A pointer is dereferenced by placing the ^ character *after* its name. Thus, the dynamically allocated variable is referred to as *AnInt^*. If you are diligently remembering to distinguish between a pointer to an object and the object itself, don't go on without looking once more at *AnInt* versus *AnInt^* to see that they differ in exactly this way.

Thus, you can initialize the integer by saying

```
AnInt^ := 5;
```

which leads to this state:

If you decide that you no longer need this dynamically allocated variable, you can tell the computer to take it back, which frees up the space it would otherwise occupy. This is accomplished by calling the standard procedure *dispose* with the pointer variable as a parameter:

```
dispose(AnInt);
```

which returns you to this state:

Notice that *dispose* leaves the pointer variable in an uninitialized state. Because *dispose* uses the pointer value to eliminate a variable, it is an error to call it with a *nil* or uninitialized pointer.

4.2.3. SELF CHECK EXERCISES

1. What are the primary advantages and disadvantages of static and dynamic variable allocation? Give one advantage and one disadvantage of each.

2. What output does the following program produce?

```
program Mystery (Output);

var
  IntPtr1, IntPtr2: ^integer;
  Num: integer;

begin
  new(IntPtr1);
  new(IntPtr2);
  Num := 100;
  IntPtr1^ := Num;
  IntPtr2^ := 100;
  writeln(IntPtr1^ = IntPtr2^);
  writeln(IntPtr1 = IntPtr2);
  writeln(IntPtr1^ = Num);
  writeln(IntPtr2^ = Num);
  IntPtr1^ := 200;
  IntPtr2 := IntPtr1;
  writeln(IntPtr1^ = IntPtr2^);
  writeln(IntPtr1 = IntPtr2);
  writeln(IntPtr1^ = Num);
  writeln(IntPtr2^ = Num);
end. (* Main *)
```

4.3. MORE LINKED LIST DETAILS

Consider the task of constructing the following linked list:

The pointer variable *Word* stores the list by pointing to its first element. What Pascal declarations would you use to define *Word*? It is a pointer to the first in a sequence of nodes, each containing a character and a pointer to another such node. Thus, each pointer references a variable whose structure is the basic linked list building block:

This is a record structure with one field for character data and another for the pointer to the next element. Suppose the record type is called *StrElement*. This is the base type of the pointer, because each points to a variable of this type. Thus, *Word* would be defined as follows:

```
type
  StringPtr = ^StrElement;

  StrElement = record
    Data: char;
    Next: StringPtr;
  end; (* StrElement *)

var
  Word: StringPtr;
```

These declarations are strange in that *StringPtr* is defined as a pointer to *StrElement* before *StrElement* is defined. This violates Pascal's rule that an identifier must be declared before used. Switching the order of the declarations doesn't help, because *StrElement* is defined in terms of *StringPtr*. To help you out of this Catch-22 situation, Pascal has a special relaxation of its normal rule that says that the base type of a pointer may be used before it is declared (provided that it is eventually declared).

So how do you construct a list using variable *Word*? Like all variables, it starts out uninitialized, meaning that it doesn't point to anything. You create the first link of the chain by calling *new* using the only pointer variable you have, the variable *Word*.

```
new(Word);
```

The base type of *Word* is *StringElement*, so the computer dynamically allocates a variable of that type and causes *Word* to point to it. Now you have two variables, one of type *StringPtr* and one of type *StringElement*:

Word is initialized to point to a dynamically allocated variable, but notice that both the *Data* and *Next* fields of the new variable are uninitialized.

You access the new variable by dereferencing *Word* with an up-arrow after its name: *Word^*. This object is a record with fields, which means it makes sense to refer to *Word^.Data* and *Word^.Next*. The following table might help to sort this out.

Variable	Type	Description
Word	StringPtr	named variable pointing to first element
Word^	StringElement	dynamically allocated record variable
Word^.Data	char	data field of first element
Word^.Next	StringPtr	pointer field of first element

Since *Word* is supposed to store `'wow'`, you want to store `'w'` in the first data field:

```
Word^.Data := 'w';
```

which leaves you in the following state:

The next step is to create another record for storing the `'o'`. That means another call on *new*. The only question is what pointer variable to use as a parameter. What about *Word*? Pointer variables can point only to one dynamically allocated variable at a time, but it is legal to call *new* more than once using the same variable:

```
new(Word);
```

The result is the following:

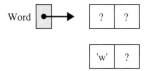

This gets you a new element, but it also destroys your previous work by losing your pointer to the `'w'` record. Instead, the new node should be linked to the first one, which can be accomplished using its field *Next* of type *StringPtr*. It is a field of an anonymous record variable, but as you saw above, you can refer to it as *Word^.Next*. Thus, you create a second variable by saying

```
new(Word^.Next)
```

A second variable of type *StringElement* is dynamically allocated with *Word^.Next* pointing to it:

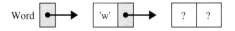

Now the references to variables and fields get even more complicated. How do you get at this new record variable? It was created using the pointer variable *Word^.Next*. That means that you get to the record by dereferencing this pointer variable to obtain *Word^.Next^*. Once dereferenced, you can get to the fields of the record using the dot notation. Here's a new table showing all the legal references you can now make:

Variable	Type	Description
Word	StringPtr	named variable pointing to first element
Word^	StringElement	first dynamically allocated variable
Word^.Data	char	data field of first element
Word^.Next	StringPtr	pointer field of first element
Word^.Next^	StringElement	second dynamically allocated variable
Word^.Next^.Data	char	data field of second element
Word^.Next^.Next	StringPtr	pointer field of second element

Thus, to store the 'o' in this new record, you would say:

```
Word^.Next^.Data  := 'o';
```

which yields:

To create the third node you call *new* again using the pointer field of the second element, which the table says is referred to as *Word^.Next^.Next*:

```
new(Word^.Next^.Next);
```

which leaves you in this state:

You should have the idea by now. The fields of this new record are referred to as *Word^.Next^.Next^.Data* and *Word^.Next^.Next^.Next*. The *Data* field should be initialized to 'w', and the *Next* field should be initialized to *nil* to indicate the end of the string. Thus, the complete main program is as follows:

```
new(Word);
Word^.Data := 'w';
new(Word^.Next);
Word^.Next^.Data := 'o';
new(Word^.Next^.Next);
Word^.Next^.Next^.Data := 'w';
Word^.Next^.Next^.Next := nil;
```

The program results in the desired structure:

This example was meant to expand your understanding of pointer variables, but as you'll soon see, there are more elegant ways to create such a structure.

4.3.1. Reversing a File of Numbers

Chapter 2 used a stack to solve the problem of reversing a file of integers. This section solves the same task using a linked list instead. Two sections from now you will see how to reimplement the stack as a linked list rather than rewriting the program.

To refresh your memory, given the following input:

```
100
32000
-20
150
```

the program should produce this output:

```
150
-20
32000
100
```

4.3.1.1. The Main Program

Each integer can be read in with a simple *readln* and then stored in a linked list. Because you want to reverse the input, each new number should be placed at the front of the list. For example, the input above would cause the list to grow as follows:

```
( )
(100)
(32000, 100)
(-20, 32000, 100)
(150, -20, 32000, 100)
```

Once you've created the list of numbers in reverse order, you can print it element by element.

The declarations used to create strings of characters can be used here as well, except that in this application the data field stores an integer instead of a character. As with the character string, a single pointer variable is declared to keep track of the list by storing a pointer to its first element. This first element is often called the *head* of the list, so it is appropriate to give your variable the same name:

```
type
  ListPtr = ^ListRec;

  ListRec = record
    Data: integer;
    Next: ListPtr;
  end; (* ListRec *)
```

```
var
  Head: ListPtr;
```

The main program can simply initialize the list to be empty and then call two procedures: one to read in the data and store it in reverse order, and one to print the numbers.

```
begin
  Head := nil;
  ReadAndStoreNumbers(Head);
  PrintNumbers(Head);
end. (* Main *)
```

4.3.1.2. Reading In the Numbers

If procedure *ReadAndStoreNumbers* is to read one number at a time, inserting it at the front of the list, then the list will go through these steps for the sample input:

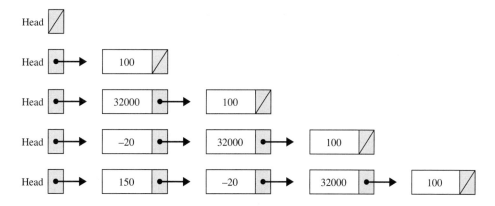

Each step involves dynamically allocating a new element, reading the next number into it, and placing it at the front of the current list. So what variable should you pass as a parameter to *new*? As the previous example pointed out, you can't use your list pointer (*Head*), because then you would lose your access to the previous list elements you've created. You need a second pointer variable to create the new element so that *Head* can keep track of the current list. This second pointer can be a local variable, because it is needed only temporarily until the new element can be integrated into the list pointed to by *Head*. Thus, the main loop of the procedure looks like this (assuming there is a local variable named *NewElemPtr* of type *ListPtr*):

```
while not eof do begin
  new(NEWELEMPTR);
  readln(NEWELEMPTR^.Data);
  <Link the new element to the front of the list>
end; (* While *)
```

All you have left to do is link this new element with the current list. For example, when processing the last number in the file, you start in this situation:

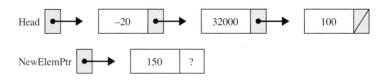

You want to insert the new value at the front, obtaining

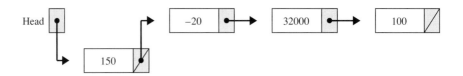

Comparing this picture with the previous one tells almost the whole story. What pointers are different? *Head* now points down to the new element instead of pointing across to the previous list, and the new element now points up to the previous list instead of having an uninitialized pointer field. Which of the two pointers should you change first? In the initial situation *Head* is the only connection to the previous list, so you can't change it first. Because the pointer field of the new element is uninitialized anyway, the obvious first step is to initialize it with the current value of *Head*:

```
NEWELEMPTR^.Next := Head;
```

Note that you *don't* want to call *new* here because you are not creating a new variable, you are only manipulating pointer values. This statement says, "*Have the Next field of the new element point to the same object that Head points to*", which leaves you in this state:

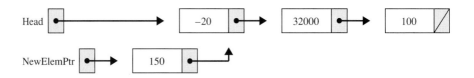

Now both *Head* and the *Next* field of the new element point to the previous list, which frees up *Head* to be reset. You would follow the same pattern to pass a heavy object to someone else, holding onto it while the person gets a good grip, so that for a moment you are both holding it, and then letting go. So *Head* can let go of the previous list and point instead to the new element:

```
Head := NEWELEMPTR;
```

Thus, these two statements combine to place the new element at the front of the list. Here is the complete procedure:

```
procedure ReadAndStoreNumbers (var Head: ListPtr);
 var
  NEWELEMPTR: ListPtr;
begin
 while not eof do begin
   new(NEWELEMPTR);
   readln(NEWELEMPTR^.Data);
   NEWELEMPTR^.Next := Head;
   Head := NEWELEMPTR;
  end; (* While *)
end; (* ReadAndStoreNumbers *)
```

4.3.1.3. Writing the Output File

Printing the list simply requires moving through the elements from first to last, printing the values as you go. If the list were an array, you would introduce a local variable of type integer and increment it in a loop to index each of the values in the array:

```
INDEX := 1;
while INDEX <= LENGTH do begin
  writeln(List[INDEX]);
  INDEX := INDEX + 1;
 end; (* While *)
```

You can write similar code for the linked list by introducing a local pointer variable called *TEMP*. Pointers are like arrows, so you want *TEMP* to be like a roving arrow, or cursor, that takes on each different pointer value in succession. Thus, it should vary as follows:

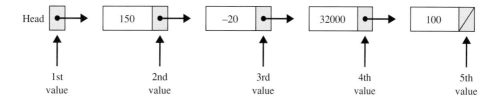

It starts out with the same value as *Head* and ends up at the *nil* stored in the last element. Thus, the loop should have this general form:

```
TEMP := Head;
while TEMP <> nil do begin
```

```
<process node>
<increment TEMP>
end; (* While *)
```

TEMP takes on each pointer value from the first to the last, which means that in the body of the loop, you can refer to the current node as *TEMP^*. The two fields of *TEMP^* can be used to complete the loop above. The node is processed by writing out the data field (*TEMP^.Data*). The next value for *TEMP* is found in the pointer field (*TEMP^.Next*). Thus, the loop can be completed as:

```
TEMP := Head;
while TEMP <> nil do begin
  writeln(TEMP^.Data);
  TEMP := TEMP^.Next;
  end; (* While *)
```

Look closely at the statement:

```
TEMP := TEMP^.Next;
```

This says, "Look inside the variable that *TEMP* is pointing to and figure out what it's pointing to. Make that the new value of *TEMP*." This is how *TEMP* is "incremented" to the next pointer value, the next arrow appearing in the list. Take note of this often puzzling statement, because you will find that it is as important to linked lists as the following often puzzling statement is to arrays:

```
INDEX := INDEX + 1;
```

Here is a complete procedure:

```
procedure PrintNumbers (Head: ListPtr);
 var
  TEMP: ListPtr;
begin
 TEMP := Head;
 while TEMP <> nil do begin
   writeln(TEMP^.Data);
   TEMP := TEMP^.Next;
   end; (* While *)
end; (* PrintNumbers *)
```

4.3.1.4. The Importance of *nil*

Remember that the main program began with the following statement:

```
Head := nil;
```

What if the main program had not initialized *Head* this way? Procedure *ReadAnd-StoreNumbers* would have used this undefined value when initializing the *Next* field of the first number read in, producing the following list:

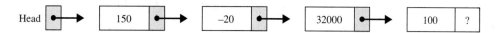

The only difference is that the list terminates with an undefined pointer rather than *nil*. That causes a problem for procedure *PrintNumbers*. With the other list, *TEMP* takes on the value *nil* the fifth time through the loop, which causes it to terminate. In this case, though, *TEMP* is set to some undefined value the fifth time through the loop, so the body of the loop is executed an extra time. The first statement tries to write out the value of *TEMP^.Data*. But *TEMP* doesn't reference any object, so *TEMP^.Data* doesn't exist! Thus, this generates an error.

To make sure that your data structure works correctly, you need to be careful to properly initialize any linked structure using a *nil* pointer.

4.3.2. Passing Pointers as Parameters

Now that you're probably pretty comfortable with parameter passing, along come pointers to ruin your day. Actually, passing pointers around isn't too bad, as long as you remember that when you pass a pointer as a parameter, you are just passing the pointer, not the object it points to. In the linked list case, passing the head of the list does not pass the list itself, only the pointer to its first element.

The simplest case is when the pointer is passed as a *var* parameter. As is always the case with *var* parameters, all changes made to the formal parameter (the one in the called procedure) will also be made to the actual parameter (the one in the procedure call). You would normally use a *var* parameter when the procedure is expected to change the pointer.

Trickier cases arise when a pointer is passed by value. In this case, the computer makes a local copy of the actual parameter so that any changes made to the formal parameter will *not* be reflected back. For example, suppose that in writing procedure *PrintNumbers*, instead of using a temporary pointer to move through the list, you use the parameter itself:

```
procedure PrintNumbers (Head: ListPtr);
begin
  while Head <> nil do begin
    writeln(Head^.Data);
    Head := Head^.Next;
  end; (* While *)
end; (* PrintNumbers *)
```

This procedure works, but is the list destroyed when *Head* is changed? The answer is no, because the value parameter protects the actual parameter from change.

The trickiest case occurs when a pointer is passed as a value parameter and the object it points to is changed. Normally the value parameter protects the actual parameter by creating a local copy, but protection breaks down here. The reason is that pointer variables provide access to other variables. So passing a pointer as a value parameter is sort of like handing a friend an extra set of keys to your car. The value parameter protects the pointer variable from change, just as the extra keys protect your originals from damage, but the procedure can use that pointer to get at the object it references, just as your friend can use the keys to get inside your car and damage it.

Consider this version of *PrintNumbers*:

```
procedure PrintNumbers (Head: ListPtr);
begin
  while Head <> nil do begin
    Head^.Data := 0;
    Head := Head^.Next;
  end; (* While *)
end; (* PrintNumbers *)
```

Instead of writing out the *Data* fields of the list elements, it changes them all to 0 with the statement

```
Head^.Data := 0;
```

This can occur because the object *Head^* is changed, causing damage to the list noticeable in the main program even though *Head* was passed as a value parameter.

4.3.3. SELF CHECK EXERCISES

1. This section read in a list of numbers and stored them in reverse order. Suppose you wanted to store the numbers in their original order instead. What problems arise?

2. Determine the output of the following program:

```
program Tester;

  type
    IntPtr = ^integer;

  var
    A, B, C: integer;
    X, Y, Z: IntPtr;

  procedure PrintOut (X, Y, Z: integer);
```

```
              begin
                writeln(X, Y, Z);
              end; (* PrintOut *)

              procedure Confuse (var X: IntPtr;
                      Y: IntPtr;
                      var Z: integer;
                      A: integer);
              begin
                C := 0;
                new(X);
                X^ := 10;
                Y^ := A;
                Z := Y^ + 4;
                A := Y^ + X^;
                PrintOut(Y^, Z, A);
              end; (* Confuse *)

          begin
            A := 1;
            B := 2;
            C := 3;
            new(X);
            X^ := 0;
            new(Y);
            Y^ := 0;
            new(Z);
            Z^ := 0;
            Confuse(X, Z, A, B);
            PrintOut(Z^, C, X^);
            X := Z;
            Confuse(Z, X, B, C);
            PrintOut(B, X^, Z^);
          end. (* Main *)
```

4.4. SAMPLE LIST OPERATIONS

When you program with linked lists for a while, you come to notice certain common patterns that appear over and over in your code and certain problems that keep surfacing. This section presents a collection of some of these common patterns and some examples that demonstrate the common pitfalls. Most programmers keep such a collection of operations in a library module so that they don't have to reimplement them every time they use a linked list in a new program.

This section presents common operations for unsorted lists. The more detailed discussion that would normally be included to explain common operations on sorted linked lists is incorporated into the reimplementation of the Table ADT that was introduced in Chapter 2. Therefore, don't consider your linked list education complete until you have also read over the section on the Table type.

For all the operations in this section, assume that linked lists are implemented using the following declarations:

```
type
  NodePtr = ^NodeRec;

  NodeRec = record
    Data: DataType;
    Next: NodePtr;
  end; (* NodeRec *)
```

4.4.1. Creating a New Node

The purpose of this procedure is to dynamically allocate a new node and initialize its fields. This is a familiar three-step process: call *new* to dynamically allocate a variable, initialize its data field, and initialize its pointer field.

This sounds like such a trivial procedure that it's not even worth writing, but you'll find that without it you often experience the tedium of writing the three lines of code to perform this operation.

```
procedure NewNode (var Head: NodePtr;
         Value: DataType;
         Link: NodePtr);
begin
 new(Head);
 Head^.Data := Value;
 Head^.Next := Link;
end; (* NewNode *)
```

4.4.2. Traversing a List

The program in the last section to reverse a sequence of numbers included a printing procedure that went through the list element by element, printing the data fields. That pattern turns out to be common enough that you will want to have it handy for other applications that require you to perform some operation as you visit each node in succession:

```
procedure Traverse (Head: NodePtr);
 var
   TEMP: NodePtr;
begin
 TEMP := Head;
 while TEMP <> nil do begin
    <perform operation on TEMP^>
    TEMP := TEMP^.Next;
```

```
          end; (* While *)
        end; (* Traverse *)
```

4.4.3. Inserting at the Front of a List

The number reversing program of the last section also had a procedure that repeatedly inserted the next value from the input file at the front of a list. The logic behind the solution was explained in that discussion.

```
procedure InsertFront (var Head: NodePtr;
        Value: DataType);
 var
  NEWELEMPTR: NodePtr;
 begin
  NewNode(NEWELEMPTR, Value, Head);
  Head := NEWELEMPTR;
 end; (* InsertFront *)
```

4.4.4. Searching for a Value at the Front of the List

You will often find yourself checking to see whether a particular value is stored as the first element of a list. This seems like a simple enough test to specify:

```
function AtFront (Head: NodePtr;
        Value: DataType): boolean;
 begin
  AtFront := (Head^.Data = Value);
 end; (* AtFront *)
```

But it's not quite this simple. What if the list is empty (*Head* is *nil*)? Then the reference to *Head^.Data* generates an error. You need to handle this special case in a separate branch so that you refer only to *Head^.Data* when you know that *Head* is not *nil*:

```
function AtFront (Head: NodePtr;
        Value: DataType): boolean;
 begin
  if Head = nil then begin
    AtFront := false;
  end
  else begin
    AtFront := Head^.Data = Value;
  end; (* If *)
 end; (* AtFront *)
```

4.4.5. Deleting from the Front of a List

The first element can be deleted from a list by resetting the list header to the value stored in the *Next* field of the first element. It is a good idea, though, to free up the variable's storage by calling *dispose*. This requires introducing a temporary variable to keep track of the rest of the list while the first element is deallocated:

```
procedure DeleteFront (var Head: NodePtr);
  var
    TEMP : NodePtr;
begin
  TEMP := Head^.Next;
  dispose(Head);
  Head := TEMP;
end; (* DeleteFront *)
```

4.4.6. Inserting at the End of a List

Unlike the problem of inserting at the front, inserting at the end of a list turns out to be rather tricky. You can start by calling *NewNode* to create the node to be inserted. Its data value is specified by a parameter and because this is to be the new last element, its *Next* field should be set to *nil*.

Then the only problem is to get to the end of the list so that you can insert this new element. A good first guess is to use the pattern from procedure *Traverse*, but not performing any action as you traverse. After the traversal, you can insert the new element at the end of the list:

```
procedure InsertBack (var Head: NodePtr;
        Value: DataType);
  var
    NEWELEMPTR, TEMP: NodePtr;
begin
  NewNode(NEWELEMPTR, Value, nil);
  TEMP := Head;
  while TEMP <> nil do begin
    TEMP := TEMP^.Next;
  end; (* While *)
  TEMP^.Next := NEWELEMPTR;
end; (* InsertBack *)
```

This version doesn't work because it scans through the list, stopping when the temporary pointer becomes *nil*. Because *TEMP* is *nil*, the reference to *TEMP^.Next* after the loop causes an error. This happens because the traversal loop not only scans *to* the end of the list, it scans *past* the end of the list. Rather than scan past the last element, you want to have *TEMP* end up pointing to this last element. How do you recognize the last element? It's the only one that has nothing after it, which means its *Next* field is *nil*. Thus, you want to scan until *TEMP^.Next* is *nil*:

```
procedure InsertBack (var Head: NodePtr;
        Value: DataType);
  var
```

```
     NEWELEMPTR, TEMP: NodePtr;
begin
 NewNode(NEWELEMPTR, Value, nil);
 TEMP := Head;
 while TEMP^.Next <> nil do begin
   TEMP := TEMP^.Next;
  end; (* While *)
 TEMP^.Next := NEWELEMPTR;
end; (* InsertBack *)
```

This version creates a new node with the given value, traverses the list until it sets *TEMP* to the last element, and links the new element as the new end of the list.

There's still a problem, though. The loop scans as long as *TEMP*ˆ.*Next* is not *nil*. This test assumes, however, that *TEMP*ˆ.*Next* exists or, more precisely, that *TEMP* is actually pointing to an object. This won't always be the case, however. If the incoming list is initially empty, then the parameter *Head* will be *nil*. This would start *TEMP* as *nil*, *TEMP*ˆ.*Next* won't exist, and an error will occur. You must handle the empty list as a special case. In that case, you can merely make *Head* point to the new node. The final version of this procedure follows:

```
procedure InsertBack (var Head: NodePtr;
        Value: DataType);
 var
   NEWELEMPTR, TEMP: NodePtr;
begin
 NewNode(NEWELEMPTR, Value, nil);
 if Head = nil then begin
   Head := NEWELEMPTR;
  end
 else begin
   TEMP := Head;
   while TEMP^.Next <> nil do begin
     TEMP := TEMP^.Next;
    end; (* While *)
   TEMP^.Next := NEWELEMPTR;
  end; (* If *)
end; (* InsertBack *)
```

4.4.7. SELF CHECK EXERCISES

1. Suppose *InsertFront* were rewritten as follows:

```
procedure InsertFront (var Head: NodePtr;
        Value: DataType);
begin
 NewNode(Head, Value, Head);
end; (* InsertFront *)
```

Will this work? Why or why not?

2. What does the following procedure do?

```
procedure XXX (var Head: NodePtr;
       Value: DataType);

begin
  if Head = nil then begin
    InsertFront(Head, Value);
  end
  else begin
    XXX(Head^.Next, Value);
  end; (* If *)
end; (* XXX *)
```

4.5. STACKS REVISITED

The major drawback to the array implementation for stacks in Chapter 2 is that the maximum size of the Stack must be specified at compile-time. This is a severe limitation, because Stacks prove useful in so many different applications, most with vastly different space requirements, that it is impossible to predict how large the stack should be nor, for that matter, even to choose one maximum size suitable for all applications. Linked lists provide an ideal solution to this problem. This section explores how to implement Stacks using a linked list instead of an array.

The program that reversed a file of numbers was originally presented in Chapter 2 as an example Stack program. Earlier in this chapter it was completely rewritten to use linked lists. Before proceeding, let's briefly review why it is better to reimplement the Stack than to rewrite the original program. Chapter 2 presented several Stack programs, and perhaps you even wrote one yourself as a homework exercise. Stacks turn out to be one of the most useful structures around. Thus, because you want to use a Stack in many different programs, it is advantageous to centralize its definition rather than including one in every program.

The reason is simple. A Stack is a useful tool for creating programs just as a broom is a useful tool for cleaning houses, so you should keep a single copy of the tool in your program utility kit, just as you keep a single broom in your broom closet. You could keep a broom in every room, but why duplicate something needlessly? The other advantage of centralization is that if you want to change your underlying implementation (e.g., by installing carpeting), you can replace one broom with one vacuum cleaner and fix the whole house all at once.

The same is true of the Stack module. Remember that if you follow a type specification completely, your high-level code becomes independent from any specific solution. Rewriting the "reverse a file" program takes almost as much time as rewriting the Stack module, but by reimplementing the Stack, you can switch *all* of your Stack programs to the new implementation with one set of changes.

As described in Chapter 2, a Stack is a *last in first out,* or *LIFO,* structure, which means that the next value returned by a Stack is always the most recent value stored in it. Its detailed specification is given in Figure 2.4 on page 76.

A Stack is simply a linear collection of data values accessed at a single point (the top of the Stack). As a result, a simple linked list is perfect for implementing a Stack. The only change necessary is to make the *Data* field of type *TableElement.Typ,* and don't forget that you have to give an appropriate value to *TableElement.Typ* before compiling and using the module.

```
type
 ElementType=   <appropriate type>
 Typ = ^StackRec;

 StackRec = record
   Data: ElementType
   Next: Typ;
  end; (* StackRec *)
```

Procedures *Push* and *Pop* have already been written in the section on common list operations, because they are simply *InsertFront* and *DeleteFront.* They merely need to be adapted to the Stack's type declarations:

```
procedure NewNode (var S: Typ;
       Item: ElementType
       Link: Typ);
begin
 new(S);
 S^.Data := Item;
 S^.Next := Link;
end; (* NewNode *)

procedure Push (var S: Typ;
       Item: ElementType);
 var
   NEWELEMPTR: Typ;
begin
 NewNode (NEWELEMPTR, Item, S);
 S := NEWELEMPTR;
end; (* Push *)

procedure Pop (var S: Typ;
       var Item: ElementType);
 var
   TEMP: Typ;
begin
 TEMP := S;
 Item := S^.Data;
 S := S^.Next;
 dispose(TEMP);
end; (* Pop *)
```

Because an empty Stack is just an empty list, initializing a Stack consists only of setting the pointer at the top of the Stack to *nil*:

```
procedure Create (var S: Typ);
begin
 S := nil;
end; (* Init *)
```

Moreover, because an empty Stack is just a *nil* pointer, the function *Empty* follows immediately:

```
function Empty (var S: Typ): boolean;
begin
 Empty := (S = nil);
end; (* Empty *)
```

Finally, *Destroy* now makes more sense than it did with the array implementation. Since you are dynamically allocating the elements in the Stack, you will need to explicitly deallocate those elements to return that memory to the system. Thus, you need to traverse the Stack, calling *dispose* on each element:

```
procedure Destroy (var S: Typ);
 var
  TEMP: Typ;
begin
 while S <> nil do begin
   TEMP := S;
   S := S^.Next;
   dispose(TEMP);
  end; (* While *)
end; (* Destroy *)
```

4.5.1. SELF CHECK EXERCISES

1. Given the abstract data type Stack, a user writes the following procedure. What does the procedure do? And what is wrong with it?

```
procedure FunStuff;
 var
  S: Stack.Typ;
  CH: char;
begin
 Stack.Create(S);
 while not (eoln) do begin
   read(CH);
   Stack.Push(S, CH);
  end;
```

```
while S <> nil do begin
  Stack.Pop(S, CH);
  write(CH);
  end;
Stack.Destroy(S);
end;
```

4.6. THE QUEUE ADT

4.6.1. Specification: What Is a Queue?

A Queue is another useful structure for storing a series of elements all of the same type. A Queue is in some respects the opposite of a Stack, because instead of using a *LIFO* strategy for storing data, it uses a *First In, First Out,* or *FIFO,* approach. Like a Stack, a Queue is defined in terms of its domain (sequences of elements of the same type) and its operations. These operations are similar to those of a Stack, except rather than inserting and removing information from only one end (the top of the Stack), data are inserted at one end (the back) and removed from the other end (the front). Thus, a Queue functions like a line, in that information goes in one end and comes out the other. Therefore, rather than having *Push* and *Pop*, a Queue has the operations *Enqueue*, which inserts an item at the end of the Queue, and *Dequeue*, which removes an item from the Queue's front. The detailed specifications of the structure Queue appear in Figure 4.1.

Like a Stack, a Queue is an abstract structure that is independent of any particular implementation, and it can be used by a wide variety of applications for storing and manipulating data. It will be used throughout the remainder of this book when an appropriate application arises. The remainder of this section focuses on two implementations of this structure that both involve linked lists.

4.6.2. Implementing a Queue as a Simple Linked List

At first glance, it appears that it would be most straightforward to implement a Queue in the same way that Stacks were implemented, by having a linked list with a pointer to one end. Thus, the data structure would be defined as follows:

```
type
Typ = ^QueueRec;

QueueRec = record
  Data: ElementType
  Next: Typ;
  end; (* QueueRec *)
```

where *ElementType* is the type of each piece of data stored in the Queue. Thus, the operations *Create, Destroy,* and *Empty* would be the same as in the *Stack* implementation:

STRUCTURE

Stores a series of elements all of type *ElementType*

Initially empty

Elements removed in FIFO order

OPERATIONS

```
procedure Enqueue (var Q: Typ; Item: ElementType);
        post    Q has Item appended to its tail

procedure Dequeue (var Q: Typ; var Item: ElementType);
        pre     not Empty(Q)
        post    The first element of Q has been removed.
                Item holds that element.

function Empty (var Q: Typ): boolean;
        post    Returns true if Q is empty, false otherwise
```

STANDARD OPERATORS

Create, Destroy

ADDITIONAL DECLARATIONS

Type *Element.Type* (default = *integer*)

FIGURE 4.1. Specification for Structure-ADT *Queue.*

```
procedure Create (var Q: Typ);
begin
 Q := nil;
end; (* Create *)

procedure Destroy (var Q: Typ);
 var
   TEMP: Typ;
begin
 while Q <> nil do begin
   TEMP := Q;
   Q := Q^.Next;
   dispose(TEMP);
  end; (* While *)
end; (* Destroy *)

function Empty (var Q: Typ): boolean;
begin
 Empty := (Q = nil);
end; (* Empty *)
```

Now comes the problem. Because a *Queue* is just a single pointer, it must reference either the front of the Queue or the back of the Queue. Say it points to the front. Then *Dequeue* is merely *DeleteFront* and *Enqueue* is *InsertBack*. But remember how *InsertBack* works. It must traverse the entire list, and is therefore slow.

```
procedure NewNode (var Q: Typ;
        Item: ElementType
        Link: Typ);
begin
 new(Q);
 Q^.Data := Item;
 Q^.Next := Link;
end; (* NewNode *)

procedure Dequeue (var Q: Typ;
        var Item: ElementType;
 var
 NEWELEMPTR, TEMP: Typ;
begin
 TEMP := Q;
 Item := Q^.Data;
 Q := Q^.Next;
 dispose(TEMP);
end; (* Dequeue *)

procedure Enqueue (var Q: Typ;
        Item: ElementType;
 var
  NEWELEMPTR, TEMP: Typ;
begin
 NewNode(NEWELEMPTR, Item, nil);
 if Q = nil then begin
  Q := NEWELEMPTR;
  end
 else begin
   TEMP := Q;
   while TEMP^.Next <> nil do begin
    TEMP := TEMP^.Next;
   end; (* While *)
   TEMP^.Next := NEWELEMPTR;
  end; (* If *)
end; (* Enqueue *)
```

Now suppose that the Queue pointer referenced the end of the Queue instead of the front. Then, *Enqueue* would be easy to write, but *Dequeue* would be difficult. In either case, one of the operations is both slow and complicated. Whenever you have this combination of problems, it's usually better to think of a different way.

4.6.3. A Better Linked List Implementation

The problems with the previous implementation arise because the Queue must be accessed at two ends, but only one of them has a direct pointer to it. Thus, these problems can be solved by keeping a pointer to both the front and the back of the list. The data structure is then a little trickier, because a Queue now consists of two pointers, but it will eliminate most of the complications and make the operations run much more quickly. The basic *Queue* type, which is available to the outside world and must encapsulate all the information about the Queue, will consist of two pointers, one to point to the front and one to point to the back. The rest of the structure will be the same as the previous implementation:

```
type
   QueuePtr = ^QueueRec;

   QueueRec = record
     Data: ElementType
     Next: QueuePtr;
     end; (* QueueRec *)

   Typ = record
     Head: QueuePtr;
     Tail: QueuePtr;
     end; (* Typ *)
```

Thus, a typical integer Queue (storing the numbers 3, 4, and 2) would look like the following:

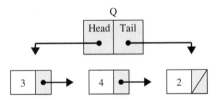

For this implementation, *Create, Destroy,* and *Empty*, while being fairly straightforward, are slightly different. An empty Queue now consists of two *nil* pointers, giving the following operations:

```
procedure Create (var Q: Typ);
begin
 Q.Head := nil;
 Q.Tail := nil;
end; (* Create  *)

procedure Destroy (var Q: Typ);
 var
  TEMP1, TEMP2: QueuePtr;
begin
  TEMP1 := Q.Head;
  while TEMP1 <> nil do begin
```

```
      TEMP2 := TEMP1;
      TEMP1 := TEMP1^.Next;
      dispose(TEMP2);
     end; (* While *)
   end; (* Destroy *)ˇ

   function Empty (var Q: Typ): boolean;
   begin
    Empty := (Q.Head = nil);
   end; (* Empty *)
```

Note that *Empty* needs to check only one of the two pointers, since if one pointer is *nil*, the other should be *nil* as well.

All that's left are *Enqueue* and *Dequeue*. To *Enqueue* an item, a new record needs to be allocated, the item stored in its *Data* field, its *Next* field set to *nil*, and it needs to be added to the end of the Queue. The previous last element pointed to by *Tail* needs to now point to this new element, and *Tail* needs to be changed to point to the new last element. Here's a first attempt at the code:

```
   procedure Enqueue (var Q: Typ;
            Item: ElementType;
     var
      NEWELEMPTR: QueuePtr;
   begin
    new(NEWELEMPTR);
    NEWELEMPTR^.Data := Item;
    NEWELEMPTR^.Next := nil;
    Q.Tail^.Next := NEWELEMPTR;
    Q.Tail := NEWELEMPTR;
   end; (* Enqueue *)
```

What's wrong with this code? The same problem exists as in the previous example: if the Queue is initially empty, then *Q.Tail^.Next* doesn't exist, which causes an error when executing:

```
   Q.Tail^.Next := NEWELEMPTR;
```

This statement should be executed only for nonempty Queues, because an empty Queue has no last element to worry about. Moreover, an empty Queue causes a further problem, in that both *Head* and *Tail* must point to this new element, because it becomes both the first *and* last element. Thus, if the Queue is nonempty, the last element should be linked up with the new element, but if it is empty, then the *Head* pointer must reference it. The following code should do the job:

```
   procedure Enqueue (var Q: Typ;
            Item: ElementType;
```

```
  var
    NEWELEMPTR: QueuePtr;
begin
  new(NEWELEMPTR);
  NEWELEMPTR^.Data := Item;
  NEWELEMPTR^.Next := nil;
  if Q.Tail <> nil then begin
    Q.Tail^.Next := NEWELEMPTR;
    end
  else begin
    Q.Head := NEWELEMPTR;
    end; (* If *)
  Q.Tail := NEWELEMPTR;
end; (* Enqueue *)
```

While this code is a little complicated, it will run significantly faster than the previous implementation, because the list never needs to be scanned at all.

Finally, *Dequeue* requires that the first item be returned through a parameter and then removed from the Queue. Since that item is referenced by the *Head* pointer, the information is easily passed back, and the *Head* pointer just needs to be advanced to the next element. The only tricky part occurs if there was only one element in the initial Queue. In this case, removing an element empties the Queue, so *Tail* must be set to *nil*:

```
procedure Dequeue (var Q: Typ;
          var Item: ElementType;
begin
  Item := Q.Head^.Data;
  Q.Head := Q.Head^.Next;
  if Q.Head = nil then begin
    Q.Tail := nil;
    end; (* If *)
end; (* Dequeue *)
```

While this change of data structure caused some complications, they weren't as drastic as the problems that arose in the first implementation. More importantly, this implementation will run significantly faster, because the list never needs to be scanned. Every operation consists of just a few pointer manipulations that are independent of the number of elements in the Queue. This form of analysis is the focus of Chapter 6, and will be covered in more detail there, but it doesn't require great insight to notice that the second implementation will run more quickly.

4.7. IMPLEMENTING THE TABLE ADT WITH A LINKED LIST

The table type discussed in Chapter 2 can be implemented using a standard linked list:

```
type
  TableElement.Typ = <appropriate type for application>;
  Typ = ^TableRec;

  TableRec = record
    Data: TableElement.Typ;
    Next: Typ;
  end; (* TableRec *)
```

Up until now all your list manipulations have been at the ends of the list. The most natural way of implementing the Table, however, is to store the information in sorted order. Thus, whenever a new item is to be inserted, it is immediately placed in its correct position in the list. This makes *FindMin* trivial to implement, because the minimum element will always be at the front of the list.

4.7.1. Keeping One Step Ahead of Yourself

Manipulating information in the middle of a list gives rise to a number of problems. The primary one is that you must always be "one step ahead of yourself." What this means is that to insert or delete an element in a list you must have access to the pointer in the position *before* the place you want to insert/delete. For example, suppose you want to insert the value 4 into the following list:

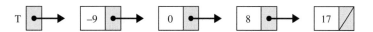

It should go between 0 and 8 because 4 is greater than 0 but less than 8. A simple algorithm for finding this position is to start a temporary pointer at the head of the list and to move it forward until you find a value that is greater than 4 (8 in this example). But you want to reach this state:

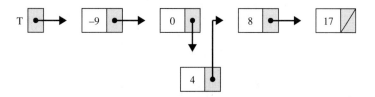

Therefore, rather than having your temporary variable end up at 8, you want it to point to 0, because you have to change its *Next* field to insert the 4.

A similar problem occurs when deleting a list element. Both involve scanning the list until a particular position is found, and then performing a manipulation to the element just before that position. Thus, it is worth creating a single utility that can be used for both insertion and deletion. It will also simplify function *InTable*, which checks to see whether an element is stored in the list, and *Extract*, which copies a sublist from the list.

Here is a first attempt. Note that the function returns a pointer, which is legal in Pascal.

```
function FindPrevToItem (T: Typ;
         Entry: TableElement.Typ): Typ;
  var
    TEMP: Typ;
  begin
    TEMP := T;
    while Compare(TEMP^.Next^.Data, Entry) = '<' do begin
      TEMP := TEMP^.Next;
    end; (* While *)
    FindPrevToItem := TEMP;
  end; (* FindPrevToItem *)
```

This function scans through the list until it finds an element greater than or equal to the new element, at which point it stops and returns a pointer to the record immediately preceding that element. There are two major problems with this function. The first occurs if all the elements in the list are less then the new element. Then the loop will never stop advancing *TEMP*. At some point, though, the last item is reached and *TEMP^.Next* becomes *nil*. Then, when the loop test is made, an error occurs, because with *TEMP^.Next* equal to *nil*, *TEMP^.Next^.Data* doesn't exist. Thus, to solve this problem you want to add another clause to your while test:

```
while (TEMP^.Next <> nil) and
      (Compare(TEMP^.Next^.Data, Entry) = '<') do begin
        TEMP := TEMP^.Next;
    end; (* While *)
```

because this should stop the loop when either the end of the list is reached or the correct position has been found. But this won't work either due to the *full evaluation problem*. The problem is that in this test, once you have reached the end of the list (and *TEMP^.Next* is *nil*) you want to stop. This should occur because the expression

```
TEMP^.Next <> nil
```

is now false. This is sufficient to make the *and* expression false, but Pascal may go ahead and check the value of the other clause anyway, causing evaluation of

```
Compare (TEMP^.Next^.Data, Entry) = '<'
```

This generates an error, because *TEMP^.Next* is *nil*. Thus, even though the first clause of the *and* will terminate the loop at this point, it happens too late because at the same time, this second clause is evaluated, generating an error.

This can be fixed by nesting the two clauses in an if/then construct so that the second clause is evaluated only if the first returns true. This test can be performed within a boolean *GoToNext* function called in the loop test. Thus, the function will return *true* if *TEMP* should be advanced, and *false* otherwise. First it will test to see if the end of the list has been reached. If so, then it will return *false*, because *TEMP* should not be advanced any further. Otherwise it will check to see if the correct position has been found, returning *false* if it has been, and *true* otherwise:

```
function GoToNext (T: Typ;
        Entry: TableElement.Typ): boolean;
begin
 if T^.Next = nil then begin
   GoToNext := false;
   end
 else begin
   GoToNext := (Compare(T^.Next^.Data, Entry) = '<');
   end; (* If *)
end; (* GoToNext *)
```

Then, the *FindPrevToItem* function would look like the following:

```
function FindPrevToItem (T: Typ;
        Entry: TableElement.Typ): Typ;
 var
   TEMP: Typ;
begin
 TEMP := T;
 while GoToNext(TEMP, Entry) do begin
   TEMP := TEMP^.Next;
   end; (* While *)
 FindPrevToItem := TEMP;
end; (* FindPrevToItem *)
```

There are still problems with this function, but fortunately they can all be addressed with one fairly simple fix. Think about what happens when you try to insert −100 into the following list:

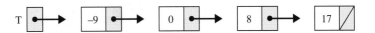

The value −100 is smaller than all these values, so it should be inserted at the front. But how can function *FindPrevToItem* return a pointer to the element just before this position? There is no such element, so it can't. This is one of the consequences of staying one step ahead. It gets even worse if the list is empty. Then, by trying to look ahead, an error is generated, since there is no next element to look at.

Because all the operations have these problems, rather than solving them individually for each routine, you can alter the data structure so that the problem goes away. Since the problems all arise when the first element needs to be examined, the solution is to ensure that the first item both *always exists* and *can always be ignored*. This is accomplished by placing a *dummy header element* at the beginning of each list.

Dummy header nodes simplify linked lists in the same way that engines simplify trains. Imagine a model railroad set with several passenger cars linked up without an engine. Instead of having the train laid out flat on the floor, think about hoisting it straight up and down by lifting the first car and allowing the others to dangle down from it. To remove the second car, you'd keep holding onto the first while you rearrange the links below. But to remove the first car, you need not only to rearrange links between cars, but also to grab onto a different part of the train. If all the cars are removed, you end up with yet another possibility where you're not holding onto anything. Thus, there are three possible ways to perform a passenger car maneuver in this scenario:

- Keep holding onto first car, rearranging links below.
- Rearrange links *and* adjust grip to a new car.
- Rearrange links and end up not holding onto anything.

This complex set of cases stems from the fact that you support the first car in a different way than you support the others, gripping it instead of maintaining a link to it. If you attach the passenger trains to an engine, suddenly things become simple because all passenger cars are supported through links. You never change your grip because the engine is always in front. That means that all manipulations of passenger cars involve the same process of rearranging links. It also means that you don't ever find yourself not holding onto anything, because even if all the passenger cars are removed, you're still holding onto the engine. Thus, the engine eliminates the second and third cases above and reduces all train maneuvers to one kind of task: rearranging links.

Similarly, in the linked lists you have seen so far, the first element is accessed in a different way from the others, through a header variable that "holds onto" the node rather than through *Next* fields that link it to the structure. Introducing a dummy header provides the same simplification as the engine does, eliminating two special cases: an empty list, and insertion/deletion at the front of the list. This greatly simplifies code, because all list rearrangements involve changing *Next* fields. Just as the engine always stays out in front, the list header always points to the same dummy header.

Up until now, an empty list has been represented by a *nil* pointer:

Head

With dummy headers, the list always has at least one element. Thus, an empty list is expressed as follows:

Head

And just as an engine doesn't carry passengers, this header node doesn't store data (which is why its *Data* field is shown to be uninitialized). That's why it's called a "dummy."

Similarly, a list of *n* elements is now stored using $n + 1$ nodes, as in the following list with five nodes storing four data values:

4.7.2. Implementing the Operations

Having solved all the major problems, it's time to implement the operations for the Table ADT. Because an empty Table consists of a single dummy header, the operation *Create* just allocates the node and initializes its *Next* field to *nil* and, correspondingly, *Empty* checks to see if the dummy's *Next* field is still *nil*. *Destroy*, then, can be implemented by disposing of all elements including the dummy header.

```
procedure Create (var T: Typ);
begin
 new(T);
 T^.Next := nil;
end; (* Create *)

function Empty (var T: Typ): boolean;
begin
 Empty := (T^.Next = nil);
end; (* Empty *)

procedure Destroy (var T: Typ);
 var
   TEMP: Typ;
begin
 while T <> nil do begin
   TEMP := T^.Next;
   dispose(T);
   T := TEMP;
  end; (* While *)
end; (* Destroy *)
```

Because the list is kept in sorted order, finding the minimum is trivial; it will always be the first element of the list. The precondition promises at least one element, so you don't have to worry about an empty list.

```
procedure FindMin (var T: Typ;
        var Item: TableElement.Typ);
begin
 Item := T^.Next^.Data;
end; (* FindMin *)
```

Procedure *Write* is also not complicated. Apart from a difference in initialization to skip over the header node, it is a standard list traversal that applies *PrintElement* to each data item:

```
procedure Write (var T: Typ);
 var
  TEMP: Typ;
begin
 TEMP := T^.Next;
 while TEMP <> nil do begin
   PrintElement(TEMP^.Data);
   TEMP := TEMP^.Next;
  end; (* While *)
end; (* Write *)
```

All that are left are *InTable*, *Insert*, *Delete*, and *Extract*, all of which require scanning the list. Using function *FindPrevToItem*, you can easily locate the pointer that needs to be changed. You can manipulate that pointer as if it were the front of a standard list, which means that the common operations can be used (here modified to the Table type declarations):

```
procedure NewNode (var T: Typ;
        Entry: TableElement.Typ;
        Link: Typ);
begin
 new(T);
 T^.Data := Entry;
 T^.Next := Link;
end; (* NewNode *)

function AtFront (var T: Typ;
        Entry: TableElement.Typ): boolean;
begin
 if T = nil then begin
   AtFront := false;
  end
  else begin
   AtFront := Compare(T^.Data, Entry) = '=';
  end; (* If *)
end; (* AtFront *)

procedure InsertFront (var T: Typ;
        Entry: TableElement.Typ);
 var
  NEWELEMPTR: Typ;
begin
 NewNode (NEWELEMPTR, Entry, T);
 T := NEWELEMPTR;
end; (* InsertFront *)
```

```
procedure DeleteFront (var T: Typ);
 var
  TEMP: Typ;
begin
 TEMP := T^.Next;
 dispose(T);
 T := TEMP;
end; (* DeleteFront *)
```

Using *FindPrevToItem* to refer to the appropriate link, *Insert*, *Delete*, and *InTable* reduce to *InsertFront*, *DeleteFront*, and *AtFront*:

```
procedure Insert (var T: Typ;
       Item: TableElement.Typ);
 var
  POSITION: Typ;
begin
 POSITION := FindPrevToItem(T, Item);
 InsertFront(POSITION^.Next, Item);
end; (* Insert *)

procedure Delete (var T: Typ;
       Item: TableElement.Typ);
 var
  POSITION: Typ;
begin
 POSITION := FindPrevToItem(T, Item);
 DeleteFront(POSITION^.Next);
end; (* Delete *)

function InTable (var T: Typ;
       Item: TableElement.Typ): boolean;
 var
  POSITION: Typ;
begin
 POSITION := FindPrevToItem(T, Item);
 InTable := AtFront(POSITION^.Next, Item);
end; (* InTable *)
```

Procedure *Extract* is a little more complicated. One simple approach is to create an empty *NewT* and move one element at a time from the original list to the new list until there are no more matching items:

```
procedure Extract (var T: Typ;
       Item: TableElement.Typ;
       var NewT: Typ);
 var
  POSITION: Typ;
```

```
begin
 Create(NewT);
 POSITION := FindPrevToItem(T, Item);
 while AtFront(POSITION^.Next, Item) do begin
   Insert(NewT, POSITION^.Next^.Data);
   POSITION := POSITION^.Next;
 end; (* While *)
end; (* Extract *)
```

The previous code has an important subtlety worth considering. Would it exhibit the same behavior if the call to *Insert* were:

```
Insert(NewT, Item);
```

The answer is no. Remember that items can be complex structures and that the ordering function might pay attention to only part of the structure. For example, the birthday records in Chapter 1 stored name, birth month, birth day, and birth year, but only birth month and birth day were used for comparisons. Thus, to extract all people born on a certain month and day, the programmer can pass *Extract* a variable whose only initialized fields are *Month* and *Day*, providing a template to match against. The matching elements should be transferred to *NewT*, as the procedure above does. Inserting *Item* into *NewT* instead creates a table whose elements are copies of the template rather than the elements it matched.

4.7.3. SELF CHECK EXERCISES

1. Procedure *Insert* doesn't work correctly if you want to insert at the front of the list, unless you use a dummy header. How would you solve this problem if you did not want to use a dummy header?

4.8. RECURSION ON LINKED LISTS

Recall that a recursive definition includes a simple base case and a recursive case that solves a complex problem by reducing it to a simpler problem from the same family of problems. Recursion also appears in data structures, as you might have noticed with the linked list definition. The base case is an empty list pointing to *nil*. A nonempty list stores a reference to the first element. Inside this element is a pointer to another linked list. Thus, the recursive case is a single element storing one data item and pointing to a simpler linked list.

The recursive nature of the linked list definition facilitates the creation of recursive solutions to linked list tasks. A recursive linked list subprogram usually tests the base case of a *nil* pointer and in the recursive case reduces the complexity of the overall problem by processing the first data item and then recursively calling itself to solve the simpler problem of processing the rest of the list. Sometimes the first data item supplies another base case, allowing the recursion to stop because a certain target value is seen.

Recursive solutions avoid many of the problems discussed in the code for the Table type. To illustrate, the next few sections describe how the complicated *Insert, Delete,* and *InTable* operations can be implemented recursively. These operations are so much easier to express recursively that this section returns to normal linked lists without header nodes. To concentrate on interesting details, this section will assume that the common list operations used in implementing the Table type are available here as well.

4.8.1. Tough Table Operations Implemented Recursively

How would you implement *Insert* recursively? By recursively calling itself, *Insert* can reduce the original list to something so simple that the task becomes trivial. But what makes insertion easy? Consider the sequence of lists that would be generated by a call on *Insert* with the following initial list:

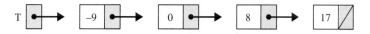

Each recursive invocation processes the first element and passes on the rest of the list in a recursive call. But the recursion cannot proceed once an empty list is encountered. Therefore, if all possible recursive calls were generated, the sequence of lists would be as follows:

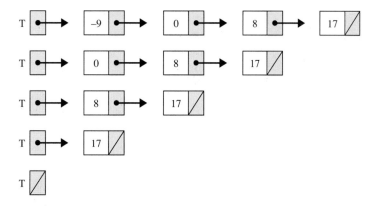

Inserting into the empty list is easy with *InsertFront,* so the last list in this sequence leads to a trivial insertion. But when would it be appropriate to insert a value there? Remember that this list follows the element 17, which means that it is appropriate to store only values there that are greater than 17. Thus, when inserting a value larger than all current values, you allow the recursion to proceed all the way to an empty list, which makes insertion trivial.

What about other values? If a value isn't greater than all list elements, there must be some first element greater than or equal to it. The value should be inserted just before this element. That's easy to do if the element appears at the beginning of the list, because then you can again use procedure *InsertFront*. Notice that each element of the list appears as the first element of some list in the preceding sequence. Eventually you will reach a recursive call where the target element is at the front of the list, allowing you to easily insert the value by calling *InsertFront*.

Thus, the procedure can be written as follows:

```
procedure Insert (var T: Typ;
        Item: TableElement.Typ);
begin
 if T = nil then begin
   InsertFront(T, Item);
  end
 else if Compare(Item, T^.Data) = '<' then begin
   InsertFront(T, Item);
  end
 else begin
   Insert(T^.Next, Item);
  end; (* If *)
end; (* Insert *)
```

Delete is even easier to write. The precondition guarantees that the entry appears somewhere in the list and each list element will be the first element of one of the lists generated by a recursive call, so you can focus on the beginning of the list and keep making recursive calls until the appropriate element makes it to the front:

```
procedure Delete (var T: Typ;
        Item: TableElement.Typ);
begin
 if Compare(T^.Data, Entry) = '=' then begin
   DeleteFront(T);
  end
 else begin
   Delete(T^.Next, Entry);
  end; (* If *)
end; (* Delete *)
```

InTable can also be written using this approach. You focus on the first element. If it has the desired value, you can return true. If not, you recursively call with the rest of the list to search it. If the value isn't there, you will eventually end up searching an empty list, at which point you can return with the answer that the value isn't in the list:

```
function InTable (var T: Typ;
        Item: TableElement.Typ): boolean;
begin
 if AtFront(T, Item) then begin
   InTable := true;
```

```
        end
      else if T = nil then begin
        InTable := false;
      end
      else begin
        InTable := InTable(T^.Next, Item);
      end; (* If *)
    end; (* InTable *)
```

Notice the difference between the first two uses of *InTable* that assign a value to the function and the third use of *InTable* that recursively calls the function to determine what value to return.

4.8.2. Mechanics of Pointers and Recursion

To better understand how a procedure like *Insert* works, consider what happens when you try to insert the value 25 into the list pointed to by variable *Tab*, assuming it stores the following values:

T is a *var* parameter, so it is set up as an alias for *Tab*:

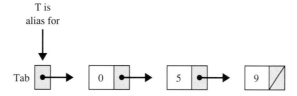

Thus, any changes to *T* also change *Tab*. This is not unusual. You have seen many examples where the list header is passed as a var parameter. *T* points to a nonempty list whose first value of 0 is not greater than 25. That means a recursive call is made passing *T^.Next* as the list parameter.

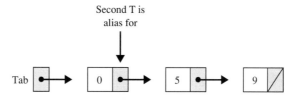

The second recursive call has its own identifier *T*. As always, these definitions do not interfere with each other and the most recent definition becomes the active one. The new *T* is aliased to the *Next* field of the first list element. This *is* unusual. By sharing the same value as *Tab^.Next*, this *T* variable points to the element 5. But more than that, this variable is bound to a link of the list in a way that surpasses what can be done with local variables. For example, you could initialize a local variable *T* using the same *Next* field:

```
T := Tab^.Next;
```

but it leads to quite a different situation:

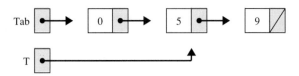

Tab^.Next and *T* point to the same place, which means they have the same focus of attention. But they are not bound in any special way. Changing *T*, for example, does not change *Tab^.Next*. To do that, you'd have to use the previous pointer. This is the classic problem of having to stay one step ahead. But notice how the problem doesn't exist in the recursion.

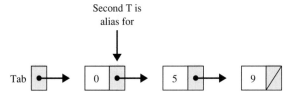

T is an alias for *Tab^.Next*, which means it's another name for it. Thus, *T* is focused on the element 5 just like *Tab^.Next* is focused on the element 5, but *T* also has the power to change *Tab^.Next* directly. For example, if the recursive procedure executes:

```
T := nil;
```

you get

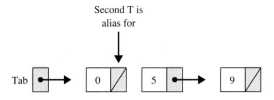

The important point is that unlike in the iterative case where you must keep track of the previous pointer in order to change the one you are focusing on, in recursive calls the power of the var parameter allows each new alias to focus on a pointer and have the ability to change it without going through the previous element.

To finish out this example, assuming *T* was not set to *nil* above, another recursive call is generated because the list is not empty and because 25 is not less than its first value, 5. This generates a third *T* alias, this time to *Tabˆ.Nextˆ.Next:*

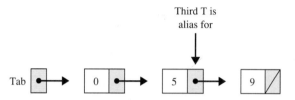

T now points to a list of one element. It's still not empty, and 25 is not less than 9, so another recursive call is generated, creating a fourth *T* alias:

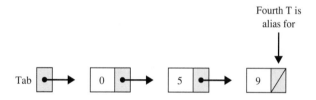

This time *T* is *nil*. Procedure *Insert* calls on procedure *InsertFront*, passing *T* as a parameter. The result is that *T* is changed to point to a new element with data value 25. Because *T* changes, the final *Next* field of the list changes as well:

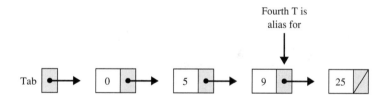

The various recursive calls then terminate in reverse order, eliminating all the *T* aliases.

The moral of the story is that even though pointer manipulations can be tedious to implement iteratively because of the need to keep one step ahead, the power of var parameters combines with the power of recursion to greatly simplify the work required to code the same manipulations recursively.

4.8.3. SELF CHECK EXERCISES

1. Why don't you need to "keep one step ahead of yourself" when you use recursion to modify a linked list?

4.9. DOUBLY LINKED LISTS AND THE DEQUE ADT

Although singly linked lists are sufficient for efficiently implementing many linked list operations, there are times when having a link in only one direction is too limiting. Singly linked lists work well when most pointer movement is forward. But when you move backward and forward often, you want links in both directions. This is known as a *doubly linked* list and is represented as follows:

Each list element now has two pointer fields, one pointing forward and one pointing backward. Thus, it is declared as

```
type
  DoublePtr = ^DoubleRec;

  DoubleRec = record
    Data: integer;
    Next, Previous: DoublePtr;
  end; (* DoubleRec *)
```

4.9.1. The Deque ADT

A *Deque* is a generalized version of a Stack and a Queue. With a Stack, items are inserted and removed from one end only, while a Queue allows items to be inserted at one end and removed from the other. With a Deque, items may be both inserted and removed from both ends.

Like Stacks and Queues, Deques can store a number of elements, each of the same type, specified by *TableElement.Typ*. The Deque's operations are similar to those of Stacks and Queues, except that items may be inserted and removed from both ends. The detailed specifications of the structure Deque appear in Figure 4.2.

4.9.2. Implementing a Deque with a Doubly Linked List

The easiest and most efficient way to implement a Deque is with a doubly linked list. To see why a singly linked list is not a good structure, consider the structure used to implement a Queue, in which pointers were maintained to both the front and the back of the list:

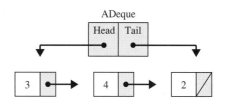

STRUCTURE

Stores a series of elements all of type *ElementType*

Initially empty

Elements added and/or removed at either the front or the back.

OPERATIONS

```
procedure PutFront (var D: Typ; Item: ElementType);
        post    D has Item appended to its front

procedure PutBack (var D: Typ; Item: ElementType);
        post    D has Item appended to its back

procedure GetFront (var D: Deque; var Item: ElementType);
        pre     not Empty(D)
        post    The front element of D has been removed.
                Item holds that element

procedure GetBack (var D: Deque; var Item: ElementType);
        pre     not Empty(D)
        post    The back element of D has been removed.
                Item holds that element

function Empty (var D: Typ): boolean;
        post    Returns true if D is empty, false otherwise
```

STANDARD OPERATORS

Create, Destroy

ADDITIONAL DECLARATIONS

Type *Element.Type* (default = *integer*)

FIGURE 4.2. Specification for Structure-ADT *Deque.*

In this case, *PutFront, GetFront*, and *PutBack* are reasonably straightforward to implement (after all, they are just *Push, Deque*, and *Enqueue* renamed), but *GetBack* is tricky. Consider what needs to be done to remove the 2 in the previous example. The *Tail* pointer must be made to reference the previous element (the one storing a 4). Because there are no backward pointers, the entire structure must be traversed to find a pointer to that element. Only then can *Tail* be reassigned. Suppose, on the other hand, you had the following structure:

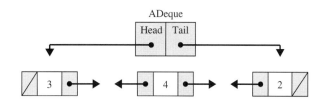

In this case, for *PutBack*, the *Tail* can just be assigned the value of the last element's previous field.

Note also that this is a symmetric structure in that every pointer in one direction has a corresponding pointer in the other direction. Thus, the operations *PutFront* and *PutBack* will be very similar, since they both just add an item onto the end of a symmetric structure. For similar reasons, *GetFront* and *GetBack* also will be "mirror images" of each other.

4.9.2.1. The Data Structure

Assuming you are implementing an integer Deque (one whose *ElementType* is *integer*), the following type definitions will yield the data structure pictured above:

```
type
  ElementType = integer;

  DequePtr = ^DequeRec;

  DequeRec = record
    Data: ElementType;
    Next, Previous: DequePtr;
  end; (* DequeRec *)

  Typ = record
    Head: DequePtr;
    Tail: DequePtr;
  end; (* Typ *)
```

To help you create new nodes of the Deque, you should create a version of *NewNode* for the doubly linked structure:

```
procedure NewNode (var D: DequePtr;
        Entry: ElementType;
        Front, Back: DequePtr);
begin
 new(D);
 D^.Data := Entry;
 D^.Previous := Front;
 D^.Next := Back;
end; (* NewNode *)
```

4.9.2.2. The Insertion Operations

PutFront inserts a value at the front. Thus, given this Deque:

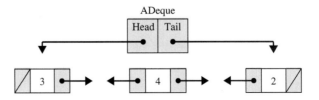

inserting a new node with value 100 leads to

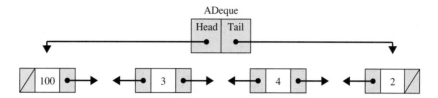

You can get most of the code from comparing the pictures. The new node is initialized with a *nil* back pointer and a front pointer referencing the old first element (old *aDeque.Head*). The old first element now points back to this new element, as does the *Head* pointer. Putting this together

```
procedure PutFront (var D: Typ;
        Item: ElementType);
  var
   NEWELEMPTR: DequePtr;
begin
  NewNode(NEWELEMPTR, Item, nil, D.Head);
  D.Head^.Previous := NEWELEMPTR;
  D.Head := NEWELEMPTR;
end; (* PutFront *)
```

As with the Queue operation *Enqueue*, however, a problem arises when inserting into an empty Deque because then the single element becomes both the *Head* and the *Tail*. Moreover, an empty Deque looks like this:

which means the statement

```
D.Head^.Previous := NEWELEMPTR;
```

will generate an error, since *D.Head^.Previous* doesn't exist. That's because when inserting into an empty Deque, there is no previous first element to point toward the new node. Thus, this special case can be handled as follows:

```
procedure PutFront (var D: Typ;
        Item: Element.Type);
  var
   NEWELEMPTR: DequePtr;
begin
```

```
NewNode(NEWELEMPTR, Item, nil, D.Head);
if D.Head <> nil then begin
  D.Head^.Previous := NEWELEMPTR;
 end
else begin
  D.Tail := NEWELEMPTR;
 end; (* If *)
D.Head := NEWELEMPTR;
end; (* PutFront *)
```

Now that *PutFront* is written, *PutBack* follows quickly, because it is basically the same operation—inserting a new element at one end of a symmetric structure. The only difference is that the *Head*'s and *Tail*'s need to be interchanged, as do the *Next*'s and *Previous*'s:

```
procedure PutBack (var D: Typ;
        Item: ElementType);
 var
  NEWELEMPTR: DequePtr;
begin
 NewNode(NEWELEMPTR, Item, D.Tail, nil);
 if D.Tail <> nil then begin
   D.Tail^.Next := NEWELEMPTR;
  end
 else begin
   D.Head := NEWELEMPTR;
  end; (* If *)
 D.Tail := NEWELEMPTR;
end; (* PutBack *)
```

4.9.2.3. Removing an Item from a Deque

Removing an item from the front of the structure involves returning the front item (through a parameter), and then advancing the *Head* pointer to the next element in the list. Further, this next element, which will become the new head of the list, must have its *Previous* field set to *nil*. This leads to the following code:

```
procedure GetFront (var D: Typ;
        var Item: Element.Type);
begin
 Item := D.Head^.Data;
 D.Head := D.Head^.Next;
 D.Head^.Previous := nil;
end; (* GetFront *)
```

But this isn't quite right. Think about what happens if, upon invocation, the *Deque* only has one element:

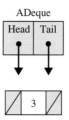

ADeque

Since removing the front element leaves the Deque empty, the *Tail* pointer must also be set to *nil*. Further, since there will be no front element upon termination of this procedure, it would be a mistake to set that element's *previous* field to *nil*. Thus, these considerations lead to the following correct implementation of *GetFront*:

```
procedure GetFront (var D: Typ;
        var Item: ElementType);
begin
 Item := D.Head^.Data;
 D.Head := D.Head^.Next;
 if D.Head = nil then begin
   D.Tail := nil;
   end
 else begin
   D.Head^.Previous := nil;
   end; (* If *)
end; (* GetFront *)
```

Because *GetFront* and *GetBack* both involve removing an item from the end of a symmetric structure, the *GetBack* procedure is just the "mirror image" of *GetFront*.

```
procedure GetBack (var D: Typ;
        var Item: ElementType);
begin
 Item := D.Tail^.Data;
 D.Tail := D.Tail^.Previous;
 if D.Tail = nil then begin
   D.Head := nil;
   end
 else begin
   D.Tail^.Next := nil;
   end; (* If *)
end; (* GetBack *)
```

4.9.2.4. The Remaining Operations

Create, *Destroy*, and *Empty* still need to be implemented. Since an empty Deque looks like the following:

ADeque

Create just needs to set the *Head* and *Tail* to *nil*, while *Empty* simply tests one of these pointers. If it is *nil*, then the Deque is empty. *Destroy* traverses the structure, deallocating each element by calling *dispose*.

```
procedure Create (var D: Typ);
begin
 D.Head := nil;
 D.Tail := nil;
end; (* Create *)

procedure Destroy (var D: Typ);
 var
   TEMP1, TEMP2: DequePtr;
begin
 TEMP1 := D.Head;
 while TEMP1 <> nil do begin
    TEMP2 := TEMP1;
    TEMP1 := TEMP1^.Next;
    dispose(TEMP2);
  end; (* While *)
end; (* Destroy *)

function Empty (var D: Typ): boolean;
begin
 Empty := (D.Head = nil);
end; (* Empty *)
```

4.10. SUMMARY OF KEY POINTS

- While you must declare most variables at compile-time, you can dynamically alllocate unnamed variables via the *new* procedure and access them through pointer variables. These dynamic variables remain allocated until they are *disposed* or the program ends.

- You can create a *linked list* by linking together dynamically allocated records that contain both data fields and a link field that points to the next element in the list.

- Linked lists are convenient for implementing many structure ADTs because they can grow and shrink as desired. Stacks, Queues, and Deques, while implementation independent, are particularly well-suited to linked list implementations because they are *positional* structure ADTs, which are manipulated only at the ends of the structure.

- You can use a sorted linked list to implement the Table ADT. Operations that may alter a linked list at any point in the structure may be written either iteratively or recursively, but iterative operations require that you keep one step ahead of yourself.

4.11. PROGRAMMING EXERCISES

1. Write a procedure that will take an input file and write that file in reverse order to an output file. You should use a linked list to store the file internally in reverse order, and then go through the linked list, writing it out. For example, given the following input file:

   ```
   Go
   Giants!
   ```

   your procedure should output the following:

   ```
   !stnaiG
   oG
   ```

2. Given a *PrintOneElement* procedure, with the header below, which will output a single element of a Stack, write a procedure *PrintStack*, whose header is also below, which will write out all the elements in the specified Stack. Upon termination of this procedure, the elements of the Stack, including their order, should be the same as they were when the procedure was invoked. You can assume that a Stack module is available for your use.

   ```
   procedure PrintOneElement (Elem: ElementType);

   procedure PrintStack (var S: Typ);
   ```

3. Given a *PrintOneElement* procedure, with the header below, which will output a single element of a Queue, write a procedure *PrintQueue*, whose header is also below, which will write out all the elements in the specified Queue. Upon termination of this procedure, the elements of the Queue, including their order, should be the same as they were when the procedure was invoked. You can assume that a Queue module is available for your use.

   ```
   procedure PrintOneElement (Elem: ElementType);

   procedure PrintQueue (var Q: Typ);
   ```

4. Given the following type declaration:

   ```
   type
     ListPtr  = ^ListType;
   ```

```
ListType = record
  Data: char;
  Next: ListPtr;
  end; (* ListType *)
```

write an *iterative* procedure, with the following header:

```
procedure DeleteAll (var Head: ListPtr; Target: char);
```

that will go through the linked list pointed to by *Head,* deleting all occurrences of *Target.*

5. Solve the previous question recursively.

6. Given the same data structure as in the previous question, write an iterative function that will return the number of nodes in a linked list.

7. Solve the previous question recursively.

8. Write a function which, given a pointer to the head of a linked list and a value stored in the list, returns a list containing all the elements in the list that precede that value.

9. Write a boolean function that takes in two linked lists as parameters and returns true if and only if the first list is "contained in" the second list. List A is contained in List B if all the elements in List A are also in List B, and they appear in List B contiguously and in the same order as in List A.

10. Write a procedure to remove duplicates from a sorted linked list.

11. Given the following data structure:

```
type
  ListPtr = ^ListRec;

  ListRec = record
    Data: integer;
    Next: ListPtr;
    end; (* ListRec *)
```

Write a procedure, with the header below, that will reverse all the elements in the linked list pointed to by the parameter List.

```
procedure Reverse (var List: ListPtr);
```

4.12. PROGRAMMING PROJECTS

1. Implement the String Package from Chapter 2 using a linked list to store the characters in a string.

2. Implement the Table ADT using a doubly linked list.

3. The Table type has the limitation that there is no notion of position within the Table, just a notion of an ordering. For applications in which a notion of position within the Table would be desirable, the Table type could be augmented by the notion of a *cursor*, which maintains a "current position." The cursor either references a particular element in the Table, or else it is "empty." This augmented Table type has all the Table operations (*Create, Destroy, Empty, Full, Insert, Delete, Find,* and *FindMin*), along with the following cursor operations:

```
procedure GoToStart (var T: Typ);
        pre     not Empty(T).
        post    T's cursor references the minimum element
                in T

procedure GoToNext (var T: Typ);
        pre     not Empty(T).
        post    T's cursor references the element in T
                which immediately follows its current
                element, according to the ordering of
                the sort keys.

procedure GoToPrev (var T: Typ);
        pre     not Empty(T).
        post    T's cursor references the element in T
                which immediately precedes its current
                element, according to the ordering of
                the sort keys.

procedure GoToKey (var T: Typ; Key: KeyType);
        post    T's cursor references the first element
                in T whose sort key has value Key.

procedure FindAtCursor (var T: Typ;
                        var Item: TableElement.Typ;
                        var IsAnElement: boolean);
        post    If T's cursor is empty, then IsAnElement
                is set to false. Otherwise, the element
                referenced by the cursor is returned via
                Item, and IsAnElement is set to true.

procedure DeleteAtCursor (var T: Typ);
        pre     T's cursor is nonempty.

        post    The element which T's cursor references
                is removed from T.
```

Further, in addition to its other actions, *Create* sets the cursor to be empty.

5
BINARY TREES

5.1. INTRODUCTION

In the previous chapter you saw how pointers can be used to create linear structures called linked lists. This chapter examines a nonlinear structure called a binary tree that can also be constructed using pointers. Unlike linked lists that always store data in a single direction (a straight line), the data in a binary tree can fan out in two different directions from any given node, generating a two-dimensional structure.

The chapter first introduces general tree terminology. Then it discusses the particular attributes of binary trees and their implementation in Pascal. Typical manipulations on binary trees are introduced through some interesting practical applications. The Table type is then reimplemented using binary trees. The chapter closes with a significant programming example that illustrates advanced binary tree manipulations and another application of the Table type.

5.2. BASIC TERMINOLOGY

The last chapter introduced the term "node," borrowed from a branch of mathematics known as *graph theory*. A *graph* is defined as a set of nodes and a set of *edges* that each connect two nodes. For example, the diagram below is a graph with nine nodes and eight edges. The edges connect nodes 1 to 2, 2 to 3, 3 to 4, 5 to 7, 7 to 6, 6 to

5, 6 to 8, and 8 to 7. As the arrows indicate, these edges are *directed*, which means they can be followed only in one direction.

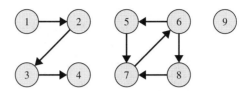

A *path* is defined as a sequence of edges that visits successive nodes. For example, there is a path from node 1 to node 4 by following the edges from 1 to 2, 2 to 3, and 3 to 4. The edges from 1 to 2, 2 to 3, and 7 to 8, however, do not constitute a path, because they don't visit successive nodes (there is a gap between 3 and 7 requiring a "jump"). As a result, there is no path connecting nodes 1 and 5 even though both have edges that touch them. A graph is called *connected* if there is a path between every pair of nodes. The preceeding graph is not connected because there is no edge joining the group of nodes on the left, the group of nodes in the middle, and the single node on the right. Nodes 1 through 4 taken by themselves, however, are connected, as are nodes 6 through 8 taken by themselves and node 9 taken by itself.

Nodes 6 through 8 in the middle of the graph above cannot be drawn in a straight line because the edges are complex enough that they require two dimensions to be drawn properly. Nodes 1 through 4 on the left are drawn in a two-dimensional way, but in fact they form a linear structure just like a linked list that can be drawn in a one-dimensional way:

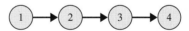

Such structures are characterized by the fact that when you put all the edges together, you get a single path, as in the graph above whose edges together form a path from 1 to 4.

A *tree* is a connected graph with the property that no pair of nodes has two paths joining them. For example, in the diagram below, nodes 1 through 4 are a tree, nodes 5 through 8 are not a tree because there are two paths from node 7 to node 6 (one through node 5 and one through node 8), and nodes 9 through 12 are not a tree because they are not connected (there is no path joining node 10 to any other node).

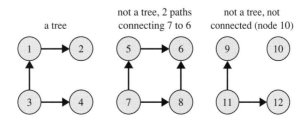

Trees are generally rearranged in a special way that makes them visually easier to comprehend by assigning each node a *height*. Every nonempty tree has exactly one node with the special property that it has no edges pointing into it (without going into an elaborate proof, suffice it to say that a graph with no such node must have two paths joining some pair of nodes and a graph with more than one such node must be disconnected). This special node is called the *root* of the tree and is drawn at the top of the diagram at what is considered height 0. All the nodes connected to the root are drawn just below it at what is considered height 1. All the nodes connected to those nodes are drawn just below them at what is considered height 2. And so on. The node appearing furthest from the root determines the tree's overall height. Those nodes that have only edges coming into them (no edges going out) are called *leaves*, because in terms of moving around the tree, they represent dead ends. The other nodes are called *branches* because they contain at least one edge that leads to some other branch of the tree.

For example, in the preceding tree, node 3 is the root (height 0) because it is the only one with no edges going into it. It is connected to nodes 1 and 4 (height 1), and node 1 in turn is connected to node 2 (height 2). The furthest node is at height 2, so the overall tree is said to have height 2. Thus, it would be drawn as follows:

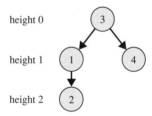

Nodes 2 and 4 are the leaves of this tree and nodes 1 and 3 are the branches.

Computer scientists tend to see the world differently from other people, so perhaps you will understand these terms better if you consider the following diagram, which is the same as the one above, but drawn upside-down. Now the root and height 0 appear at the bottom, where you might expect to see the ground in a picture. The parts of the picture toward the top are at a higher height, as in the real world. Branches extend from the root upwards, just as with nature's trees. And leaves appear on top of branches, representing the uppermost edge of the tree, just as in nature.

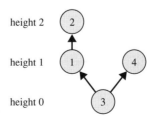

Computer scientists don't purposely try to make things confusing. Probably the standard orientation for a tree comes from conventions used to record family trees. In fact, the terminology used with such trees is also used for these mathematical trees. The nodes below the root are considered its *children* and it is considered their *parent*. Similarly, for any node, the nodes connected to it one level below are its children and it is their parent. The children of a node are called *siblings*; children of children are called *descendants*; and parents of parents are called *ancestors*. If you think about it, you'll realize that the root is the ancestor of all other nodes, sort of like Adam and Eve rolled into one.

Putting these concepts in graph terms, edges define parent/child relationships and paths define ancestor/descendant relationships. The root is connected to every other node by some path (if there is no path at all then the graph is disconnected, and if the path were from the node to the root then the root would have an edge going into it, both of which are disallowed by definition), so it is the ancestor of all other nodes. The stipulation that no pair of nodes have two paths joining them implies that each node has a unique ancestral trail back to the root. For example, the illegal tree with two paths from the previous diagram would look like this if drawn like a tree:

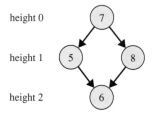

In this structure, node 6 has two ways of tracing its ancestry to the root. Because such structures are not considered trees, you know that every node in a tree has a single ancestral trail back to the root, which means it has one parent, who has one parent, who has one parent, and so on back to the root. In terms of family trees, a crossover like this occurs when siblings or cousins produce a child, introducing two paths back to a common ancestor.

This allows you to see an important property of trees, namely that each child of the root is the root of a smaller tree (called a *subtree* of the original). Unique ancestry means that each of the root's children will have only one edge pointing into it, the parental connection from the root. Thus, when the root is taken away, the child takes on the special property associated with roots that they have no edges pointing into them. In family terms, this is like saying that each couple has its own lineage, which means that Adam and Eve don't have a monopoly on family trees. Every couple causes a new family tree to "sprout" with them at the top.

Trees in general are two-dimensional structures. If, however, all nodes of the tree appear on a single path, then its data values appear in a linear sequence that can be drawn in a straight line. The linear graph example from the beginning of this section fits the definition of a tree and would be drawn as follows:

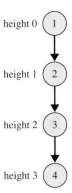

Notice that what would be the head of a linked list storing this data is the root of this tree and what would be the last node of such a list is the only leaf of this tree. Although a linear structure like the one above is by definition a tree, it is often called *degenerate* because all branching is absent. In fact, degenerate trees become quite important when you analyze the efficiency of tree algorithms because they often exhibit worst case behavior.

5.2.1. Terminology of Binary Trees

The general notion of a tree does not impose any restriction on how many children a node might have. But just as changing the number of links in a linked list structure can drastically change its character (going from a singly linked to a doubly linked list), so changing the number of links included in a tree structure can drastically change its character. If generality were critical, you could devise a way to store an indefinite number of links in each tree node. But in fact, two links is often what you want and its simplicity leads to a certain elegance of code that more than makes up for loss of generality. [1]

Thus, this book concentrates on a special class of trees called *binary trees* that share the property that all nodes have no more than two children. Furthermore, the notion of binary trees presented in this book and understood by most programmers involves one other minor stipulation that the trees be *ordered*. That means that the children of a node appear in a specific order that must be maintained. With binary trees the children are referred to as the *left child* and *right child*, which automatically introduces a distinction. Thus, the following two trees do not represent the same binary

---

[1] In fact, a node with two links *can* be used to store general trees with one link pointing down to the first child of the node and the other pointing across to the next sibling.

tree because their left and right children are reversed.

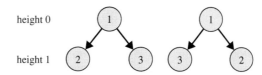

Similarly, a node with one child is not quite as simple in an ordered tree. For binary trees, the child has to be either to the left or to the right. It is not legal for it to be in the middle, as indicated in the samples below.

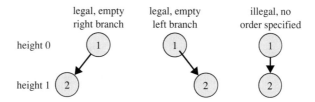

5.2.2. SELF CHECK EXERCISES

These questions all refer to the following binary tree:

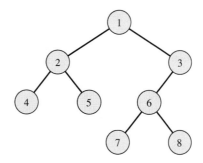

1. Which nodes are branches?

2. Which nodes are leaves?

3. Which node is the root?

4. Which nodes are at height 2?

5. What is the height of the overall tree?

6. Which node is node 6's parent?

7. Which nodes are node 1's children?

5.3. BUILDING BINARY TREES

Binary trees are built the same way that linked lists are, using many elements all with the same basic structure. Just as a linked list can be described in terms of its basic building block, so too a binary tree can be described using its building block. The atomic unit of storage in a binary tree is a single node, which means that the basic building block must be a node with a space for data (here an integer) and links for its left and right children:

Putting a few of these together, you might construct the following:

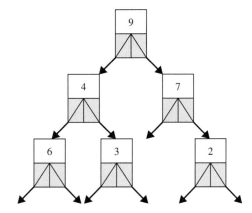

But just as the linked list pattern is slightly different for the last node of the list (using *nil* to avoid an arrow pointing off into space), so the binary tree pattern is slightly different at the edges of the tree where one or more children are empty (again, using *nil* to avoid arrows pointing off into space):

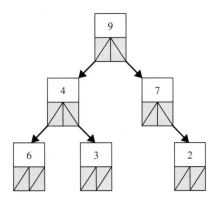

If you compare the diagram above with that of a simple linked list you'll notice that it is much more cluttered. That happens because it is two-dimensional, it has a more complex record structure, and it has many *nil* pointers versus the one that appears at the end of a linked list. As a result, the binary tree diagrams that follow use an abbreviated format that shows just the nonempty links (the assumption being that branches not shown are set to *nil*). For example, the diagram above becomes:

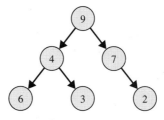

This format allows you to concentrate on the actual structure of the tree and the data it stores without having to be reminded of the internal node structure and the numerous *nil* values indicating unused branches.

The appropriate type declarations are not difficult to deduce from the picture of the basic building block. Each node stores three elements: data, a left pointer, and a right pointer. The pointers are to other nodes, which leads to declarations quite similar to those of a linked list:

```
type
  TreePtr = ^TreeNode;

  TreeNode = record
    Data: integer;
    Left, Right: TreePtr;
  end; (* TreeNode *)
```

The recursive nature of these declarations mirrors the observation made earlier that the left and right pointers store references to structures that are legal trees, subtrees of the original. This fact is heavily exploited in recursive subprograms to manipulate binary trees.

5.3.1. Adding a Leaf

Given this definition, a tree can be constructed through successive calls on *new*, each of which allocates a new node for the tree. Procedure *NewNode* was helpful for creating linked list nodes (most often at the end of the list), so it seems prudent to create a parallel procedure for binary trees. Trees are most often grown at the leaves, so a procedure for creating a new leaf with a specified data value is helpful. As always, *nil* should be stored in the unused links so that your programs can properly identify unused branches. As long as we're creating a procedure for creating a leaf, we might as well also create a function for testing to see if a node is a leaf. It also proves very useful.

```
procedure NewLeaf (var NewElemPtr: TreePtr;
        Num:integer);
begin
 new(NewElemPtr);
 NewElemPtr^.Data := Num;
 NewElemPtr^.Left := nil;
 NewElemPtr^.Right := nil;
end; (* NewLeaf *)

function IsLeaf (aNode: TreePtr): boolean;
begin
 if aNode = nil then begin
   IsLeaf := false;
   end
 else begin
   IsLeaf := (aNode^.Left = nil) and (aNode^.Right = nil);
   end;
end; (* IsLeaf *)
```

5.3.2. Building a Tree the Hard Way

Trees can be built one leaf at a time using *NewLeaf* to create leaves and then calling it again to attach new leaves as children of the previous leaf. For example, the following code will create the binary tree used as an example on page 213.

```
procedure BuildATree (var Root: TreePtr);
begin
 NewLeaf(Root, 9);
 NewLeaf(Root^.Left, 4);
 NewLeaf(Root^.Right, 7);
 NewLeaf(Root^.Left^.Left, 6);
 NewLeaf(Root^.Left^.Right, 3);
 NewLeaf(Root^.Right^.Right, 2);
end; (* BuildATree *)
```

As with linked list programs, you only have one pointer variable available at the beginning, so about the only thing you can do is to create a leaf using variable *Root*.

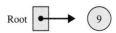

Now that you have a root node, the following references are legal:

Variable	Type	Description (* means currently empty)
Root	TreePtr	named variable pointing to root node
Root^	TreeNode	root node
Root^.Data	integer	data field of root node
Root^.Left	TreePtr	* left subtree of root
Root^.Right	TreePtr	* right subtree of root

As the asterisks above indicate, you now have two empty pointer variables to work with. You can grow the tree either to the left or to the right. The program calls *NewLeaf* with *Root^.Left* as its pointer parameter, so it chooses to grow to the left first. This attaches a new leaf as the left child of the root:

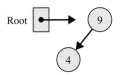

which makes the following references now legal:

Variable	Type	Description (* means currently empty)
Root	TreePtr	named variable pointing to root node
Root^	TreeNode	root node
Root^.Data	integer	data field of root node
Root^.Left	TreePtr	left subtree of root
Root^.Right	TreePtr	* right subtree of root
Root^.Left^	TreeNode	root's left child node
Root^.Left^.Data	integer	data field of root's left child
Root^.Left^.Left	TreePtr	* left subtree of root's left child
Root^.Left^.Right	TreePtr	* right subtree of root's left child

This opens up even more options for where to grow the tree. You can still grow to the right of the root, or now you can grow to either the left or right of the root's left child. The main program uses *Root^.Right*, which means that it chooses to grow to the right of the root:

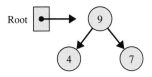

which makes these references legal:

Variable	Type	Description (* means currently empty)
Root	TreePtr	named variable pointing to root node
Root^	TreeNode	root node
Root^.Data	integer	data field of root node
Root^.Left	TreePtr	left subtree of root
Root^.Right	TreePtr	right subtree of root
Root^.Left^	TreeNode	root's left child node
Root^.Left^.Data	integer	data field of root's left child
Root^.Left^.Left	TreePtr	* left subtree of root's left child
Root^.Left^.Right	TreePtr	* right subtree of root's left child
Root^.Right^	TreeNode	root's right child node
Root^.Right^.Data	integer	data field of root's right child
Root^.Right^.Left	TreePtr	* left subtree of root's right child
Root^.Right^.Right	TreePtr	* right subtree of root's right child

This completes height 1 for the tree, because there can be only two children of the root. It leaves you with four places where you might decide to grow: the left and right pointers of the two nodes at level 1. The rest of the main program simply goes left to right adding three more leaves at level 2 and leaving you with this structure:

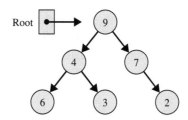

Now that you've had some experience with the tedious approach to binary trees, you're ready to look at some elegant code.

5.3.3. SELF CHECK EXERCISES

These questions all refer to the following binary tree:

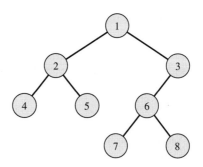

1. Which nodes are in node 2's left subtree?

2. Which nodes are in node 3's left subtree?

3. Write a procedure, with the header below, that uses procedure *NewLeaf* to create the tree above, with the parameter *Root* pointing to the new tree's root.

   ```
   procedure BuildATree (var Root: TreePtr);
   ```

5.4. TREE TRAVERSALS

Programs that store data values in a structure often need to perform some operation on each individual value (e.g., printing them out). Binary trees are no exception. You will often need to do something to each of the node values in the tree. This is usually referred to as *visiting* the nodes of the tree or *traversing* the tree. Unlike linked lists, binary trees don't really have a first value, second value, third value, and so on. You could argue that the root should come first, but what comes next? Different traversal methods will visit the nodes in different orders. Most binary tree applications are quite sensitive to the order in which nodes are visited, so you usually need to choose your traversal carefully.

Several standard traversal strategies follow naturally from the recursive nature of binary trees. Each node stores:

1. Its own data.
2. A reference to its left subtree.
3. A reference to its right subtree.

If you use recursive calls to traverse the subtrees, then you have only three steps to carry out: process the data, process the left subtree, and process the right subtree. With typical Western bias, computer scientists always process from left to right, leading to this starting pseudocode:

```
process left subtree
process right subtree
```

The only variation in standard traversals is when to process the data. It can be done either before, in between, or after the two calls. Using the prefixes pre-, in-, and post-, these traversal strategies are referred to as *preorder, inorder,* and *postorder.*

←processing data here yields
preorder traversal

```
process left subtree
```

←processing data here yields
inorder traversal

```
process right subtree
```

←processing data here yields
postorder traversal

Consider the task of writing out the data values stored in a tree using a preorder traversal. That means you want this pseudocode:

```
process data
process left subtree
process right subtree
```

Because the left and right subtrees *are* trees, recursion can be applied to process them. Each is simpler than the original, so the recursion will tend toward the base case. Processing the data simply involves writing it out. All that's left is the base case, which is the simplest version of the problem that can be solved directly. Since an empty tree requires no work, the base case is reached when an attempt is made to print an empty tree. Thus, the following code will print a binary tree using preorder traversal:

```
procedure PrintPreorder (aNode: TreePtr);
begin
  if aNode <> nil then begin
    writeln(aNode^.Data);
    PrintPreorder(aNode^.Left);
    PrintPreorder(aNode^.Right);
  end; (* If *)
end; (* PrintPreorder *)
```

The procedure is so short that you might find it easy to understand, but just in case, consider some of its subtleties. When you stand in line to get food you can be deceived by a single customer who appears to be alone but in fact is ordering for a large group of people, which keeps you waiting as if all those people had actually been in line. This procedure is similarly deceptive. The code seems to print the left *node* followed by the right *node*, when in fact it prints the left *subtree* followed by the right *subtree*. If there are one thousand nodes in the left subtree, nothing from the right will be printed until all those one thousand nodes are processed.

Consider the recursive calls generated by a tree of four nodes. Notice that at each level, the entire left subtree is processed before the right subtree is even considered. The following table uses notations like "right, left, left" to indicate the right subtree's left subtree's left subtree (i.e., from the root turn right, then left, then left). As indicated in the table, nine calls are generated (two recursive calls for each node plus the initial call). A trace of its execution is shown in the following diagram.

If you understand how the basic recursive structure of procedure *PreorderTraversal* allows it to traverse all the tree's nodes, then you should have no trouble seeing that the other two traversals are obtained simply by moving the *writeln* statement. Moving it around relative to the two recursive calls produces the other two traversals:

```
procedure PrintInorder (aNode: TreePtr);
begin
  if aNode <> nil then begin
    PrintInorder(aNode^.Left);
    writeln(aNode^.Data);
    PrintInorder(aNode^.Right);
  end; (* If *)
end; (* PrintInorder *)
```

Call	Description	Structure
1	original tree	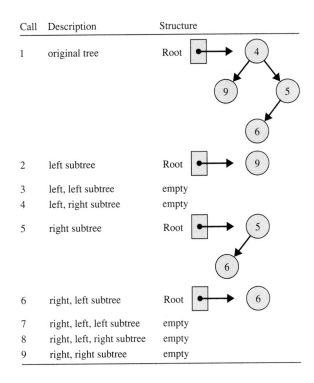
2	left subtree	
3	left, left subtree	empty
4	left, right subtree	empty
5	right subtree	
6	right, left subtree	
7	right, left, left subtree	empty
8	right, left, right subtree	empty
9	right, right subtree	empty

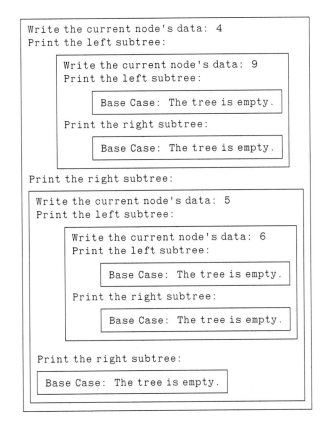

```
Write the current node's data:  4
Print the left subtree:

    Write the current node's data:  9
    Print the left subtree:

        Base Case:  The tree is empty.

    Print the right subtree:

        Base Case:  The tree is empty.

Print the right subtree:

Write the current node's data:  5
Print the left subtree:

    Write the current node's data:  6
    Print the left subtree:

        Base Case:  The tree is empty.

    Print the right subtree:

        Base Case:  The tree is empty.

Print the right subtree:

Base Case:  The tree is empty.
```

```
procedure PrintPostorder (aNode: TreePtr);
begin
  if aNode <> nil then begin
    PrintPostorder(aNode^.Left);
    PrintPostorder(aNode^.Right);
    writeln(aNode^.Data);
  end; (* If *)
end; (* PrintPostorder *)
```

Using the same sample tree as with *PreorderTraversal*, these procedures would produce this output:

```
PrintInorder:     9 4 6 5
PrintPostorder:   9 6 5 4
```

5.4.1. SELF CHECK EXERCISES

1. Write a procedure that will print out the elements of an integer binary tree using an inorder traversal, except that the tree is printed from right to left, instead of left to right.

2. Given the following binary tree:

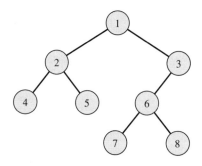

in which order are the nodes traversed using

a. preorder traversal

b. inorder traversal

c. postorder traversal

5.5. FUNCTIONS ON BINARY TREES

Frequently you will want to analyze a binary tree and determine some property of that tree. For example, you might want to know the height of a particular tree. Because these problems involve analyzing a structure and returning a value, a function is the appropriate mechanism for this task.

As an example, consider the problem of determining the height of a binary tree. As stated earlier, the height of a tree is the height of the node furthest from the root, where the root has a height of zero. The height of a tree is thus the length of the longest path from the root to a leaf.

Although you could traverse every path in the tree iteratively, the number of branches makes this quite difficult. Instead, you should take advantage of the recursive nature of binary trees and let recursive calls do most of the work for you. Given a tree, you want to discover the longest path from the root to a leaf. If the tree is nonempty, then the root has three properties:

1. Itself.
2. Its left subtree.
3. Its right subtree.

You know that the height of the current tree is one greater than the height of the larger of its two subtrees. Thus, if you can determine the height of each of the subtrees, it is simple to determine the height of the entire tree. You have thus reduced the problem of finding the height of the entire tree to one of finding the height of the two subtrees. Since these are each simpler versions of the original problem, you can assume that you can make recursive calls to solve these subproblems. All that remains is the base case. Since an empty tree doesn't even have a root node, the recursive case cannot be used to find an empty tree's height. Since the height of a tree with just one node is zero (there is no path from the root to a leaf, since the root is a leaf), then the height of an empty tree must be -1. This is the base case. These ideas lead to the following pseudocode:

```
function Height (Root: TreePtr): integer;
begin
 if Root is an empty tree then begin
   Height := -1
   end
 else begin
   Find Height of left subtree;
   Find Height of right subtree;
   Height := max ( left height, right height ) + 1;
   end; (* If *)
end; (* Height *)
```

Given a *max* function, which takes two values and returns the larger of the two:

```
function Max (First, Second: integer): integer;
begin
 if First > Second then begin
   Max := First;
   end
 else begin
   Max := Second;
   end; (* If *)
end; (* Max *)
```

you can turn the pseudocode into Pascal. Because the function returns a value, you can use the values returned by the recursive calls directly in the statement that determines the tree's height:

```
function Height (Root: TreePtr): integer;
begin
  if Root = nil then begin
    Height := -1;
  end
  else begin
    Height := Max(Height(Root^.Left),
               Height(Root^.Right)) + 1;
  end; (* If *)
end; (* Height *)
```

5.5.1. SELF CHECK EXERCISES

1. Write a function that takes an integer binary tree as a parameter and returns the sum of the data in all the nodes in the tree.

2. Write a function that returns the length of the shortest path from the root to a leaf.

5.6. MANIPULATING ARITHMETIC EXPRESSIONS

Consider the problem of reading and manipulating ordinary arithmetic expressions composed of unsigned integer constants, operators ($+$, $-$, $*$, and $/$), and parentheses. Figuring out how different parts of an expression should be grouped together is tricky, so let's begin by considering expressions that include a set of parentheses for each arithmetic operator.

The set of legal expressions of this form can be described recursively by saying that a legal expression must match one of these patterns:

* *<an unsigned integer constant>*
* *(<legal expression> <operator> <legal expression>)*

as in

```
((84/9) * (18/4))
((3 * (2 + 2))/(49 - 18))
((4 + (3 * (8 - (7/(1 + 1))))) * 18)
```

This is a recursive definition with integer constants as the base case and operators defining the recursive case. For example, you can apply these rules to build more and more complex expressions:

Number	Expression	Explanation
1	100	integer constant
2	(100 + 100)	basic form with expr #1 twice
3	8	integer constant
4	7	integer constant
5	(8×7)	basic form with exprs #3, #4
6	((100 + 100)/(8×7))	basic form with exprs #2, #5
7	((8× 7)+100)	basic form with exprs #5, #1
8	(((100 + 100)/(8×7))−((8×7) + 100))	basic form with exprs #5, #1

Notice that the following are not legal expressions by these rules:

Expression	Explanation
100.0	only integer expressions allowed
−38	no sign allowed
2 + 2	missing parens
(2 + 3 + 4)	only one operator for each paren pair
(3 + 4)/(8 × 9)	no outer parens for / operator
(z + (x × y))	basic forms, but exprs are not legal
−(2 × 3)	no rule for this kind of negation operator
(3 + (4 − 8) + 6)	only one operator for each paren pair
(18 − 9) + 3)	missing left paren
(18)	no operator and only one integer

Although this constructive technique can be used to define the set of legal expressions, programming usually involves the opposite kind of work: taking something complex and reducing it to simpler components. For example, consider the following expression:

```
(((3*4)+(4*8))/169)
|                 |
|_____|
       expr
```

Its outer parentheses enclose the / operator:

```
(   ((3*4)+(4*8))   /   169   )
    |           |   |   |
    |_____|   |   |
        expr       oper  expr
|                            |
|_____|
            expr
```

This leads to two subexpressions, one complex and one simple. The outer parentheses for the complex subexpression enclose the + operator:

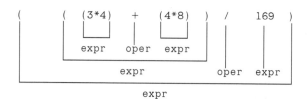

And each of these subsubexpressions can be expanded into subsubsubexpressions.

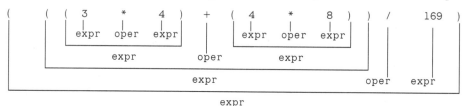

This completes the analysis of the structure of this expression because all expressions have now been broken down into their simplest components.

5.6.1. Parsing Expressions

5.6.1.1. What Is Parsing?

Parsing, in this book, refers to decomposing some input into its constituent parts. Typically, an input is decomposed and stored in a *parse tree*, which represents the parsed input internally. For example, one of the first things a compiler must do is take your program as input and decompose it into a more meaningful form, which usually means parsing the program and storing it in a parse tree. Luckily, working with expressions is somewhat easier than parsing a Pascal program. In fact, a binary tree is perfect for storing an expression.

Each of the two rules used to define expressions leads to a different tree pattern. Integer constants are stored in leaf nodes. For example, the complex expression from the last section generates five leaf nodes:

$$(((3 * 4) + (4 * 8)) / 169)$$

Operators are stored in branch nodes with their subexpressions stored in the subtrees.

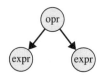

For example, the two subsubsubexpressions in the complex expression each leads to a simple pattern like the one above, where the *expr* nodes are leaves that store integer constants. You put an expression into tree format by moving the operator into a branch node, deleting its parentheses, and connecting its subexpressions as its children. This leads to

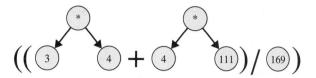

You can turn the + operator to its tree form also by connecting these two branch nodes to a third branch node that stores the +. Finally, the / operator can be turned into its tree form by putting it into a branch node and connecting it to the + node and the 169 node. The final result is

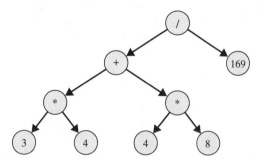

This is a parse tree for the complex expression. It is equivalent to the expression in that its nodes store the individual operators and integers that make up the expression and its structure reflects the grouping of operators specified by the parentheses. This is the one and only parse tree equivalent to that expression. As you will soon see, expressions like these are much easier to manipulate when you first change them to this form.

5.6.1.2. Building the Parse Tree

The appropriate data structure for a parse tree is a slight variation of the normal binary tree. Every node has two pointers and a piece of data, but the leaf nodes store integers as data while the branches store characters that represent operators. The simplest way to accommodate this is to include one of each kind of data field in every node. Another approach is to use a construct known as a variant record, but to keep things simple for your reading, you can experiment with that on your own.

```
type
  TreePtr = ^TreeNode;

  TreeNode = record
    Number: integer;
    Operator: char;
    Left, Right: TreePtr;
  end; (* TreeNode *)
```

The recursive definition of an expression in terms of an operator and two subexpressions fits beautifully with the recursive definition of a tree in terms of a root and two subtrees. As a result, recursion is particularly helpful when creating and manipulating parse trees.

Consider the task of reading a legal arithmetic expression and trying to build the appropriate parse tree for it. How many cases do you have to consider? There seem to be many kinds of expressions, subexpressions, subsubexpressions, and so on. But fortunately you have only two cases to consider: one for each of the rules that define an expression. Thus, you expect to process either a simple integer or input of the form

(\<expression\> \<operator\>\<expression\>)

How do you know which kind you've got? The pattern above is easy to spot because it starts with a left parenthesis. Thus, all you need to do is look ahead on the input line to see if what follows is a left parenthesis or a number. This allows you to distinguish the cases, and the rules themselves describe how to process each case.

```
procedure Parse(Tree);
begin
  if (no left parenthesis ahead) then begin
    read the integer into a leaf node
    end
  else begin
    Allocate a branch node
    Skip the left parenthesis
    Parse first subexpression (store as left child)
    Read the operator
    Parse second subexpression (store as right child)
    Skip the right parenthesis
    end; (* If *)
end; (* Parse *)
```

Most of this is easily translated into Pascal:

```
procedure Parse (var Tree: TreePtr);
var
 VALUE: integer;
 PAREN: char;
begin
  if (no left parenthesis ahead) then begin
    read (VALUE);
    NewLeaf(Tree, VALUE);
    end
  else begin
    new(Tree);
    read (PAREN);
    Parse(Tree^.Left);
    read(Tree^.Operator);
    Parse(Tree^.Right);
    read (PAREN);
    end; (* If *)
end; (* Parse *)
```

5.6.1.3. Procedure Parse and I/O

The only remaining detail for procedure *Parse* is the test to see if there is a left parenthesis ahead. You might at first think that you can read one character ahead and test the result. But that backfires when the next character is the first digit of an integer constant. For example, if when *Parse* is called the next few characters in the input stream are "2485", then the procedure should simply perform an integer read. But how do you *know* that you're dealing with the integer constant case and not a parenthesized expression? If you read a character to find out, you process "2" from the input file. This allows you to decide that it's the integer constant case, but it also means that your subsequent integer read will obtain 485 rather than 2485.

Standard Pascal specifies a remedy called *INPUT^*, but unfortunately Turbo Pascal does not implement this feature. Besides, if you pursue this line of reasoning much further, you'll realize that other input bugs exist. For example, if the input stream is positioned at a space when you perform the character read meant to process the operator or the parentheses, you will end up reading the wrong thing and throwing off the entire calculation.

The easiest fix is to abandon standard reading operations and make use of a utility module whose reading conventions are more appropriate for solving this problem. Chapter 1 presented several such modules. Module *CharBuff* is used to allow one-character lookahead. If you're interested in the details, you might want to review the module specification on page 28. Here is the resulting procedure:

```
procedure Parse (var Tree: TreePtr);
  var
    VALUE: integer;
    PAREN: char;
begin
  if (CharBuff.Window <> '(') then begin
    CharBuff.ReadInt(VALUE);
    NewLeaf(Tree, VALUE);
  end
  else begin
    new(Tree);
    CharBuff.ReadChar(PAREN);
    Parse(Tree^.Left);
    CharBuff.ReadChar(Tree^.Operator);
    Parse(Tree^.Right);
    CharBuff.ReadChar(PAREN);
  end; (* If *)
end; (* Parse *)
```

5.6.1.4. Tracing Through the Recursion

To help you understand how this procedure works, think about parsing the following expression:

```
(8 * (3 + 4))
```

When first called, *Parse* applies the recursive case because the next input character is a left parenthesis. It allocates a new node that will serve as the root of the overall parse tree, skips past the left parenthesis, and makes its first recursive call to parse the first subexpression, which it stores in its left subtree:

(expr)

On the next call, *Parse* doesn't see a left parenthesis, so it reads an integer (the number 8) and stores it in a leaf node:

This concludes the root node's first recursive call. Proceeding with the remaining instructions in the recursive case, it next reads and stores its operator (*), and then it makes the second recursive call, this time to evaluate the second subexpression and store the result in the right subtree:

On this call to *Parse*, the next character from the input file is again a left parenthesis, which causes the procedure to perform the recursive case. It allocates a node that will serve as the root of this new subexpression, it skips past the left parenthesis, and it makes its first recursive call to store the first subexpression in its left subtree:

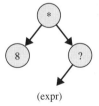

(expr)

Now you're back to the base case because the next input value to be read is the integer 3. Thus, this call on *Parse* creates a new leaf node storing the value 3. This concludes the right subtree's first recursive call. It next reads the operator it should store (+) and makes its second recursive call to store the second subexpression in the right subtree:

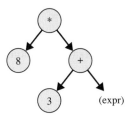

The next input value is 4, so the base case is again applied, creating a node with the value 4. This concludes the right subtree's second recursive call. It finishes up by reading the right parenthesis that marks the end of the + expression. This, then, concludes the second recursive call being made by the root, which causes it to finish up by reading its right parenthesis. Thus, the tree ends as follows:

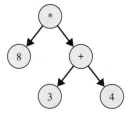

In summary, *Parse* is called a total of five times. Each call processes either an integer (leading to a leaf node) or an operator (leading to a branch node). The diagram below summarizes which recursive call generates each node:

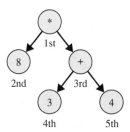

Here is a trace of the execution:

```
Allocate branch node for operator
Parse first subexpression as left child
     Allocate leaf node for 8
Assign node the value '*'
Parse second subexpression as right child
     Allocate branch node for operator
     Parse first subexpression as left child
          Allocate leaf node for 3
     Assign node the value '+'
     Parse second subexpression as right child
          Allocate leaf node for 4
```

5.6.2. Printing Expressions

Having built a parse tree for such an expression, it is fairly simple to manipulate that expression. For example, printing out the tree using an inorder traversal recreates the original expression. If you just write the values, you'll get something like this:

```
8 * 3 + 4
```

instead of this:

```
(8 * (3 + 4))
```

This isn't right, because without the parentheses, most people would interpret this as first performing the multiply and then the addition. Thus, you need to include the parentheses if you want to be sure to show unambiguously how the expression is grouped. Thus, you should write the traversal as follows:

```
procedure PrintInorder (aNode: TreePtr);
begin
  if aNode <> nil then begin
    if IsLeaf(aNode) then begin
      write(aNode^.Number : 1);
    end
    else begin
      write ('(');
      PrintInorder(aNode^.Left);
      write(' ', aNode^.Operator, ' ');
      PrintInorder(aNode^.Right);
      writeln (')');
    end; (* If *)
  end; (* If *)
end; (* PrintInorder *)
```

The other traversals can also be used to write the parse tree, but the result is quite different. Preorder traversal produces something called prefix notation, and postorder traversal produces something called postfix notation. Unlike infix notation, prefix and postfix are unambiguous even when no parentheses are written out. For example, the expression above would produce the following prefix output:

```
* 8 + 3 4
```

5.6.3. Evaluating Expressions

Now that the expression has been stored in a convenient internal form, it should be reasonably straightforward to evaluate it. An *Eval* function again is most easily written recursively.

Consider the two tree patterns for expressions:

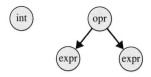

These two forms map directly into the structure of a recursive function. A leaf node containing an integer constant just evaluates to that number. This is the base case, because all expressions are eventually reduced to single numbers. The second form maps to the recursive case, in which each subexpression is evaluated recursively, and then the result is computed by applying the appropriate operation to those values. Putting these cases together yields the following pseudocode:

```
function Eval(Tree) : integer;
begin
  if <Tree is a leaf node> then begin
    return the value of the number;
  end
  else begin
    Evaluate left subexpression;
    Evaluate right subexpression;
    Apply Tree's operator to the subexpressions and return
    result;
  end; (* If *)
end; (* Eval *)
```

which can be refined into the following Pascal function. Notice that as a function, the two recursive calls can appear in an expression rather than as a sequence of steps as indicated in the pseudocode above.

```
function Eval (Tree: TreePtr): integer;
begin
  if IsLeaf(Tree) then begin
    Eval := Tree^.Number;
  end
  else begin
    case Tree^.Operator of
      '+' :
      Eval := Eval(Tree^.Left) + Eval(Tree^.Right);
      '-' :
      Eval := Eval(Tree^.Left) - Eval(Tree^.Right);
      '*' :
      Eval := Eval(Tree^.Left) * Eval(Tree^.Right);
      '/' :
      Eval := Eval(Tree^.Left) div Eval(Tree^.Right);
    end; (* Case *)
  end; (* If *)
end; (* Eval *)
```

To make things easier, this function assumes that you want to perform only integer arithmetic.

5.6.3.1. Parsing without Parentheses

Parsing becomes more complicated when only some of the operators are parenthesized, as in

```
3 * (2 + 4)
8 * 2 * 4 * (2 + 2)
```

For this kind of complex parsing, it is usually best to write short rules that specify the set of legal inputs and then translate those rules into Pascal. Such rules are often expressed using Backus–Naur Form (BNF). You might remember using BNF when you studied grammar. For example, the following BNF rules describe a set of simple English sentences:

```
<sentence>     ::= <noun phrase> <verb phrase>
<noun phrase> ::= the <noun> ! <noun>
<noun>         ::= man ! woman ! baby ! time
<verb phrase> ::= <verb> <noun phrase> ! <verb>
<verb>         ::= helps ! hurts ! kills
```

Each line is a different BNF rule. Rules are composed of terminals and nonterminals. Terminals represent actual elements of the language you are trying to describe. In the example above, the terminals are words like "the," "man," "woman," "baby." Nonterminals are enclosed in brace characters (e.g., <sentence>) and are used to describe the structure of the language. Each rule specifies possible replacements for a nonterminal (when there is more than one possible replacement, they are separated by the "!" character). For example, using the replacement rules above you can derive the following sentence:

```
<sentence>
<noun phrase> <verb phrase>
the <noun> <verb phrase>
the baby <verb phrase>
the baby <verb> <noun phrase>
the baby kills <noun phrase>
the baby kills <noun>
the baby kills time
```

Some BNF rules are recursive. For example, instead of defining a noun as

```
<noun>          ::= man ! woman ! baby ! time
```

you might include the following recursive replacement rule:

```
<noun>          ::= <adjective> <noun> ! man ! woman ! baby
                    ! time
```

```
<adjective>   ::= nice ! attractive ! smart ! furry
```

This allows you to include as many adjectives as you want in front of a noun. For example

```
<sentence>
<noun phrase> <verb phrase>
the <noun> <verb phrase>
the <adjective> <noun> <verb phrase>
the nice <noun> <verb phrase>
the nice <adjective> <noun> <verb phrase>
the nice attractive <noun> <verb phrase>
the nice attractive <adjective> <noun> <verb phrase>
the nice attractive furry <noun> <verb phrase>
the nice attractive furry man <verb phrase>
the nice attractive furry man <verb> <noun phrase>
the nice attractive furry man helps <noun phrase>
the nice attractive furry man helps the <noun>
the nice attractive furry man helps the baby
```

This recursive rule also allows you to form repetitious phrases, as in "The nice nice nice nice nice man helps the furry furry furry baby."

How would you describe parenthesized expressions using BNF? A direct translation of the two rules we have been using leads to

```
<expression> ::= <number> !
                 (<expression> <operator> <expression>)
<operator>   ::= + ! - ! * ! /
```

You could write a BNF description of <number>, but because the parsing procedure reads an entire number at once, you don't need rules for parsing it. How do you describe expressions that don't always have parentheses? First consider the case of expressions with no parentheses. You might try simply removing the parentheses from the rules above, defining them as follows:

```
<expression> ::= <number> !
                 <expression> <operator> <expression>
<operator>   ::= + ! - ! * ! /
```

There are two problems, however, with this definition. First, consider what happens with an expression like

```
2 + 3 - 4
```

There are two ways to derive this expression. You might think of it as $2 + $ <expression>, which groups it as $2 + (3 - 4)$, or you might think of it as <expression> $- 4$, which groups it as $(2 + 3) - 4$. You didn't have such ambiguity before because parentheses were always present to specify how to group operators. But these two approaches would lead to two different parse trees. You can't parse with such ambiguity, so you need to refine the description. The fix is to introduce another nonterminal to represent a simple expression (i.e., one with no operators). To have operators applied left to right, you specify that simple expressions appear on the right-hand side:

```
<expression> ::= <simple> ¦ <expression> <operator>
                 <simple>
<simple>     ::= <number>
<operator>   ::= + ¦ - ¦ * ¦ /
```

Because a simple expression must be a number, when parsing $2 + 3 - 4$, you are forced to parse the expression in this way:

```
<expression>
<expression> <operator> <simple>
<expression> - 4
  . . .
```

Thus, the subexpression $2 + 3$ is grouped together. Similarly, by putting the simple expression on the left

```
<expression> ::= <simple> ¦ <simple> <operator>
                 <expression>
<simple>     ::= <number>
<operator>   ::= + ¦ - ¦ * ¦ /
```

you force right to left grouping. When parsing $2 + 3 - 4$, because the simple expression on the left must be a number, the only possible interpretation is

```
<expression>
<simple> <operator> <expression>
2 + <expression>
  . . .
```

which groups $3 - 4$. Left to right grouping is more commonly used, but it leads to a more complex definition in Pascal. Thus, to keep this introduction to parsing simple, we will use the right to left definition above.

This definition can be translated into Pascal by creating a procedure for each nonterminal. Parsing a simple expression involves simply reading a number and turning it into a leaf. There are two definitions for an expression, but they both start with <simple>. Thus, you can read a simple expression, and then look for an operator to see whether you should apply the first replacement rule or the second. This leads to the following code:

```
procedure ParseSimple (var Tree: TreePtr);
  var
```

```
     VALUE: integer;
begin
 CharBuff.ReadInt(VALUE);
 NewLeaf(Tree, VALUE);
end; (* ParseSimple *)

procedure ParseExpr (var Tree: TreePtr);
 var
   SimpleExpr: TreePtr;
begin
 ParseSimple(SimpleExpr);
 if CharBuff.Window in ['+', '-', '*', '/'] then begin
   new(Tree);
   Tree^.Left := SimpleExpr;
   CharBuff.ReadChar(Tree^.Operator);
   ParseExpr(Tree^.Right);
   end
 else begin
   Tree := SimpleExpr;
   end; (* If *)
end; (* ParseExpr *)
```

Notice how *ParseExpr* exactly parallels the rule:

```
<expression> ::= <simple> ¦ <simple> <operator>
                 <expression>
```

Each nonterminal is replaced by the appropriate procedure call. How would you modify this BNF to deal with parentheses? Normally the rule above determines how numbers are grouped with their operators. To override this rule, you want to consider a parenthesized expression to be automatically grouped as one item, which means that it has the same atomic status as a number. Thus, you want to introduce parentheses in the definition of a simple expression. Because you can include arbitrarily complex subexpressions inside parentheses, you want to define a simple expression as follows:

```
<simple> ::= <number> ¦ (<expression>)
```

This changes the definition of procedure *ParseSimple* to:

```
procedure ParseSimple (var Tree: TreePtr);
 var
   PAREN: char;
   VALUE: integer;
begin
 if CharBuff.Window = '(' then begin
   CharBuff.ReadChar(PAREN);
   ParseExpr(Tree);
```

```
      CharBuff.ReadChar(PAREN);
    end
  else begin
    CharBuff.ReadInt(VALUE);
    NewLeaf(Tree, VALUE);
  end; (* If *)
end; (* ParseSimple *)
```

Now procedure *ParseSimple* calls *ParseExpr*, and *ParseExpr* calls *ParseSimple*. This is called *mutual recursion*. It causes a problem in Pascal because procedures are supposed to be declared before they are called. You get around this by using a *forward* declaration. With a *forward* declaration, you define the calling conventions of a procedure with its header and the word `forward` in place of its body. You can include the actual definition of the procedure anywhere later in the program, but because this second definition is only defining the body of the procedure, the header should have no parameters in it. To allow the mutual recursion of *ParseSimple* and *ParseExpr*, you would include the following declaration before *ParseSimple*:

```
procedure ParseExpr (var Tree: TreePtr);
forward;
```

and would replace the header in its later definition by

```
procedure ParseExpr;
```

This definition still has a problem. What happens with expressions like

```
2 * 3 + 4
```

Right to left grouping interprets this as `2 * (3 + 4)`. Normally the multiplicative operators (* and /) are given a higher precedence than the additive operators (+ and −). To accomplish this, you need one more nonterminal to distinguish between close-binding operators and loose-binding operators. Instead of defining an expression as a series of simple expressions separated by operators, you define it as a series of subexpressions separated by loose-binding operators that each contain nothing but close-binding operators. These subexpressions are then defined as a series of simple expressions separated by close-binding operators. This leads to the following rules:

```
<expression>       ::= <close> |
                       <close> <loose operator> <expression>
<close>            ::= <simple> |
                       <simple> <close operator> <close>
<simple>           ::= <number> | (<expression>)
<loose operator> ::= + | -
<close operator> ::= * | /
```

This is somewhat counterintuitive. The close-binding operators are said to be of "higher precedence" than the loose-binding operators. Yet, the loose-binding operators appear at the higher level in this definition, which means that they will appear higher in the parse tree. That's because the word "higher" is being used in two different ways. Appearing higher in the parse tree actually means being further away from the actual numbers being bound together. You might describe an auditorium as being divided into rows each of which are divided into seats. The "higher" level of description is the division into rows, but that means that people will end up grouped more closely in the lower level structure (i.e., within a single row).

These definitions are easily translated into Pascal by again writing one procedure paralleling each nonterminal:

```
procedure ParseExpr (var Tree: TreePtr);
forward;

procedure ParseSimple (var Tree: TreePtr);
 var
  PAREN: char;
  VALUE: integer;
begin
 if CharBuff.Window = '(' then begin
   CharBuff.ReadChar(PAREN);
   ParseExpr(Tree);
   CharBuff.ReadChar(PAREN);
  end
 else begin
   CharBuff.ReadInt(VALUE);
   NewLeaf(Tree, VALUE);
  end; (* If *)
end; (* ParseSimple *)

procedure ParseClose (var Tree: TreePtr);
 var
  SimpleExpr: TreePtr;
begin
 ParseSimple(SimpleExpr);
  if CharBuff.Window in ['*', '/'] then begin
   new(Tree);
   Tree^.Left := SimpleExpr;
   CharBuff.ReadChar(Tree^.Operator);
   ParseClose(Tree^.Right);
   end
  else begin
   Tree := SimpleExpr;
  end; (* If *)
end; (* ParseClose *)

procedure ParseExpr;
```

```
        var
          CloseExpr: TreePtr;
        begin
         ParseClose(CloseExpr);
         if CharBuff.Window in ['+', '-'] then begin
           new(Tree);
           Tree^.Left := CloseExpr;
           CharBuff.ReadChar(Tree^.Operator);
           ParseExpr(Tree^.Right);
           end
         else begin
           Tree := CloseExpr;
           end; (* If *)
        end; (* ParseExpr *)
```

5.7. BINARY SEARCH TREES

Now that trees can be seen to have order, the notion of a sorted binary tree makes sense. One such tree is known as a *binary search tree*, which has the property that, given a node, all the data in the left subtree are less than the data in that node, whereas all the data in the right subtree are greater than its own data. Thus, this tree

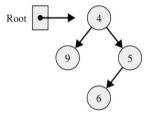

is *not* a binary search tree, because 9 is not less than 4, but the node containing it is in 4's left subtree. Further, 6 is in 5's left subtree, which further violates the rule for binary search trees. For example, the following are two binary search trees that both contain the same data as the above tree:

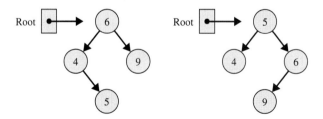

To see why binary search trees are useful, think about an inorder traversal. With an inorder traversal, all the elements in the left subtree are first accessed, followed by the current node, followed by the nodes in the right subtree. Thus, the *PrintInorder* procedure first prints out all the data in the left subtree, then the data in the current node, and last the data in the right subtree. In a binary search tree, though, all the nodes in the left subtree are less than the current node, which is less than all the nodes in the right subtree. Thus, the data in the three parts of the node (the left subtree, the right subtree, and the node itself) will all be output *in order*, relative to each other. Further, since each subtree is also a binary search tree, *PrintInorder* will also print each subtree in order. Thus, given a binary search tree, an inorder traversal will traverse the tree in order. For example, *PrintInorder* called with either of the above binary search trees would yield the following output, which is in sorted order:

    4 5 6 9

5.7.1. Creating a Binary Search Tree

Suppose you want to store the numbers

    8 3 1 20 10 5 4

in a binary search tree. Remember, the rule is that, given a node in the tree, all the data to the left must be less than the current node's data, while all the data to the right must be larger than that data. Initially the tree is empty and you want to insert the 8. The only choice is to just store the 8 in the root:

Next comes the 3. Because 3 is less than 8, the 3 goes in the left subtree:

One is less than 8, so it must go to the left of the 8, and since 1 is also less than 3, it goes to the left of the 3:

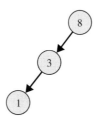

Now, 20 is greater than 8, so it goes to the right of the 8:

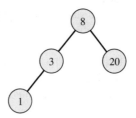

Note that each new element is inserted *as a leaf* in the tree. Although this is not the only way to construct a binary search tree, this method is simple because you simply scan for the correct position and add a leaf. You never need to rearrange the internal structure of the tree. Here are the rest of the steps you would go through to construct the binary search tree for the given data:

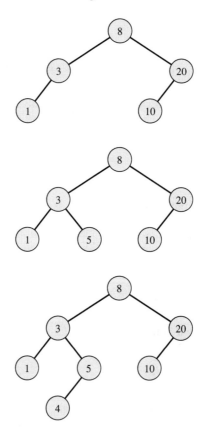

Of course, this is not the only binary search tree for the given data, since binary search trees are not unique. But this one does follow the rule and it is easy to construct.

The code for building a binary search tree in this manner will be discussed in the next section.

5.7.2. Handling Equality

Before writing the code, think about what should happen if two equal numbers are in the binary search tree. Should equal numbers be put in the right or left subtree? Suppose they are put in the left subtree. Now all the numbers in that subtree are less than or equal to the current number. Since they are less than or equal, the numbers that are equal, being the largest numbers, will be visited last in an inorder traversal of that subtree. In fact, they will be traversed just before the current node is, and therefore those equal numbers will be output just before the current node. Since they are equal to the number in the current node, though, that's when they should be output to maintain the order. So placing equal data in the left subtree works fine.

What if, on the other hand, equal numbers are placed in the right subtree? In this case, the right subtree now contains only numbers greater than or equal to the current number, and thus all the numbers that are equal to the current number will be the smallest numbers in that subtree. Thus, an inorder traversal will output them first. Because the procedure will have just output the current node, outputting these equal numbers first will result in a sorted output.

Thus, it doesn't matter in which subtree the equal numbers are placed. The traversal will still access the elements in the correct order.

5.7.3. SELF CHECK EXERCISES

1. Starting with the leftmost number, place the following numbers into a binary search tree. Then output the tree using preorder, inorder, and postorder traversals.

   ```
   20 5 3 25 6 3 1 100
   ```

2. Write a procedure that will output the contents of a binary search tree in *descending* order.

5.8. IMPLEMENTING THE TABLE ADT AS A BINARY SEARCH TREE

You should be growing accustomed to the Table type after learning some of its applications in Chapter 2 and seeing how it can be reimplemented using linked lists in Chapter 4. This chapter shows yet another technique for implementing tables. The next chapter presents an analysis of these different implementations where you'll see that this one is much more efficient than arrays or linked lists for certain critical operations.

Just as the table can be implemented using fairly standard array and linked list implementations, you can use the standard binary tree declarations for this implementation. The basic idea is the same as the binary search trees presented in the previous section. For example, to store a table of simple integers, you would use the following declarations:

```
type
  Typ = ^TableRec;

  TableRec = record
    Data: TableElement.Typ;
    Left, Right: Typ;
  end; (* TableRec *)
```

Some of the table operations are so easy to implement that it makes sense to knock them off immediately. Because an empty tree is represented by a *nil* pointer, *Create* and *Empty* follow easily:

```
procedure Create (var T: Typ);
begin
 T := nil;
end; (* Create *)


function Empty (var T: Typ): boolean;
begin
 Empty := (T = nil);
end; (* Empty *)
```

Most of the other operations are considerably more complex, but you shouldn't move on without first considering how you might adapt existing code to these tasks. First, the simple leaf operations prove useful in almost any tree program, so adapting them to these declarations will probably pay off.

```
procedure NewLeaf (var NewElemPtr: Typ;
        Item: TableElement.Typ);
begin
 new(NewElemPtr);
 NewElemPtr^.Data := Item;
 NewElemPtr^.Left := nil;
 NewElemPtr^.Right := nil;
end; (* NewLeaf *)


function IsLeaf (T: Typ): boolean;
begin
 IsLeaf := (T^.Left = nil) and (T^.Right = nil);
end; (* IsLeaf *)
```

You've actually seen three different traversals for printing the contents of a tree, so *Write* can be obtained simply by choosing the appropriate technique and making the minor adjustments necessary to match these specific declarations. As you saw in the last section, the inorder traversal is the appropriate choice to cause the elements of a binary search tree to be printed in sorted order. Thus, *Write* is implemented as

```
procedure Write (var T: Typ);
begin
 if T <> nil then begin
   Write(T^.Left);
   PrintElement(T^.Data);
   Write(T^.Right);
  end; (* If *)
end; (* Write *)
```

You can easily move through the elements of a linked list, but binary trees are more formidable. As a result, the pattern you see in procedure *Write* can prove helpful in implementing other operations that require visiting all elements of the structure. In particular, the task of cleaning up after a large tree has been grown boils down to finding a way to apply *dispose* to each and every node of the tree. If you think about what happens when you dispose a node, you'll realize that the order you choose for doing so is highly important. If nodes were people, it would be fair to consider the binary tree structure as delicate as the dangerous configuration of having one person holding onto a bar high above the ground with two people hanging onto that person, and four more hanging onto them, eight more hanging onto them, and so on. Obviously, the only orderly way to take apart such a structure is from the bottom up. For example, the root should be the last element disposed. The postorder traversal is just what you need for this application, because it processes both subtrees before the node itself. Thus, *Destroy* can be written as follows.

```
procedure Destroy (var T: Typ);
begin
 if T <> nil then begin
   Destroy(T^.Left);
   Destroy(T^.Right);
   dispose(T);
  end; (* If *)
end; (* Destroy *)
```

This about exhausts the "easy" operations. As with the other table implementations, the operations for finding, deleting, and inserting, prove to be more complex.

5.8.1. Inserting into a Table

Think about how *Insert* might work. Because each subtree of a binary search tree is also a binary search tree, inserting a value into a tree can be reduced to inserting it into one of the subtrees. Following the rule for binary search trees, if a value is less than the current element, it goes to the left. Otherwise it goes to the right.

This process breaks down if the current tree is empty, because there is no current element to compare the value against. Thus, in this case (the base case), you can just insert the new value as the root of the tree. Note that the new element is a leaf in this tree, which means that *NewLeaf* can be used to initialize it.

Thus, inserting a new element into a binary search tree reduces to inserting that element into one of the root's subtrees, unless the tree is empty, in which case the new element is inserted directly:

```
procedure Insert (var T: Typ;
      Item: TableElement.Typ);
begin
 if T = nil then begin
   NewLeaf(T, Item);
   end
 else if Compare(Item, T^.Data) = '<' then begin
   Insert(T^.Left, Item);
   end
 else begin
   Insert(T^.Right, Item);
   end; (* If *)
end; (* Insert *)
```

Notice that function *Compare* is used for comparisons. Recall that using this function instead of direct comparisons increases the flexibility of the Table type, allowing it to store complex data elements and to define unusual definitions for ordering.

5.8.2. Deleting from a Table

Deleting a node from a binary search tree is tricky and involves several steps. First, the desired node must be found. Either the root of the tree is the desired node, or it's in the left or right subtree (if it's in the tree at all). Thus, the problem of finding the node reduces to checking to see if it is the root. If it is, then the node has been found. Otherwise it can be found in one of the two subtrees, and the correct subtree can be determined by comparing the desired value with the root's value.

Because searching a subtree for a given node is just a simpler version of the original problem, a recursive call can be used to search the subtrees. This recursive case breaks down if the tree is empty, because then there is no root node to compare with. In this case, the given node is clearly not in the tree and the recursion stops.

Thus, there are four cases:

1. The given value is equal to the root, which means that the desired node has been found.

2. The given value is less than the root, in which case it must be in the left subtree.

3. The given value is greater than or equal to the root, and so it must be to the right.

4. The tree is empty, in which case the given value is not in the tree.

The fourth case is not supposed to happen, because the precondition of *Delete* promises that the value appears somewhere in the table. Thus, this procedure does not handle this case. Error detection and recovery issues are discussed in detail in Chapter 8. Thus, these cases produce the following code:

```
procedure Delete (var T: Typ;
      Item: TableElement.Typ);
begin
  if Compare (Item, T^.Data) = '=' then begin
    <Delete the node referenced by T>
  end
  else if Compare (Item, T^.Data) = '<' then begin
    Delete(T^.Left, Item);
  end
  else begin
    Delete(T^.Right, Item);
  end; (* If *)
end; (* Delete *)
```

Consider the problem of deleting 9 from the following tree. You start at the root and compare it to 7. It's greater, so a recursive call is made using the right pointer. On that recursive call, the new root to compare against is 9, and a match is found. At that point, the parameter *T* corresponds to the overall root's *Right* pointer field, pointing to the 9 node.

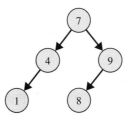

The tricky thing about deleting a node is that the resulting tree must also be a binary search tree. There are again four cases to consider:

1. The node is a leaf, in which case it can be deleted because the resulting tree, an empty tree, is clearly a binary search tree.

2. The node has only a left subtree (its right subtree is empty). Then the resulting tree just becomes the left subtree, which, because it was a binary search tree before the deletion, must still be a binary search tree.

3. The node has only a right subtree, in which case the right subtree becomes the new tree.

4. The last, and trickiest, case occurs when neither subtree is empty. This case will be dealt with momentarily.

Thus, putting these cases together yields the following procedure that, given a pointer to a node in a binary search tree, deletes that node while preserving sorted order. Notice that the procedure must be careful in how it disposes of *BadNode* because some of the cases require assigning *BadNode* a new value using its left and right subtrees. If you dispose first, you lose the subtrees, and if you assign first, you lose the node. This problem often comes up when disposing of nodes and is easily solved by introducing a local variable for temporary storage.

```
procedure Remove (var BadNode: Typ);
 var
  TEMPNODE: Typ;
begin
 TEMPNODE := BadNode;
 if IsLeaf(BadNode) then begin
   BadNode := nil;
  end
 else if (BadNode^.Left = nil) then begin
   BadNode := BadNode^.Right;
  end
 else if (BadNode^.Right = nil) then begin
   BadNode := BadNode^.Left;
  end
 else begin
   <Delete the node for the case of two non-empty
   subtrees>
  end; (* If *)
 dispose(TEMPNODE);
end; (* Remove *)
```

The problem is that the final case generates two separate binary search trees that must be merged into one. Suppose you want to delete the value 5 from the following tree:

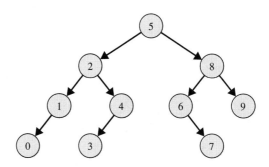

For this tree, an inorder traversal yields the following ordering:

    0, 1, 2, 3, 4, 5, 6, 7, 8, 9

which is the correct ordering of values from lowest to highest. Thus, when 5 is deleted, the ordering must be maintained, and an inorder traversal should visit elements in this order:

    0, 1, 2, 3, 4, 6, 7, 8, 9

The key to a simple solution is to recognize that this ordering is the only constraint you are bound by. It doesn't matter what node ends up at the root or what structure the tree has as long as it produces this sequence from an inorder traversal.

You are considering the case of removing a branch node. This is inherently difficult because pulling out such a central node leaves you two potentially large subtrees to put back together. The simpler approach is to find a node in a less central position to switch places with the node you're deleting, allowing you to leave the current structure mostly intact by deleting a different node whose disappearance is easier to manage. This is the same strategy any sane business follows when a high-level administrator leaves the company. Such a loss often generates chaos, but rather than trying to rearrange the entire staff into a brand new structure, most often the company will find someone to replace the person who left.

A good strategy for locating a suitable replacement in a binary search tree is to look for a node that is close in magnitude to the other node, but still somewhat smaller, similar to the usual business practice of looking for a "junior" version of the same person. For example, where would you find the node just smaller than the one you're trying to delete (i.e., the one visited just before this one by an inorder traversal)? Because it's smaller, it must appear in the left subtree. But to be the largest value in the left subtree, it must appear more to the right than to the left of other nodes in the left subtree. Thus, it is the rightmost node of the left subtree. Moreover, it is guaranteed to be easy to delete, because it's right subtree must be empty. [2]

This pinpoints a node that can trade places with the node to be deleted, allowing it to be deleted instead. Thus, in the example, 5 can be easily removed by having it switch places with the 4 node and then deleting that node instead of the root. After switching places you get The first tree shown at the top of page 248, and then you can easily delete the value 5 now that it has an empty right subtree (although notice that because its left subtree is not empty, it moves up to replace the deleted node):

---

[2] If not, that subtree would contain values larger than the parent's that are also contained in the left subtree of the node to be deleted, which means they would have been selected instead of the parent in the first place.

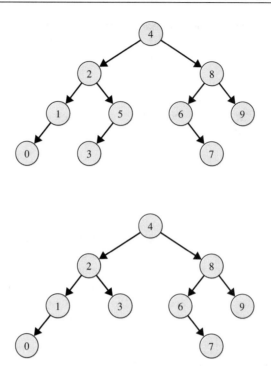

The original 5's node is therefore not actually deleted. To program a solution for this approach you have to locate the rightmost node in the left subtree. Once you've found the proper node, you might as well process it entirely. Therefore, instead of actually swapping its value with the root's value, you might as well go ahead and delete it, returning its data field so that the root can be assigned the proper new value. In the above example, the procedure would delete the 4 node and return its value so that the root can be given the value 4. This slightly different formulation produces a procedure that performs a general enough manipulation that it might find application in solving other binary tree tasks. For this particular task the procedure is used to delete nodes from subtrees, but in essence, the procedure deletes the maximum value stored in any binary search tree, returning its data value.

Finding the rightmost node is fairly easy. Once you position yourself at the root of the left subtree, just go right as many times as you can. This can be solved using a loop, but as with linked lists, the powerful combination of var parameters and recursion leads to a more elegant solution. The base case is when you have nothing more to pursue in the right direction (i.e., when the right pointer is *nil*). In the recursive case, you simply follow the right branch in search of a solution (a simpler problem because it places you closer to the desired node). The node you're searching for has no right subtree, but because it might have a left subtree, you have to reset it to whatever value its left subtree has. As with *Remove*, to both process the node and dispose of it, this procedure requires a temporary variable.

```
procedure DeleteMax (var Tree: Typ;
        var ItsValue: TableElement.Typ);
var
  TEMPNODE: Typ;
begin
  if Tree^.Right <> nil then begin
    DeleteMax(Tree^.Right, ItsValue);
    end


  else begin
    ItsValue := Tree^.Data;
    TEMPNODE := Tree;
    Tree := Tree^.Left;
    dispose(TEMPNODE);
    end; (* If *)
  end; (* DeleteMax *)
```

Applying this procedure, you can easily complete procedures *Remove* and *Delete*. But because this procedure does its own disposing, you have to rework procedure *Remove* to place this case in its own branch, allowing the other three branches to continue to directly dispose of *BadNode*.

```
procedure Remove (var BadNode: Typ);
  var
    TEMPNODE: Typ;
    ITSVALUE: TableElement.Typ;
begin
  if (BadNode^.Left <> nil) and (BadNode^.Right <> nil)
  then begin
    DeleteMax(BadNode^.Left, ITSVALUE);
    BadNode^.Data := ITSVALUE;
    end
  else begin
    TEMPNODE := BadNode;
    if IsLeaf(BadNode) then begin
      BadNode := nil;
      end
    else if (BadNode^.Left = nil) then begin
      BadNode := BadNode^.Right;
      end
    else if (BadNode^.Right = nil) then begin
      BadNode := BadNode^.Left;
      end;
    dispose(TEMPNODE);
    end; (* If *)
  end; (* Remove *)
```

```
            procedure Delete (var T: Typ;
                  Item: TableElement.Typ);
            begin
             if Compare(Item, T^.Data) = '=' then begin
               Remove(T);
             end
             else if Compare(Item, T^.Data) = '<' then begin
               Delete(T^.Left, Item);
             end
             else begin
               Delete(T^.Right, Item);
             end; (* If *)
            end; (* Delete *)
```

5.8.3. Searching a Table

InTable and *FindMin* are almost the only operations left to implement. They turn out to be easier than deleting, because they don't require reorganizing a tree. Also, deleting involves locating a value and then removing it, which means that *InTable* is, in fact, simply a subtask of *Delete*. Thus, you can generate *InTable* with almost no effort by adapting *Delete*. The only differences are that you immediately return when you find the value or hit a dead end rather than proceeding to delete that node, and you are defining a function rather than a procedure, which leads to slightly different recursive calls. Thus, *InTable* can be written as follows:

```
            function InTable (var T: Typ;
                  Item: TableElement.Typ): boolean;
            begin
             if T = nil then begin
               InTable := false;
             end
             else if Compare(Item, T^.Data) = '=' then begin
               InTable := true;
             end
             else if Compare(Item, T^.Data) = '<' then begin
               InTable := InTable(T^.Left, Item);
             end
             else begin
               InTable := InTable(T^.Right, Item);
             end; (* If *)
            end; (* InTable *)
```

It is generally not a good idea to have two subprograms with such obvious duplication. But the task of generalizing them is complex, and most approaches fail to yield satisfying results. This is partly due to the fact that one is a procedure and one is a function, but it has more to do with a certain tedious property of programming with pointers. This is easiest to explain through example.

The simplest approach would be to factor out the common code that determines a value's location: either a pointer to the node or *nil* if it isn't present. Thus, you might try writing a function *Location* called by both *Delete* and *InTable* to avoid the redundant code. Unfortunately, *InTable* can be written this way, but not *Delete*. It isn't enough for *Delete* to know the location of a node. That provides only a *copy* of the actual tree pointer and, thus, changing it does not change the tree. Section 4.8.2 used a linked list example to explain in detail this confusing and frustrating limitation of pointer structures. *Delete* gets around the problem by using recursion and var parameters. There are ways to solve this problem, but most lead to even more tedious and dangerous repetition than you see in these two subprograms. For example, you could return the location of the *parent* of the node you're looking for, allowing you to make references to *Parentˆ.Left* and *Parentˆ.Right*, just as you solved this problem with linked lists by referring to *Tempˆ.Next* rather than *Temp*. But then you have to decide whether the node is to the left or to the right, and you have to deal with nasty special cases where the parent doesn't exist or the where the tree is empty.

5.8.4. Finishing the Table Implementation

Only two operations remain: *FindMin* and *Extract*. *FindMin* is related to *DeleteMax* in the same way that *InTable* is related to *Delete*, with one extra complication that it wants to search in the opposite direction. The reversal is accomplished by using the opposite tests in if/then/else constructs and by interchanging left and right. If you do this to *DeleteMax* and eliminate its code for deleting the node, you get

```
procedure FindMin (var T: Typ;
          var Item: TableElement.Typ);
begin
 if Tˆ.Left <> nil then begin
   FindMin(Tˆ.Left, Item);
  end
 else begin
   Item := Tˆ.Data;
  end; (* If *)
end; (* FindMin *)
```

Procedure *Extract* simply involves initializing the new table to be empty and then recursively searching the table for all elements to be extracted:

```
procedure Extract (var T: Typ;
        Item: TableElement.Typ);

  procedure Explore (T: Typ);
    begin
     if T <> nil then begin
```

```
      if Compare(Item, T^.Data) <> '>' then begin
        if Compare(Item, T^.Data) = '=' then begin
          Insert(NewT, T^.Data);
        end; (* If *)
        Explore(T^.Left);
        Explore(T^.Right);
      end; (* If *)
    end; (* If *)


  begin
    NewT := nil;
    Explore(T);
  end; (* Extract *)
```

5.8.5. SELF CHECK EXERCISES

1. The *Delete* procedure, when asked to delete a node with two nonempty children, instead deletes the rightmost node of the desired node's left subtree, moving that item into the desired node. What other node could be used instead of the rightmost node of the left subtree? Why?

5.9. SUMMARY OF KEY POINTS

- A *tree* is a connected graph with the property that no pair of nodes has two paths joining them. Every tree has a single *root* node, which is the only node that has no *parent*. Nodes in *binary trees* may have at most two children, the *left child* and the *right child*. *Branch* nodes have children whereas *leaves* do not.

- Since trees are nonlinear structures, they do not have the natural ordering that linked lists have, and thus there is no single obvious way to traverse the structure. *Preorder, inorder,* and *postorder* are the most common traversal strategies.

- *Parsing* consists of verifying correct input while transforming it into a more convenient form. You can easily represent arithmetic expressions using binary trees in which the operators are stored in the branch nodes and the numbers are stored in the leaves.

- Binary trees can be used to efficiently store information by imposing an "ordering" on the data in the tree. A *binary search tree* is a binary tree in which every node exhibits the property that all nodes to the left of the node contain data whose value is less than that node's data, while the nodes to the right store the data larger than the current node's data. Thus, an inorder traversal will traverse a binary search tree in sorted order. Binary search trees provide efficient insert, delete, and lookup of data.

- A binary search tree implementation of the Table ADT is more efficient than a linked list implementation. Efficiency considerations are the focus of the next chapter.

5.10. PROGRAMMING EXERCISES

All the following problems, unless otherwise stated, assume the following data structure definition:

```
type
  TreePtr = ^TreeRec;

  TreeRec = record
    Data: integer;
    Left, Right: TreePtr;
  end; (* TreeRec *)
```

1. A node in a binary tree is a *left child* if it is to the left of its parent. For example, in the following diagram the nodes containing **5, 3, 1, 6,** and **9** are the five left children.

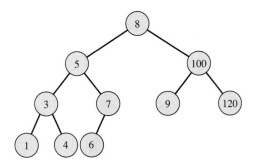

Write a function, with the header below, which takes a tree as input and returns the number of left children in the tree.
Here is the header:

```
function NumLeft (Tree: TreePtr): integer;
```

2. You are to write a procedure, with the header below, which will take in a binary tree whose *Data* fields are uninitialized and will set them such that an inorder traversal

will produce a "countdown," (i.e., an inorder traversal of a tree of n nodes will first visit a node numbered n, then a node numbered $n - 1$, etc., and ending with a node numbered one). For example, given the following tree:

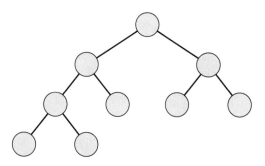

your procedure would number the nodes as follows:

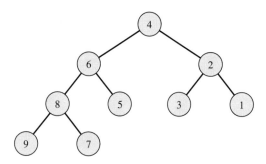

Here is the header:

```
procedure NumberTree (Tree: TreePtr);
```

As a hint, you may find writing an auxiliary procedure helpful.

3. Write a procedure with the following header:

```
procedure Mirror (TreeIn: TreePtr; var TreeOut: TreePtr);
```

which takes a tree pointed to by the *TreeIn* parameter and returns a tree, via the *TreeOut* parameter, which is the mirror image. As an example, suppose *TreeIn* initially points to the following tree:

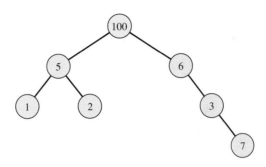

When the procedure terminates, *TreeIn* should still be pointing to the same tree, and *TreeOut* should be pointing to the following tree:

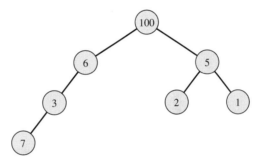

4. A *complete* binary tree is one in which every node either

   a. is a leaf, or

   b. has two nonempty children.

   Write a boolean function that is passed a pointer to a binary tree and returns *true* if the tree is complete and *false* otherwise.

5. A *completely balanced* binary tree is one with the following characteristics:

   a. The root is complete (see the above question for a definition of a complete node).

   b. The root's subtrees have equal height (see above for definition of the height of a node).

   c. The root's subtrees are both completely balanced.

Write a boolean function that is passed a pointer to a binary tree and returns *true* if that tree is completely balanced and *false* otherwise.

6. Write a procedure that will print out the data in a tree in *breadth-first* order, i.e., each level is printed out from left to right before the next level. As a hint, you might find a Queue useful.

7. Write a procedure that, given a postorder and an inorder traversal of a binary tree as input, will output the corresponding preorder traversal. For example, if the input file contains

```
BADECHGF
ABCDEFGH
```

these traversals correspond to the following tree:

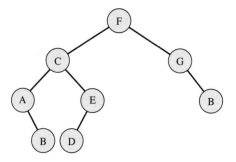

and you would thus output the following preorder traversal:

```
FCABEDGH
```

8. A *fully parenthesized logical expression* is defined by the following grammar:

```
<exp> ::= (<exp> V <exp>) ¦ (<exp> ^ <exp>) ¦
          (~ <exp>) ¦ T ¦ F
```

For example

```
T     (TVF)     ((~F)^T)     (~(FV(F^T)))
```

are all legal fully parenthesized logical expressions. A parse tree storing an expression has the following components:

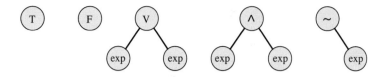

For example, $(\text{T}^\wedge(\sim\text{T}))$ has the following parse tree:

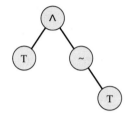

9. a. Show parse trees for each of the given expressions:

```
1) Expression:    T
2) Expression:   (TVF)
3) Expression:  ((~F)^T)
4) Expression:  (~(FV(F^T)))
```

b. Suppose you are given the following data structure definition:

```
type
  TreePtr = ^TreeRec;
  TreeRec = record
    Data: char;
    Left, Right: TreePtr;
  end; (* TreeRec *)
```

Write a procedure, with the header below, that will read a fully parenthesized logical expression in from a file and will build a parse tree for that expression. Here is the procedure header:

```
procedure Parse (var Infile: text; var Root: TreePtr);
```

c. Write a procedure, with the header below, which takes a parse tree of a fully parenthesized logical expression in as a parameter and writes out the expression to an output file. The procedure has the following header:

```
procedure PrintExpression (var Outfile: text; Root: TreePtr);
```

d. A logical expression is either *true (T)* or *false (F)*. The values *T* and *F* are the atomic values in this system. The logical connectives *and* (^), *or* (V), and *not* (~) combine expressions to form a single truth value, as shown by the following truth tables (where *p* and *q* are arbitrary logical expressions):

p	q	(p∧q)
T	T	T
T	F	F
F	T	F
F	F	F

p	q	(p∨q)
T	T	T
T	F	T
F	T	T
F	F	F

p	(~p)
T	F
F	T

For example, the expression

```
((~F)V(F^T))
```

evaluates to *true*. Write a function, with the header below, that takes a parse tree containing a logical expression (using the data structure from part *b*) and returns the truth value of that expression.

```
function Eval (Root: TreePtr) : boolean;
```

5.11. PROGRAMMING PROJECTS

1. Implement the *Cursor-Table* ADT described in the Chapter 4 Programming Projects, except use a binary search tree as the underlying structure, rather than a linked list.

2. Before telephones and computers, people used the telegraph to communicate over distances. Because the telegraph could only beep, they used sequences of short and long beeps (dots and dashes), encoded according to Morse Code, to transmit meaningful messages. In Morse Code, each letter is assigned a unique combination of dots and dashes. For this project, your program will take in two input files. The first will contain the Morse Code, with one letter per line. Each line will contain the letter, followed by a space, and ending with that letter's code. The second file will contain a number of lines, each of which will be either a line of Morse Code, or a line of English text. Your program should generate an output file that contains the translation of the "phrases" file. Although translating English to Morse Code

is relatively fast with an array, translating Morse Code to English efficiently is somewhat more difficult. Rather than storing the code in a linked list or an array and searching that structure for each letter, you can instead store the code in a binary tree. Each node in the tree will have two pointers, one going toward the *dot* side and one toward the *dash*. These are analogous to the *left* and *right* pointers used in the book. For example, consider this mini-tree:

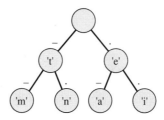

By following the pointers (dash is left and dot is right) you can see that the code for 'm' is '- -', the code for 'a' is '.-', and so on. This tree has 6 letters. Yours will have all 26.

3. For this project you're going to write a guessing game; the game will ask the player to think of an animal and then will try to determine which animal the player has in mind by asking certain yes/no questions. Based on the answers to the early questions, the game can refine its guesses until it's asking very specific questions about the animal's characteristics. Of course, since the players will probably be somewhat sophisticated, there's a good chance they may have in mind some animal with which the game is not familiar; the game may exhaust its knowledge base without having guessed the animal. That's when your friends get to teach the game about the animal they've chosen.

Here's an example of what part of a game session might look like:

```
Please think of an animal . . .

Is it a dog
Y or N > n
I give up then.
What is your animal?
salmon
Please give me a yes/no question that will distinguish your
animal from a dog.
Does it live in the water?
And what would the answer be for your animal?
Y or N > y
Had enough for today?
Y or N > n
Please think of an animal . . .
```

```
Does it live in the water?
Y or N > y

Is it a fish
Y or N > n
I give up then.
What is your animal?
whale
Please give me a yes/no question that will distinguish your
animal from a fish.
Does it breathe under water?
And what would the answer be for your animal?
Y or N > n
Had enough for today?
Y or N > y
```

The data structure used by the program is a binary tree. Each branch node of the tree contains a yes/no question, with one branch representing animals for which the answer to the question is yes, and the other branch representing animals for which the answer to the question is no. The animals are stored in the leaves.

4. Fully parenthesized logical expressions were defined in the Programming Exercises. You can also define non-fully parenthesized logical expressions, in which *not* ($\sim$) has the highest precedence, followed by *and* ($\char94$) and then *or* (V). Moreover, these expressions may include *logical variables*, which are represented by lowercase letters and may be either *true* or *false*. The following grammar defines legal expressions of this form:

```
<expr>    ::= <close> V <expr> ¦ <close>

<close>   ::= <simple> ^ <close> ¦ <simple>

<simple>  ::= <lowercase letter> ¦ T ¦ F ¦ ~ <simple> ¦
              ( <expr> )
```

The operators ($\char94$, V, $\sim$) yield the same results that they did in the Programming Exercise for fully parenthesized expressions. Because these expressions contain variables, you cannot always know the value of an expression without knowing the values of the variables. A *truth table* shows all the possible assignments of logical values to the variables, and thus shows all the values an expression can have. For example, the following expression:

```
aVb^~a
```

has this truth table:

a	b	$(a \lor (b \land (\sim a)))$
T	T	T
T	F	T
F	T	T
F	F	F

You are to write a program that will read in legal expressions from a file, with one expression per line, and generate a truth table for each expression.

6

SORTING, SEARCHING, AND ALGORITHM ANALYSIS

6.1. INTRODUCTION

Most of the material in the previous chapters focused on software engineering principles and new programming techniques. This chapter provides your first concentrated exposure to the kind of analysis more typical of computer science by introducing the notion of program and algorithm *efficiency*.

EFFICIENCY

. . . .

A relative measure of the resources consumed by a program or algorithm. A program that runs quickly is said to be *time efficient*, whereas one that requires a minimal amount of memory is considered *space efficient*.

The details of formal analysis often obscure the highly intuitive techniques used to determine efficiency. Thus, the chapter begins by informally introducing basic terminology, using simple examples that illustrate fundamental concepts. These ideas are further explained by examining the two most common strategies used when searching a list for a specific value. Again, these algorithms are sufficiently straightforward that they can be analyzed using an intuitive rather than a formal approach.

Building on the conceptual framework you will acquire in these early sections, the chapter then introduces formal methods for the analysis of time efficiency. You will see how to analyze iterative algorithms by applying fairly simple counting techniques. You will then spend considerable time learning a somewhat more complicated counting technique that greatly simplifies the analysis of many recursive algorithms.

The latter half of the chapter demonstrates how these formal techniques can be applied to the previously discussed searching algorithms and to common sorting algorithms. The discussion of sorting concludes with a technique called *hashing*, which greatly improves the normal efficiency of sorting and searching by creating a special structure called a *hash table*. The chapter closes with a last look at the Table ADT, analyzing the efficiency of a hash table implementation and the various implementations you have seen previously.

6.2. ANALYZING TIME EFFICIENCY

As computers have become more and more a part of everyday life, virtually everyone has been exposed to the notion of fast versus slow programs. For example, microcomputer owners are frequently frustrated by the amount of time some of their seemingly simple programs require. Because most of these personal computers can perform only one task at a time, their owners are acutely aware of how long they are forced to sit idle by their machine, waiting for a program to finish executing.

As a result, almost every software company goes out of its way to stress that its program is "fast and efficient, the best product of its kind." Such statements are meaningless because marketing people who find the marketplace competitive and uncertain will usually spout such phrases with the same kind of instinctual reaction that causes most of us to pull back when we touch something very hot.

So how can you make a truly meaningful statement about the speed of a program? The computer science approach starts with simple scientific inquiry. Rather than relying on anecdotal evidence, you go out into the real world and collect real data. Then you look for observable trends and hypothesize about their causes. Given a program, you could observe how its execution time varies when executed on different computers, or given an algorithm, you could observe how its execution time varies when coded in different programming languages. Such observations might tell you about the efficiency of specific computers or specific programming languages, but they won't shed any light on the efficiency of the underlying program or algorithm. Instead, you should limit yourself to one computer and one programming language and observe how execution time varies with different inputs.

6.2.1. Growth Rate as a Measure of Efficiency

As the size of program input grows, so, generally, does the running time. By observing how execution time varies with input size, you can determine the *growth rate* of the program or algorithm, usually expressed in terms of n, where n is a measure of input size or complexity.

The growth rate of a program is an important measure of efficiency because it predicts how much time will be required for very large inputs. For example, the following table compares execution times of different length inputs for three sorting techniques presented later in the chapter.

Execution Time (seconds) versus Input Size for Sorting Algorithms

Algorithm	10	100	250	500	1,000	2,500	5,000	10,000
Merge sort	0.012	0.043	0.109	0.234	0.497	1.38	2.99	6.33
Quicksort	0.011	0.031	0.070	0.138	0.284	0.74	1.56	3.31
Selection Sort	0.011	0.053	0.266	1.020	4.030	25.00	102.00	410.00

For small n the times are nearly identical, but as n gets larger, there is a difference. From this table it appears that for large sorting tasks, Quicksort is better than merge sort and merge sort is better than selection sort. This is the most direct conclusion you can draw from the table. But if you analyze the data carefully enough, you can discover other significant trends.

One way to categorize objects is by their function: clothing, food, books, and so on. Computer scientists categorize algorithms and subprograms the same way: sorting procedures, searching procedures, numerical functions, and so on. People also categorize by similar strengths and weaknesses: washable items, fragile objects, flammable materials, and so on. The story of the three little pigs explains why straw houses can fall down easily while wooden houses withstand almost anything but a huff-and-a-puff, and brick houses are best of all because they survive even that punishment.

Algorithms can also be categorized in this way, grouping together those with similar limitations or similar resilient behavior under stress. In particular, algorithms are grouped by their growth rate. For example, look at what you get when, for each input size, you calculate the ratio of execution times for the different algorithms.

Ratios for Sorting Times

Ratio	10	100	250	500	1,000	2,500	5,000	10,000
Merge/Quick	1.09	1.39	1.56	1.70	1.75	1.86	1.92	1.91
Selection/Quick	1.00	1.71	3.81	7.38	14.20	33.70	65.60	1243.00
Selection/Merge	0.92	1.22	2.44	4.36	8.10	18.20	34.30	64.90

Because the ratio between selection sort and the other two sorts gets progressively worse, you know that it must differ in a fundamental way (like a straw house that blows down while two brick houses remain standing). The opposite is true of the ratio of merge sort to Quicksort, which seems to be converging to a value around 2.2. Despite the fact that these two algorithms are quite different, they exhibit *identical* growth rates (like two houses that withstand the same pressures because they are both made of brick, even though they might be quite different in design). This similarity is much more important than the fact that Quicksort is usually twice as fast. You can worry about how to make your straw house twice as strong, but you won't beat The Big Bad Wolf until you realize that you can accomplish more by switching to a new *kind* of house, recognizing that wooden houses are *by nature* stronger than straw houses, and that brick houses are by nature stronger still.

This allows you to group algorithms by growth rate, but how do you characterize such groups? The data above is again useful, but this time, instead of comparing different algorithms for similarity, you should compare different times for the same algorithm to better understand its growth. The following tables list the ratios that result when the input is doubled and when it is increased tenfold.

Sorting Growth Rates for Doubling Input

Algorithm	500/250	1,000/500	5,000/2,500	10,000/5,000
Merge sort	2.14	2.05	2.17	2.12
Quicksort	1.98	2.05	2.10	2.12
Selection Sort	3.83	3.95	4.09	4.01

Sorting Growth Rates for Tenfold Increase of Input

Algorithm	100/10	1,000/100	2,500/250	5,000/500	10,000/1,000
Merge sort	3.58	11.56	12.66	12.78	12.74
Quicksort	2.82	9.16	10.57	11.30	11.65
Selection Sort	4.82	76.04	93.98	100.00	101.70

These tables exhibit a highly uniform pattern. The first column of the second table doesn't fit the rest of the data, but that merely indicates that these algorithms need to warm up a bit before they hit their stride and settle into the pattern you see everywhere else. Merge sort and Quicksort have identical growth rates. Twice as much input requires a little more than twice as much time while ten times as much input takes about 12 or 13 times longer. For selection sort, twice as much input takes 4 times longer while 10 times as much input takes 100 times longer.

The fact that squaring 2 yields 4 and squaring 10 yields 100 is too much of a coincidence to ignore. It implies that the growth rate for selection sort can be characterized as n^2. A quick check of other values verifies that increasing input by a factor of 4 increases time by about 16 (15.15 going from 250 to 1,000 and 16.4 going from 2,500 to 10,000), increasing input by a factor of 5 increases time by about 25 (25.3 from 1,000 to 5,000), and so on.

The growth rate of selection sort can, in fact, be characterized as n^2. More precisely, increasing the input by a factor of m increases the time required by approximately m^2. Later in the chapter you'll see how you could figure this out without making any tables, analyzing the code itself.

Characterizing an algorithm's efficiency using a function like n^2 is another application of abstraction. Rather than analyzing specific properties of specific algorithms, computer scientists use growth rate functions to consider general properties common to all algorithms with a certain growth rate. Thus, as you'll see in the next section, analyzing the efficiency of a program or algorithm reduces to finding an appropriate characterization for the growth rate.

Before leaving this subject, though, consider the aspects of running time that are ignored by growth rate. For example, most routines have an initialization segment that must execute regardless of the size of the input. For small *n*, this (and other) fixed costs can dominate the running time. Thus, it is not always inappropriate to choose an algorithm with a larger growth rate (a straw house), because for small applications it might prove more useful either because of its simplicity or because it actually performs better for small inputs.

6.2.2. Big Oh and the Notion of Complexity

When analyzing the efficiency of an algorithm or program, your goal is to find a function $f(n)$ that expresses the growth rate. This function is used to describe the *complexity* of the algorithm and is sometimes referred to as the *complexity function*.

> **COMPLEXITY**
> . . . .
> A measure of efficiency, usually understood to mean time efficiency, although the concept applies equally well to memory efficiency. Specified by the mathematical function that best characterizes how time varies as a function of input (usually in terms of n, the size of input).

Given an algorithm, how do you choose the function that "best" characterizes how time varies with input? You might think it best to provide as many details as possible. With this approach, you would realize that no simple mathematical function will give the exact running time for every possible input, so you might instead list actual times for each possible input, as in the previous tables. This is a mistake, because "characterizing" is not the same as "describing."

You should apply abstraction principles when characterizing so that you eliminate unimportant details, presenting only essential information. If someone asks you to characterize how you spend your days, you wouldn't say, "I'm usually in school, except for when I'm on vacation and traveling, and except for days when I'm sick, and except for that day I skipped class to listen to Jesse Jackson, and except for gorgeous days that I might choose to spend with my significant other (if I ever manage to find one), and except for my baby years before kindergarten which I don't remember very well, and except for . . ." In this case, the "best" response is probably something simple, as in, "I go to school." This is the most accurate and succinct description of how you spend most days and what you see as your primary activity.

The same is true with complexity functions. You should simplify whenever possible. Here are some general guidelines for doing so:

- The real world is an uncertain place, so even if you are willing to gather the details, you won't be able to predict running time precisely. Describe the most general pattern. Imagine a scatter plot of times for various values of n. You want to do the equivalent of *curve fitting*, finding the smooth curve suggested by the pattern of points.

- If one of the larger linebackers from your school's football team is going to step on a scale while dressed in street clothes and reading a textbook, what would you concentrate on to predict the weight reported by the scale:

the clothes, the textbook, or the linebacker? The football player dominates the result, so you pay attention to him. Similarly, if your function has more than one additive term, eliminate all but the most significant. For example, $0.0001x^2 + 999x + 3497$ should be simplified to $0.0001x^2$ because for large values of x, x^2 far exceeds the other terms in magnitude, even when it is multiplied by a small number and x is multiplied by a large number.

- Even if you could exactly predict the execution time of your program, you'd have to give different answers for different computers. For example, a large mainframe might require $2.34n^2$ seconds whereas a microcomputer requires $974.6n^2$ seconds. Constants like these detract from the overall function. Thus, you should eliminate constants, reporting the complexity function as simply n^2.

- Logarithms in one base can be converted to another base with an appropriate constant multiplier ($\log_b(x) = \log_c(x)/\log_c(b)$). You don't care about constants, so you should generally use the function log even if you know a specific base, as in $\log_2$ or ln.

In essence, the complexity function, as in the football player example, is the "heaviest" term—the greatest single predictor of execution time for large values of n. The complexity function is usually expressed using *Big Oh notation* where $f(n)$ is listed instead as $O(f(n))$.

The formal definition of Big Oh is not presented here because it is somewhat confusing and not terribly important to the presentation in this chapter. All you need to understand is that Big Oh is used to express the idea of complexity. Saying "This algorithm is $O(n^2)$" is equivalent to saying, "The complexity function of this algorithm is n^2," or that, "The growth rate of this algorithm is *on the order of n^2*," or that, "This algorithm grows no faster than n^2."

By simplifying complexity functions as much as possible, you find that some of them appear over and over again as the complexity of many different algorithms. Each such function defines a *complexity class* of algorithms with similar growth rates. For example, merge sort and Quicksort discussed previously are in one complexity class, which explains why they exhibit similar behavior, while selection sort is in another, which explains why it behaves so differently.

6.2.3. Typical Complexity Classes

Within a single complexity class, some algorithms will be faster than others (e.g., the previous data suggest that Quicksort is twice as fast as merge sort). But as in the three little pigs example, you can achieve much more drastic improvements in efficiency by choosing an algorithm from a different complexity class. For example, the following table shows how five of the most common complexity classes grow. It indicates how long ago you would have had to start a program executing in order to have it finish now, assuming each step requires one microsecond (μsec means microsecond, msec means millisecond).

Runtime to Finish Now, 1 μsec Operation, Various Complexity Classes

n	$O(log(n))$	$O(n)$	$O(n\ log(n))$	$O(n^2)$	$O(n^3)$	$O(2^n)$
10	3.3 μsec	10 μsec	33 μsec	100.0 μsec	1 msec	1 msec
20	4.3 μsec	20 μsec	86 μsec	400.0 μsec	8 msec	1 sec
30	4.9 μsec	30 μsec	147 μsec	900.0 μsec	27 msec	18 min
40	5.3 μsec	40 μsec	213 μsec	1.6 msec	60 msec	13 days
50	5.6 μsec	50 μsec	282 μsec	2.5 msec	125 msec	36 years
60	5.9 μsec	60 μsec	354 μsec	3.6 msec	216 msec	since Cro-Magnon Man
70	6.1 μsec	70 μsec	429 μsec	4.9 msec	343 msec	since last dinosaur
80	6.3 μsec	80 μsec	506 μsec	6.4 msec	512 msec	two big bangs ago
90	6.5 μsec	90 μsec	584 μsec	8.1 msec	729 msec	39 billion millenia
100	6.7 μsec	100 μsec	664 μsec	10.0 msec	1 sec	402 trillion centuries
1,000	10.0 μsec	1 msec	10 msec	1.0 sec	16.7 min	3×10^{298} years
10,000	13.0 μsec	10 msec	132 msec	1.7 min	11.6 days	beginning of time
100,000	17.0 μsec	100 msec	1.7 sec	2.8 hr	31.7 years	pre-time void

You can see that some functions grow much more rapidly than others and, in fact, the running time for algorithms which are $O(2^n)$ grows so quickly that they are considered *intractable,* meaning that it is not possible to solve a nontrivial problem completely because of the time required. These complexity classes are so common that virtually all of the programs in this book are from one of them.

The complexity "log (n)" is sometimes harder to recognize than the others, so it deserves special comment. It most often occurs when the problem size is halved on each step.

```
    n    n/2  n/2/2  n/2/2/2   ...   n/2/2/2.../2
    ↑    ↑     ↑       ↑                   ↑
  start  1st   2nd     3rd      ...       kth
         step  step    step               step
```

Once you reduce to a problem size of 1, you can't reduce any further. In worst case, then, the kth step is dealing with a problem of size 1. That means that n divided by 2 k times is 1, or $2^k = n$. By definition, $k = log_2(n)$. Thus, log (n) is the complexity of operations like these because that's how many times you must divide n by 2 to get 1.

Here is a brief summary of the major complexity classes:

• *Constant Time (O(1)).* This is the first mention of this class. It contains programs whose running time is independent of the input size. For example, a program that takes no input is said to be O(1).

• *Logarithmic Time (O(log(n))).* These algorithms grow slowly. They usually result when, on each step, you reduce by half the magnitude of the overall problem being solved. For example, when inserting into a binary search tree with n nodes, the correct position is found by comparing the new element with data in the current node, and then branching either left or right. Because roughly half the tree is contained in each of these branches, each such move eliminates half the search space.

- *Linear Time (O(n))*. Execution time for these algorithms is directly related to input size. For example, doubling the input doubles the time required. Linear time is typically the product of a traversal of the data that visits each element exactly once. For example, you saw with linked lists an insertion algorithm that scans a sorted list for the proper place to insert a new value.

- *n log(n) Time (n log(n))*. No simple word names this class. These algorithms most typically are the result of n executions of an operation, each of which requires $\log(n)$ work. Most of the more sophisticated sorting techniques belong to this class. For example, a list of numbers can be sorted by inserting them one at a time into a binary search tree. As you saw above, insertion requires $\log(n)$ work. Performing n of these leads to an overall complexity of $n\log(n)$.

- *Quadratic Time (O(n²))*. These algorithms generally act on all pairs of input items, and often become too slow for reasonably large n. One hundred steps for $n = 10$ is okay, ten thousand steps for $n = 100$ is unpleasant but workable, but even for $n = 1000$ the time required to perform the resulting million steps begins to put the algorithm off limits. As with the previous complexity class, this one often results from n steps being performed, but in this case, each step requires work proportional to n rather than $\log(n)$, leading to $n \times n$ or n^2 steps in all. For example, inserting into a sorted linked list generates this complexity because of its n steps each of which potentially scans the entire list (also n steps).

- *Cubic Time (O(n³))*. Algorithms in this (and similar) complexity classes tend to run quite slowly even for moderate values of n (e.g., 125 million steps for 500 input items).

- *Exponential Time (O(cⁿ) for some constant c)*. These algorithms grow so rapidly that even for small values of n, execution time can be expressed as a multiple of the age of the universe. The Towers of Hanoi solution is one such algorithm. In this example, a problem of size n generates two problems of size $n - 1$, four problems of size $n - 2$, eight of size $n - 3$, and so on. Problems that "try all possibilities," such as Cave Search and Eight Queens, also grow exponentially.

6.2.4. Three Cases

Three cases can be analyzed: *best case, worst case,* and *average case.*

Best case analysis is usually not very useful, since most algorithms can become trivial under certain rare conditions. For example, sorting is $O(n)$ in the best case (which occurs when you scan the list and find it already in sorted order), but this doesn't tell you much about the general nature of the algorithm.

Worst case analysis is somewhat more valuable, since it is often important to have a good upper bound on the running time, particularly in sensitive real-time applications (e.g., a program used in a hospital or aircraft where execution time must *always* be within certain limits to guarantee safety).

Frequently, though, it is the "average" case that you want to understand. This will tell you how the algorithm will "generally" behave. As you might imagine, however, defining the "average" is often quite tricky. For example, what is the "average" array of numbers? Your answer will vary from application to application.

Another way of understanding these three cases is to consider who cares about each. Marketing people are the only ones who pay attention to best case, always on the lookout for good demos, even if they are misleading. "Real" programmers generally care about average case, because they are interested in what is likely to actually happen. Computer scientists generally consider worst case because, as theoreticians, they prefer something well-defined and they enjoy searching for obscure cases that bring algorithms to their knees.

6.2.5. SELF CHECK EXERCISES

1. What other factors, besides growth rate, influence running time? Under what conditions might these factors be more important when comparing two algorithms?

2. When analyzing the complexity of an algorithm, you do so in terms of some parameter. For example, the complexity of the Towers of Hanoi routine was analyzed in terms of the number of disks. For the following algorithms, what is the significant parameter that determines the growth rate of that algorithm's running time, and in which complexity class does the algorithm belong?

   a. Printing all the elements in a linked list.
   b. Printing the elements in a binary tree using an inorder traversal.
   c. Finding an element in a linked list.
   d. Finding an element in a binary search tree.
   e. The recursive *WriteStars* procedure from Chapter 3.

6.3. SEARCHING

Being able to search a structure quickly is essential to many applications. This section presents two techniques for searching an array. They produce the same results, but because they fall into different complexity classes, they execute at considerably different rates.

Consider looking for a particular element in a sorted array. If found, you return its index. Otherwise, you return zero. Thus, given the following type declarations:

```
const
  MaxList = 100;

type
  ListArray = array [1..MaxList] of integer;

  ListRec = record
    Data: ListArray;
    NumElems: integer;
  end; (* ListRec *)
```

where a *ListRec* stores a list of integers along with the number of elements in the list, your procedure will have the following header:

```
procedure Search (var List: ListRec;
          Target:integer;
          var Index:integer);
```

6.3.1. Linear Search

The obvious method is to simply start with the first element and scan the array one by one, until the desired element is found. Because the list is sorted, if you reach a number larger than the given number, then it is not in the list. Here is a first attempt at the code:

```
procedure Search (var List: ListRec;
          Target: integer;
          var Index: integer);
begin
 Index := 1;
 with List do begin
   while Data[Index] < Target do begin
     Index := Index + 1;
   end; (* While *)
   if Data[Index] <> Target then begin
     Index := 0;
   end; (* If *)
  end; (* With *)
end; (* Search *)
```

This code breaks down, however, if *all* the elements in the list are less than the given number. In this case, the procedure will scan past the end of the list, resulting in an "index out of bounds" error. Thus, you also need to make sure that you stop at the end of the list:

```
procedure Search (var List: ListRec;
          Target: integer;
          var Index: integer);
begin
 Index := 1;
 with List do begin
   while (Data[Index] < Target) and (Index < NumElems) do
   begin
     Index := Index + 1;
   end; (* While *)
   if Data[Index] <> Target then begin
     Index := 0;
   end; (* If *)
```

```
    end; (* With *)
  end; (* Search *)
```

Because this code involves scanning potentially all elements of the array, it is O(n).

6.3.2. Binary Search

How do you search through a phone book? Probably you don't start with the first name on the first page and scan each name until you find the one you're looking for. Instead, you flip to the middle of the book, check the name there, and then flip again, going to the left or right depending on whether your person's name is less than or greater than the name in the middle. You repeat this process until you find the page you're looking for. Thus, every time you flip you eliminate approximately half the search space, instead of just one element (as with linear search).

Consider applying this technique to the array search problem. Instead of starting with the first element, start in the middle and compare the number at that position with your number. Because the array is sorted, you know that all the numbers less than the middle number are to its left, and all the numbers greater than it are to the right. There are three possibilities: either you've found the number, in which case there is nothing left to do; or the number is less than the middle number, in which case it must be in the left half; or the number is greater than the middle number, in which case it must be in the right half. With one comparison you can eliminate one half of the search space. This process continues until you either find the number you're looking for, or discover that the number is not in the array.

Suppose you want to find the value 30 in the following sorted array:

10	20	30	40	50	60	70	80	90

You first check the middle value:

Since 30 is less than 50, you know it must be in the left half. You can therefore eliminate the entire right half (including the middle element):

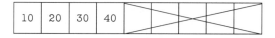

You again look at the middle element of your search space. Because there are an even number of elements, there are actually two "middles." It doesn't matter which you select, so suppose you choose the smaller one:

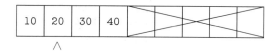

Since 30 is greater than 20, you know that your number must be to the right, and can therefore eliminate the left half:

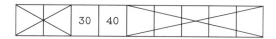

Again you examine the middle element of your (greatly reduced) search space:

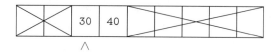

In this case the middle element is the number you're looking for, so you're done. Think about how you might encode this algorithm. You start by looking at the entire array, and then continuously eliminate half of your search space until you find your number, as shown in the following pseudocode:

```
procedure Search (var List: ListRec;
        Target: integer;
        var Index: integer);
begin
  Initialize search space to the entire list;
  Index := 0;
  while (Index = 0) do begin
    if Target = middle number of search space then begin
      Set Index to index of middle of search space;
      end else if Target < middle number of search space then
      begin
      Eliminate right half of search space;
      end else
    begin
      Eliminate left half of search space;
    end; (* If *)
  end; (* While *)
end; (* Search *)
```

The search space consists of consecutive elements in the array, and can therefore be defined by its starting and ending indexes. You can therefore represent the current search space by storing these indexes. Because the middle index is also significant, you can use three integer variables (for the start, middle, and end) to represent this space.

```
procedure Search (var List: ListRec;
      Target: integer;
      var Index: integer);
 var
  FIRST, MIDDLE, LAST: integer;
begin
 with List do begin
   FIRST := 1;
   LAST := NumElems;
   Index := 0;
   while (Index = 0) do begin
     MIDDLE := (FIRST + LAST) div 2;
        if Target = middle number then begin
        Set Index to index of middle of search space;
        end else if Target < middle number then begin
        Eliminate right half of search space;
        end else begin
        Eliminate left half of search space;
        end; (* If *)
    end; (* While *)
  end; (* With *)
end; (* Search *)
```

Eliminating one half simply requires moving either *FIRST* or *LAST* past the middle. For example, the left half of the search space can be eliminated by moving *FIRST* to the right of the middle, since the search space will then begin with the first element to the right of the old middle element. This leads to the following (nearly correct) code:

```
procedure Search (var List: ListRec;
      Target: integer;
      var Index: integer);
  var
   FIRST, MIDDLE, LAST: integer;
begin
 with List do begin
   FIRST := 1;
   LAST := NumElems;
   Index := 0;
   while (Index = 0) do begin
     MIDDLE := (FIRST + LAST) div 2;
     if Target = Data[MIDDLE] then begin
       Index := MIDDLE;
      end
     else if Target < Data[MIDDLE] then begin
       LAST := MIDDLE - 1;
      end
     else begin
       FIRST := MIDDLE + 1;
```

```
        end; (* If *)
      end; (* While *)
    end; (* With *)
  end; (* Search *)
```

This code works provided that the number you're looking for actually appears in the list. Think about what should happen, however, if it's not there. Suppose you're given the same array as before:

| 10 | 20 | 30 | 40 | 50 | 60 | 70 | 80 | 90 |

but this time you're searching for 35 instead of 30. You will make the same steps as you did previously:

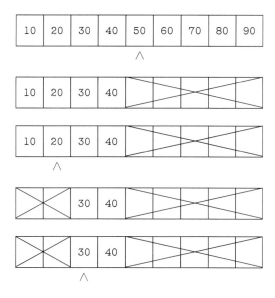

This time, however, you are looking for 35, which is larger than 30 (the middle element), and so you eliminate the left half and continue searching:

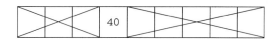

The middle element (indeed, the only element) is now 40, and so you compare it with 35:

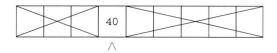

Since 35 is less than 40 you eliminate the right half of the search space:

In so doing, however, you leave yourself with an empty search space. Thus, your number cannot be in the array. To see how to integrate this into your code, consider how the search space is defined. You have stored the first and last indexes of the search space. These indexes define a legal search space as long as the first index comes before (or is equal to) the last index. If the first index comes after the last index, then clearly the search space is no longer well-defined. In fact, this is the condition that occurs when the search space becomes empty, for it will go from consisting of a single element to an empty space by eliminating either the left or the right half of the single element. This will cause either *FIRST* to move past *LAST* or *LAST* to move behind *FIRST*. Thus, this consideration leads to the following version of the code:

```
procedure Search (var List: ListRec;
        Target: integer;
        var Index: integer);
  var
   FIRST, MIDDLE, LAST: integer;
begin
  with List do begin
    FIRST := 1;
    LAST := NumElems;
    Index := 0;
    while (Index = 0) and (FIRST <= LAST) do begin
      MIDDLE := (FIRST + LAST) div 2;
      if Target = Data[MIDDLE] then begin
        Index := MIDDLE;
       end
      else if Target < Data[MIDDLE] then begin
        LAST := MIDDLE - 1;
       end
      else begin
        FIRST := MIDDLE + 1;
       end; (* If *)
     end; (* While *)
   end; (* With *)
 end; (* Search *)
```

Although this code is significantly trickier than the linear search code, the speed increase is considerable, especially for large lists. Its complexity is $O(\log(n))$ because each step eliminates half of the search space. Here are sample running times for these algorithms for various values of n, the number of items in the list. All times are in milliseconds:

n	Linear Search ($O(n)$)	Binary Search ($O(\log n)$)
10	1	1
100	2	1
1000	6	1
10000	87	2
50000	341	2
100000	800	2

You can see that the running time for binary search grows so slowly that a millisecond clock is too slow to supply data that can demonstrate this growth rate in a meaningful way.

6.3.3. SELF CHECK EXERCISES

1. Why does binary search require that the data are sorted?

2. Show the steps that binary search would go through to find the number 8 in the following arrays:

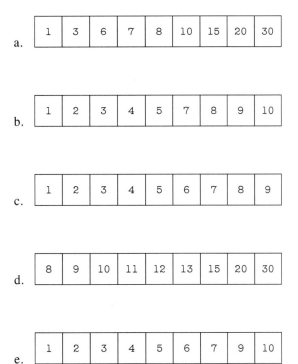

6.4. SOME ANALYSIS TECHNIQUES

Thus far the analysis has been on a very intuitive level. At this point you should understand the concept of a complexity class and its relationship to an algorithm's time efficiency, and you can see why certain algorithms fall into their respective complexity classes. This section expands on these intuitive notions, providing a more rigorous basis for algorithm analysis.

6.4.1. Basic Rules for Big Oh Notation

You have already seen that you pay attention only to the most significant term in characterizing the complexity function (e.g., using $O(n^2)$ instead of $O(n^2 + 3n + 4)$). More formally, the *addition rule* states that if an algorithm is $O(f(n) + g(n))$, then it is $O(max(f(n),g(n)))$. This rule has important implications, even beyond allowing you to ignore most of the terms in an expression.

Consider one code fragment that follows another in a program. If the first is $O(f(n))$ and the second is $O(g(n))$, then the running time for both fragments together is $O(f(n)+g(n))$. By the addition rule, however, this is just $O(max(f(n),g(n)))$. Think about what this means. The complexity for any program is determined by the complexity of its slowest fragment. Thus, the complexity of an algorithm is determined by the complexity of its most frequently executed statement.

The other rule that helps simplify program analysis is the *multiplication rule*, which states that, for any two program fragments, if one is $O(f(n))$ and the other is $O(g(n))$, then the running time of their product is $O(f(n)g(n))$. This rule has significant implications for loops, in which the number of times one code fragment executes is determined by another code fragment. For example, if one fragment is $O(n)$, and each time it executes it performs an $O(n^2)$ operation, then the combination is $O(n^2n)$, or $O(n^3)$.

6.4.2. Analyzing Iterative Routines

6.4.2.1. Some Useful Techniques

These rules lead to some basic techniques for analyzing nonrecursive code fragments. They essentially reduce to determining the complexity class of the most frequently executed statement, which requires both identifying that statement and determining the number of times it executes as a function of the size of the input. Because counting statement executions in a recursive routine is quite tricky, another technique will be introduced later to deal with this case.

The following are some general guidelines for analyzing iterative code fragments:

1. Simple statements, such as assignment statements (except for those involving arrays and function calls), and I/O routines are $O(1)$, since their execution time is independent of any external factor.

2. The running time for a procedure (or function) call is just the running time for the procedure's (or function's) body, plus the time to set up the parameters.

Setting up the parameters is O(1), unless a large structure is passed as a value parameter, in which case that structure must be copied into the parameter. It is for this reason that large structures should be passed as *var* parameters even if they are not modified. For example, in the preceding *Search* procedures the list was passed as a *var* parameter.

3. In an *if/then/else* statement, the test (which is usually O(1)) and one of the conditional statements are executed. Since you generally cannot determine the result of the test ahead of time, you should assume the worst case, and thus the running time of the *if/then/else* will be the sum of the running time of the test and the running time of the worst-case statement.

4. The running time for a loop is determined by the multiplication rule. You need to determine the running time for the loop's body and the number of times the loop iterates. The loop's running time is then the sum, over all iterations, of the running time of the body. Frequently you can just multiply the running time of the body by the number of iterations.

5. You can combine sequences of statements by using the addition rule, which states that the running time of a sequence of statements is just the maximum of the running time of each individual statement.

6.4.2.2. Analyzing Some Example Code Fragments

To get the feel for analyzing code using these rules, consider some examples.

```
(1)      K := 0;
(2)      for I := 1 to N do
(3)          for J := 1 to N do
(4)              K := I * J + N;
```

This fragment consists of two statements at the outermost level, an assignment statement (1) and a loop (2). Because these are two sequential statements, the running time for the entire fragment is just the maximum of the running times of each statement (according to the addition rule). You can therefore break this fragment into the following parts:

```
(1)      K := 0;          (2)      for I := 1 to N do
                          (3)          for J := 1 to N do
                          (4)              K := I * J + N;
```

Statement (1) is just an assignment statement, and so it is O(1). Statement (2) is a loop, and so you determine its running time by figuring out both the running time of its body and the number of times it iterates, and then applying the multiplication rule. The body of this loop (statement (3)) is also a loop, but its body (statement (4)) is just an O(1) assignment statement. Thus, statement (3) executes an O(1) statement n times, and is therefore O(n). This loop is the body of statement (2), however, which also executes n times. Since its body is O(n), and it iterates n times, the entire loop is O(n^2). Thus, statement (1) is O(1) and statement (2) is O(n^2), and therefore this entire fragment is O($max(1, n^2)$), or O(n^2).

The next fragment is somewhat trickier:

```
(1)      K := 0;
(2)      while N > 1 do begin
(3)          N := N div 2;
(4)          K := K + 1;
         end;  (*While*)
```

Again, there are two statements at the outermost level, an assignment statement and a loop. The assignment statement is O(1), as are the assignment statements in the loop's body (statements (3) and (4)):

```
(1)      K := 0;                    O(1)
(2)      while N > 1 do begin
(3)          N := N div 2;          O(1)
(4)          K := K + 1;            O(1)
         end;  (*While*)
```

Thus, because the body of the loop consists of two O(1) statements, by the addition rule the entire body is O(1). Given the running time for the loop's body, you now need to determine the number of times it iterates. This is the tricky part. Every time through the loop the value of n is cut in half, and the loop continues executing as long as n is greater than one. This is the familiar pattern that leads to $\log_2(n)$. Each of these steps is an O(1) operation, so the loop is O(log (n)). Since statement (1) is O(1) and statement (2) is O(log (n)), the entire fragment is O(log (n)).

The final example is also a little tricky, but is simple to analyze once you see the trick:

```
(1)      K := 0;
(2)      for I := 1 to 500 do
(3)          K := K + N;
```

Again, this fragment is made up of two statements, one an assignment statement and one a loop. The body of the loop is O(1) and the loop executes exactly 500 times. Thus, the loop is O(500 × 1), or O(1). The weird thing is that even though there is a loop, its running time is O(1). This loop, however, executes the same number of times, regardless of the value of n. Thus, as n changes, the running time remains constant.

The following table compares sample running times for these three fragments for various values of n (all times are in milliseconds):

n	$O(n^2)$ Fragment	$O(\log n)$ Fragment	$O(1)$ Fragment
10	1	1	2
100	59	1	2
1000	5873	1	2
10000	599658	1	2

6.4.2.3. Another Look at the Searching Algorithms

This section applies this new analysis technique to the searching algorithms discussed earlier. By reasoning about the nature of the algorithms, it was determined that linear search is O(n) and binary search is O(log (n)). Here is the code for linear search:

```
procedure Search (var List: ListRec;
          Target: integer;
          var Index: integer);
begin
 Index := 1;
 with List do begin
    while (Data[Index] < Target) and (Index < NumElems)
    do begin
       Index := Index + 1;
     end; (* While *)
    if Data[Index] <> Target then begin
      Index := 0;
     end; (* If *)
   end; (* With *)
 end; (* Search *)
```

Consider all the statements in this procedure. The *with* statement can be ignored, since it is not an executable statement. Further, all the assignment statements are O(1), as is the *if/then*, since both the test and the body are O(1):

```
procedure Search (var List: ListRec;
          Target: integer;
          var Index: integer);
begin
O(1)Index := 1;
     with List do begin
         while (Data[Index] < Target) and (Index < NumElems)
         do begin
O(1)           Index := Index + 1;
         end; (* While *)
O(1)       if Data[Index] <> Target then begin
O(1)           Index := 0;
         end; (* If *)
     end; (* With *)
 end; (* Search *)
```

All that remains is the *while* loop. Its body is O(1), so you just need to determine the number of times the loop iterates. This is quite tricky, however, because it depends on the data. If the number you're looking for is the first item in the list, then the loop won't iterate at all. If it's not in the list, though, it will iterate n times. The complexity of the algorithm, then, varies drastically depending on the state of the data. Thus, the analysis must take the data into account.

The algorithm is O(1) in the best case (which occurs when the desired number is first in the list), since it then becomes irrelevant how many numbers are in the list. In the worst case it is O(n), since all n elements in the array must be searched. For average case, you can generally assume that all numbers in the array are equally likely to be requested, and thus you need to search through half the array, on average. Thus, in the average case, the loop will iterate $n/2$ times, and is therefore O($n/2$), which is just O(n). Thus, using this definition of "average," linear search is O(n) in the average case.

Binary search can be analyzed in a similar way. All the assignment statements are O(1):

```
      procedure Search (var List: ListRec;
              Target: integer;
              var Index: integer);
      var
       FIRST, MIDDLE, LAST: integer;
      begin
          with List do begin
O(1)      FIRST := 1;
O(1)      LAST := NumElems;
O(1)      Index := 0;
          while (Index = 0) and (FIRST <= LAST) do begin
O(1)          MIDDLE := (FIRST + LAST) div 2;
              if Target = Data[MIDDLE] then begin
O(1)              Index := MIDDLE;
              end else if Target < Data[MIDDLE] then begin
O(1)              LAST := MIDDLE - 1;
              end else begin
O(1)              FIRST := MIDDLE + 1;
              end; (* If *)
          end; (* While *)
        end; (* With *)
      end; (* Search *)
```

The *if/then/else* statement is also O(1), since both its test and statements are O(1).

```
      procedure Search (var List: ListRec;
              Target: integer;
              var Index: integer);
       var
        FIRST, MIDDLE, LAST: integer;
      begin
          with List do begin
O(1)      FIRST := 1;
O(1)      LAST := NumElems;
O(1)      Index := 0;
          while (Index = 0) and (FIRST <= LAST) do begin
O(1)          MIDDLE := (FIRST + LAST) div 2;
```

```
O(1)            if Target = Data[MIDDLE] then begin
O(1)                Index := MIDDLE;
                end else if Target < Data[MIDDLE] then begin
O(1)                LAST := MIDDLE - 1;
                end else begin
O(1)                FIRST := MIDDLE + 1;
                end; (* If *)
            end; (* While *)
        end; (* With *)
    end; (* Search *)
```

Note that the running time for most of the code can be determined almost immediately. All that remains is the running time for the loop. Since every statement in the loop's body is O(1), the entire body (by the addition rule) is O(1). Thus, you just have to determine the number of times the loop iterates, and the analysis is complete. Again, though, this is tricky, because the number of iterations depends on the data involved.

In the best case, the number you're looking for is always the middle number, and so the loop doesn't have to iterate at all. Thus, in this case, binary search is O(1).

The worst case occurs if the number is not in the array and you must search the entire list. Because of the way binary search works, though, this requires only $\log_2(n)$ iterations. Since the loop executes $\log_2(n)$ times, each time performing an O(1) operation, the loop is O(log (n)), and so the entire procedure is O(log (n)).

Again, the average case is difficult to analyze, because "average" is difficult to define. A reasonable definition would be that all the numbers in the array are equally likely to be sought. Given this definition, binary search is still O(log (n)), since half the numbers will not be found until the last iteration of the loop.

6.4.3. Analyzing Recursive Routines

The essence of the foregoing analysis is to determine how the running time for the most frequently executed instruction changes as the size of the input grows. The difficult part is nearly always determining how many times a loop iterates.

The same techniques can be applied to recursive routines, but in these cases it is the recursion, and not a loop, that causes the iteration. Thus, to determine a recursive routine's complexity class, you need to know how many recursive calls that routine will generate. This is usually quite tricky, but fortunately there is a reasonably straightforward method that works nicely in a large number of cases. As a word of warning, this method appears a little intimidating at first, since it is somewhat mathematical, but with a little practice you should get the hang of it.

6.4.3.1. Recurrence Relations

A recursive routine consists of two parts—the base case and the recursive case. Because the base case must be nonrecursive, it can be analyzed using the techniques discussed in the previous section. The running time of the recursive case is determined by the following factors:

1. The number of recursive calls at each level of recursion.
2. The reduction done by each of those calls.
3. The running time for the nonrecursive part of the recursive case. This can be analyzed using the foregoing techniques.

A *recurrence relation* is a formal method for expressing these factors. For example, consider the following recurrence relation:

$$T(1) = c_1$$
$$T(n) = 2T(n - 1) + c_2$$

Within a recurrence relation, the notation $T(n)$ represents *the amount of time necessary to solve a problem of size n.* Thus, this relation implies the following:

1. The amount of time to solve a problem of size one is a constant.
2. The amount of time to solve a problem of size n is twice the time to solve a problem of size $n - 1$, plus another constant.

6.4.3.2. Setting Up Recurrence Relations

This relation is a convenient way of expressing the running time of a recursive routine because its form follows from the structure of recursive procedures. A recursive procedure has a base case and a recursive case, as does a recurrence relation. The "base case" of the recurrence relation expresses the running time for the base case of the recursive procedure, which is nearly always just some constant value. The "recursive case" of the recurrence relation reflects the recursive case of the code in that it expresses the running time in recursive terms. It is therefore fairly straightforward to set up these relations.

Here are a few example recursive procedures and their recurrence relations. First, the following is the procedure that solves the Towers of Hanoi problem:

```
procedure MoveDisks (Num: integer;
      Source, Dest, Temp: char);
begin
  if Num <> 0 then begin
    MoveDisks(Num - 1, Source, Temp, Dest);
    writeln('Move disk from ', Source, ' to ', Dest, '.');
    MoveDisks(Num - 1, Temp, Dest, Source);
  end; (* If *)
end; (* MoveDisks *)
```

The recurrence relation has two parts. The first equation expresses the running time of the base case. In this example, the base case just consists of evaluating a test (Num <> 0) and then doing nothing. Thus, it takes some constant amount of time to execute the base case, since the amount of time to evaluate this test does not vary with the number of disks. The amount of time to move zero disks (a problem of size zero) is, therefore, some constant:

$$T(0) = c_1$$

The second equation is somewhat trickier, since the running time for recursive case *does* vary with the number of disks. A problem of size n, where n is the number of disks, is solved by taking the following steps:

1. Move $n - 1$ disks from *Source* to *Temp*.
2. Move 1 disk from *Source* to *Destination*.
3. Move $n - 1$ disks from *Temp* to *Destination*.

Thus, solving a problem of size n involves solving two problems of size $n - 1$. There are therefore two recursive calls at each level, each of which reduces the problem by one. The recursive part of the recursive case therefore yields the following equation:

$$T(n) = 2T(n - 1)$$

This states that the amount of time to solve a problem of size n is the same as the amount of time to solve two problems of size $n - 1$. There is, however, more to the recursive case than just the two recursive calls. The nonrecursive work done at each level consists of evaluating the test (Num <> 0) and writing out a single move. The running time for these operations is fixed, regardless of the number of disks. Thus, the running time for the recursive case is equal to the running time for the recursive calls, plus some constant:

$$T(n) = 2T(n - 1) + c_2$$

These two equations yield the following recurrence relation for the Towers of Hanoi procedure:

$$T(0) = c_1$$
$$T(n) = 2T(n - 1) + c_2$$

As another example, consider insertion into a binary search tree:

```
procedure Insert (var T: Typ;
        Item: TableElement.Typ);
begin
  if T = nil then begin
    NewLeaf(T, Item);
  end
  else if Compare(Item, T^.Data) = '<' then begin
    Insert(T^.Left, Item);
```

```
      end
    else begin
      Insert(T^.Right, Item);
    end; (* If *)
  end; (* Insert *)
```

The base case again just takes a constant amount of time:

$$T(1) = c_1$$

The recursive case is the interesting one. There are two recursive calls in this procedure, but because they appear in an *if/then/else,* only one of them will be executed at any particular level of recursion. Thus, the problem of inserting a new node into a tree of n nodes is solved by inserting that node into a smaller tree. But how small is that tree? It depends on the data. Usually, about half the tree will be in each subtree, but in some degenerate cases one of the subtrees can contain all the nodes, with the other subtree being empty. Thus, most of the time each recursive call cuts the problem in half, but it may just reduce it by one in these degenerate cases. Because the amount of reduction done at each level plays a significant role in forming the recurrence relation, each of these cases will have a different recurrence relation that expresses its running time.

Having determined the number of recursive calls and the reduction they perform at each level, all that's left is to analyze is the nonrecursive work done in the recursive case. Besides the recursive calls, the only work consists of evaluating two conditionals, both of which are O(1), and so the running time will be some fixed constant. Putting this all together you get the following recurrence relations, depending on how much reduction is done at each level.

Assuming that each call reduces the problem by half yields the following relation:

$$T(1) = c_1$$
$$T(n) = T(n/2) + c_2$$

If each call just reduces the problem by one, you get the following recurrence relation:

$$T(1) = c_1$$
$$T(n) = T(n - 1) + c_2$$

6.4.3.3. Determining the Running Time

At first glance the recurrence relation doesn't appear to give much useful information. There is an equation for $T(n)$, the running time of the routine with respect to n, the size of the input, which is what you are looking for. But it expresses $T(n)$ in terms of the running time for simpler problems, rather than in more concrete terms. For example, you want an expression for $T(n)$ like the following:

$$T(n) = 5n^3 + 3n^2 + 10$$

which would tell you that the corresponding routine is $O(n^3)$. Fortunately, there is a technique that will often allow you to derive such an expression from a recurrence relation. This technique is probably best illustrated by example. The Towers of Hanoi procedure has the following recurrence relation:

$$T(0) = c_1$$
$$T(n) = 2T(n - 1) + c_2$$

The problem is that $T(n)$ is specified in terms of $T(n - 1)$. You need to eliminate this term and get an expression for $T(n)$ that involves only constants and functions of n.

You start by noticing that the recurrence relation gives a value for the running time of any subproblem of the original problem. For example, since

$$T(n) = 2T(n - 1) + c_2$$

you can substitute $n - 1$ in for n and get the following equation:

$$T(n - 1) = 2T(n - 2) + c_2$$

This equation results from the straight substitution. Now note, however, that you have an expression for $T(n - 1)$ in terms of $T(n - 2)$. But the original equation expressed $T(n)$ in terms of $T(n - 1)$. Thus, you can substitute this new expression into the original equation and get an expression for $T(n)$ in terms of $T(n - 2)$, instead of $T(n - 1)$. These steps are summarized below:

$$T(n) = 2T(n - 1) + c_2.$$

Substituting in $(n - 1)$ for (n):

$$T(n - 1) = 2T(n - 2) + c.$$

Substituting for $(n - 1)$ in the original equation:

$$T(n) = 2T(n - 1) + c_2$$
$$= 2[2T(n - 2) + c_2] + c_2$$
$$= 4T(n - 2) + 3c_2$$

This set of substitutions is tricky, but the technique just involves repeating these steps a number of times, until a pattern emerges. You now have an expression for $T(n)$ in terms of $T(n - 2)$. You can get an expression for $T(n - 2)$ by substituting in $n - 2$ for n in the original equation:

$$T(n) = 2T(n - 1) + c_2.$$

Substituting in $(n - 2)$ for n:

$$T(n - 2) = 2T(n - 3) + c_2.$$

Given that you have an expression for $T(n)$ in terms of $T(n - 2)$:

$$T(n) = 4T(n - 2) + 3c_2$$

you can now derive an expression for $T(n)$ in terms of $T(n - 3)$:
Given

$$T(n - 2) = 2T(n - 3) + c_2$$

and

$$T(n) = 4T(n - 2) + 3c_2$$

you get

$$T(n) = 4[2T(n - 3) + c_2] + 3c_2$$
$$= 8T(n - 3) + 7c_2$$

By applying this technique repeatedly you get the following expressions for $T(n)$:

$$T(n) = 2T(n - 1) \quad + c_2$$
$$T(n) = 4T(n - 2) \quad + 3c_2$$
$$T(n) = 8T(n - 3) \quad + 7c_2$$
$$T(n) = 16T(n - 4) + 15c_2$$
$$T(n) = 32T(n - 5) + 31c_2$$
$$\vdots$$

In fact, you can get an expression for $T(n)$ in terms of $T(n - i)$, for any i. The trick is to deduce this general equation from the above specific equations. In this case, the pattern is fairly straightforward. Every expression involving $T(n - i)$ has the form:

$$T(n) = 2^i T(n - i) + (2^i - 1)c_2$$

For example, the next equation in the series would be

$$T(n) = 64T(n - 6) + 63c_2$$

Now comes the *coup de grace*. As seen previously, you can derive an equation for

$T(n)$ in terms of $T(n - i)$, *for any i*, from the following formula:

$$T(n) = 2^i T(n - i) + (2^i - 1)c_2$$

Suppose you choose an i such that $n - i$ is zero. Then, you will have an expression for $T(n)$ in terms of $T(0)$. But you know that the amount of time to move zero disks is just a constant:

$$T(0) = c_1$$

Thus, you can eliminate the recursive term on the right-hand side of the equation. You want

$$n - i = 0 \rightarrow n = i$$

By choosing n for i you get the following expression for $T(n)$:

$$T(n) = 2^i T(n - i) + (2^i - 1)c_2.$$

Choose $i = n$.

$$T(n) = 2^n T(n - n) + (2^n - 1)c_2$$
$$= 2^n T(0) + (2^n - 1)c_2.$$

But

$$T(0) = c_1$$

and therefore

$$T(n) = 2^n c_1 + (2^n - 1)c_2$$

Thus, you have an expression for $T(n)$ in terms of functions of n and constants. Since the maximum function of n is 2^n, you have shown that the *MoveDisks* procedure is $O(2^n)$.

This is a lot of information to absorb. To help you get the feel for this technique, the running time for insertion into a binary search tree, in the case where half the nodes are contained in each subtree, is found below. Finding the running time for the degenerate case is left as an exercise.

Given the following recurrence relation (which was derived above):

$$T(1) = c_1$$
$$T(n) = T(n/2) + c_2$$

Here are the steps used to find the running time:

$$T(n) = T(n/2) + c_2. \quad \text{But} \quad T(n/2) = T(n/4) + c_2 \longrightarrow$$
$$T(n) = T(n/4) + 2c_2. \quad \text{But} \quad T(n/4) = T(n/8) + c_2 \longrightarrow$$
$$T(n) = T(n/8) + 3c_2. \quad \text{But} \quad T(n/8) = T(n/16) + c_2 \longrightarrow$$
$$T(n) = T(n/16) + 4c_2. \quad \text{But} \quad T(n/16) = T(n/32) + c_2 \longrightarrow$$
$$T(n) = T(n/2^i) + ic_2. \quad \text{for any } i.$$

Because you know that

$$T(1) = c_1$$

you can choose an i such that

$$n/2^i = 1, or$$
$$n = 2^i, or$$
$$i = \log_2 n$$

Substituting into the general equation for $T(n)$ you get:

$$T(n) = T(n/2^i) + ic_2. \quad \text{Choosing } i = \log_2 n \longrightarrow$$
$$T(n) = T(1) + (\log_2 n)c_2$$
$$= c_1 + (\log_2 n)c_2$$

Thus, in this case, insertion into a binary search tree is O(log(n)).

6.4.4. SELF CHECK EXERCISES

1. In Big Oh notation, what is the running time for the following procedure, with respect to n?

```
procedure GoGiants (N: integer);
 var
 I, J: integer;
begin
 for I := 1 to N - 1 do begin
   J := N;
   while J > 1 do begin
     J := J div 2;
     writeln(J);
   end; (* While *)
 end; (* For *)
end; (* GoGiants *)
```

2. In Big Oh notation, what is the running time for the following procedure, with respect to *n*?

```
procedure GoGiants (N: integer);
 var
 I, J: integer;
 SUM: integer;
begin
 SUM := 0;
 for I := 1 to N - 1 do begin
   SUM := SUM + I;
  end; (* For *)
 J := N;
 while J > 1 do begin
   J := J div 2;
   writeln(J);
  end; (* While *)
end; (* GoGiants *)
```

3. Suppose you want to determine the growth rate of the running time for the following function, with respect to *n*.

```
function YeaGiants (N: integer): integer;
begin
 if N <= 1 then begin
   YeaGiants := 1;
  end
 else begin
   YeaGiants := 2 * YeaGiants(N div 3);
  end; (* If *)
end; (* YeaGiants *)
```

a. Show a recurrence relation that expresses the running time in terms of *n*.

b. Use this recurrence relation to get an expression for the running time for this function in terms of constants and functions of *n*.

c. Express, in Big Oh notation, the growth rate of the running time of this function, with respect to *n*.

4. Suppose you want to determine the growth rate of the running time for the following function, with respect to *n*.

```
function YeaGiants (N: integer): integer;
 var
  I: integer;
begin
 if N <= 1 then begin
   YeaGiants := 1;
```

```
      end
    else begin
      for I := 1 to N do begin
        writeln(N);
        end; (* For *)
      YeaGiants := 2 * YeaGiants(N - 1);
      end; (* If *)
  end; (* YeaGiants *)
```

a. Show a recurrence relation that expresses the running time in terms of *n*.

b. Use this recurrence relation to get an expression for the running time for this function in terms of constants and functions of *n*.

c. Express, in Big Oh notation, the growth rate of the running time of this function, with respect to *n*.

6.5. SORTING

Sorting, along with searching, has a wide variety of applications, and a great deal of thought has gone into developing efficient sorting techniques. In fact, you have already seen two sorting algorithms in previous chapters. In the linked list implementation of the Table ADT you used *insertion sort* to maintain a sorted list of elements. This technique involves inserting each new element into its correct position in the list. Then, when implementing the Table with a binary search tree, you took advantage of the nature of the tree to efficiently sort the elements. This section presents three new sorting algorithms, using the foregoing analysis techniques to compare their efficiency.

6.5.1. Selection Sort

Selection sort, like other sorting algorithms, takes in a list of elements and returns that list in sorted order. Although all these sorting techniques will work for any lists of ordered data, the examples assume that the elements are integers.

6.5.1.1. The General Algorithm

Selection sort maintains two lists, one sorted and one unsorted. Initially, the sorted list is empty and the unsorted list contains all the numbers. On each iteration, the smallest number in the unsorted list is removed from that list and placed at the end of the sorted list. Thus, on each pass, the sorted list grows by one element, while the unsorted list similarly shrinks by one. Thus, if there are *n* numbers, the sorted list will hold them all after *n* iterations. For example, suppose the initial list contains the following numbers:

8, 3, 20, 1, 5, 4

Then, the algorithm will go through the following six steps:

Iteration	Sorted List	Unsorted List
0	()	(8, 3, 20, 1, 5, 4)
1	(1)	(8, 3, 20, 5, 4)
2	(1, 3)	(8, 20, 5, 4)
3	(1, 3, 4)	(8, 20, 5)
4	(1, 3, 4, 5)	(8, 20)
5	(1, 3, 4, 5, 8)	(20)
6	(1, 3, 4, 5, 8, 20)	()

It is called "selection" sort because, on each pass through the unsorted list, you select the smallest element in that list.

6.5.1.2. Implementing Selection Sort

While selection sort will work for any "list" structure, the code will be implemented assuming that the list is represented as follows:

```
const
  MaxList = 100;

type
  ListArray = array[1..MaxList] of integer;

  ListRec = record
    Data: ListArray;
    NumElems: integer;
  end; (* ListRec *)
```

This is the same structure that was used to implement the search algorithms. The list is maintained by a record, which stores the numbers in an array and the size of the list in the *NumElems* field.

The selection sort procedure takes in a list and returns that list with the numbers in sorted order. The basic algorithm is as follows:

1. Initialize the sorted and unsorted lists.
2. Iterate *n* times. On each iteration:
   (a) Remove the smallest number from the unsorted list.
   (b) Insert that number at the end of the sorted list.
3. Return the sorted list.

Fortunately, the array can be used to store both lists, since if *n* is the number of elements in the list, the sum of the sizes of both lists will always be *n* (since the lists just contain those numbers). The sorted list will grow from left to right, with the shrinking unsorted list next to it. On each iteration you will find the smallest number in the unsorted list and swap it with the the first element in that list. Thus, that smallest number from the unsorted list will become the largest number in the sorted list. Here is a first attempt at pseudocode:

```
procedure SelectionSort (var List: ListRec);
 var
  I: integer;
begin
 with List do begin
   for I := 1 to NumElems - 1 do begin
     Find index of smallest number in array from
     indexes [I..n];
     Swap this smallest number with the I'th number;
   end; (* For *)
 end; (* With *)
end; (* SelectionSort *)
```

For example, given the following initial list:

8	3	20	5	1	4

the algorithm will process the array as follows:

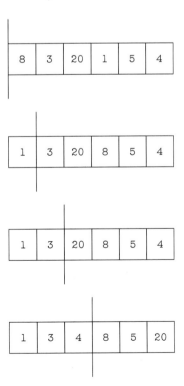

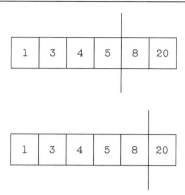

At this point, there is only one number in the unsorted list. Since that number must be the largest number in the array, the entire list is therefore sorted. This is the reason the loop only needs to iterate $n - 1$, rather that n, times.

Continuing with the code, you next need to find the index of the smallest number in the unsorted list. This is done by scanning through the list, maintaining a "current smallest" number. You compare each new number with that current smallest. If the new number is less than the current smallest, it becomes the current smallest. Thus, the pseudocode can be further refined:

```
procedure SelectionSort (var List: ListRec);
 var
  I, J, MININDEX: integer;
begin
 with List do begin
   for I := 1 to NumElems - 1 do begin
     MININDEX := I;
     for J := I + 1 to NumElems do begin
       if Data[J] < Data[MININDEX] then begin
           MININDEX := J;
         end; (* If *)
       end; (* For *)
     Swap this smallest number with the I'th number;
     end; (* For *)
   end; (* With *)
end; (* SelectionSort *)
```

All that remains is to swap the two array elements. The following is a general procedure that will swap the values of two variables:

```
procedure Swap (var First, Second: integer);
 var
  TEMP: integer;
begin
 TEMP := First;
 First := Second;
```

```
      Second := TEMP;
   end; (* Swap *)
```

Thus, given this procedure, you can complete the code for selection sort:

```
procedure SelectionSort (var List: List Rec);
 var
   I, J, MININDEX: integer;
begin
 with List do begin
    for I := 1 to NumElems - 1 do begin
       MININDEX := I;
       for J := I + 1 to NumElems do begin
         if Data[J] < Data[MININDEX] then begin
            MININDEX := J;
         end; (* If *)
       end; (* For *)
       Swap(Data[I], Data[MININDEX]);
    end; (* For *)
 end; (* With *)
end; (* SelectionSort *)
```

6.5.1.3. Analyzing Selection Sort

First, think about the general algorithm and try to develop an intuitive understanding of the running time. It performs n iterations, each time scanning the unsorted list looking for the smallest number. On average, the unsorted list will contain $n/2$ numbers. Thus, selection sort does $n^2/2$ operations, and is therefore $O(n^2)$.

Now analyze the code more formally. First, the *Swap* procedure just consists of three $O(1)$ assignment statements:

```
procedure Swap (var First, Second: integer);
 var
   TEMP: integer;
begin
 TEMP := First;        O(1)
 First := Second;      O(1)
 Second := TEMP;       O(1)
end; (* Swap *)
```

and therefore, by the addition rule, the procedure as a whole is $O(1)$. Looking at the selection sort code itself, every assignment statement is $O(1)$, as is the *if/then* and the call on *Swap*:

```
procedure SelectionSort (var List: ListRec);
 var
   I, J, MININDEX: integer;
begin
```

```
         with List do begin
           for I := 1 to NumElems - 1 do begin
O(1)    MININDEX := I;
           for J := I + 1 to NumElems do begin
O(1)      if Data[J] < Data[MININDEX] then begin
O(1)        MININDEX := J;
             end; (* If *)
           end; (* For *)
O(1)    Swap(Data[I], Data[MININDEX]);
         end; (* For *)
       end; (* With *)
     end; (* SelectionSort *)
```

All that remains are the loops. Think about how many times the inner loop iterates, remembering that on each iteration it performs an O(1) operation. On the first pass it looks through $n - 1$ numbers. The second time it looks at $n - 2$ numbers. Finally, the last time it just looks at one number. In general it looks at $n - i$ numbers, where i varies from 1 to $n - 1$.

Thus, the running time is

$$(n - 1) + (n - 2) + (n - 3) + \cdots + 2 + 1$$

This sum can be expressed in closed form as $(n)(n - 1)/2$, which is $O(n^2)$.

6.5.2. Merge Sort

There are many times when selection sort is an appropriate sorting technique. It is simpler and easier to code than the more efficient algorithms, and it works quite well for small n. When n is large, however, the $O(n^2)$ sorts become prohibitively expensive. In this case, more efficient sorts, such as merge sort, become essential.

6.5.2.1. The Algorithm

Suppose you are given two *sorted* sublists:

(1, 3, 5, 6)
(2, 4, 4, 7, 8)

Since these lists are sorted, it is easy to create one sorted list from these two sublists. You simply maintain two pointers, one at the front of each sublist, and compare their corresponding numbers. You take the smaller of the two, and advance that pointer. The steps you would take given the above lists are shown in the table on the following page. At this point all the numbers in the first sublist have been transferred, and so you can just fill up the new list with the remaining numbers in the second list, which are already in sorted order.

Given that you can merge two sorted sublists into a single sorted list, the rest of merge sort follows quite easily (assuming that you find recursion "easy"). The above

First List	Second List	Take From	Final List
(1, 3, 5, 6)	(2, 4, 4, 7, 8)		()
(3, 5, 6)	(2, 4, 4, 7, 8)	first	(1)
(3, 5, 6)	(4, 4, 7, 8)	second	(1, 2)
(5, 6)	(4, 4, 7, 8)	first	(1, 2, 3)
(5, 6)	(4, 7, 8)	second	(1, 2, 3, 4)
(5, 6)	(7, 8)	second	(1, 2, 3, 4, 4)
(6)	(7, 8)	first	(1, 2, 3, 4, 4, 5)
()	(7, 8)	first	(1, 2, 3, 4, 4, 5, 6)

merge algorithm requires two sorted sublists and, given those lists, will yield a single sorted list. The goal of merge sort, however, is to create a sorted list from unsorted data. When using recursion, however, you *assume* that your procedure will work on simpler versions of the same problem. Thus, you can assume that your procedure will sort smaller lists, and can therefore create two sorted sublists from the original unsorted data. The merge algorithm will then combine these two sorted sublists into one sorted list, and the problem is solved.

Thus, you can sort a list of numbers by

1. Recursively sorting the first half of the list.
2. Recursively sorting the second half of the list.
3. Merging these two (now sorted) sublists together.

All that's left is the base case. If the list contains fewer than two elements, then you can't generate two sublists, and so you can't apply the recursive case. A list that contains zero or one elements, however, is already in sorted order, and so no work has to be done in this case.

For example, suppose you wanted to sort the following list:

(8, 3, 1, 20, 10, 5, 4)

Merge sort would sort this list as follows:

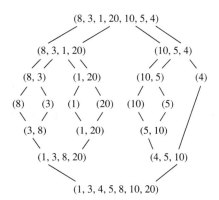

6.5.2.2. Writing the Code

This algorithm, like the previous one, will be implemented using the following data structure:

```
const
 MaxList = 100;

type
 ListArray = array[1..MaxList] of integer;
 ListRec = record
   Data: ListArray;
   NumElems: integer;
  end; (* ListRec *)
```

This structure, combined with the merge sort algorithm, leads to the following first attempt at pseudocode:

```
procedure Mergesort(List)
begin
 if (List contains 2 or more elements) then begin
   Mergesort(first half of List);
   Mergesort(second half of List);
   Merge these two sorted sublists into one sorted list;
   list;
  end; (* If *)
end; (* Mergesort *)
```

Because the list is represented by an array, it is easy to compute the midpoint of the list and determine which elements comprise the first half and which are in the second half. Because this procedure will be sorting these sublists, it must be able to sort any part of the array, and therefore must be told which elements in the array comprise the current list. Thus, you need to pass in both the array itself, as well as the starting and ending indexes of the current list.

```
procedure Mergesort (var Data: ListArray;
       First, Last: integer);
 var
  MIDPOINT: integer;
begin
 if (List contains 2 or more elements) then
 begin
  MIDPOINT := (First + Last) div 2;
  Mergesort(Data, First, MIDPOINT);
  Mergesort(Data, MIDPOINT + 1, Last);
  Merge these two sorted sublists into one sorted list;
 end; (* If *)
end; (* Mergesort *)
```

Since *First* and *Last* are the indexes of the first and last elements in the list, respectively, you know that the list contains at least two elements if *First* is less than *Last*.

To make the recursion work, moreover, you needed to change the parameters. But you don't want to write a procedure that sorts some part of an array. You want a procedure that sorts an entire list. Thus, you should "wrap" this recursive procedure inside another procedure, which takes a list as input and makes the initial recursive call:

```
procedure Mergesort (var List: ListRec);

  procedure MSort (var Data: ListArray;
        First, Last: integer);
    var
     MIDPOINT: integer;
  begin
   if First < Last then begin
     MIDPOINT := (First + Last) div 2;
     MSort(Data, First, MIDPOINT);
     MSort(Data, MIDPOINT + 1, Last);
     Merge these two sorted sublists into one sorted list;
     list;
   end; (* If *)
  end; (* MSort *)

begin (* Mergesort *)
 MSort(List.Data, 1, List.NumElems);
end; (* Mergesort *)
```

All that's left is the *Merge* routine. While the algorithm is fairly straightforward, the code is a little tricky. You are given two sorted sublists and are to combine them into a single sorted list. Here is a first attempt at pseudocode:

```
procedure Merge (var List1, List2);
begin
 Set pointers to the beginning of List1 and List2;
 while (pointers aren't at the end of their lists) do begin
   Move smaller referenced number into sorted list;
   Advance appropriate pointer;
 end; (* While *)
 Fill in sorted list with remainder of leftover list;
end; (* Merge *)
```

This can be further refined as follows:

```
procedure Merge(var List1, List2);
begin
```

```
                    Set LEFT pointer to beginning of List1;
                    Set RIGHT pointer to beginning of List2;
                    while (pointers aren't at the end of their lists) do begin
                      if LEFT number < RIGHT number then begin
                        Move LEFT number into sorted list;
                        Advance LEFT pointer;
                      end else begin
                        Move RIGHT number into sorted list;
                        Advance RIGHT pointer;
                      end; (* If *)
                    end; (* While *)
                    Fill in sorted list with remainder of leftover list;
                  end; (* Merge *)
```

Because the list is being implemented with an array, the pointers will be *integers* that will store the index of the corresponding element. These pointers should initially hold the first index of each list. If you pass in the first and last indexes of the entire list, you can compute the starting and ending indexes of each sublist (since the sublists are half the size of the entire list). These observations lead to the following pseudocode:

```
                  procedure Merge (var Data: ListArray;
                        First, Last: integer);
                    var
                     MIDPOINT, LEFT, RIGHT: integer;
                  begin
                  MIDPOINT := (First + Last) div 2;
                  LEFT := First;
                  RIGHT := MIDPOINT + 1;
                  while (LEFT <= MIDPOINT) and (RIGHT <= Last) do begin
                    if Data[LEFT] < Data[RIGHT] then begin
                      Move LEFT number into sorted list;
                      LEFT := LEFT + 1;
                    end
                    else begin
                      Move RIGHT number into sorted list;
                      RIGHT := RIGHT + 1;
                    end; (* If *)
                  end; (* While *)
                  Fill in sorted list with remainder of leftover list;
                end; (* Merge *)
```

You now run into the problem of where to store the sorted list. You need a set of contiguous elements in which to store the list, but because of the way the two sublists occupy the elements of the array, such contiguous elements are not available. Thus, you need a temporary array to store the sorted list as it is being constructed, and then need to copy this array back into the original list when you're done:

```
procedure Merge (var Data: ListArray;
        First, Last: integer);
 var
  MIDPOINT, LEFT, RIGHT, COUNT: integer;
  TEMPLIST: ListArray;
begin
 COUNT := First;
 MIDPOINT := (First + Last) div 2;
 LEFT := First;
 RIGHT := MIDPOINT + 1;
 while (LEFT <= MIDPOINT) and (RIGHT <= Last) do begin
   if Data[LEFT] < Data[RIGHT] then begin
     TEMPLIST[COUNT] := Data[LEFT];
     LEFT := LEFT + 1;
    end
   else begin
     TEMPLIST[COUNT] := Data[RIGHT];
     RIGHT := RIGHT + 1;
    end; (* If *)
   COUNT := COUNT + 1;
  end; (* While *)
 Fill in sorted list with remainder of leftover list;
 Copy TEMPLIST[First:Last] back into Data[First:Last];
end; (* Merge *)
```

The rest of the code consists of copying elements from one array to another. The following is a general-purpose utility that will copy a range of items from one array to another, starting at one position in one array, and beginning at another position in the other:

```
procedure Transfer (var FromList, ToList: ListArray;
        FromFirst, FromLast, ToFirst: integer);
 var
  I: integer;
begin
 for I := FromFirst to FromLast do begin
   ToList[ToFirst + (I - FromFirst)] := FromList[I];
  end; (* For *)
end; (* Transfer *)
```

Now you can use this utility to copy the leftover elements from the appropriate sublist to the temporary, and then copy the temporary back to original list when it's all sorted:

```
procedure Merge (var Data: ListArray;
        First, Last: integer);
 var
  MIDPOINT, LEFT, RIGHT, COUNT: integer;
  TEMPLIST: ListArray;
```

```
begin
 COUNT := First;
 MIDPOINT := (First + Last) div 2;
 LEFT := First;
 RIGHT := MIDPOINT + 1;
 while (LEFT <= MIDPOINT) and (RIGHT <= Last) do begin
   if Data[LEFT] < Data[RIGHT] then begin
     TEMPLIST[COUNT] := Data[LEFT];
     LEFT := LEFT + 1;
    end
   else begin
     TEMPLIST[COUNT] := Data[RIGHT];
     RIGHT := RIGHT + 1;
    end; (* If *)
   COUNT := COUNT + 1;
  end; (* While *)
 if (LEFT <= MIDPOINT) then begin
   Transfer(Data, TEMPLIST, LEFT, MIDPOINT, COUNT);
  end
 else begin
   Transfer(Data, TEMPLIST, RIGHT, Last, COUNT);
  end; (* If *)
 Transfer(TEMPLIST, Data, First, Last, First);
end; (* Merge *)
```

Putting this all together you get the following code:

```
procedure Mergesort (var List: ListRec);

 procedure Transfer (var FromList, ToList: ListArray;
       FromFirst, FromLast, ToFirst: integer);
  var
   I: integer;
 begin
  for I := FromFirst to FromLast do begin
    ToList[ToFirst + (I - FromFirst)] := FromList[I];
   end; (* For *)
 end; (* Transfer *)

 procedure Merge (var Data: ListArray;
       First, Last: integer);
  var
   MIDPOINT, LEFT, RIGHT, COUNT: integer;
   TEMPLIST: ListArray;
 begin
  COUNT := First;
  MIDPOINT := (First + Last) div 2;
  LEFT := First;
  RIGHT := MIDPOINT + 1;
```

```
        while (LEFT <= MIDPOINT) and (RIGHT <= Last) do begin
          if Data[LEFT] < Data[RIGHT] then begin
            TEMPLIST[COUNT] := Data[LEFT];
            LEFT := LEFT + 1;
           end
          else begin
            TEMPLIST[COUNT] := Data[RIGHT];
            RIGHT := RIGHT + 1;
           end; (* If *)
          COUNT := COUNT + 1;
         end; (* While *)
        if (LEFT <= MIDPOINT) then begin
          Transfer(Data, TEMPLIST, LEFT, MIDPOINT, COUNT);
         end
        else begin
          Transfer(Data, TEMPLIST, RIGHT, Last, COUNT);
         end; (* If *)
        Transfer(TEMPLIST, Data, First, Last, First);
       end; (* Merge *)

      procedure MSort (var Data: ListArray;
            First, Last: integer);
        var
         MIDPOINT: integer;
      begin
        if First < Last then begin
          MIDPOINT := (First + Last) div 2;
          MSort(Data, First, MIDPOINT);
          MSort(Data, MIDPOINT + 1, Last);
          Merge(Data, First, Last);
         end; (* If *)
       end; (* MSort *)

      begin (* Mergesort *)
       MSort(List.Data, 1, List.NumElems);
      end; (* Mergesort *)
```

6.5.2.3. Tracing Through the Recursion

Suppose you are given the following list:

(8, 3, 1, 20, 10, 5, 4)

Here is a trace of the execution of the merge sort procedure on that list:

```
    Mergesort (8, 3, 1, 20, 10, 5, 4)
        Mergesort (8, 3, 1, 20)
            Mergesort (8, 3)
                Mergesort (8).  Base Case.
```

```
              Mergesort (3).  Base Case.
              Merge (8) and (3) into (3, 8)
        Mergesort (1, 20)
              Mergesort (1).  Base Case.
              Mergesort (20).  Base Case.
              Merge (1) and (20) into (1, 20)
          Merge (3, 8) and (1, 20) into (1, 3, 8, 20)
        Mergesort (10, 5, 4)
              Mergesort (10, 5)
                  Mergesort (10).  Base Case.
                  Mergesort (5).  Base Case.
                  Merge (10) and (5) into (5, 10)
              Mergesort (4).  Base Case.
              Merge (5, 10) and (4) into (4, 5, 10)
        Merge (1, 3, 8, 20) and (4, 5, 10) into (1, 3, 4, 5, 8,
  10, 20)
```

6.5.2.4. Analyzing the Running Time of *Mergesort*

Because merge sort is recursive you should analyze it with recurrence relations. To refresh your memory, this technique has the following steps:

1. Set up the recurrence relation.
2. Expand this relation, looking for a general pattern.
3. Having found this pattern, choose i such that the $T(f(n, i))$ term on the right-hand side of the equation corresponds to the base case.
4. Substitute in the known running time for the base case and find an expression for $T(n)$ in terms of functions of n and constants.
5. Express the running time for this routine in Big Oh notation.

For merge sort, the base case occurs when there is only one element in the list. This case consists solely of a single boolean test, and it therefore takes some constant amount of time to execute:

$$T(1) = c_1$$

Setting up the equation for the recursive case involves analyzing the following three factors:

1. The number of recursive calls at each level of recursion.
2. The reduction done by each of those calls.
3. The running time for the nonrecursive part of the recursive case.

Here is the basic mergesort procedure:

```
procedure MSort (var Data: ListArray;
        First, Last: integer);
```

```
var
  MIDPOINT: integer;
begin
  if First < Last then begin
    MIDPOINT := (First + Last) div 2;
    MSort(Data, First, MIDPOINT);
    MSort(Data, MIDPOINT + 1, Last);
    Merge(Data, First, Last);
  end; (* If *)
end; (* MSort *)
```

There are two recursive calls, each of which solve half of the problem. Thus, the amount of time it takes to sort n items is twice the amount of time it takes to sort $n/2$ items, plus the time to perform the nonrecursive part. This part involves some simple O(1) operations, but also includes merging the two sorted sublists. When you merge these sublists together, you pass through every element in the list, copying it to the temporary array. You then copy all these elements back to the original list. *Merge* is thus O($2n$), which is O(n). Thus, the nonrecursive part takes O(n) time, yielding the following equation:

$$T(n) = 2T(n/2) + nc_2$$

Merge sort therefore has the following recurrence relation:

$$T(1) = c_1$$
$$T(n) = 2T(n/2) + nc_2$$

As discussed before, given this recurrence relation, you use the following steps to find the running time for mergesort:

$T(n) = 2T(n/2) + nc_2.$ But $T(n/2) = 2T(n/4) \quad +(n/2)c_2 \rightarrow$
$T(n) = 4T(n/4) + 2nc_2.$ But $T(n/4) = 2T(n/8) \quad +(n/4)c_2 \rightarrow$
$T(n) = 8T(n/8) + 3nc_2.$ But $T(n/8) = 2T(n/16) \quad +(n/8)c_2 \rightarrow$
$T(n) = 16T(n/16) + 4nc_2.$ But $T(n/16) = 2T(n/32) +(n/16)c_2 \rightarrow$

$$\vdots$$

$T(n) = 2^i T(n/2^i) + i(n)c_2$ for any i.

Because you know that

$$T(1) = c_1$$

you can choose an i such that

$$n/2^i = 1, \quad \text{or}$$
$$n = 2^i, \quad \text{or}$$
$$i = \log_2 n$$

Substituting into the general equation for $T(n)$ you get:

$$T(n) = 2^i T(n/2^i) + i(n)c_2. \quad \text{Choosing } i = \log_2 n \rightarrow$$
$$T(n) = nT(1) + (\log_2 n)(n)c_2$$
$$= nc_1 + (n)(\log_2 n)c_2$$

Thus, merge sort is $O(n \log(n))$.

6.5.3. Quicksort

While selection sort is $O(n^2)$ and merge sort is $O(n \log(n))$, Quicksort is a strange combination of the two. It is usually $O(n \log(n))$, but is $O(n^2)$ in the worst case. Moreover, even though Quicksort can be $O(n^2)$, it is actually faster than merge sort most of the time.

6.5.3.1. The Quicksort Algorithm

Consider the following list of numbers:

(8, 3, 1, 20, 10, 5, 4)

You can choose any one of these numbers, called the *pivot,* and *partition* this list into two sublists, one containing all the numbers less than or equal to the pivot, and the other containing all the numbers greater than the pivot. Suppose you select the first number, the 8, as the pivot. Then you can partition this list into the following sublists:

(3, 1, 5, 4)   and   (20, 10)

While these sublists are not individually sorted, they are sorted relative to each other, i.e., all the numbers in the first sublist are less than the numbers in the second sublist. Thus, if you sort each of these sublists individually, you can then combine these two lists with the pivot, and the entire list will be sorted:

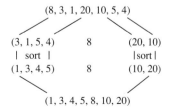

You have therefore reduced the problem of sorting one list to one of sorting two sublists, both of which are smaller than the original list. If you solve this problem recursively, however, you can assume that your procedure will solve these simpler problems. Thus, the recursive case has the following steps:

1. Select one element as the pivot and remove that element from the list.
2. Partition the list into two sublists, one containing all the numbers less than or equal to the pivot, and the other containing all the numbers greater than the pivot.
3. Recursively sort the "less than or equal to" list.
4. Recursively sort the "greater than" list.
5. Recombine these two lists, along with the pivot, into a single, sorted list.

The base case occurs when you try to sort an empty list, since you can't select a pivot from such a list. Sorting an empty list is trivial, though. Thus, the following pseudocode describes the Quicksort algorithm:

```
procedure Quicksort(List);
begin
  if (List isn't empty) then begin
    Select a pivot and remove it from the List;
    Partition into two sublists, based on the pivot;
    Quicksort the ''less than or equal to'' sublist;
    Quicksort the ''greater than'' sublist;
    Combine these two sublists and the pivot;
  end; (* If *)
end; (* Quicksort *)
```

Assuming that you just choose the first number in the list as the pivot, Quicksort will go through the following steps on the example list:

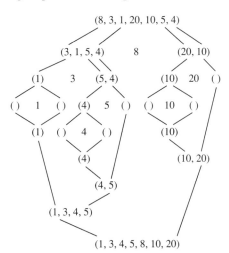

6.5.3.2. Implementing Quicksort

All these sorting algorithms are independent of any particular data structure. They will work on any structure in which you can implement a "list." You have seen an $O(n^2)$ sort implemented on linked lists (insertion sort) and one implemented with an array (selection sort). Since you have also seen merge sort $[O(n \log(n))]$ on arrays, why not implement this $O(n \log(n))$ [or, at least, $O(n \log(n))$ in most cases] sort on linked lists? Below is the data structure definition, which is just a standard linked list structure:

```
type
  ListPtr = ^ListRec;

  ListRec = record
    Data: integer;
    Next: ListPtr;
    end; (* ListRec *)
```

Here is the pseudocode for Quicksort from above:

```
procedure Quicksort(List);
begin
 if (List isn't empty) then begin
    Select a pivot and remove it from the List;
    Partition into two sublists, based on the pivot;
    Quicksort the ''less than or equal to'' sublist;
    Quicksort the ''greater than'' sublist;
    Combine these two sublists and the pivot;
    end; (* If *)
end; (* Quicksort *)
```

Going through this line by line, the *List* parameter will just be a pointer to the head of a linked list, which is empty when this variable is *nil*:

```
procedure Quicksort (var List: ListPtr);
begin
 if List <> nil then begin
    Select a pivot and remove it from the list;
    Partition into two sublists, based on the pivot;
    Quicksort the ''less than or equal to'' sublist;
    Quicksort the ''greater than'' sublist;
    Combine these two sublists and the pivot;
    end; (* If *)
end; (* Quicksort *)
```

Choosing the pivot is tricky, because the pivot could be any element in the list. Ideally, you would always select the median number as the pivot, since in this case both partitions would be the same size (each would contain half the elements). Finding the median, however, is a very slow process (the most popular method is to sort the data (!) and take the middle number). Instead, it is generally better just to pick any number as the pivot. This will rarely be the median, but it does tend to divide the list into roughly equally sized partitions, especially for large *n*. Since it is much faster to select a number than to search for the median, this method is almost always more time efficient. The first number in the list is the easiest to select and remove from the list:

```
procedure FindPivot (var List, Pivot: ListPtr);
begin
 Pivot := List;
 List := List^.Next;
end; (* FindPivot *)
```

This procedure removes the first number from *List* and returns it as the pivot. You now have the following pseudocode:

```
procedure Quicksort (var List: ListPtr);
 var
   PIVOT: ListPtr;
begin
 if List <> nil then begin
   FindPivot(List, PIVOT);
   Partition into two sublists, based on the pivot;
   Quicksort the ''less than or equal to'' sublist;
   Quicksort the ''greater than'' sublist;
   Combine these two sublists and the pivot;
  end; (* If *)
end; (* Quicksort *)
```

The next, and trickiest, step is to partition the list into the two sublists, one containing all the numbers less than or equal to the pivot, and one containing all the numbers greater than the pivot. This procedure will thus take in the original list and the pivot and will return two new sublists. It will go through the original list, compare each number with the pivot, and transfer the numbers to the appropriate sublist:

```
procedure Partition (var List, LessEq, Greater: ListPtr;
        Pivot: integer);
begin
 LessEq := nil;
 Greater := nil;
 while List <> nil do begin
   if List^.Data <= Pivot then begin
     Transfer(List, LessEq);
    end
   else begin
```

```
        Transfer(List, Greater);
      end; (* If *)
    end; (* While *)
  end; (* Partition *)
```

To transfer an item from one list to another you just need to remove it from the
head of one list and place it on the front of the other. It's similar in spirit to the *Swap*
procedure you saw earlier:

```
procedure Transfer (var FromList, ToList: ListPtr);
 var
  TEMP: ListPtr;
begin
 TEMP := FromList;
 FromList := FromList^.Next;
 TEMP^.Next := ToList;
 ToList := TEMP;
end; (* Transfer *)
```

This gives you the following pseudocode for Quicksort:

```
procedure Quicksort (var List: ListPtr);
 var
  PIVOT, LESSEQ, GREATER : ListPtr;
begin
  if List <> nil then begin
    FindPivot(List, PIVOT);
    Partition(List, LESSEQ, GREATER, PIVOT^.Data);
    Quicksort the ''less than or equal to'' sublist;
    Quicksort the ''greater than'' sublist;
    Combine these two sublists and the pivot;
  end; (* If *)
end; (* Quicksort *)
```

Sorting the two sublists just requires two recursive calls, one on each of the lists:

```
procedure Quicksort (var List: ListPtr);
 var
  PIVOT, LESSEQ, GREATER: ListPtr;
begin
 if List <> nil then begin
   FindPivot(List, PIVOT);
   Partition(List, LESSEQ, GREATER, PIVOT^.Data);
   Quicksort(LESSEQ);
   Quicksort(GREATER);
   Combine these two sublists and the pivot;
  end; (* If *)
end; (* Quicksort *)
```

Finally, you have to put these two (now sorted) sublists, along with the pivot, back together into a single list. You can easily link the pivot and the "greater" list, but you need to scan through the entire "less than or equal to" list to link it with the pivot:

```
procedure Combine (var List, LessEq,
        Pivot, Greater: ListPtr);
begin
 List := LessEq;
 Pivot^.Next := Greater;
 AddToEnd(List, Pivot);
end; (* Combine *)
```

The following recursive procedure scans through a list until it reaches the end, and then appends the second list to it:

```
procedure AddToEnd (var ToList: ListPtr;
        AddList: ListPtr);
begin
 if ToList <> nil then begin
   AddToEnd(ToList^.Next, AddList);
  end
 else begin
   ToList := AddList;
  end; (* If *)
end; (* AddToEnd *)
```

Thus, here is the final version of the Quicksort procedure:

```
procedure Quicksort (var List: ListPtr);
 var
  PIVOT, LESSEQ, GREATER: ListPtr;
begin
 if List <> nil then begin
   FindPivot(List, PIVOT);
   Partition(List, LESSEQ, GREATER, PIVOT^.Data);
   Quicksort(LESSEQ);
   Quicksort(GREATER);
   Combine(List, LESSEQ, PIVOT, GREATER);
  end; (* If *)
end; (* Quicksort *)
```

6.5.3.3. Tracing Through the Recursion

Below is a trace of the execution of this procedure on the example list.

```
Quicksort (8, 3, 1, 20, 10, 5, 4)
   Select pivot = 8
```

```
        Partition (3, 1, 20, 10, 5, 4) into (4, 5, 1, 3) and
                (10, 20)
    Quicksort (4, 5, 1, 3)
        Select pivot = 4
        Partition (5, 1, 3) into (3, 1) and (5)
        Quicksort (3, 1)
            Select pivot = 3
            Partition (1) into (1) and ()
            Quicksort (1)
                Select pivot = 1
                Partition () into () and ()
                Quicksort ().  Base case.
                Quicksort ().  Base case.
                Combine (), 1, and () into (1)
            Quicksort ().  Base case.
            Combine (1), 3, and () into (1, 3)
        Quicksort (5)
            Select pivot = 5
            Partition () into () and ()
            Quicksort ().  Base case.
            Quicksort ().  Base case.
            Combine (), 5, and () into (5)
        Combine (1, 3), 4, and (5) into (1, 3, 4, 5)
    Quicksort (10, 20)
        Select pivot = 10
        Partition (20) into () and (20)
        Quicksort ().  Base case.
        Quicksort (20)
            Select pivot = 20
            Partition () into () and ()
            Quicksort ().  Base case.
            Quicksort ().  Base case.
            Combine (), 20, and () into (20)
        Combine (), 10, and (20) into (10, 20)
    Combine (1, 3, 4, 5), 8, and (10, 20) into
            (1, 3, 4, 5, 8, 10, 20)
```

6.5.3.4. Time Analysis for Quicksort

As stated earlier, Quicksort is difficult to analyze. Since it is recursive, you want to analyze it by finding its recurrence relation and using that relation to derive the running time. Since the base case, which occurs when sorting an empty list, is O(1), you get the following "base case" equation for the recurrence relation:

$$T(0) = c_1$$

The "recursive case" in the recurrence relation involves analyzing the following factors:

1. The number of recursive calls at each level of recursion.
2. The reduction done by each of those calls.
3. The running time for the nonrecursive part of the recursive case.

Looking at the nonrecursive part, selecting the pivot is $O(1)$, partitioning is $O(n)$, and combining the partitions is also $O(n)$. Thus, by the addition rule, the nonrecursive part of the recursive case is $O(n)$. Furthermore, there are two recursive calls made at each level of the recursion. It is the reduction made by each call that is difficult to specify. In the best case, in which the median is always chosen as the pivot, both partitions will be half the size of the original list, and you will get the following recurrence relation:

$$T(0) = c_1$$
$$T(n) = 2T(n/2) + nc_2$$

This relation is identical to merge sort's relation, and so Quicksort is $O(n \log(n))$ in this case. The reason that Quicksort generally runs faster than merge sort is that the constants for Quicksort are much smaller.

In the worst case, however, the pivot will be either the largest or smallest number in the list, *at every level,* and one sublist will therefore have $n - 1$ elements and the other will be empty, yielding the following recurrence relation:

$$T(0) = c_1$$
$$T(n) = T(n - 1) + T(0) + nc_2$$
$$= T(n - 1) + c_1 + nc_2$$

If you work through this relation it turns out that Quicksort is $O(n^2)$ in this case. Nevertheless, it is very rare that the pivot will be the largest or smallest number in the list at every level of the recursion.

Generally, what you want to know is an algorithm's complexity in the "average" case, where this case represents the expected behavior under typical circumstances. The "average" is difficult to define, however, and analyzing this case is often challenging. If you assume that all possible orderings of the numbers in the list are equally likely, then tedious calculations can show that Quicksort is average case $O(n \log(n))$. Regardless, experience shows that Quicksort is the fastest sort on unconstrained data in nearly all cases.

6.5.4. SELF CHECK EXERCISES

1. Given the following list:

(5, 13, 8, 1, 4, 6)

Use pictures to show the steps that each of the following algorithms would use to sort this list:

a. Selection sort

b. Merge sort

c. Quicksort

2. When coding merge sort (Section 6.5.2), a local variable *TempList* was declared in the *Merge* procedure. If this variable is instead declared local to the *Merge sort* procedure, and therefore nonlocal to *Merge,* you get a significant increase in speed. Explain.

3. Show that Quicksort is $O(n^2)$ in the worst case.

4. Show that partitioning in Quicksort is $O(n)$.

6.6. HASHING

6.6.1. Introduction

One of the main reasons for sorting information is to obtain fast lookup. For example, given a sorted array, binary search can be used to quickly find a particular item. Similarly, placing data into a binary search tree permits rapid searching. Both of these techniques provide $O(\log(n))$ lookup and provide the extra benefit that the data are sorted.

Often, though, sorted data are unnecessary, and only fast lookup is required. In these cases, another method, known as *hashing,* will allow you to search for an item in $O(1)$ time.

6.6.2. Hashing Fundamentals

6.6.2.1. The Basics

Suppose you are storing information about students in a class. You want to be able to insert a student into the database, delete a student, and find the information about any particular student. Each student has a unique ID number, which is a seven-digit number. Because this number is unique, it can serve as the sort key.

Rather than placing these students into a binary search tree or some other structure, in which you would have to search for a particular student, you could have a huge array that could store information about all the students. Since the ID number has seven digits, an array with 10,000,000 elements would have a slot for all possible students. For example, if you wanted to look up the student with ID number 3290135, you would just use that number as the index into the array, and your student's information would be there. Because no search is required, *Insert, Delete,* and *Find* are all $O(1)$.

Clearly, though, it is unreasonable to have a 10,000,000 element array when there will probably be only 100 students in the class. If there are 100 students, you would like a 100 element array. This would work fine if you had a function that mapped each student to a unique array element. For example, if student 3290135 mapped to the third element in the array, and no other students map to that element, then you could simply pass 3290135 to this function, get back the 3, and go immediately to the third element. Again, no search is required, and so the operations would still be O(1).

Such a function is known as a *perfect hashing function* because every key is mapped to its own array element. Unfortunately, unless the data are known beforehand, perfect hashing functions are very difficult (and usually impossible) to write. A more reasonable function is one that "usually" maps each key to a unique array element. While these hashing functions aren't as nice as perfect hashing functions, they're nearly as good and not too difficult to create.

For example, suppose you have 100 students, each of whom has a seven-digit ID number. You therefore have an array with 100 elements, and you need to be able to map from ID number to array index. One easy method for fitting numbers to a specific range is Pascal's *mod* function. Any expression of the form

```
x mod y
```

will return a value from 0 to $(y - 1)$. Thus, the function

```
function Hash (ID: integer): integer;
begin
 Hash := ID mod 100;
end; (* Hash *)
```

will take in any integer and return a number from 0 to 99. You could therefore store the students in the following structure:

```
StudentArray = array[0..99] of StudentRec;
```

Such an array is known as a *hash table,* since the index for each student is found by passing the student's ID number to some *hash function.* For example, the above function returns 35 when passed 3290135, and thus you would store this student in element number 35 in the array.

6.6.2.2. Handling Collisions with Open Hashing

A problem arises when two keys map to the same array index. For example, given the above hash function, students 3290135 and 3290235 will both hash to index 35. Thus, if both of these students are in your class, you will have a *collision*, since you have two keys that have the same hash value. While your hash function hopefully minimizes these *collisions*, you need to have some strategy for *collision resolution*. One technique, known as *open hashing,* uses a structure like the following diagram. Thus, the 10,000,000 ID numbers are partitioned into 100 *buckets,* each of which is a linked list containing all the students that hash to the same value.

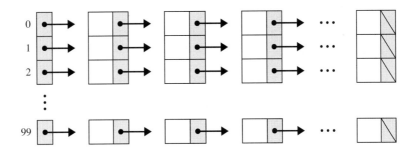

6.6.2.3. An Example

Suppose you have a class of five students and you want to store each student's grade. You thus want a hash table with 5 buckets:

```
const
 MaxHash = 4;

type
 BucketPtr = ^BucketRec;

 BucketRec = record
   ID: integer;
   Grade: char;
   Next: BucketPtr;
  end; (* BucketRec *)

 HashTable = array [0..MaxHash] of BucketPtr;
```

Since there are five buckets, the following is an appropriate hash function:

```
function Hash (ID: integer): integer;
begin
 Hash := ID mod (MaxHash + 1);
end; (* Hash *)
```

Here are the students:

ID Number	Grade	Hash Value
3453212	A	2
3290135	B	0
3323434	A	4
3290235	C	0
3436576	C	1

Initially, the hash table is empty:

The first three students can be inserted into the table without any collisions:

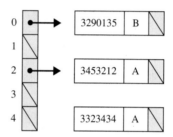

At this point, however, you try to insert 3290235, who also hashes to zero. Handling the collision, though, is simple. You just stick this new record onto the front of the appropriate linked list and continue. Thus, the final table looks as follows:

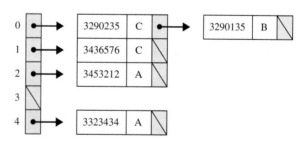

Any of these students can be found by passing their ID number to the hash function, which returns the corresponding array index. The item can then be immediately found at that index (with only a very brief search if more than one item hashed to that position).

6.6.2.4. Other Hash Functions

The foregoing hash functions all involve mapping integers to array indexes. Since array indexes are just a subrange of the integers, these functions are fairly simple. It gets more complicated when your keys are nonnumeric. Furthermore, you want a hash function that will minimize the number of collisions, so that each key is generally assigned to a unique bucket, and when collisions do occur, the subsequent linked lists are small. Although without a priori knowledge about your data you cannot come up with the "best" hash function, there has been considerable research into what constitutes good hash functions. Unfortunately, the mathematics behind this research is beyond the scope of this book, and so only relatively simple hash functions are presented here.

In any case, the most frequently used keys are integers (for which you have already seen how to develop a hash function) and strings. At first it seems quite difficult to hash a string, since a string is made up of characters, and the hash function returns an integer. The key is that since each character has a position in the character set, this position can be used as an integer value. Pascal's built-in *ord* function will take in a character and return the appropriate integer. Since a string is a collection of characters, each of which has an integer value, the entire string can be given an integer value by summing up the values of each of the string's characters. Thus, given the following string declaration:

```
type    String = array[1..25] of char;
```

Here is a simple, but reasonable, hash function:

```
function Hash (Str: String): integer;
 var
  I, SUM: integer;
begin
 SUM := 0;
 for I := 1 to 25 do begin
   SUM := SUM + ord(Str[I]);
  end; (* For *)
 Hash := SUM mod MaxHash;
end; (* Hash *)
```

where *MaxHash* is some constant that specifies that maximum array index. Once again, there are "better" hash functions that will generally result in fewer collisions, but the important thing is to understand that a hash function partitions a set of keys into a set of buckets.

6.6.3. Writing the Code

Given a hash function (named *Hash*) and the maximum array index (specified by a constant *MaxHash*), the hashing routines are fairly simple to write. You want to be able to *create* an empty table, *insert* items into the table, *delete* items from the table, and *find* a specific item, given that item's sort key.

More formally, assuming you have the following data structure definition:

```
type
 TableElement.Typ = record
   Key: KeyType;
                .
                .
                .

  end; (* TableElement.Typ*)

BucketPtr = ^BucketRec;

BucketRec = record
  Data: TableElement.Typ;
  Next: BucketPtr;
 end; (* BucketRec *)

HashTable = array[0..MaxHash] of BucketPtr;
```

here are the desired operations:

```
procedure Create (var T: HashTable);
        post     T is initialized and empty

procedure Insert (var T: HashTable; Item: TableElement.Typ);
        pre      T is not full
        post     Item is added to T such that T remains
                 sorted.

procedure Delete (var T: HashTable;
         Key: KeyType; var Success: boolean);
        post     The first element in T whose key is equal
                 to Key is removed.  If such an Item exists,
                 then Success is set to true.  Otherwise
                 Success is set to false and T is
                 unchanged.

procedure Find (T: HashTable; Key: KeyType;
         var Item: TableElement.Typ; var Success: boolean);
        post     The first element in T whose key is equal
                 to Key is returned via Item.  If such an
                 element exists, then Success is set to
                 true.  Otherwise it is set to false.
```

Note that this hash table is similar to the Table ADT discussed in previous chapters. This similarity is not a coincidence and is discussed in some detail later.

The code follows from basic linked-list management techniques discussed in Chapter 4:

```
procedure Create (var T: HashTable);
 var
  I: integer;
begin
 for I := 0 to MaxHash do begin
   T[I] := nil;
  end; (* For *)
end; (* Create *)

procedure Insert (var T: HashTable;
       Item: TableElement.Typ);
 var
  INDEX: integer;
  NEWELEMPTR: BucketPtr;
begin
 INDEX := Hash(Item.Key);
 new(NEWELEMPTR);
 NEWELEMPTR^.Data := Item;
 NEWELEMPTR^.Next := T[INDEX];
 T[INDEX] := NEWELEMPTR;
end; (* Insert *)

procedure ListDelete (var List: BucketPtr;
       Key: KeyType;
       var Success: boolean);
begin
 if List <> nil then begin
   if List^.Data.Key = Key then begin
     Success := true;
     List := List^.Next;
    end
    else begin
     ListDelete(List^.Next, Key, Success);
    end; (* If *)
  end
 else begin
   Success := false;
  end; (* If *)
end; (* ListDelete *)

procedure Delete (var T: HashTable;
       Key: KeyType;
       var Success: boolean);
begin
    ListDelete(T[Hash(Key)], Key, Success);
end; (* Delete *)

procedure ListFind (List: BucketPtr;
       Key: KeyType;
```

```
                   var Item: TableElement.Typ;
                   var Success: boolean);
         begin
           if List <> nil then begin
             if List^.Data.Key = Key then begin
               Success := true;
               Item := List^.Data;
             end
             else begin
               ListFind(List^.Next, Key, Item, Success);
             end; (* If *)
           end
           else begin
             Success := false;
           end; (* If *)
         end; (* ListFind *)

         procedure Find (T: HashTable; Key: KeyType;
                   var Item: TableElement.Typ;
                   var Success: boolean);
         begin
             ListFind(T[Hash(Key)], Key, Item, Success);
         end; (* Find *)
```

6.6.4. Time Analysis

6.6.4.1. Analyzing Hashing

Hashing techniques are somewhat difficult to analyze because their success relies heavily on the data. The idea is that n items of data are partitioned into b buckets. If you have a hash function that results in few collisions, then the n items will be distributed roughly uniformly over the b buckets, with each bucket storing approximately n/b items. Further, if you choose $n \approx b$, then each bucket will have approximately n/n, or one, item. Thus, under these conditions, the standard hash table operations (*Insert, Delete,* and *Find*) will all be O(1), since they will just require computing the item's index and immediately finding that item. The data do not need to be searched at all. Of course, these are all optimistic assumptions, but they tend to hold up quite well in practice.

6.6.4.2. Hashing and the Table ADT

You've probably noticed a resemblance between using hash tables to store information and the Table ADT discussed in previous chapters. The Table ADT provides basic storage-management operations for maintaining data items of the same type. The Table ADT provides all the basic operations that hashing does, along with a notion of "order," in that there is a *FindMin* operation that returns the item in the Table with the smallest value. Such a function could be written for a hash table, but because the table has no notion of order, you would have to search the entire table. Thus, this operation would be O(n).

Nevertheless, it is inappropriate to implement the Table ADT as a hash table. Because an ADT is, by nature, an abstraction, an implementation should not rely heavily on advance knowledge of the particular data it will store. In particular, the Table ADT is useful largely because it can be used efficiently by many applications. For hashing to work efficiently, however, the implementation must mirror the data in several ways. You need to choose a hashing function that maps sort keys to array indexes. Thus, you obviously need to know the ordering function in advance. Further, the size of the array should approximately equal the number of data items. Thus, while the code for the operations will remain roughly the same, there are many details that are application specific.

In any case, because hash tables and the Table ADT perform roughly the same goals, you can compare their running times for each of the operations. This table assumes that the hash function partitions the data uniformly across the bucket space, and that the number of buckets roughly equals the number of data items.

Operation	Linked List Table Implementation	Binary Search Tree Table Implementation	Hash Table
Create	$O(1)$	$O(1)$	$O(n)$
Empty	$O(1)$	$O(1)$	$O(n)$
Full	$O(1)$	$O(1)$	$O(1)$
Insert	$O(n)$	$O(\log n)$	$O(1)$
Delete	$O(n)$	$O(\log n)$	$O(1)$
Find	$O(n)$	$O(\log n)$	$O(1)$
FindMin	$O(1)$	$O(\log n)$	$O(n)$

6.6.5. SELF CHECK EXERCISES

1. Given the following hash function:

```
function Hash (ID: integer): integer;
begin
 Hash := ID mod 6;
end; (* Hash *)
```

and a hash table with 6 buckets, show the state of the table after the following data have been inserted (in the given order):

ID Number	Grade
3243245	D
3453213	A
3465478	B
3214324	A
3543234	C
3653213	C

2. *Open hashing* has been presented here. Another form of hashing, known as *closed hashing,* differs from open hashing in the way collisions are resolved. Rather than having each bucket reference a linked list, as in open hashing, there are no linked lists in closed hashing. Instead, when a collision occurs, the new item is *rehashed,* in that a new position in the array is found for that item. One common rehashing strategy is to scan the array until an empty slot is found and store the new item in that slot. What are the problems with this strategy? Discuss other rehashing strategies.

3. Is there a limit on the number of items that can be stored in a hash table that uses open hashing? What about one that uses closed hashing?

6.7. SUMMARY OF KEY POINTS

- The *time efficiency* of an algorithm is measured by analyzing the rate at which the running time grows with respect to the size of the input. Algorithms belong to *complexity classes,* which are denoted using *Big Oh notation.* An algorithm's complexity class is specified by the mathematical function that best characterizes how time varies as a function of input size. Algorithms are frequently analyzed in terms of *best case, worst case,* and *average case* behavior.

- You can easily search a linear structure using the *linear search* technique, which runs on $O(n)$ time, but you can search in $O(\log (n))$ time using *binary search* provided the data are sorted.

- You can analyze the running time of nonrecursive routines by analyzing each statement and applying the addition and multiplication rules. Because loops are the only constructs whose running time can vary, they tend to determine the running time for nonrecursive operations.

- In recursive routines the recursive calls play a large role in determining the routine's running time. You can establish a *recurrence relation* for the running time of recursive routines and can often simplify these relations using the *expanding recurrences* technique to solve for the running time directly.

- Selection sort is simple to code and is one of the better $O(n^2)$ sorts, but merge sort will sort data in $O(n \log(n))$ time, whereas quicksort is usually $O(n \log(n))$ but is $O(n^2)$ in the worst case.

- For data that are not required to be sorted you can achieve $O(1)$ lookup by putting the data into a *hash table,* in which each data element is assigned to its own bucket, and the number of buckets is approximately equal to the number of elements.

6.8. PROGRAMMING EXERCISES

1. Given the following data structure definition:

```
type
  ListPtr = ^ListRec;
```

```
ListRec = record
  Data: integer;
  Next: ListPtr;
end; (* ListRec *)
```

implement merge sort with linked lists.

2. Given the following data structure definition:

```
const

MaxList = 100;

type
ListArray = array[1..MaxList] of integer;

ListRec = record
  Data: ListArray;
  NumElems: integer;
end; (* ListRec *)
```

implement Quicksort for this structure.

3. Implement Quicksort on Queues.

6.9. PROGRAMMING PROJECTS

1. In this project you are going to work on the classic knapsack problem. The problem is stated as follows: You wish to fill up your knapsack with items under some weight constraint (the total weight may not exceed a fixed maximum) so as to maximize the total calorie count of the items in the knapsack. You will have "n" items to choose from, each with an associated weight and calorie count. *Each item may appear no more than once in the knapsack.* All solutions that are *guaranteed* to give the optimal answer for this problem are believed to be exponential time algorithms. Because exponential time algorithms are very slow, you are to come up with an algorithm that will give a "good" solution in polynomial time (something like n^2, n^3, $n \log_2 n$, etc.). Be creative in your solutions. While you should certainly consider important properties of the items such as calorie density, adding a little randomness will allow you to generate different solutions each time, which can increase your chances of finding better solutions.

GRAPHS

Although linked lists and trees allow you to represent relationships among data elements, sometimes the relationships are too complex to be represented using these structures. Both linked lists and trees are subsets of the more general *graph* structure, which is the subject of this chapter. This chapter also uses most of the abstract data types defined in the previous chapters, demonstrating how using ADTs can make the programming process easier (by allowing the programmer to think at a higher level of abstraction), and can make programs both more efficient and easier to understand.

First let's quickly review the basic terminology introduced in Section 5.2. A *graph* is defined formally as a set of *nodes* and a set of *edges*. A sequence of edges that visits successive nodes is a *path,* and a path that has the same starting and ending node is a *cycle*. A *connected graph* is one where each pair of vertices is joined by a path. A *tree* is a connected graph with no pair of nodes joined by two distinct paths. An edge is specified as an ordered pair of distinct vertices (v_1, v_2), indicating that it is legal to start at v_1 and follow the edge to v_2.

The graphs described earlier are called *directed graphs* or *digraphs,* meaning that each edge has a specific direction from one node to another. For example, the following digraph indicates which people like which other people:

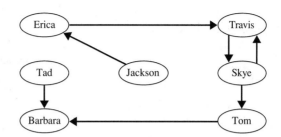

Thus, Erica likes Travis, Jackson likes Erica, Skye likes Tom, and so on. Because this is a digraph, each edge indicates only one direction of attraction. In fact, the only couple who are mutually attracted in this graph are Travis and Skye. In all, this graph has seven nodes and seven edges. The edges can be specified in set notation as follows: {(Erica, Travis), (Travis, Skye), (Skye, Travis), (Jackson, Erica), (Skye, Tom), (Tad, Barbara), (Tom, Barbara)}. The order of edges in this set is unimportant, but because this is a digraph, the order of the two nodes for each edge is significant.

Another kind of graph is represented in the same way, but the order of nodes making up an edge is irrelevant. Such a graph is called an *undirected* graph. For example, the following graph indicates which couples have been married at one time or another, which leads to an undirected graph because it is a two-way correspondence in all cases:

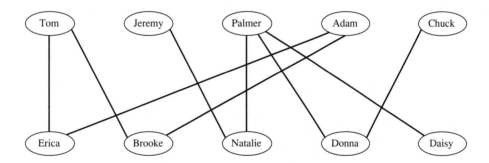

Thus, Tom and Erica were married, as were Tom and Brooke, as were Chuck and Donna, and so on. This graph consists of ten nodes and nine edges.

7.1. THE ADJACENCY MATRIX

It is possible to represent a graph in many different ways. The most straightforward approach from a mathematical point of view is to number the nodes of the graph with consecutive integers and then store the information about edges using what is known as the *adjacency matrix*. It is a two-dimensional grid of boolean values. If the value stored at position $[i,j]$ is True, then you know there is an edge connecting node i to j. Conversely, if position $[i,j]$ is False, then you know that there is no edge between nodes i and j.

For example, in the last graph example showing current and former marriage partners, you could number the nodes as follows:

Node	Number	Node	Number
Tom	1	Erica	6
Jeremy	2	Brooke	7
Palmer	3	Natalie	8
Adam	4	Donna	9
Chuck	5	Daisy	10

leading to this adjacency matrix:

	1	2	3	4	5	6	7	8	9	10
1	F	F	F	F	F	T	T	F	F	F
2	F	F	F	F	F	F	F	T	F	F
3	F	F	F	F	F	F	F	T	T	T
4	F	F	F	F	F	T	T	F	F	F
5	F	F	F	F	F	F	F	F	T	F
6	T	F	F	T	F	F	F	F	F	F
7	T	F	F	T	F	F	F	F	F	F
8	T	T	T	F	F	F	F	F	F	F
9	F	F	T	F	T	F	F	F	F	F
10	F	F	T	F	F	F	F	F	F	F

For example, element [1, 7] is True in this grid because nodes 1 and 7 (Tom and Brooke) are connected by an edge.

For a digraph, you wouldn't necessarily expect element $[j,i]$ to be True when element $[i,j]$ is True. But for an undirected graph, element $[j,i]$ is *always* True when element $[i,j]$ is True. For example, because the matrix above represents an undirected graph, the fact that element [1, 7] is True indicates that element [7, 1] should also be True, which it is.

Thus, for an undirected graph, if you divide its adjacency matrix along the diagonal stretching from the upper-left corner to the lower-right corner, you get two halves that are "mirror images" of each other. You might think that this redundancy should be eliminated. In general, this is not a good idea. If you store the matrix in a two-dimensional array, you can only get rectangular blocks anyway, not the triangular blocks you obtain along the diagonal. If you store the matrix in a linked structure instead, you often risk losing significant execution efficiency unless you go ahead and duplicate.

The most compelling reason for allowing the unnecessary duplication for undirected graphs, however, is that it allows you to store both digraphs and undirected
graphs in exactly the same way. Thus, you can write a single set of subprograms that
can be applied to either kind of graph.

This generalization can easily be taken one step further. The edges of a graph
are often assigned a numeric weighting factor. For example, a traveler, using a map
to help choose what path to follow, expects the edges that connect cities to somehow
indicate the relative cost of that edge. The number might represent how many miles
separate the cities, the expected amount of time to travel between them, the amount
of money required for that route, or some other relative measure that will enable the
traveler to look for the most convenient route.

Graphs whose edges are assigned numeric values are called *weighted graphs*.
One way to store the weighting information for such a structure is to store not only a
True/False value for each element of the adjacency matrix, but also a corresponding
weight. Often these two values can be collapsed into one. For example, it is safe to
assume in many applications that no edge will have weight 0. Thus, the adjacency
matrix can simply store the weights, a value of 0 indicating that no edge exists.

It is once again possible to accommodate both weighted and unweighted graphs
in the same structure, again allowing a single set of subprograms to be applied to
each. Instead of storing boolean True/False values for an unweighted graph, you can
simply store numeric 1/0 values.

7.2. THE GRAPH ADT

A graph is a high-level mathematical abstraction that is useful for representing complex
relationships among data elements. As such, graphs are valuable structures for storing
data in a computer. It is therefore desirable to make this high-level structure available
to programmers by designing an abstract data type with appropriate graph manipulation
operations.

The Graph ADT must be able to store nodes and the edges that connect them.
It should also be able to deal with both directed and undirected graphs, as well as
weighted and unweighted graphs.

First, consider how the ADT should maintain edges. Since edges connect nodes,
there must be an operation for adding both weighted and unweighted edges. The
ADT need only allow adding directed edges, since undirected edges can be created
by adding two directed edges. Operations must also exist for removing an edge, for
determining whether or not a connection exists, and for retrieving an edge's weight
in a weighted graph.

The nodes present more of a problem. The data stored in the nodes will vary greatly
from application to application, and the ADT therefore cannot provide any operations
on node data apart from data storage and retrieval. In any case, the value of the graph
lies not in its ability to store data, but instead in its ability to represent the relationships
among the data elements. Thus, it is the way in which the edges connect the nodes,
and not the nodes themselves, that is the essential information stored in a graph.

Nevertheless, given that a graph consists of nodes, there must be operations in the Graph ADT that provide access to the nodes. For example, to add an edge to a graph the programmer must be able to specify which two nodes the edge connects. The most straightforward approach would be to identify a node by the data it stores. Since node data may not be unique, however, this method will not suffice. For example, if two nodes stored the name *Skye,* then one of those nodes cannot be uniquely determined by specifying the node data. Another, trickier method for finding a desired node would be to define an abstract *NodeType* and give the programmer access to one node in the graph. This node could then be used to traverse the graph, enabling the client to search for the desired node. For this method to work, though, the start node must be connected to all the nodes in the graph, which may not be the case for any node in the graph, particularly since graphs may not even be connected. Further, even if this method were viable, it would not be desirable since it would require traversing the graph every time the client wanted access to the data in a node. Since it is unlikely that the graph is organized for efficient searches of the node data, this would be a very inefficient mechanism.

A better method, and the one used in the Graph ADT, is to simply number the nodes with positive integers and have the client maintain a mapping from these node numbers to the data stored in the nodes. This mechanism provides a unique identifier for each node, permits access to every node independent of the edges in the graph, and allows the client to organize the data efficiently outside of the graph. Thus, the nodes of the graph do not store any data, and are identified by consecutive positive integers (starting with 1). Further, nodes are only added to a graph implicitly, as there is no *AddNode* operation. Nodes are implicitly added when an edge connecting two nodes is added to the graph. This gives the client control over the numbering of the nodes. Each graph therefore has explicit knowledge about only those nodes that have edges.

While the nodes do not store data, a number of graph algorithms need to be able to *mark* a node in some way for the algorithm to perform correctly. For example, when traversing a graph each visited node must be marked to prevent infinite loops. Thus, the Graph ADT associates an integer value (which has no relationship to the node's number) with each node, and allows clients to set and retrieve the value of that mark.

Finally, since the connectivity of the nodes is the primary information stored by a graph, there should be an easy way to find the neighbors of a given node. The Graph ADT provides such an operation, which, given a node number, returns the node numbers for all of that node's neighbors. It does this by passing back to the client a Stream that contains the neighbors' node numbers. The Stream type was introduced in Chapter 2 and will be used repeatedly in this chapter for storing collections of node numbers.

The detailed specifications of the Graph ADT appear in Figure 7.1.

7.2.1. An Example Graph: The Roman Gods

Before discussing various implementations of the Graph ADT, consider a simple application in which the ADT is used to store graphs like the following, in which the

STRUCTURE

Stores nodes and the edges which connect them

Initially empty

The edges, identified by the nodes they connect, may be weighted

The nodes, identified by positive integers, may have an integer mark value

OPERATIONS

```
procedure AddEdge (var G: GraphTyp;
                   FromNode, ToNode: integer);
      post    There is an edge from FromNode to
              ToNode in G

procedure AddWeightedEdge (var G: Typ;
                           FromNode, ToNode: integer;:
                           Weight: integer);
      post    There is an edge with weight Weight from
              FromNode to ToNode
```

(continued)

FIGURE 7.1. Specification for Structure-ADT Graph

nodes store the names of Roman gods and the edges represent the "parent" relationship (e.g., Vulcan is the parent of Cupid):

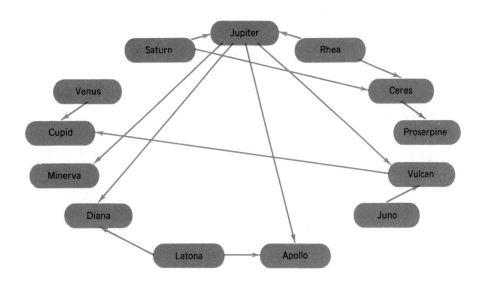

OPERATIONS (CONTINUED)

```
procedure RemoveEdge (var G: Typ;
                        FromNode, ToNode: integer);
        pre     There is an edge from FromNode to
                ToNode in G
        post    There is not an edge from FromNode to
                ToNode in G

function GetWeight (var G: Typ;
                        FromNode, ToNode: integer): integer;
        pre     There is an edge from FromNode to
                ToNode in G
        post    Returns the weight of the edge from
                FromNode and ToNode in G

function ConnectionExists (var G: Typ;
                            FromNode, ToNode: integer):
                            boolean;
        post    Returns TRUE if there is an edge from
                FromNode to ToNode in G

function NumNodesWithEdges (var G: Typ): integer;
        post    Returns the number of nodes in G that
                are connected to other nodes by edges

procedure ZeroAllMarks (var G: Typ);
        post    The marks of all the nodes in G are set
                to zero

procedure SetMark (var G: Typ;
                    Node: integer;
                    Value: integer);
        post    The mark of node Node in G is set to Value

function GetMark (var G: Typ;
                    Node: integer): integer;
        pre     The mark of node Node in G has been set
        post    Returns the mark of node Node in G

procedure Neighbors (var G: Typ;
                        var S: StreamTyp;
                        Node: integer);
        pre     S is initialized
        post    S contains the node numbers of Node's
                neighbors
                S is in the Reading mode
                S's position pointer references its first element
```

STANDARD OPERATORS
Create, Destroy

FIGURE 7.1. Specification for Structure-ADT Graph *(continued)*

Since the names are not actually stored in the nodes, the programmer must store the names elsewhere, in the process associating node numbers with the names. A simple approach is to use an array of Strings, using the String ADT defined in Chapter 2. The following type definitions describe such a structure:

```
const
  MaxGods = 30;

type
  GodsArray = array[1..MaxGods] of String.Typ;
  GodsRec = record
    Data: GodsArray;
    Num: integer;
  end; (* GodRec * )
```

Suppose the data for the graph are stored in a file in which each line contains two names, the first being the parent and the second the child. For example, the following data represents the preceding graph of Roman gods:

```
Saturn Jupiter
Rhea Jupiter
Saturn Ceres
Rhea Ceres
Ceres Proserpine
Jupiter Vulcan
Juno Vulcan
Jupiter Apollo
Latona Apollo
Jupiter Diana
Latona Diana
Jupiter Minerva
Vulcan Cupid
Venus Cupid
```

A program to store this information in a graph could read the file in line by line. For each name it would check to see if that node already exists. If it doesn't yet exist, the node's name is added to the array and, in doing so, it is assigned a node number. The given "parent" edge is then added to the graph. The following code builds up a graph from such a file:

```
function Locate (Nodes: GodsRec;
    Name: String.Typ): integer;
  var
    COUNT: integer;
    FOUND: boolean;

begin
  Locate := 0;
```

```
    COUNT := 0;
    FOUND := false;
    while (COUNT < Nodes.Num) and (not FOUND) do begin
      COUNT := COUNT + 1;
      FOUND := (String.Compare(Nodes.Data[COUNT],
                Name) = '=');
    end; (* While *)
    if FOUND then begin
      Locate := COUNT;
    end; (* If *)
  end; (* Locate *)


  procedure ComputeNodeNum (var Infile: text;
      var Nodes: GodsRec;
      var Num: integer);
   var
    NAME: String.Typ;
  begin
   String.Create(NAME);
   String.Read(Infile, NAME);
   Num := Locate(Nodes, NAME);
   if Num = 0 then begin
     Nodes.Num := Nodes.Num + 1;
     Num := Nodes.Num;
     String.Copy(Nodes.Data[Num], NAME);
   end; (* If *)
   String.Destroy(NAME);
  end; (* ComputeNodeNum *)


  procedure BuildGraph (var Infile: text;
      var RomanGraph: Graph.Typ;
      var Nodes: GodsRec);
   var
    PNUM, CNUM: integer;
  begin
   while not eof(Infile) do begin
     ComputeNodeNum(Infile, Nodes, PNUM);
     ComputeNodeNum(Infile, Nodes, CNUM);
     readln(Infile);
     Graph.AddEdge(RomanGraph, PNUM, CNUM);
   end; (* While *)
  end; (* BuildGraph *)
```

Suppose you wanted to find all the children of a particular god? You would look up that god in the array, find its node number, and then use the Graph ADT's *Neighbors* operation to find all of that node's neighbors. Since the edges represent the parent relationship, these nodes are the god's children. You could then print out the children's names by looking the names up in the array. The following program builds a graph from an input file (named *gods* in this example), asks the user for the name of a god, and then prints out the names of that god's children:

```
program Romans;
 uses
  StreamADT, GraphADT, StringADT;

 const
  MaxGods = 30;

 type
  GodsArray = array[1..MaxGods] of String.Typ;
  GodsRec = record
    Data: GodsArray;
    Num: integer;
   end; (* GodRec *)

 var
  Infile: text;
  RomanGraph: Graph.Typ;
  Nodes: GodsRec;

 procedure Init (var Infile: text;
     var RomanGraph: Graph.Typ;
     var Nodes: GodsRec);
  var
   I: integer;
 begin
  assign(Infile, 'gods');
  reset(Infile);
  Graph.Create(RomanGraph);
  Nodes.Num := 0;
  for I := 1 to MaxGods do begin
    String.Create(Nodes.Data[I]);
   end; (* For *)
  String.DefineIllegal([' ']);
  String.SkipJunk(true);
  String.IgnoreCase(true);
 end; (* Init *)

 function Locate (Nodes: GodsRec;
     Name: String.Typ): integer;
 begin
    (* Same code as above *)
 end; (* Locate *)

 procedure ComputeNodeNum (var Infile: text;
     var Nodes: GodsRec;
     var Num: integer);
```

```
        begin
           (* Same code as above *)
        end; (* ComputeNodeNum *)

        procedure BuildGraph (var Infile: text;
              var RomanGraph: Graph.Typ;
              var Nodes: GodsRec);
        begin
           (* Same code as above *)
        end; (* BuildGraph *)


        procedure PrintChildren (var Outfile: text;
              RomanGraph: Graph.Typ;
              Nodes: GodsRec);
         var
          NODESTREAM: Stream.Typ;
          NODENUM: integer;
          NAME: String.Typ;
        begin
         Stream.Create(NODESTREAM);
         write('Give me the name of a god>  ');
         String.Read(input, NAME);
         readln;
         NODENUM := Locate(Nodes, NAME);
         Graph.Neighbors(RomanGraph, NODESTREAM, NODENUM);
         while not Stream.AtEnd(NODESTREAM) do begin
           Stream.Read(NODESTREAM, NODENUM);
           String.Write(Outfile, Nodes.Data[NODENUM]);
           writeln(Outfile);
          end; (* While *)
         Stream.Destroy(NODESTREAM);
        end; (* PrintChildren *)

      begin
       Init(Infile, RomanGraph, Nodes);
       BuildGraph(Infile, RomanGraph, Nodes);
       PrintChildren(output, RomanGraph, Nodes);
       Graph.Destroy(RomanGraph);
      end. (* Main *)
```

Here is a sample execution of the program:

```
Give me the name of a god>  Jupiter
Vulcan
Apollo
Diana
Minerva
```

Keep this example in mind because it will resurface in the discussion of useful graph algorithms later in this chapter.

7.2.2. Implementing the Graph ADT

7.2.2.1. A Matrix Implementation

To implement the Graph ADT you must first decide how to structure the graph data. The adjacency matrix abstraction of a graph leads to a straightforward and very time-efficient implementation in which the graph is represented as an array of nodes, with each node storing an array of possible edges, thus yielding what is essentially a two-dimensional array. Each node will also need to store its mark value, and you can make searches for a node's neighbors more efficient by also storing the largest of its neighbor's node numbers. These considerations lead to the following type definitions:

```
const
  NoConnection = 0;
  MaxNodes = 40;

type
  ConnectArray = array[1..MaxNodes] of integer;
  NodeRec = record
    LastConnection: integer;
    MarkVal: integer;
    Connections: ConnectArray;
  end; (* NodeRec *)
  NodeArray = array[1..MaxNodes] of NodeRec;
  Typ = record
    NumNodes: integer;
    Nodes: NodeArray;
  end; (* Typ *)
```

Each node thus has an array of integers that stores the weight of the edge connecting the given node to the node identified by the array's index. As a simplification, this implementation will assume that no edge has a weight of zero, and thus will store zero to indicate that no connection exists. Correcting this problem is left as an exercise.

The ADT has four "categories" of operations: the standard operations, the edge operations, the node operations, and the *Neighbors* procedure that bridges edges and nodes. First, consider the standard operations *Create* and *Destroy*. *Create* is responsible for initializing a graph to the empty state. As such it should ensure that there are no nodes in the graph. Since only nodes that have edges will be known to the ADT, Create must also zero-out all the connections, so that nodes with no edges will be represented as such. Finally, *Create* sets all the marks to zero:

```
procedure Create (var G: Typ);
  var
    I, J: integer;
```

```
begin
 G.NumNodes := 0;
 for I := 1 to MaxNodes do begin
   G.Nodes[I].LastConnection := 0;
   G.Nodes[I].MarkVal := 0;
   for J := 1 to MaxNodes do begin
     G.Nodes[I].Connections[J] := NoConnection;
     end; (* For *)
   end; (* For *)
end; (* Create *)
```

The *Destroy* operation deallocates the memory used by a graph. Since arrays cannot be deallocated, *Destroy* does nothing.

```
procedure Destroy(var G:Typ);
begin
end; (* Destroy *)
```

The edge operations allow the client to add directed edges that are either weighted or unweighted. Clients can also remove an edge, retrieve an edge's weight, and test whether or not an edge from one node to another exists. In this implementation, unweighted edges are represented by an edge with a weight of one, and thus adding an edge simply requires storing the edge's weight at the appropriate array index. Since the ADT also maintains the total number of known nodes (which is just the largest node number of a node with an edge), adding an edge may also update this value. Finally, the ADT also maintains the last connection of each node:

```
function Max (First, Second: integer): integer;
begin
 if First > Second then begin
   Max := First;
   end
 else begin
   Max := Second;
   end; (* If *)
end; (* Max *)

procedure AddWeightedEdge (var G: Typ;
    FromNode, ToNode: integer;
    Weight: integer);

begin
 G.NumNodes := Max(G.NumNodes, FromNode);
 G.NumNodes := Max(G.NumNodes, ToNode);
 with G.Nodes[FromNode] do begin
   Connections[ToNode] := Weight;
   LastConnection := Max(LastConnection, ToNode);
   end; (* With *)
end; (* AddWeightedEdge *)
```

```
procedure AddEdge (var G: Typ;
   FromNode  ToNode: integer);
begin
 AddWeightedEdge(G, FromNode, ToNode, 1);
end; (* AddEdge *)
```

Since the information about edge connectedness and weight is stored in each node's array, the remaining edge operations are all straightforward:

```
procedure RemoveEdge (var G: Typ;
   FromNode, ToNode: integer);
begin
 G.Nodes[FromNode].Connections[ToNode] := NoConnection;
end; (* RemoveEdge *)

function GetWeight (var G: Typ;
   FromNode, ToNode: integer): integer;
begin
 GetWeight := G.Nodes[FromNode].Connections[ToNode];
end; (* GetWeight *)

function ConnectionExists (var G: Typ;
   FromNode, ToNode: integer): boolean;
begin
 ConnectionExists := G.Nodes[FromNode].Connections[ToNode]
                   <> NoConnection;
end; (* ConnectionExists *)
```

The node operations allow the client to retrieve the largest node number of all the nodes with edges (which represents the number of nodes known to the ADT), as well as manipulate the nodes' marks:

```
function NumNodesWithEdges (var G: Typ): integer;
begin
 NumNodesWithEdges := G.NumNodes;
end; (* NumNodesWithEdges *)

procedure ZeroAllMarks (var G: Typ);
 var
  I: integer;
begin
 for I := 1 to MaxNodes do begin
   G.Nodes[I].MarkVal := 0;
  end; (* For *)
end; (* ZeroAllMarks *)

procedure SetMark (var G: Typ;
   Node:integer;
   Value:integer);
```

```
begin
 G.Nodes[Node].MarkVal := Value;
end; (* SetMark *)

function GetMark (var G: Typ;
    Node: integer): integer;
begin
 GetMark := G.Nodes[Node].MarkVal;
end; (* GetMark *)
```

Finally, the *Neighbors* operation returns the node numbers of a given node's neighbors. It returns these numbers by means of a stream, which it assumes has been initialized. It first puts this stream into the Writing mode (which, in the process, erases any previous contents), adds the node numbers to the stream, and then puts the stream into the Reading mode, so that the client can immediately access the stream data:

```
procedure Neighbors (var G: Typ;
    var S: Stream.Typ;
    Node: integer);
 var
  I: integer;
begin
 Stream.Rewrite(S);
 for I := 1 to G.Nodes[Node].LastConnection do begin
   if ConnectionExists(G, Node, I) then begin
     Stream.Write(S, I);
   end; (* If *)
  end; (* For *)
 Stream.Reset(S);
end; (* Neighbors *)
```

7.2.2.2. A More Space-Efficient Implementation

The foregoing implementation is excellent for small graphs, or for graphs with extremely high connectivity. It is very space-inefficient for a large number of graph applications, however, since many of these applications involve adjacency matrices that are very *sparse,* meaning that most of the values in the matrix are zero. For example, the graph used to store current and former marriages becomes more and more sparse as the number of people increases. It seems unlikely that many people would ever marry more than 10 times (even Elizabeth Taylor hadn't reached that mark as of our publication date). Even assuming that the *average* number of marriages is ten, look at how the density of the adjacency matrix shown in the table on the following page quickly approaches zero.

As a result, the two-dimensional array might be prohibitively inefficient for many graph applications. For a sparse matrix, it makes more sense to use a linked structure so that all or most of the "0" elements can be eliminated. You could link in both directions, but that will generally not pay off if the edges are fairly evenly distributed across rows and columns. In the marriage problem above, no matter how low the

People	Matrix Elements	Edges	Density
10	100	100	100%
20	400	200	50%
30	900	300	33%
40	1,600	400	25%
50	2,500	500	20%
100	10,000	1,000	10%
500	250,000	5,000	2%
1,000	1,000,000	10,000	1%

density goes, each row and each column will still, on average, have 10 elements (because each person has, on average, 10 marriages). Thus, it makes most sense to preserve the fast access time possible with the array for either the rows or for the columns, and use linking in the other dimension. An array of linked lists is perfect for this application.

```
const
  MaxNodes = 40;

type
  EdgePtr = ^EdgeRec;
  EdgeRec = record
    EdgeTo: integer;
    Next: EdgePtr;
  end; (* EdgeRec *)
  NodeRec = record
    MarkVal: integer;
    Connections: EdgePtr;
  end; (* NodeRec *)

  NodeArray = array[1..MaxNodes] of NodeRec;
  Typ = record
    NumNodes: integer;
    Nodes: NodeArray;
  end; (* Typ *)
```

Although this structure will lead to a reasonable implementation, you will find that to implement the operations you will need to duplicate most of the tricky linked list operations from Chapter 4. If you'll recall, though, those operations were written in the context of the Table type. Thus, the Table already includes the desired operations, and so the Graph ADT can be implemented using the Table instead of having to rewrite all the linked list operations. Moreover, if the Graph ADT is implemented in terms of the Table, then it will work with all the Table implementations, including the binary tree implementation from Chapter 5. Thus, you get the increased efficiency of binary trees with no extra work! Using the Table instead of a linked list to store the edges leads to the following type definitions:

```
const
 MaxNodes = 40;

type
 NodeRec = record
   MarkVal: integer;
   Connections: Table.Typ;
  end; (* NodeRec *)
 NodeArray = array[1..MaxNodes] of NodeRec;
 Typ = record
   NumNodes: integer;
   Nodes: NodeArray;
  end; (* Typ *)
```

Since the Table is a generic structure, you must first specify the type for the elements of the Table. This Table stores edges from one node to another, and thus needs to store the node to which the edge points, along with the edge's weight. You must then also specify the *PrintElement* and *Compare* operations. *PrintElement* won't be used, so you could just have it print out the basic information to use while debugging. Since the edges will be looked up based on node number, this value should be the basis for the comparison. These considerations lead to the following unit encapsulating the *TableElement* information:

```
unit TableElement;

interface

 type
  Typ = record
    EdgeTo, Weight: integer;
   end; (* Typ *)

 procedure PrintElement (var Outfile: text;
     var Entry: Typ);

 function Compare (var Data1, Data2: Typ): char;

implementation

 procedure PrintElement (var Outfile: text;
     var Entry: Typ);
 begin
  write(Outfile, '(', Entry.EdgeTo : 1, ', ',
     Entry.Weight : 1, ')');
 end; (* PrintElement *)
```

```
function Compare (var Data1, Data2: Typ): char;
begin
 if Data1.EdgeTo < Data2.EdgeTo then
  Compare := '<'
 else if Data1.EdgeTo = Data2.EdgeTo then
  Compare := '='
 else
  Compare := '>';
 end; (* Compare *)
end. (* TableElement *)
```

Now consider how to implement the Graph ADT using the Table. Remember, there are four categories into which the operations fall: the standard operations, the edge operations, the node operations, and the *Neighbors* procedure. Since the structure for the nodes is unchanged, the node operations (*NumNodesWithEdges*, *ZeroAllMarks*, *GetMark*, and *SetMark*) are the same as in the foregoing implementation.

The standard operations *Create* and *Destroy* are responsible for allocating and deallocating space, and initializing variables. *Create* should empty the graph, set all the marks to zero, and initialize the tables that represent the edges. *Destroy* deallocates the space occupied by those tables by calling *Table.Destroy*:

```
procedure Create (var G: Typ);
 var
  I: integer;
begin
 G.NumNodes := 0;
 for I := 1 to MaxNodes do begin
   Table.Create(G.Nodes[I].Connections);
   G.Nodes[I].MarkVal := 0;
  end; (* For *)
end; (* Create *)

procedure Destroy(var G:Typ);
 var
  I: integer;
begin
 for I := 1 to MaxNodes do begin
   Table.Destroy(G.Nodes[I].Connections);
  end; (* For *)
end; (* Destroy *)
```

The edge operations allow the user to add edges, remove edges, get an edge's weight, and test whether or not an edge exists. To add an edge you must create a new Table element storing the desired edge information. Then, if an edge connecting the desired nodes already exists, you must remove it. Finally, you insert the new edge into the table. You must also update the number of known nodes in the graph, if necessary:

```
function Max (First, Second: integer): integer;
begin
 if First > Second then begin
   Max := First;
   end
 else begin
   Max := Second;
   end; (* If *)
end; (* Max *)

procedure AddWeightedEdge (var G: Typ;
    FromNode, ToNode: integer;
    Weight: integer);
 var
  NewElem: TableElement.Typ;
begin
 G.NumNodes := Max(G.NumNodes, FromNode);
 G.NumNodes := Max(G.NumNodes, ToNode);
 with G.Nodes[FromNode] do begin
   NewElem.EdgeTo := ToNode;
   NewElem.Weight := Weight;
   if Table.InTable(Connections, NewElem) then begin
     Table.Delete(Connections, NewElem);
     end; (* If *)
   Table.Insert(Connections, NewElem);
   end; (* With *)
end; (* AddWeightedEdge *)

procedure AddEdge (var G: Typ;
    FromNode, ToNode: integer);
begin
 AddWeightedEdge(G, FromNode, ToNode, 1);
end; (* AddEdge *)
```

Retrieving an edge's weight is a little tricky. If the edge is in the graph, then you need to look up that edge's weight. Since the weight is stored in a table, however, you must first use *Table.Extract* to store that edge's record in a new table, and then use *Table.FindMin* to get that record. Then you can return the weight. If the edge is not in the graph, this routine returns a weight of zero:

```
function GetWeight (var G: Typ;
    FromNode, ToNode: integer): integer;
 var
  NewTable: Table.Typ;
  Elem: TableElement.Typ;
begin
 Elem.EdgeTo := ToNode;
 if Table.InTable(G.Nodes[FromNode].Connections, Elem) then
 begin
   Table.Create(NewTable);
```

```
             Table.Extract(G.Nodes[FromNode].Connections, Elem,
                           NewTable);
             Table.FindMin(NewTable, Elem);
             GetWeight := Elem.Weight;
             Table.Destroy(NewTable);
           end
         else begin
           GetWeight := 0;
         end; (* If *)
     end; (* GetWeight *)
```

To remove an edge you delete it from the appropriate table, and you can determine whether or not an edge exists by using the *Table.InTable* function. As an aside, since only existing edges are stored, this implementation allows edges with weights of zero.

```
     procedure RemoveEdge (var G: Typ;
         FromNode, ToNode: integer);
       var
         OldElem: TableElement.Typ;
     begin
       OldElem.EdgeTo := ToNode;
       Table.Delete(G.Nodes[FromNode].Connections, OldElem);
     end; (* RemoveEdge *)

     function ConnectionExists (var G: Typ;
         FromNode, ToNode: integer): boolean;
       var
         Elem: TableElement.Typ;
     begin
       Elem.EdgeTo := ToNode;
       ConnectionExists :=
             Table.InTable(G.Nodes[FromNode].Connections, Elem);
     end; (* ConnectionExists *)
```

Finally, the *Neighbors* procedure needs to go through the given node's table, returning the node numbers that table contains. Since the Table ADT does not allow clients to traverse its contents nondestructively, you must remove each element from that table, store its node number in the stream, and then store the element in a temporary table. When all the node numbers have been stored in the stream, you must then copy the elements back from the temporary table to the original table.

```
     procedure Neighbors (var G: Typ;
         var S: Stream.Typ;
         Node: integer);
       var
         TempTable: Table.Typ;
         Elem: TableElement.Typ;
     begin
```

```
            Table.Create(TempTable);
            Stream.Rewrite(S);
            with G.Nodes[Node] do begin
              while not Table.Empty(Connections) do begin
                Table.FindMin(Connections, Elem);
                Table.Delete(Connections, Elem);
                Table.Insert(TempTable, Elem);
                Stream.Write(S, Elem.EdgeTo);
                end; (* While *)
              while not Table.Empty(TempTable) do begin
                Table.FindMin(TempTable, Elem);
                Table.Delete(TempTable, Elem);
                Table.Insert(Connections, Elem);
                end; (* For *)
            end; (* With *)
          Stream.Reset(S);
          Table.Destroy(TempTable);
        end; (* Neighbors *)
```

Neither of these implementations is better than the other. As with most design decisions in engineering, the decision about which structure to use will vary depending on what is known about typical patterns of use (how sparse the structure will be, how often edges will be checked, etc.).

7.2.3. SELF CHECK EXERCISES

1. The Graph ADT permits edges to have only a single weight. Sometimes, though, it is useful to have multiple weights. For example, maps often have a graph of cities showing both distance and travel time between cities. How could you change the specification of the Graph ADT so that it would permit edges to have multiple weights?

2. The array implementation of the Graph ADT does not allow edges with a weight of zero. What change to the data structure would permit you to distinguish edges with a weight of zero from nonexistent edges?

7.3. THE GRAPH LIBRARY

The remainder of this chapter is devoted to developing a library of useful graph algorithms. All the operations in the libary will be based on the Graph ADT, and will thus be independent of any particular implementation.

7.3.1. Displaying Graphs

Although display algorithms that graphically depict a graph's structure are beyond the scope of this book, it is useful to be able to display graphs in a simple manner for both demonstration and debugging purposes. The following procedure prints out the adjacency matrix of a given graph, adding in the mark values of each node:

```
procedure DisplayGraph (var Outfile: text;
    var G: Graph.Typ);
 var
  Row, Col: integer;
begin
 write(Outfile, '     Mark ');
 for Col := 1 to Graph.NumNodesWithEdges(G) do begin
   write(Outfile, Col : 2, ' ');
  end; (* For *)
 writeln(Outfile);
 write(Outfile, '   +------+');
 for Col := 1 to Graph.NumNodesWithEdges(G) do begin
   write(Outfile, '---+');
  end; (* For *)
 writeln(Outfile);
 for Row := 1 to Graph.NumNodesWithEdges(G) do begin
   write(Outfile, Row : 2, ' |');
   write(Outfile, Graph.GetMark(G, Row) : 6, '|');
   for Col := 1 to Graph.NumNodesWithEdges(G) do begin
     write(Outfile, Graph.GetWeight(G, Row, Col) : 2,
          ' |');
    end; (* For *)
   writeln(Outfile);
  end; (* For *)
 writeln(Outfile);
end; (* DisplayGraph *)
```

For example, the following graph of the Roman gods (which includes each node's node number):

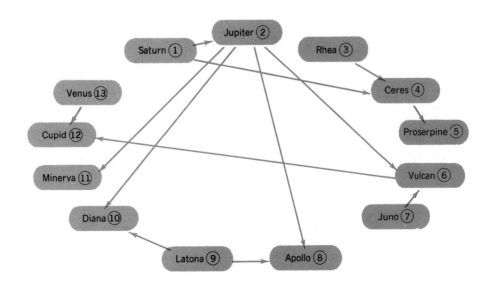

would generate the following output:

	Mark	1	2	3	4	5	6	7	8	9	10	11	12	13
1	0	0	1	0	1	0	0	0	0	0	0	0	0	0
2	0	0	0	0	0	0	1	0	1	0	1	1	0	0
3	0	0	1	0	1	0	0	0	0	0	0	0	0	0
4	0	0	0	0	0	1	0	0	0	0	0	0	0	0
5	0	0	0	0	0	0	0	0	0	0	0	0	0	0
6	0	0	0	0	0	0	0	0	0	0	0	0	1	0
7	0	0	0	0	0	0	1	0	0	0	0	0	0	0
8	0	0	0	0	0	0	0	0	0	0	0	0	0	0
9	0	0	0	0	0	0	0	0	1	0	1	0	0	0
10	0	0	0	0	0	0	0	0	0	0	0	0	0	0
11	0	0	0	0	0	0	0	0	0	0	0	0	0	0
12	0	0	0	0	0	0	0	0	0	0	0	0	0	0
13	0	0	0	0	0	0	0	0	0	0	0	0	1	0

In this example, the rows represent children and the columns represent parents.

7.3.2. Copying a Graph

Another useful operation is one that copies the contents of one graph to another. The following procedure performs this operation. Note that it first reinitializes the destination graph, so that it will contain only the contents of the original graph.

```
procedure CopyGraph (var FromG, ToG: Graph.Typ);
  var
   I, J: integer;
  begin
   Graph.Destroy(ToG);
   Graph.Create(ToG);
    for I := 1 to Graph.NumNodesWithEdges(FromG) do
      for J := 1 to Graph.NumNodesWithEdges(FromG) do
        if Graph.ConnectionExists(FromG, I, J) then begin
          Graph.AddWeightedEdge(ToG, I, J,
                          Graph.GetWeight (FromG, I, J));
      end; (* If *)
  end; (* CopyGraph *)
```

7.3.3. Graph Traversals

Given a structure, it is useful to be able to traverse all the nodes in that structure. You have seen the standard methods for traversing the nodes of linked lists and binary trees. While graphs do not in general have "root" nodes from which you can find a path to every other node, being able to start at a node and traverse the set of nodes that can be reached from that node is a frequently used operation. Such traversals are typically performed in one of two ways: either *depth-first* or *breadth-first*. The difference between the two traversals is derived from the order in which neighbors are processed versus the neighbors of those neighbors. Consider the starting node. It has a set of neighbors to be traversed, and each neighbor, potentially, has a set of neighbors to be traversed. In depth-first traversal, as each neighbor of the current node is processed, all its neighbors are also processed. In breadth-first traversal, all neighbors of the current node are processed before any of the neighbors of those neighbors.

For example, consider a traversal that starts with the node for Jupiter in the sample graph from the last section:

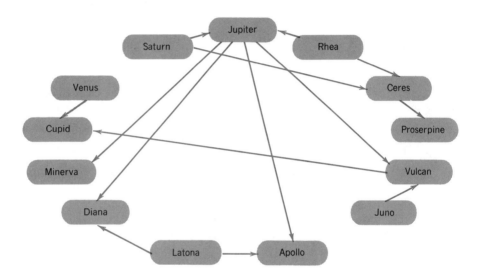

Jupiter has four neighbors (representing his children): Vulcan, Apollo, Diana, and Minerva. In a depth-first traversal, one of the neighbors (say, Vulcan) is traversed along with all of its neighbors, and then the second neighbor (in this case, Apollo) is traversed *along with all of its neighbors*, and so on. In breadth-first traversal, the above four neighbors are traversed before any of their neighbors. For example, the following is a depth-first traversal of this graph, starting with Jupiter:

```
Jupiter Vulcan Cupid Diana Apollo Minerva
```

whereas a breadth-first traversal might result in the following ordering:

```
Jupiter Vulcan Diana Apollo Minerva Cupid
```

Note that both of these traversals yield the same nodes; it's just their ordering that differs. Further, these traversals are not unique, since a node's neighbors are not ordered in any way (unlike the left–right ordering of a binary tree). For example,

```
Jupiter Minerva Apollo Diana Vulcan Cupid
```

represents a legal ordering of both a depth-first and a breadth-first traversal. For another view of the difference between the two traversals, consider the meaning of the two traversals on the foregoing graph. A depth-first traversal of a god will always visit all that god's descendants before visiting any of the god's siblings. A breadth-first traversal, on the other hand, will visit all of a god's siblings before visiting any of his/her children.

These traversals are among the most useful graph algorithms and thus belong in the library. To function as library routines, though, they must be able to pass the traversed nodes back to the caller. These operations therefore work in the same way that the *Neighbors* routine in the Graph ADT works: given a node, return a set of node numbers "related" to that node. Thus, these traversals will take in a graph and a node number and will return a stream containing the numbers of the traversed nodes.

Consider first depth-first traversal, as it is somewhat easier to implement. As each node is visited it is added to the stream, and then each of its neighbors is, in turn, recursively traversed. The problem is that in a graph, unlike in a tree, many nodes may connect to a single node. Thus, it is possible to visit a node more than once, which would lead to infinite recursion. The solution to this problem is to mark each node as it is visited, and traverse a node only if it is unmarked. Finally, since the marks are just used to prevent infinite recursion, and their values are meaningless, you might as well take advantage of the marks set during traversal. A useful value to store is the number of times the node is reached. This indicates the number of nodes in the traversal that have that node as a neighbor. A recursive implementation of depth-first traversal appears below:

```
procedure DepthFirstTrav (var G: Graph.Typ;
        var NodeStream: Stream.Typ;
        StartNode: integer);

  procedure DoDepthFirst (Node: integer);
   var
    NeighborStream: Stream.Typ;
    Neighbor: integer;
  begin
   Stream.Create(NeighborStream);
   Graph.SetMark(G, Node, Graph.GetMark(G, Node) + 1);
   if Graph.GetMark(G, Node) = 1 then begin
     Stream.Write(NodeStream, Node);
     Graph.Neighbors(G, NeighborStream, Node);
     while not Stream.AtEnd(NeighborStream) do begin
       Stream.Read(NeighborStream, Neighbor);
       DoDepthFirst(Neighbor);
     end; (* While *)
   end; (* If *)
```

```
        Stream.Destroy(NeighborStream);
        end; (* DoDepthFirst *)

    begin
      Stream.Rewrite(NodeStream);
      Graph.ZeroAllMarks(G);
      DoDepthFirst(StartNode);
      Graph.SetMark(G, StartNode,
      Graph.GetMark(G, StartNode) - 1);
      Stream.Reset(NodeStream);
    end; (* DepthFirstTrav *)
```

Note that the main program subtracts one from the original node's mark value, since when it is first traversed its mark is incremented, even though no node referenced it.

As an example, using this procedure to traverse the graph of Roman gods, starting with Jupiter (node 2) would yield a stream containing the node numbers 2, 6, 12, 8, 10, and 11 (for Jupiter, Vulcan, Cupid, Apollo, Diana, and Minerva, respectively), and would result in the graph whose nodes are marked as follows (where the marks, in this case, represent the number of the god's parents that are in the traversal):

	Mark	1	2	3	4	5	6	7	8	9	10	11	12	13
1	0	0	1	0	1	0	0	0	0	0	0	0	0	0
2	0	0	0	0	0	0	1	0	1	0	1	1	0	0
3	0	0	1	0	1	0	0	0	0	0	0	0	0	0
4	0	0	0	0	0	1	0	0	0	0	0	0	0	0
5	0	0	0	0	0	0	0	0	0	0	0	0	0	0
6	1	0	0	0	0	0	0	0	0	0	0	0	1	0
7	0	0	0	0	0	0	1	0	0	0	0	0	0	0
8	1	0	0	0	0	0	0	0	0	0	0	0	0	0
9	0	0	0	0	0	0	0	0	1	0	1	0	0	0
10	1	0	0	0	0	0	0	0	0	0	0	0	0	0
11	1	0	0	0	0	0	0	0	0	0	0	0	0	0
12	1	0	0	0	0	0	0	0	0	0	0	0	0	0
13	0	0	0	0	0	0	0	0	0	0	0	0	1	0

This straightforward recursive method won't work for breadth-first traversal, since you need to traverse all of a node's neighbors before traversing any of their neighbors. You thus add the current node to the stream, and then store its neighbors in an auxiliary structure. You can then visit each of those nodes in turn, every time adding the node to the stream and adding all of its neighbors to the end of the auxiliary structure. This results in a breadth-first traversal, since a node isn't visited until all the nodes before it in the auxiliary structure have been visited. Since this auxiliary structure must provide FIFO access to the nodes, you can use a Queue (as defined in Chapter 4) to perform this service:

```
      procedure BreadthFirstTrav (var G: Graph.Typ;
          var NodeStream: Stream.Typ;
          StartNode: integer);

      var
        NeighborStream: Stream.Typ;
        Node, Neighbor: integer;
        Storage: Queue.Typ;

      begin
        Stream.Rewrite(NodeStream);
        Stream.Create(NeighborStream);
        Queue.Create(Storage);
        Graph.ZeroAllMarks(G);
        Queue.Enqueue(Storage, StartNode);
        while not Queue.Empty(Storage) do begin
          Queue.Dequeue(Storage, Node);
          Graph.SetMark(G, Node, Graph.GetMark(G, Node) + 1);
          if Graph.GetMark(G, Node) = 1 then begin
            Stream.Write(NodeStream, Node);
            Graph.Neighbors(G, NeighborStream, Node);
            while not Stream.AtEnd(NeighborStream) do begin
              Stream.Read(NeighborStream, Neighbor);
              Queue.Enqueue(Storage, Neighbor);
            end; (* While *)
          end; (* If *)
        end; (* While *)
        Queue.Destroy(Storage);
        Stream.Destroy(NeighborStream);
        Graph.SetMark(G, StartNode,
                    Graph.GetMark(G, StartNode) - 1);
        Stream.Reset(NodeStream);
      end; (* BreadthFirstTrav *)
```

As an interesting aside, think again about how the foregoing procedure works. Every time it visits a node, it adds that node's neighbors to the end of a queue, thereby yielding a breadth-first traversal. If the neighbors were instead pushed onto a stack, then all a node's neighbors would be visited *before* any other nodes in the graph, rather than *after* the other nodes that were already in the auxiliary structure, as is the case with a queue. Thus, replacing all the queue references in the foregoing procedure with stack references results in an iterative procedure that traverses the nodes of a graph in depth-first order:

```
      procedure DepthFirstWithStack (var G: Graph.Typ;
          var NodeStream: Stream.Typ;
          StartNode: integer);
```

```
                          var
                            NeighborStream: Stream.Typ;
                            Node, Neighbor: integer;
                            Storage: Stack.Typ;

                          begin
                            Stream.Rewrite(NodeStream);
                            Stream.Create(NeighborStream);
                            Stack.Create(Storage);
                            Graph.ZeroAllMarks(G);
                            Stack.Push(Storage, StartNode);
                            while not Stack.Empty(Storage) do begin
                              Stack.Pop(Storage, Node);
                              Graph.SetMark(G, Node, Graph.GetMark(G, Node) + 1);
                              if Graph.GetMark(G, Node) = 1 then begin
                                Stream.Write(NodeStream, Node);
                                Graph.Neighbors(G, NeighborStream, Node);
                                while not Stream.AtEnd(NeighborStream) do begin
                                  Stream.Read(NeighborStream, Neighbor);
                                  Stack.Push(Storage, Neighbor);
                                end; (* While *)
                              end; (* If *)
                            end; (* While *)
                            Stack.Destroy(Storage);
                            Stream.Destroy(NeighborStream);
                            Graph.SetMark(G, StartNode,
                                      Graph.GetMark(G, StartNode) - 1);
                            Stream.Reset(NodeStream);
                          end; (* DepthFirstWithStack *)
```

7.3.4. Analyzing Pairs of Nodes

This section examines various algorithms that analyze all pairs of nodes in a graph. They are useful for undertanding the connectivity properties of these pairs.

7.3.4.1. Matrix Multiplication

Representing a graph via an adjacency matrix has advantages beyond being a simple and precise depiction of the graph's structure. To understand the power of the adjacency matrix, however, you must first understand how to multiply two matrices. The fundamental operation in a matrix multiplication is the *dot product* of two *vectors*, where a vector is a matrix with either a single row or a single column. You can take the dot product of two vectors if one has a single row and the other has a single column, and if the number of columns in the first vector is the same as the number of rows in the second vector. You compute the dot product by multiplying each element in the first vector by the element in the corresponding position in the second vector, and then adding up these products. An example should make this clear:

$$[3\ 4\ 10\ 2\ 6] \begin{bmatrix} 8 \\ 12 \\ 4 \\ 0 \\ 2 \end{bmatrix} \begin{array}{l} = [(3*8) + (4*12) + (10*4) + (2*0) + (6*2)] \\ = \quad 124 \end{array}$$

To multiply two $n \times n$ matrices, you perform n^2 dot product operations, each one computing an element of the $n \times n$ matrix that represents the product of the two original matrices. To compute the element in row i, column j of the product matrix, you take the dot product of the ith row in the first matrix and the jth column of the second matrix. For example,

$$\begin{bmatrix} 4\ 3\ 2 \\ 8\ 3\ 0 \\ 6\ 1\ 3 \end{bmatrix} \times \begin{bmatrix} 8\ 2\ 3 \\ 7\ 6\ 7 \\ 5\ 6\ 2 \end{bmatrix} = \begin{bmatrix} 63\ 38\ 37 \\ 85\ 34\ 45 \\ 70\ 36\ 31 \end{bmatrix}$$

In this example, the value in row 2, column 1 of the product was computed by taking the dot product of the second row of the first matrix and the first column of the second matrix:

$$[8\ 3\ 0] \times \begin{bmatrix} 8 \\ 7 \\ 5 \end{bmatrix} = [(8*8) + (3*7) + (0*5)] = 85$$

The remaining elements of the product were computed in the same way.

7.3.4.2. The Adjacency Matrix and Matrix Multiplication

Applying matrix multiplication to adjacency matrices yields an interesting and useful result. Think about what it means to multiply an adjacency matrix by itself. In an adjacency matrix, each row represents the edges from a particular node to all other nodes, while each column represents the edges from all nodes to a particular node. For example, row 5 shows whether or not there is an edge *from* node 5 to all other nodes, while column 3 shows which nodes have edges leading *to* node 3. Now think about the dot product of row 5 with column 3 (in an $n \times n$ matrix). This value is determined by multiplying the value of the ith column in row 5 with the value of the ith row of column 3, for i going from 1 to n, and then summing up these products. This value will therefore be nonzero only if there is a path from node 5 to some node k, and from node k to node 3. In other words, this value will be nonzero only if there is a path of length 2 going from node 5 to node 3. The consequence of this is that if you square an adjacency matrix (which shows all the paths of length 1), then the resulting matrix shows all the paths of length 2. Further, if you multiply this product by the adjacency matrix, the result shows all the paths of length 3, and so on.

To help understand this rather surprising result, consider the graph of the Roman gods:

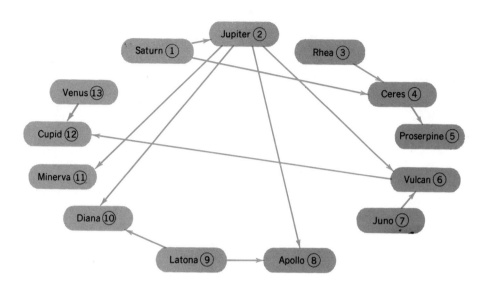

which has the following adjacency matrix:

	1	2	3	4	5	6	7	8	9	10	11	12	13
1	0	1	0	1	0	0	0	0	0	0	0	0	0
2	0	0	0	0	0	1	0	1	0	1	1	0	0
3	0	1	0	1	0	0	0	0	0	0	0	0	0
4	0	0	0	0	1	0	0	0	0	0	0	0	0
5	0	0	0	0	0	0	0	0	0	0	0	0	0
6	0	0	0	0	0	0	0	0	0	0	0	1	0
7	0	0	0	0	0	1	0	0	0	0	0	0	0
8	0	0	0	0	0	0	0	0	0	0	0	0	0
9	0	0	0	0	0	0	0	1	0	1	0	0	0
10	0	0	0	0	0	0	0	0	0	0	0	0	0
11	0	0	0	0	0	0	0	0	0	0	0	0	0
12	0	0	0	0	0	0	0	0	0	0	0	0	0
13	0	0	0	0	0	0	0	0	0	0	0	1	0

While squaring this matrix, you will take the dot product of row 2 (showing all of Jupiter's children) with column 12 (which represents Cupid's parents):

$$[0\ 0\ 0\ 0\ 0\ 1\ 0\ 1\ 0\ 1\ 1\ 0\ 0] \times \begin{bmatrix} 0 \\ 0 \\ 0 \\ 0 \\ 0 \\ 1 \\ 0 \\ 0 \\ 0 \\ 0 \\ 0 \\ 0 \\ 1 \end{bmatrix} = \begin{aligned} &0 + 0 + 0 + 0 + 0 + 1 + 0 + 0 + 0 + 0 \\ &+ 0 + 0 + 0 = 1 \end{aligned}$$

This value is nonzero because there is an edge from Jupiter (node 2) to Vulcan (node 6), and an edge from Vulcan to Cupid (node 12). Thus, Cupid is Jupiter's grandchild, and the square of this adjacency matrix (shown below) shows the "grandparent" relationship:

	1	2	3	4	5	6	7	8	9	10	11	12	13
1	0	0	0	0	1	1	0	1	0	1	1	0	0
2	0	0	0	0	0	0	0	0	0	0	0	1	0
3	0	0	0	0	1	1	0	1	0	1	1	0	0
4	0	0	0	0	0	0	0	0	0	0	0	0	0
5	0	0	0	0	0	0	0	0	0	0	0	0	0
6	0	0	0	0	0	0	0	0	0	0	0	0	0
7	0	0	0	0	0	0	0	0	0	0	0	1	0
8	0	0	0	0	0	0	0	0	0	0	0	0	0
9	0	0	0	0	0	0	0	0	0	0	0	0	0
10	0	0	0	0	0	0	0	0	0	0	0	0	0
11	0	0	0	0	0	0	0	0	0	0	0	0	0
12	0	0	0	0	0	0	0	0	0	0	0	0	0
13	0	0	0	0	0	0	0	0	0	0	0	0	0

Similarly, the matrix on the following page is the cube of the adjacency matrix, and shows all the paths of length 3 (the "great-grandparent" relationship).

Since this information may be useful, it would be nice to have a routine in the library that takes in a graph and an integer n and returns a new graph that represents the graph whose adjacency matrix is the adjacency matrix of the original graph raised to the nth power. Thus, in this graph, all edges will represent paths of length n in the original graph. To perform this computation you must first be able to compute the dot product of two vectors. The following function returns the dot product of a row of

	1	2	3	4	5	6	7	8	9	10	11	12	13
1	0	0	0	0	0	0	0	0	0	0	0	1	0
2	0	0	0	0	0	0	0	0	0	0	0	0	0
3	0	0	0	0	0	0	0	0	0	0	0	1	0
4	0	0	0	0	0	0	0	0	0	0	0	0	0
5	0	0	0	0	0	0	0	0	0	0	0	0	0
6	0	0	0	0	0	0	0	0	0	0	0	0	0
7	0	0	0	0	0	0	0	0	0	0	0	0	0
8	0	0	0	0	0	0	0	0	0	0	0	0	0
9	0	0	0	0	0	0	0	0	0	0	0	0	0
10	0	0	0	0	0	0	0	0	0	0	0	0	0
11	0	0	0	0	0	0	0	0	0	0	0	0	0
12	0	0	0	0	0	0	0	0	0	0	0	0	0
13	0	0	0	0	0	0	0	0	0	0	0	0	0

one graph with a column of another:

```
function DotProduct (var G1, G2: Graph.Typ;
        Row, Col: integer): integer;
  var
    I, SUM: integer;
  begin
    SUM := 0;
    for I := 1 to Graph.NumNodesWithEdges(G1) do begin
      SUM := SUM + Graph.GetWeight(G1, Row, I)
                 * Graph.GetWeight(G2, I, Col);
    end; (* For *)
    DotProduct := SUM;
  end; (* DotProduct *)
```

Next, you need to perform this operation over all the rows of the first matrix and the columns of the second matrix, storing the results in the product matrix:

```
procedure MatrixMultiply (var G1, G2, Result: Graph.Typ);
  var
    ROW, COL, VALUE: integer;
  begin
    for ROW := 1 to Graph.NumNodesWithEdges(G1) do begin
      for COL := 1 to Graph.NumNodesWithEdges(G1) do begin
        VALUE := DotProduct(G1, G2, ROW, COL);
        if VALUE <> 0 then begin
          Graph.AddEdge(Result, ROW, COL);
        end; (* If *)
      end; (* For *)
    end; (* For *)
  end; (* MatrixMultiply *)
```

Finally, you need to perform this operation n times. Doing this is actually a little tricky. Since the *MatrixMultiply* procedure takes three graph parameters (the two operands and the result), the procedure below uses a temporary graph to store the intermediate multiplication results. It copies the original graph to the temporary and then loops $n - 1$ times, each time multiplying the original graph by the temporary, and copying that result back to the temporary. In this way, iterations of the loop yield the adjacency matrix raised to successively higher powers. This procedure assumes that $n > 1$.

```
procedure PathsOfLength (var G, Result: Graph.Typ;
         Length: integer);
  var
   I: integer;
   Temp: Graph.Typ;
  begin
   Graph.Create(Temp);
   CopyGraph(G, Temp);
   for I := 1 to (Length - 1) do begin
     Graph.Destroy(Result);
     Graph.Create(Result);
     MatrixMultiply(G, Temp, Result);
     CopyGraph(Result, Temp);
   end; (* For *)
   Graph.Destroy(Temp);
  end; (* PathsOfLength *)
```

7.3.4.3. The Connectivity Matrix and Matrix Multiplication

The *connectivity matrix* is the same as the adjacency matrix except that it has ones along the *diagonal*, where the diagonal contains all the elements in row i and column j where $i = j$. These are all zero in the adjacency matrix unless the graph contains a node with an edge to itself (such a graph is known as a *pseudograph*). For example, here is the connectivity matrix for the graph of the Roman gods:

	1	2	3	4	5	6	7	8	9	10	11	12	13
1	1	1	0	1	0	0	0	0	0	0	0	0	0
2	0	1	0	0	0	1	0	1	0	1	1	0	0
3	0	1	1	1	0	0	0	0	0	0	0	0	0
4	0	0	0	1	1	0	0	0	0	0	0	0	0
5	0	0	0	0	1	0	0	0	0	0	0	0	0
6	0	0	0	0	0	1	0	0	0	0	0	1	0
7	0	0	0	0	0	1	1	0	0	0	0	0	0
8	0	0	0	0	0	0	0	1	0	0	0	0	0
9	0	0	0	0	0	0	0	1	1	1	0	0	0
10	0	0	0	0	0	0	0	0	0	1	0	0	0
11	0	0	0	0	0	0	0	0	0	0	1	0	0
12	0	0	0	0	0	0	0	0	0	0	0	1	0
13	0	0	0	0	0	0	0	0	0	0	0	1	1

Although the connectivity matrix doesn't usually represent the structure of the graph, as the adjacency matrix does, multiplying these matrices by themselves does yield an interesting result. Squaring a connectivity matrix, like squaring an adjacency matrix, shows all the paths of length 2, but it also preserves all the paths of length 1. Similarly, cubing the connectivity matrix shows all the paths *up to* length 3, rather than all the paths of *exactly* length 3, as does cubing the adjacency matrix. To see why this occurs, think about taking the dot product of Jupiter's row (row 2) and Cupid's column (column 12). This result is nonzero, as it was with the adjacency matrix, since there is a path from Jupiter to Vulcan (node 6), and a path from Vulcan to Cupid. Now think about the dot product of Jupiter's row and Vulcan's column. This value was zero with the adjacency matrix, but it is nonzero in this case because there is a path from Jupiter to Jupiter, and a path from Jupiter to Vulcan. Thus, putting a one on the diagonal creates a path from each node to itself, which in turns allows matrix multiplication to preserve information about existing paths. For example, the following is the square of the foregoing connectivity matrix, which contains edges from each node to itself (paths of length zero) and to the nodes representing that god's children and grandchildren:

	1	2	3	4	5	6	7	8	9	10	11	12	13
1	1	1	0	1	1	1	0	1	0	1	1	0	0
2	0	1	0	0	0	1	0	1	0	1	1	1	0
3	0	1	1	1	1	1	0	1	0	1	1	0	0
4	0	0	0	1	1	0	0	0	0	0	0	0	0
5	0	0	0	0	1	0	0	0	0	0	0	0	0
6	0	0	0	0	0	1	0	0	0	0	0	1	0
7	0	0	0	0	0	1	1	0	0	0	0	1	0
8	0	0	0	0	0	0	0	1	0	0	0	0	0
9	0	0	0	0	0	0	0	1	1	1	0	0	0
10	0	0	0	0	0	0	0	0	0	1	0	0	0
11	0	0	0	0	0	0	0	0	0	0	1	0	0
12	0	0	0	0	0	0	0	0	0	0	0	1	0
13	0	0	0	0	0	0	0	0	0	0	0	1	1

Given the above *PathsOfLength* procedure it is now easy to write a *PathsUpToLength* procedure. You simply add ones to the diagonal (thereby creating the connectivity matrix) and raise that matrix to the desired power:

```
procedure PathsUpToLength (var G, Result: Graph.Typ;
        Length: integer);
  var
    Temp: Graph.Typ;
    I: integer;

  begin
    Graph.Create(Temp);
    CopyGraph(G, Temp);
```

```
      for I := 1 to Graph.NumNodesWithEdges(G) do begin
        Graph.AddEdge(Temp, I, I);
      end; (* For *)
    PathsOfLength(Temp, Result, Length);
  end; (* PathsUpToLength *)
```

7.3.4.4. Transitive Closure

Consider the problem of finding out for each pair of nodes in a graph whether it is possible to travel from the first node to the second node. Suppose you are looking at nodes numbered x and y. If there is an edge from x to y, then it is certainly possible to make the trip.

Similarly, if there is a node z such that there is an edge from x to z and an edge from z to y, then there it is also possible to make the trip:

Or if there are nodes z and w such that x goes to z, z goes to w, and w goes to y.

In mathematical terms, all this means is that getting from one node to another is a *transitive* relationship. More formally, transitivity is the property that for any x and y, x is always related to y whenever x is related to some z and z is related to y.

Determining all potential paths in a graph involves following all the simple edges from one node to another, all of the paths of length 2 that you get from transitivity connecting nodes through a "middleman," all of the paths of length 3 that you get from transitivity connecting nodes through two "middlemen," and so on. If you wanted to keep track of all possible paths, you would want to take the union of all of these connections. Mathematicians call that the *transitive closure* because it involves applying the property of transitivity over and over again until you've found every path that can be generated that way.

One way of computing the transitive closure of a graph is to multiply the connectivity matrix by itself repeatedly, until the result is the same as the previous result. Although this method works, it is very inefficient. A computer scientist named Warshall devised a fairly clever technique for calculating the transitive closure. The problem is managing the complexity of all the potential middlemen transitivity introduces. The trick is to construct a loop where each iteration considers how just one node changes things if it is allowed to be a middleman. So you start with the connections that can be made with no middlemen at all (i.e., the original edges). Then you consider, say, what new connections you get if you allow node number 1 to be a middleman. Then you consider what new connections you get if you allow node number 2 to be a middleman. In pseudocode:

```
start with just simple edge connections.
for k := 1 to (number of nodes in the graph) do begin
    add any new connections that can be formed using
      node number k as a middleman;
end;
```

More specifically:

```
start with just simple edge connections.
for k := 1 to (num nodes in graph) do begin
  for i := 1 to (num nodes in graph) do begin
    for j := 1 to (num nodes in graph) do begin
      if (i and j are not connected) and (node k
        connects them) then begin
        consider i and j connected;
      end;
    end;
  end;
end;
```

This is easily translated into a Pascal procedure that can be added to the library:

```
procedure TransitiveClosure (var G, Closure: Graph.Typ);
var
  I, J, K: integer;
begin
CopyGraph(G, Closure);
for K := 1 to Graph.NumNodesWithEdges(G) do
  for I := 1 to Graph.NumNodesWithEdges(G) do
    for J := 1 to Graph.NumNodesWithEdges(G) do
      if (not Graph.ConnectionExists(Closure, I, J)) and
        (Graph.ConnectionExists(Closure, I, K)) and
        (Graph.ConnectionExists(Closure, K, J)) then begin
        Graph.AddEdge(Closure, I, J);
      end; (* If *)
end; (* TransitiveClosure *)
```

For example, consider the graph of Roman gods. You start with the original graph:

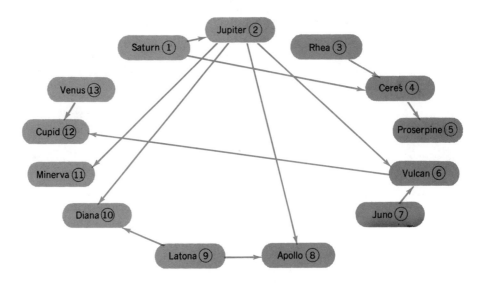

You then try and see if node 1 (Saturn) can be a middleman. To do this, you go through each node and see if it has an edge to node 1. If it does, you then go through all the nodes to which node 1 has an edge and create an edge from your original node to those nodes. Since no nodes have an edge to node 1, however, the result at this point is the same as the original graph:

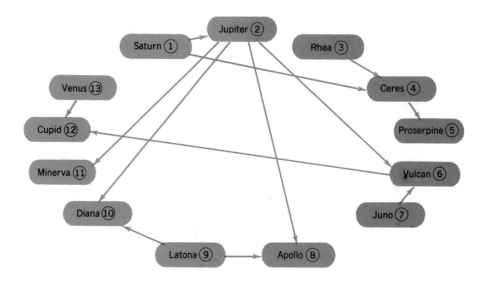

You now try the same thing with node 2 (Jupiter). Both nodes 1 (Saturn) and 3 (Rhea) have an edge to node 2. Further, node 2 has edges to nodes 6 (Vulcan), 8 (Apollo), 10 (Diana), and 11 (Minerva). You therefore create edges from both Saturn and Rhea to each of these four nodes, yielding the following result:

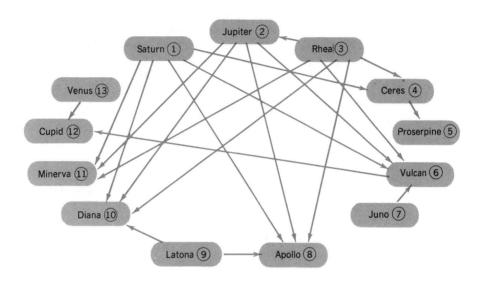

Carrying this to its conclusion you get the following graph, which represents the transitive closure of the original graph:

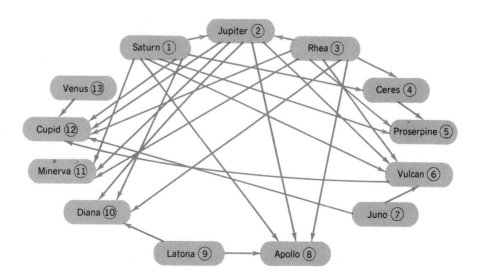

Thus, in this graph each node has an edge to all of its god's descendants, rather than just to the god's children.

7.3.5. All Shortest Paths

Floyd developed an algorithm similar to Warshall's, in which the weights of the resulting graph, instead of just being one to indicate the transitive closure, represent instead the cost of the shortest path from one node to another. For example, if an edge connects node i to node j, and that edge has a weight of 5, then the cost of traversing that edge is 5. Further, if there is an edge from i to k with weight 2, and an edge from k to j with weight 1, then the cost of going from i to j along this path is 3. Since this cost is less than the cost of going from i to j directly, Floyd's algorithm would indicate that there is indeed a path from i to j, and, moreover, that the path with the minimum cost has a cost of 3 (assuming there aren't other paths whose cost is less).

Floyd's algorithm computes these minimal-cost paths by starting with the original edges, as does Warshall's algorithm. Also like Warshall's algorithm, it then considers the paths you get by allowing each node, successively, to be a middleman connecting two other nodes. Unlike Warshall's algorithm, it computes the cost for all the paths in which that node is a middleman. If this cost is less than the weight of the edge currently connecting the two nodes, or if no such edge exists, then an edge connecting those nodes, with the given cost as the weight, is added to the graph. This algorithm leads to the following code:

```
procedure AllShortestPaths (var G, Shortest: Graph.Typ);
var
  I, J, K, NewVal: integer;
begin
 CopyGraph(G, Shortest);
 for K := 1 to Graph.NumNodesWithEdges(G) do
  for I := 1 to Graph.NumNodesWithEdges(G) do
   for J := 1 to Graph.NumNodesWithEdges(G) do
     if (Graph.ConnectionExists(Shortest, I, K)) and
        (Graph.ConnectionExists(Shortest, K, J)) and
        (i <> j) then begin
       NewVal := Graph.GetWeight(Shortest, I, K)
                 + Graph.GetWeight(Shortest, K,
        if (not Graph.ConnectionExists(Shortest, I, J)) or
        (NewVal < Graph.GetWeight(Shortest, I, J)) then
          Graph.AddWeightedEdge(Shortest, I, J, NewVal);
      end; (* If *)
 end; (* AllShortestPaths *)
```

For example, consider again the graph of the Roman gods shown on the following page. This graph is represented by the following adjacency matrix, which shows the weights of each edge (which are all zero or one at this point).

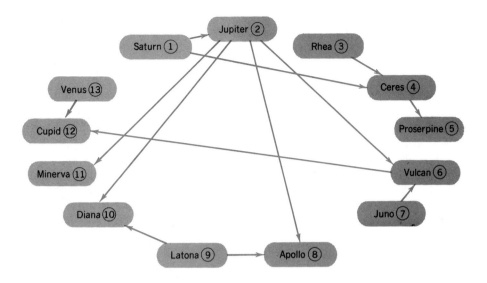

	1	2	3	4	5	6	7	8	9	10	11	12	13
1	0	1	0	1	0	0	0	0	0	0	0	0	0
2	0	0	0	0	0	1	0	1	0	1	1	0	0
3	0	1	0	1	0	0	0	0	0	0	0	0	0
4	0	0	0	0	1	0	0	0	0	0	0	0	0
5	0	0	0	0	0	0	0	0	0	0	0	0	0
6	0	0	0	0	0	0	0	0	0	0	0	1	0
7	0	0	0	0	0	1	0	0	0	0	0	0	0
8	0	0	0	0	0	0	0	0	0	0	0	0	0
9	0	0	0	0	0	0	0	1	0	1	0	0	0
10	0	0	0	0	0	0	0	0	0	0	0	0	0
11	0	0	0	0	0	0	0	0	0	0	0	0	0
12	0	0	0	0	0	0	0	0	0	0	0	0	0
13	0	0	0	0	0	0	0	0	0	0	0	1	0

Floyd's algorithm starts with this graph. It then considers all nodes that have edges to node 1. Since none does, it next looks at all nodes that have edges to node 2 (Jupiter's node). In this case, both Saturn and Rhea have edges to Jupiter, since they are Jupiter's parents. It then computes the cost of the path from Saturn and Rhea's four children. For example, since the cost to go from Saturn to Jupiter is 1, and the cost to go from Jupiter to Vulcan is 1, then the cost to go from Saturn to Vulcan is 2. Since there was no edge from Saturn to Vulcan, such an edge is created whose weight is 2. Similarly, edges from Saturn and Rhea to the remainder of Jupiter's children are created, each of which has a weight of 2. When this algorithm is carried to completion, the result is a graph with the following adjacency matrix:

	1	2	3	4	5	6	7	8	9	10	11	12	13
1	0	1	0	1	2	2	0	2	0	2	2	3	0
2	0	0	0	0	0	1	0	1	0	1	1	2	0
3	0	1	0	1	2	2	0	2	0	2	2	3	0
4	0	0	0	0	1	0	0	0	0	0	0	0	0
5	0	0	0	0	0	0	0	0	0	0	0	0	0
6	0	0	0	0	0	0	0	0	0	0	0	1	0
7	0	0	0	0	0	1	0	0	0	0	0	2	0
8	0	0	0	0	0	0	0	0	0	0	0	0	0
9	0	0	0	0	0	0	0	1	0	1	0	0	0
10	0	0	0	0	0	0	0	0	0	0	0	0	0
11	0	0	0	0	0	0	0	0	0	0	0	0	0
12	0	0	0	0	0	0	0	0	0	0	0	0	0
13	0	0	0	0	0	0	0	0	0	0	0	1	0

Think about the meaning of this graph. Where Warshall's algorithm resulted in a graph in which every node had an edge to all of its descendants, this graph does that and also tells you how distant those descendants are from that node. For example, since there is an edge of length 2 from node 3 (Rhea) to node 6 (Vulcan), Vulcan must be Rhea's grandchild! You can therefore find all a god's descendants by finding its node's neighbors, and you can then tell how the two gods are related by examining the weights of the edges connecting them.

7.3.6. Topological Sort

The previous several algorithms were similar in that they analyzed all pairs of nodes in a graph. The next algorithm, however, instead looks at the *dependencies* between the nodes of a graph. A node is said to depend on another node if there is an edge from the second node to the first. Thus, dependencies are meaningful only in a directed graph. The topological sort algorithm computes an ordering of the nodes in a graph such that every node comes before all the nodes that depend on it. Such an ordering can exist only in an acyclic graph, since cycles introduce mutual dependencies. Thus, topological sort is defined for directed acyclic graphs, or DAGs.

7.3.6.1. The Algorithm

As an example, consider how cells in a spreadsheet are recalculated when a cell value changes. A spreadsheet consists of a collection of cells, each of which may contain either a *number* or a *formula* (as well as other items that are irrelevant to this example). A formula represents a calculation that may depend on the values of other cells. Thus, when the value of one cell changes, that may result in a large number of changes being propagated through the spreadsheet. For example, a spreadsheet may have the following cells:

Cell Number	Contents	Value
1	100	100
2	(Cell One) + 10	110
3	(Cell One) × 20	2000
4	(Cell One) + (Cell Two) + (Cell Three)	2210

Thus, cells 2 and 3 depend on the value of cell 1, whereas cell 4 depends on cells 1, 2, and 3. The following graph depicts these dependencies:

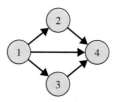

Given these dependencies, there are two possible topologically sorted orderings: (1, 2, 3, 4) and (1, 3, 2, 4). This is precisely the order in which the cells must be recalculated when the value in cell 1 changes. Any other order of recalculation will result in a cell temporarily holding an incorrect value. Thus, topological sort is an appropriate technique for computing the recalculation order of cells in a spreadsheet.

To topologically sort a graph, you first determine each node's set of dependencies. Thus, for the preceding graph, you would compute the following information:

```
Node      Dependencies
 1        None
 2        {1}
 3        {1}
 4        {1, 2, 3}
```

Given this initial state, you repeatedly traverse the nodes, each time removing a node that depends on none of the remaining nodes. When you remove that node, you must also remove it from every other node's set of dependencies. You repeat this until you have removed all the nodes. For example, on the first pass over the foregoing graph you will remove node 1 (since it has no dependencies) and set the dependency lists of the remaining nodes as follows:

```
Node      Dependencies
 2        None
 3        None
 4        {2, 3}
```

You can then remove either node 2 or node 3. Suppose you remove node 2. This leaves you with the following:

```
Node      Dependencies
 3        None
 4        {3}
```

You then remove node 3, leaving only node 4, which doesn't depend on any remaining nodes (since there aren't any). You thus remove node 4, and the algorithm terminates. The order in which the nodes have been removed is a topologically sorted order.

7.3.6.2. Implementing the Algorithm

Given the Graph ADT, there is a convenient way of implementing this algorithm without requiring each node to store a set of dependencies. Instead, you initially set each node's mark value to the number of that node's dependencies. Thus, a node that has a zero mark has no dependencies. When you remove such a node, you then go through all its neighbors and decrement their mark values. This effectively removes that node from the dependency lists of all the nodes that depend on it. This implementation is summarized in the following pseudocode. Note that it returns the topologically sorted ordering via a Stream:

```
procedure TopologicalSort (var G: Graph.Typ;
        var S: Stream.Typ);
begin
   Set marks of nodes in G to their number of dependencies
   for I := 1 to (number of nodes in G)
      Z := Node number of a node in G with mark of zero
      Set Z's mark to a nonzero number
      Decrement Z's neighbors marks by one
      Add Z to S
   end; (* For *)
end; (* TopologicalSort *)
```

As an aside, note that when a node with a mark value of zero is added to the Stream, its mark value is set to some nonzero number, so that it won't be added again on subsequent iterations of the loop. Since this value can be any nonzero value, you might as well set it to the value of the loop control variable *I*, which represents the position of that node in the ordering. Thus, when the algorithm terminates, the mark of every node in the graph indicates that node's position in the topologically sorted order.

To complicate things a bit, there are actually two "topological sorts" that may be of interest. You may want to sort every node in the graph, as the foregoing pseudocode describes, or you may want to "topological subsort" a subset of those nodes. For example, when you change the value of a cell in a spreadsheet you only want to recalculate the values of the cells that depend on the changed cell, and you are not concerned with the rest of the cells in the spreadsheet. You thus want to find all the cells that depend on the changed cell and topologically sort that subgraph. The following pseudocode summarizes such an algorithm:

```
procedure TopologicalSubsort (var G: Graph.Typ;
        N: integer;
        var S: Stream.Typ);
begin
   L := List of nodes in G that depend on N (including N)
   Set marks of nodes in L to their number of
   dependencies on nodes in L
   for I := 1 to (number of nodes in L)
```

```
      Z := Node number of a node in L with mark of zero
      Set Z's mark to I
      Decrement Z's neighbors marks by one
      Add Z to S
  end; (* For *)
end; (* TopologicalSubsort *)
```

First, consider implementing this "topological subsort" algorithm. You can determine the nodes that depend on the given node *n* by traversing the graph starting with
that node. This will yield a stream containing all the nodes that depend on *n* and,
as a bonus, will set the marks of those nodes to the number of their dependencies
(if you'll recall, that was a side effect of the traversals). This leads to the following
code:

```
procedure TopologicalSubsort (var G: Graph.Typ;
    var SortStream: Stream.Typ;
    StartNode: integer);
  var
   TempStream: Stream.Typ;
begin
 Stream.Create(TempStream);
 DepthFirstTrav(G, TempStream, StartNode);
 DoSort(G, TempStream, SortStream);
 Stream.Destroy(TempStream);
end; (* TopologicalSubsort *)
```

The *DoSort* procedure must first therefore determine the number of nodes in the
traversal. It then loops that many times, each time finding a node with a zero mark,
changing that mark, decrementing the dependencies of that node's neighbors, and
adding that node to *SortStream*:

```
procedure DoSort (var G: Graph.Typ;
    var NodeStream, SortStream: Stream.Typ);
  var
   I, NextNode: integer;
begin
 Stream.Rewrite(SortStream);
 for I := 1 to NumElems(NodeStream) do begin
   GetZeroMarkNode(G, NodeStream, NextNode);
   Graph.SetMark(G, NextNode, I);
   DecNeighborMarks(G, NextNode);
   Stream.Write(SortStream, NextNode);
  end; (* For *)
end; (* DoSort *)
```

You can determine the number of nodes in a Stream simply by traversing that Stream
and maintaining a counter:

```
function NumElems (var S: Stream.Typ): integer;
 var
   COUNT, DUMMY: integer;
begin
 Stream.Reset(S);
 COUNT := 0;
 while not Stream.AtEnd(S) do begin
    COUNT := COUNT + 1;
    Stream.Read(S, DUMMY);
   end; (* While *)
 NumElems := COUNT;
end; (* NumElems *)
```

Finally, finding a node with a mark value of zero just requires scanning all the nodes that are being sorted, and you can decrement the mark value of a node's neighbors by first determining those neighbors using the *Graph.Neighbors* routine, and then subtracting one from each of their mark values:

```
procedure GetZeroMarkNode (var G: Graph.Typ;
      NodeStream: Stream.Typ;
      var NextNode: integer);
 var
  Found: boolean;

begin
 Stream.Reset(NodeStream);
 Found := false;
 while (not Stream.AtEnd(NodeStream)) and (not Found) do
 begin
   Stream.Read(NodeStream, NextNode);
   Found := (Graph.GetMark(G, NextNode) = 0);
   end; (* While *)
end; (* GetZeroMarkNode *)
```

```
procedure DecNeighborMarks (var G: Graph.Typ;
      Node: integer);
 var
  NeighborStream: Stream.Typ;
  Neighbor: integer;
begin
 Stream.Create(NeighborStream);
 Graph.Neighbors(G, NeighborStream, Node);
 while not Stream.AtEnd(NeighborStream) do begin
   Stream.Read(NeighborStream, Neighbor);
   Graph.SetMark(G, Neighbor,
              Graph.GetMark(G, Neighbor) - 1);
   end; (* While *)
 Stream.Destroy(NeighborStream);
end; (* DecNeighborMarks *)
```

For example, given the following graph:

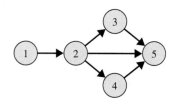

a topological subsort starting at node 1 would yield the ordering (1, 2, 3, 4, 5), while a subsort starting from node 4 would yield (4, 5).

This *DoSort* procedure makes implementing full topological sort straightforward. You first need to build a Stream that contains the node numbers of all the nodes in the graph, and you must set the marks of those nodes appropriately:

```
procedure PrepForFullSort (var G: Graph.Typ;
    var S: Stream.Typ);
 var
  I, J: integer;

begin
 Stream.Rewrite(S);
 Graph.ZeroAllMarks(G);
 for I := 1 to Graph.NumNodesWithEdges(G) do begin
   Stream.Write(S, I);
   for J := 1 to Graph.NumNodesWithEdges(G) do begin
     if Graph.ConnectionExists(G, I, J) then begin
       Graph.SetMark(G, J, Graph.GetMark(G, J) + 1);
     end; (* If *)
   end; (* For *)
 end; (* For *)
end; (* PrepForFullSort *)
```

The *TopologicalSort* procedure follows directly:

```
procedure TopologicalSort (var G: Graph.Typ;
    var SortStream: Stream.Typ);
 var
  I: integer;
  TempStream: Stream.Typ;
begin
 Stream.Create(TempStream);
 PrepForFullSort(G, TempStream);
 DoSort(G, TempStream, SortStream);
 Stream.Destroy(TempStream);
end; (* TopologicalSort *)
```

Given the previous example graph, this procedure will return (1, 2, 3, 4, 5) as the topologically sorted ordering of the graph.

7.3.7. Minimal-Cost Spanning Tree

The final algorithm discussed in this chapter computes a *minimal-cost spanning tree* for a graph. A spanning tree is a collection of edges such that every node in the graph can be reached from every other node by following some path of edges. Such a set of edges is called a spanning tree because it is said to "span" the nodes of the graph. Thus, all connected graphs have at least one spanning tree, consisting of its complete set of edges. Prim's algorithm takes a connected graph and returns the spanning tree with the minimal cost, where the cost is the sum of the weights of the edges.

For example, for the following undirected graph:

Prim's algorithm would return the graph below, which contains the minimal spanning tree (whose cost is 30):

This algorithm has a large number of applications, including highway planning, laying cable for computer networks and cable TV, and positioning phone and power lines. In each of these examples, the nodes represent locations, with the edges connecting those locations and serving as conduits for shared resources.

7.3.7.1. The Algorithm

Prim's algorithm builds the minimal-cost spanning tree one edge at a time, each time taking the edge with the minimal cost that leads from a node already in the tree to a node not in the tree. In this way, the resulting spanning tree is guaranteed to be both connected and have minimal cost. For *undirected* graphs, you first select an arbitrary node and find its minimum-weight edge. You add this edge to the spanning tree, and then look through the two nodes now in the tree, scanning for the minimum edge that connects one of those nodes with a new node. You add this edge to the tree, giving you a tree with three nodes. You then look through those three nodes for the smallest edge connecting one of those nodes to a new node, add that edge to the tree, and so on. You repeat this until all the nodes from the original graph are reachable in the spanning tree.

For example, suppose you are given the following undirected graph:

You first select an arbitrary node, say node 1. You then choose its minimum-weight edge, which is the edge to node 2, and add this edge to the spanning tree:

You then select the minimum edge connecting either node 1 or node 2 to a node not already in the spanning tree and add that edge to the tree:

Finally, you select the smallest edge connecting either nodes 1, 2, or 3 to some other node and add that edge to the spanning tree:

The resulting graph contains exactly the edges that constitute the minimal-cost spanning tree.

7.3.7.2. Implementing the Algorithm

Once again, the marking capability of the Graph ADT will prove useful. Rather than maintaining a separate list of nodes that have been added to the tree, you can simply mark those nodes in the original graph. Thus, each time through the loop, you want to find the minimal-cost edge connecting a marked node with an unmarked node, mark that node, and add that edge to the spanning tree you are constructing. This leads to the following procedure (keeping in mind that since these are undirected graphs the edges must point in both directions):

```
procedure MinimalSpanningTree (var G, Span: Graph.Typ);
 var
   Node1, Node2, Weight, I: integer;
begin
 Graph.ZeroAllMarks(G);
 Graph.SetMark(G, 1, 1);
 for I := 2 to Graph.NumNodesWithEdges(G) do begin
   FindNextEdge(G, Node1, Node2, Weight);
   Graph.SetMark(G, Node2, 1);
   Graph.AddWeightedEdge(Span, Node1, Node2, Weight);
   Graph.AddWeightedEdge(Span, Node2, Node1, Weight);
 end; (* For *)
end; (* MinimalSpanningTree *)
```

To find the next edge on each loop iteration, you simply scan through all the nodes in the original graph. For each marked node, you scan across all its edges, looking for the edge to an unmarked node with the smallest weight. You then return the smallest such edge:

```
procedure MinWeightForNode (var G: Graph.Typ;
     Node: integer;
     var MinWeight, ToNode: integer;
     var Found: boolean);
 var
   NeighborStream: Stream.Typ;
   EdgeWt, Neighbor: integer;
begin
 Stream.Create(NeighborStream);
 MinWeight := maxint;
 Found := false;
 Graph.Neighbors(G, NeighborStream, Node);
 while not Stream.AtEnd(NeighborStream) do begin
   Stream.Read(NeighborStream, Neighbor);
   if Graph.GetMark(G, Neighbor) = 0 then begin
     EdgeWt := Graph.GetWeight(G, Node, Neighbor);
     if EdgeWt <= MinWeight then begin
```

```
                              Found := true;
                              ToNode := Neighbor;
                              MinWeight := EdgeWt;
                           end; (* If *)
                        end; (* If *)
                     end; (* While *)
                  Stream.Destroy(NeighborStream);
                  end; (* MinWeightForNode *)

               procedure FindNextEdge (var G: Graph.Typ;
                     var Node1, Node2: integer;
                     var Weight: integer);
                  var
                  Node, Neighbor, NodeMinWt, CurrMin: integer;
                  Found: boolean;

               begin
                  Weight := maxint;
                  for Node := 1 to Graph.NumNodesWithEdges(G) do begin
                     if Graph.GetMark(G, Node) <> 0 then begin
                        MinWeightForNode(G, Node, NodeMinWt, Neighbor, Found);
                        if (Found) and (NodeMinWt <= Weight) then begin
                           Node1 := Node;
                           Node2 := Neighbor;
                           Weight := NodeMinWt;
                        end; (* If *)
                     end; (* If *)
                  end; (* While *)
               end; (* FindNextEdge *)
```

Note that this routine sets the marks of all the nodes in the original graph to 1.

7.3.8. SELF CHECK EXERCISES

1. Two versions of depth-first traversal are shown, a recursive version and a stack-based version. The order in which the nodes are output, though, differs for these versions. Why?

2. In the recursive implementation of depth-first traversal, why must *NeighborStream* be a local variable?

3. Given the array implementation of the Graph ADT, negative weights can lead to a problem with the algorithms that rely on matrix multiplication. What is this problem?

4. Rather than using Prim's algorithm, why can't you find a minimal-cost spanning tree by simply selecting the minimum edge leading to each node? Answer this question for both directed and undirected graphs.

5. Chapter 5 discussed three binary free traversal; preorder, inorder, and postorder. And these traversals breadth-first or depth-first?

7.4. SUMMARY OF KEY POINTS

- Graphs consist of a set of *nodes* and a set of *edges* connecting those nodes. Graphs may be *connected, directed, cyclic,* and/or *weighted.* They are useful for representing complex relationships among data elements.

- The Graph ADT provides high-level operations for manipulating a graph's structure while giving the client responsibility for the data stored in the nodes. Two implementations are shown, one of which is suitable for small graphs or for graphs with high connectivity, whereas the other is more appropriate for large, sparsely-connected graphs.

- The *adjacency matrix* is a representation of a graph in which the value at row i, column j is nonzero if there is an edge from node i to node j. For weighted graphs, the value stored in that position is the corresponding edge's weight. Raising an adjacency matrix to the nth power yields a matrix whose nonzero elements correspond to the paths of length n in the original graph.

- The *connectivity matrix* of a graph is identical to that graph's adjacency matrix, except that it has ones down the diagonal. Raising a connectivity matrix to the nth power yields a matrix whose nonzero elements correspond to the paths of length up to n in the original graph.

- *Warshall's algorithm* determines the *transitive closure* of a graph, which shows the connectivity of each pair of nodes. *Floyd's algorithm* also reveals a graph's transitive closure, and additionally indicates the cost of the shortest path from each node to every other node.

- The *topological sort* algorithm orders the nodes of an acyclic graph such that each node comes before all the nodes that *depend* on it.

- *Prim's algorithm* find the *minimal-cost spanning tree* of a connected graph.

7.5. PROGRAMMING EXERCISES

1. Since graph data may change during a program's execution, it is useful to be able to save the state of a graph to an external file and then retrieve that information. Implement procedures with the following headers that will perform these functions:

   ```
   procedure ArchiveGraph (var Outfile: text; var G: Graph.Typ);
   procedure RestoreGraph (var Infile: text; var G: Graph.Typ);
   ```

2. The example program in Section 7.2.1 that showed the children of Roman gods used an array to associate a god's name with that god's node number. Rewrite this code using the Table ADT instead of an array.

3. Modify the Roman gods program from Section 7.2.1 to show all of a god's descendants, rather than just a god's children.

4. Modify the Roman gods program from Section 7.2.1 to show all of a god's descendants, and to specify the relationship of each of those descendants to the given god.

5. Write a procedure to detect whether or not a graph has a cycle.

6. Implement Prim's algorithm for directed graphs.

7.6. PROGRAMMING PROJECTS

1. Reimplement the array version of the Graph ADT so that weights of zero are permitted.

2. Modify the Graph ADT specification so that it permits an edge to have multiple weights and then implement this new Graph ADT.

3. The section on topological sort discusses using this algorithm in a spreadsheet recalc engine. Implement a simple spreadsheet that provides a two-dimensional array of cells and allows the user to enter either a *label,* a *number,* or a *formula* into each cell. Each cell is numbered using the capital letters vertically and consecutive integers horizontally. For example, cell A1 is in the upper-left-hand corner of the spreadsheet. A label is just a string, numbers are the spreadsheet's raw data, and formulas allow the user to compute new data based on old data. For example, the formula '= A1 + B1' has as its value the sum of the contents of cells A1 and B1.

4. For this assignment, you have been hired by a cable TV company to help bring HBO and MTV to every building on campus. This will involve drilling a lot of tunnels and laying a lot of cables. We will assume that someone has figured out the cost of drilling a tunnel between every pair of buildings on campus. You are given this information in a file such as the one below:

```
Wilbur Stern 5
Branner Stern 1
Stern Meyer 2
. . .
```

The file contains a series of lines. Each line denotes one possible edge (tunnel) between two nodes (buildings). The first line in the preceding example means it is possible to connect Wilbur to Stern for a cost of 5 thousand dollars. Of course, this connection works both ways; it could just as easily have been listed as "Stern Wilbur 5." If the cost of laying a cable between two buildings is prohibitively expensive, it is not listed in the file. Luckily, you do not have to connect every building to every other building. You just have to make sure that each building is connected to at least one other building, and that by following enough connections you can eventually get from each building to every other building. Your job is to find the least expensive network that satisfies these conditions. Your program should print a list of the necessary tunnels, and the total cost of the project.

8

ADVANCED TOPICS

This chapter presents a quick overview of some advanced material not covered in depth in this book.

8.1. ADVANCED TECHNIQUES FOR ADT MODULES

Chapter 2 used the analogy that using the operations supplied by an ADT module for manipulating variables is similar to a scientist handling radioactive isotopes using a robot arm. The analogy is particularly helpful in pointing out that manipulating variables in this way will inevitably be somewhat clumsy and inefficient. Working through the procedures and functions included in the ADT specification will always be like handling an object while wearing gloves. Without the gloves, the ADT, you know that you can always perform tasks in the simplest and most efficient manner possible. Constrained by the ADT, however, you might find that simple things become complex or that efficiency becomes impossible to achieve. Thus, it is not always desirable to formally abstract a type used in a program by specifying an ADT for it.

This section begins by reviewing the pros and cons of the ADT approach to give you a context for deciding when to apply and when to avoid this technique. Then it introduces a few "fancy" techniques for handling some of the most significant cons even in the ADT approach. These techniques are helpful on those occasions when the cons don't manage to outweigh the pros, but nevertheless prove significant and worthy of attention. The section closes with two other advanced ADT techniques, one to enhance the integrity of the ADT's isolation (i.e., strengthening "the wall") and another that can enhance the usefulness of an ADT that is often manipulated using a similar sequence of actions.

8.1.1. Pros and Cons of the ADT Approach

Having read the examples in previous chapters, you should by now recognize some of the benefits of the ADT approach. The Table ADT introduced in Chapter 2, for example, proves useful in so many different programs that encapsulating its definition in an ADT module that can easily be applied multiple times saves considerable programming effort. Furthermore, because the table ends up being used so often, the added benefit of being able to reimpliment it without rewriting any of the programs that use it makes the job of software maintenance much simpler.

You have also seen examples where the ADT approach is helpful even for a highly specific structure. As Chapter 3 pointed out, the data structure details implicit in the eight queens and maze-search problems are sufficiently complex that creating ADT modules greatly simplifies the task of writing and debugging the recursive procedures that solve the overall tasks. For those two problems, the data structures are so specific to the applications at hand that it is possible to isolate not only the details of data structure manipulation, but also the type and variable declarations for the structure itself. This greatly simplifies the ADT interface, allowing the author of the high-level code to manipulate the "implied" or "understood" structure maintained by the ADT module without having to actually understand or specify such details.

There is a host of minor benefits of the ADT approach, not least of which is the fact that for those who understand and use the methodology, it serves as one more potential starting point for solving a challenging problem. Nevertheless, the only major benefit of the ADT approach not demonstrated in this book is that of project management.

All managers of software development teams have the unenviable task of handling the group dynamics of their staff. Managers of all kinds understand the simple principle that people work best when they know that interference from other staff members cannot interrupt or jeopardize their work. In this context, the independence of ADT modules allows a software manager to divide up a project into chunks that can be developed independently from the others, allowing all staff members to have their own chunks to work on, guaranteed to be free from interference. When this technique is applied, the work of the software manager, as is often the case with managers in general, reduces to one of overall planning and design of the project in the early stages and, as the project progresses, resolution of disputes between staff members. Because of the independence of ADT details, resolution of conflicts most often takes the form of a modification or clarification of module interfaces.

In summary, the primary benefits of the ADT approach are as follows:

- Easy reuse and maintenance of a general-purpose structure or type.
- As an aid in decomposition, separating from the program details a complex

set of data details and possibly even the structure itself (leading to an implied
but undeclared data structure).

• As an aid in project management, by reducing human interface problems to
software interface issues.

For the program examples in this book, ADT modules are introduced only when
one of these advantages is likely to be gained. The benefit of easy manipulation is more
important for such types than the potential benefits of using the ADT
approach.

Anyone who applies the ADT approach quickly becomes aware of its drawbacks.
For example, suppose that you have implemented the Table ADT as a record containing
an array of items and a corresponding length variable, as indicated below:

```
const
 MaxEntries = 500;

type
 TableElement.Typ = <appropriate type>;
 Typ = record
    Entries: array[1..MaxEntries] of TableElement.Typ;
    Length: integer;
  end;
```

If you are writing a program that uses this version of the table module, you *know* that
it is much easier to empty the table simply by saying

```
Table.Length := 0;
```

rather than

```
while not Table.Empty(Table) do begin
   Table.FindMin(Table, Next);
   Table.Delete(Table, Next);
end; (* While *)
```

Another major drawback of the ADT approach is that the specification limits what
you can do. That is why it is so essential to anticipate *in advance* all the operations that
you might want to perform on variables of a given type. It is not humanly possible to
anticipate everything, which means that ADTs are inevitably incomplete. For example,
suppose you are using the array implementation and you want to check to make sure
that you don't try to add an element to the table when it is full. If you are willing to
violate the interface specification (the wall), you could say

```
if (Table.Length < MaxEntries) then begin
   Table.Insert(Table, Item);
 end; (* If *)
```

Unfortunately, there is no way to easily express the test using the specified Table operations (about the only thing you can do is to calculate the length of the table by repeatedly moving its elements into a temporary table until the original becomes empty, and then restore the original using the temporary table).

Providing sufficient but not overly complex facilities for recognizing errors is, in fact, one of the more difficult aspects of ADT design. Recovering from errors is an equally "messy" task in Pascal because it has no special language support for doing so. That is why this book has basically ignored the issue of error recovery until now. Later in this section, however, you will find some suggestions for accommodating error-handling when using the ADT approach.

One other major drawback of the ADT approach that hasn't been discussed much in this book is inefficiency. For example, consider the application of the Table ADT described in Section 2.3.1.

```
program SortNumbers (input, output);
var
 Numbers: Table.Typ;
 NEXT: integer;
begin (* Main *)
 Table.Create(Numbers);
 while not eof do begin
   readln(NEXT);
   if not Table.InTable(Numbers, NEXT) then begin
     Table.Insert(Numbers, NEXT);
     end; (* If *)
   end; (* While *)
 Table.Write(Numbers);
 Table.Destroy(Numbers);
end. (* Main *)
```

Consider what happens when the table is implemented using a linked list, as described in Section 4.7, and the input file is known to be sorted, as in the example below.

```
49
52
56
57
58
```

It is impossible to take advantage of the knowledge that the data appear in sorted order in the input file. In fact, this actually causes the program to perform at its *worst*. Think, for example, of what happens when the value 58 is processed by the program. The first four values are already stored in the table (remember that this implementation involved a dummy header node):

Numbers

The program first calls *InTable* to find whether 58 is already in the table. This requires traversing all four list elements to return the answer *False*. Then it calls *Insert*. This also requires traversing all four list elements before finding the appropriate place for inserting 58. A minor concern is that this approach requires twice as much work as is required in that both the call on *InTable* and the call on *Insert* have to locate the appropriate place for the value in the table. Of even greater concern is the fact that for *n* items to be inserted, the total number of items traversed is $O(n^2)$, when it could optimally be just $O(n)$.

Again, if you were willing to violate the interface specification, you could build the linked list much more efficiently by introducing two temporary linked-list variables and rewriting the initialization and while loop of the main program as follows:

```
begin (* Main *)
  Table := nil;
  while not eof do begin
    new(CURR);
    readln(CURR^.Data);
    CURR^.Next := nil;
    if Table = nil then begin
      Table := CURR;
    end
    else begin
      PREV^.Next := CURR;
    end; (* If *)
    PREV := CURR;
  end; (* While *)
end. (* Main *)
```

A later part of this section shows a better way to solve this problem without violating the ADT interface.

There are several other drawbacks to the ADT approach that are straightforward enough that they don't need to be explained in detail. In summary, the advantages of direct manipulation over the ADT approach are as follows:

- Some simplification of ADT operations, generally for those aspects of the problem that are directly represented in the underlying implementation (e.g., manipulating a length field of a record rather than having to perform abstract manipulations to change the length).

- Complete freedom to manipulate the data, even in ways that were not originally anticipated (e.g., facilitating the addition of error-handling that was not originally anticipated).

- Ability to optimize how operations are performed for a specific program and a specific implementation of the type.

- Simplifying the design process and potentially eliminating unnecessary coding by avoiding the need to guarantee that the set of ADT operations is "complete," allowing the programmer to handle such details "on the fly" whenever, and only whenever, they are needed.

- Elimination of the overhead of calling procedures and functions for all ADT manipulations, increasing overall execution efficiency.

8.1.2. Checking for Errors

The previous section pointed out that this book has ignored the issue of error-recovery in sample programs. Anticipating and handling errors is, in fact, of great importance for a software engineer. The facilities for recovering from errors, however, vary significantly from programming language to programming language. Demonstrating at least as much diversity as the programming languages themselves, current "software experts" differ tremendously on the subject of what basic philosophy should be applied when considering error detection and handling.

Because Pascal has no special support for either error detection or error recovery and because neither of your authors is expert in this field, this section merely presents a few different approaches for incorporating such error-checking into the kind of Pascal ADT modules included in this book.

If an ADT interface is not violated, then error conditions will generally become apparent inside the ADT module itself (e.g., when it is asked to insert a new value into a table that is filled to capacity). Thus, the author of the ADT module must anticipate and check for errors. But error recovery varies so much from program to program that including appropriate error-handling code in the ADT module itself is generally not advisable (e.g., when the table becomes too full, should a warning be appended to an errors file, should an error message be printed to the terminal screen, should program execution be terminated, or should some other action be taken?). Thus, the author of the program or code segment that makes use of the ADT module should, in general, be responsibile for recovering from errors.

That means that the real issue to be addressed in ADT module design is how you can best facilitate communication between the error-checking code in the ADT module and the error-recovery code in the code segment that uses the module. Obviously the only way to add this extra dimension of communication is to modify the ADT interface.

One approach is to incorporate error-checking information in the parameters of the ADT operations. For example, instead of specifying table insertion as follows:

```
procedure Insert (var T: Typ; Item: TableElement.Typ);
        post    Item is added to T such that T remains
                sorted.
```

you could add a third parameter and change the specification to the following:

```
procedure Insert (var T: Typ; Item: TableElement.Typ;
                  var Success: boolean);
        post    If T is not full, Item is added to T such
                that T remains sorted and Success is set
                to True; otherwise, T is unchanged and
                Success is set to False.
```

The problem with this approach is that it significantly complicates the interface. Every call on an ADT operation that might produce an error would have to be modified in a similar manner. That means that the many calls on ADT operations in the many programs that make use of the ADT have to be changed by introducing boolean variables for recording error status and including such variables in the list of parameters passed to the ADT.

A simple calculation on the resulting impact should tell you that this is the wrong approach. After all, there is only one ADT module versus many different existing and potential programs that use the module. Does it make more sense to burden the single author of the single module or the many authors of the many programs using the module? Unless you have a trace of dictator in you, you should realize that burdening the module author is most appropriate for preserving "global harmony."

Instead of having the programs that use the ADT declare and pass boolean error variables, you can add boolean functions to the set of basic ADT operations. For example, you can introduce a function for testing whether a table is full and change the specification of procedure *Insert* as follows:

```
function Full (var T: Typ): boolean;
        post    returns True if T is full; otherwise,
                returns False.

procedure Insert (var T: Typ; Item: TableElement.Typ);
        pre     not Full(T)
        post    Item is added to T such that T remains
                sorted.
```

For an implementation using dynamic allocation (e.g., a linked list), the error condition *Full* would never become true, leading to this definition:

```
function Full (var T: Typ): boolean;
begin
 Full := false;
end; (* Full *)
```

For the array implementation described in the last section, however, the function would contain a meaningful test that allows the user of the module to detect when a table implemented in this way has been filled to capacity.

```
function Full (var T: Typ): boolean;
begin
 Full := (T.length = MaxEntries);
end; (* Full *)
```

A boolean function like *Full* is similar to the colored indicators manufacturers sometimes include in the dashboard of an automobile to assist consumers in identifying minor problems early enough to correct them before a serious problem occurs. For example, an indicator might turn on or change from green to red when you are running out of gas, or if you have too little oil, or if your mileage indicates that it's once again time to rotate your tires.

Thus, to use a function like *Full*, you must *anticipate* the error and be sure not to proceed once you detect it. For example, suppose that you are processing an input file that indicates for a series of years which days of that year were particularly rainy. Suppose that each line of the file stores a year followed by a series of integers between 1 and 365 (366 for leap years) indicating the rainy days for that year, as in

```
1961 28 29 43 57 58 59 ...
1989 3 4 5 34 35 44 55 ...
```

You might write the following code to read in this file and produce a list of all the years followed by a list of the rainy days (with days that were rainy in more than one year appearing as duplicates).

```
begin
 Table.Create(Years);
 Table.Create(Days);
 while not eof do begin
    read(Next);
    Table.Insert(Years, Next);
    while not eoln do begin
       read(NEXT);
       Table.Insert(Days, Next);
      end; (* While *)
    readln;
  end; (* While *)
 writeln('Years:');
 Table.Print(Years);
 writeln('Days:');
 Table.Print(Days);
 Table.Destroy(Years);
 Table.Destroy(Days);
end. (* Main *)
```

Using function *Full*, to avoid overflow problems, you would change the two calls on *Insert* above to the following:

```
if not Table.Full(Years) then begin
  Table.Insert(Years, Next);
 end; (* If *)
 ...
if not Table.Full(Days) then begin
  Table.Insert(Days, Next);
 end; (* If *)
```

And you would want to add some code that reports the error before the program terminates, as in:

```
writeln('Years:');
Table.Print(Years);
if Table.Full(Years) then begin
  writeln('This table overflowed.');
 end; (* If *)
writeln('Days:');
Table.Print(Days);
if Table.Full(Days) then begin
  writeln('This table overflowed.');
 end; (* If *)
```

Function *Full* can best be described as an early-warning device. It provides a facility for the author of code that uses the ADT to easily detect impending problems. It also means that many of the ADT operations have added preconditions involving the warning messages (e.g., procedure *Insert* cannot be called if *Full* is *True*). Although this is an intuitive approach, it has several drawbacks:

- It adds the burden of paying attention to a warning as soon as the warning is issued. Thus, the user of the ADT must carefully check all calls on sensitive operations like *Insert*.
- It leaves the author of the ADT module no reasonable alternative when warnings are ignored. For example, what should *Insert* do if it is called when *Full* is *True*? If it tries to insert, an execution error occurs and the program terminates abnormally. If it ignores the request to insert, then authors of code using the module will not realize that their programs contain bugs that cause them to attempt to insert values into tables that are full. The only other alternative is for the ADT module to try to handle the error, but as mentioned earlier, there is no way to know what action is appropriate.
- It leads to subtle bugs where errors are confused with near-errors. For example, the previous program actually does not work correctly in the case where the data causes one or both tables to be filled exactly to capacity. The program reports overflow in this case, even if no attempt was made to insert a value after the table filled.

Thus, you will often find that another approach is desirable.

Another alternative is to make the ADT operations more robust by allowing them to be called even if an error state is about to be reached or has previously been reached. Instead of supplying functions for detecting potential future errors, you supply functions for detecting previous actual errors. This can best be described as an error-resistant approach.

This closely parallels how fuses and circuit-breakers work, as well as the function of the "Tilt" light on a pinball machine. If there is a sudden surge of power in your house (e.g., if it's just been struck by lightning), you don't want a warning bell to sound to inform you that all of your electrical equipment plugged into outlets is about to be fried to ashes. What you want is something like a fuse or circuit-breaker to make your electrical system robust enough to shut itself off when an error like that occurs. Pinball machines do the same thing when they shut themselves off because a player has cheated by tilting it. And just as the pinball machine has to flash the message "Tilt" for the bewildered player to figure out what happened, any such system must allow previous errors to be reported.

Using an error-resistant approach, you would introduce a function *Overfull* instead of a function *Full* and would specify *Insert* as follows:

```
function Overfull (var T: Typ): boolean;
        post    returns True if an attempt was previously
                made to add an element to T when it was
                full; otherwise, returns False.

procedure Insert (var T: Typ; Item: TableElement.Typ);
        post    if T is not full, Item is added to T such
                that it remains sorted; otherwise, T is
                unchanged and subsequent calls on
                Overfull will return True.
```

Using this approach, the original file-processing program remains exactly the same, except in the final reporting of results:

```
writeln('Years:');
Table.Print(Years);
if Table.Overfull(Years) then begin
  writeln('This table overflowed.');
 end; (* If *)
writeln('Days:');
Table.Print(Days);
if Table.Overfull(Days) then begin
  writeln('This table overflowed.');
 end; (* If *)
```

The benefits of the error-resistant approach are most significant when, as in the previous example, the programmer using the ADT module wants to first manipulate the structure in a complex way without paying attention to errors, and then as a second step, handle any errors.

The error-resistant approach has two subtleties that need to be mentioned. First, unlike the early-warning approach, it often means introducing error variables because the data themselves are generally sufficient for issuing warnings while additional memory is usually required to remember previous errors. For example, for the array implementation of the Table mentioned in the last section, you would add an extra field to the record:

```
Typ = record
  Entries: array[1..MaxEntries] of TableElement.Typ;
  Length: integer;
  Overfull: boolean;
end;
```

This extra field would have to be initialized to *False* and procedures like *Insert* that might cause this error would have to be modified to change it to *True* when the error occurs. Function *Overfull* itself, then, would simply be defined as

```
function Overfull (var T: Typ): boolean;
begin
 Overfull := T.Overfull.;
end; (* Overfull *)
```

The other problem with the error-resistant approach is that you probably will want to include some mechanism for resetting the error variable after it has been set. This is like being able to turn the circuit-breaker back on after you have solved whatever problem caused the error. This can be accomplished by adding another operation to the ADT specification and modifying the specification of *Overfull* slightly, as in

```
function Overfull (var T: Typ): boolean;
            post    returns True if an attempt was previously
                    made to add an element to T when it was
                    full and procedure ClearOverfull was not
                    subsequently called; otherwise, returns
                    False.

procedure ClearOverfull(var T:Typ);
            post    subsequent calls on Overfull will return
                    False.
```

8.1.3. Improving Efficiency of ADT Operations

Consider the problem introduced in Section 8.1.1 where the following program is executed on an input file that is known to be in sorted order:

```
program SortNumbers (input, output);
var
 Numbers: Table.Typ;
 NEXT: integer;
begin (* Main *)
 Table.Create(Numbers);
 while not eof do begin
   readln(NEXT);
   if not Table.InTable(Numbers, NEXT) then begin
     Table.Insert(Numbers, NEXT);
   end; (* If *)
```

```
      end; (* While *)
   Table.Write(Numbers);
   Table.Destroy(Numbers);
end. (* Main *)
```

Two inefficiencies were pointed out for the following linked list implementation:

```
type
   TableElement.Typ = <appropriate type>;

   Typ = ^TableRec;

   TableRec = record
      Data: TableElement.Typ;
      Next: Typ;
   end; (* TableRec *)
```

First, the calls on *InTable* and *Insert* double the amount of work required to build the list because each has to perform the exact same search for the value's appropriate position in the structure. Second, there is no way to take advantage of the knowledge that the file is already sorted. In fact, instead of helping, it actually leads to worst case behavior.

When you recognize a potential efficiency problem in an application of the ADT that you can anticipate, it is usually possible to optimize the ADT to actually perform efficiently even without changing the ADT interface. For example, the problems cited above both occur because of excessive scanning of the linked list to locate a position.

It turns out that both inefficiencies come about because the most recent position examined in the list often turns out to be either the position that will be desired next time, or one away from that position. The call on *InTable* to determine whether the element is already in the list will always end up at the exact position where the value should be inserted by a subsequent call on *Insert*. And for input data that appears in sorted order, each new value should be inserted exactly one position after the previous value.

Thus, the key to increased efficiency is to keep track of the most recent table location. In this case, a table will consist of not just a pointer to the head of the list, but also a pointer to the most recent position examined. The obvious implementation is to include both pointers in a record structure, requiring the type *Typ* to be renamed to something else (say, *RecPtr*) so that the new definition of *Typ* can be included.

```
type
   TableElement.Typ = <appropriate type>;

   RecPtr = ^TableRec;

   TableRec = record
      Data: TableElement.Typ;
```

```
     Next: Typ;
   end; (* TableRec *)

Typ = record
  head: RecPtr;
  recent: RecPtr;
  end;
```

One pervasive change this introduces is that every reference in the implementation to a variable of type *Typ* (e.g., *T*) has to be changed to instead make reference to the *Head* field of the record (e.g., *T^.Head*). Furthermore, local variables and private functions used to maintain list positions have to be changed from type *Typ* to type *RecPtr*. For example, the old definitions of procedure *Create* and function *FindPrevToItem* are as follows:

```
procedure Create (var T: Typ);
begin
  new(T);
  T^.Next := nil;
end; (* Create *)

function FindPrevToItem (T: Typ;
       Entry: TableElement.Typ): Typ;
 var
  TEMP: Typ;
begin
 TEMP := T;
 while GoToNext(TEMP, Entry) do begin
   TEMP := TEMP^.Next;
   end; (* While *)
 FindPrevToItem := TEMP;
end; (* FindPrevToItem *)
```

In this new implementation they would have to be rewritten as

```
procedure Create (var T: Table);
begin
 new(T.Head);
 T.Head^.Next := nil;
end; (* Create *)

function FindPrevToItem (T: Table;
       Entry: TableElement.Typ): RecPtr;
 var
  TEMP: RecPtr;
begin
 TEMP := T.Head;
 while GoToNext(TEMP, Entry) do begin
   TEMP := TEMP^.Next;
   end; (* While *)
```

```
FindPrevToItem := TEMP;
end; (* FindPrevToItem *)
```

The changes necessary to make use of the most recent position are actually quite simple and are isolated to *Create* and *FindPrevToItem*, mostly because all three operations involving position (insertion, deletion, and check for inclusion in the table) are implemented using procedure *FindPrevToItem* to determine the appropriate position. Initially the most recent position should simply be set to the header node. But inside procedure *FindPrevToItem*, if the most recent position stores a value less than or equal to the target value, then it should start searching from that position rather than starting all the way back at the beginning of the list. Finally, procedure *FindPrevToItem* needs to remember its final value as the new value stored in the table's *Recent* field.

Thus, the operations are rewritten as follows:

```
procedure Create (var T: Table);
begin
 new(T.Head);
 T.Head^.Next := nil;
 T.Recent := T.Head;
end; (* Create *)

function FindPrevToItem (T: Table;
        Entry: TableElement.Typ): RecPtr;
  var
   TEMP: RecPtr;
begin
 if (T.Head = T.Recent) then begin
   TEMP := T.Head;
  end
 else if Less(T.Recent^.Data, Entry) then begin
   TEMP := T.Recent;
  end
 else begin
   TEMP := T.Head;
  end; (* If *)
 while GoToNext(TEMP, Entry) do begin
   TEMP := TEMP^.Next;
  end; (* While *)
 FindPrevToItem := TEMP;
 T.Recent := TEMP;
end; (* FindPrevToItem *)
```

To understand how this solves the efficiency problems, let's trace through a few insertions using the sample input file of 49, 52, 56, 57, and 58. The table is created empty, meaning that both the *Head* and *Recent* fields of the record point to the dummy header node:

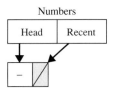

Both fields point to the same position, so it doesn't matter which is used as the starting point when the table is searched for the first value 49. The appropriate position turns out to be the dummy header node (because function *FindPrevToItem* returns the position just *before* where it is to be inserted). Thus, the value 49 is inserted after the dummy header node. The *Recent* field still points here, because it was the last position explored.

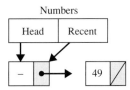

The value 52 is not found in the table, but when the search is performed, the appropriate position is found to be just after the node storing 49. Thus, after the call on *InTable*, the *Recent* field will be updated to reflect a new most recent position:

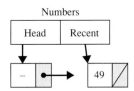

Thus, the subsequent call on *Insert* does not need to search, because it discovers immediately that the most recent position is the correct place to insert the new value. This leads to a new node in the list, but the most recent position is not updated because the very same location is used for insertion as was used when checking for inclusion in the table.

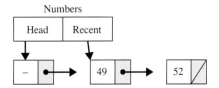

The next value to process is 56. By noticing that the most recent position was at the value 49, a number less than 56, the search for the appropriate position for 56 can proceed from the node storing 49 rather than having to start from the beginning of the list. The correct position is found right next to this node, right after the node storing 52.

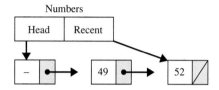

Again, the subsequent call on *Insert* does not have to scan the list for the location for insertion, because it should be performed in the exact same spot most recently examined by the call on *InTable*.

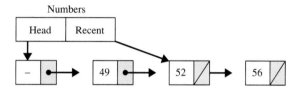

The processing of the value 57 follows the same pattern. The call on *InTable* needs to scan only one node to the right, because the previous position was one before where the new element belongs.

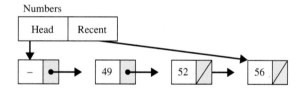

and the subsequent call on *Insert* finds that the most recent position is the exact place where the new node should be inserted.

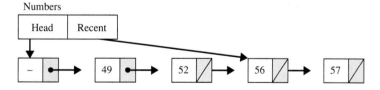

Thus, keeping track of the most recently explored table position eliminates both inefficiencies described above. It turns out that keeping track of the most recent position solves many potential efficiency problems, because many algorithms involve multiple operations all performed in the same general location in the data structure.

The same idea can be used to keep track of more than just the most recently explored position. For example, in a linked list application where the ADT specification includes a function *Length*, actually storing a length variable along with a pointer to the head of the list allows you to return the length directly rather than calculating it by scanning the list.

In general, if you can anticipate these kind of inefficiencies, you can usually safeguard against them. It is not always possible, however, to anticipate all such problems or even to solve them when they are known.

For example, consider what happens when the sample table program tries to build a table given an input file with values that are sorted, except that each successive pair is reversed in order. For example, instead of storing the sequence (1, 2, 3, 4, 5, 6, 7, 8), such an input file would store the sequence (2, 1, 4, 3, 6, 5, 8, 7).

Such an input file with n items exhibits the worst-case behavior of $O(n^2)$ even with the enhancement of keeping track of the most recent position, because for every other element the search for its position requires starting back at the beginning of the list. A clever programmer who could manipulate the structure directly could optimize the program to run in $O(n)$ time. Then again, if this possibility were really considered realistic, the ADT module could be optimized to be just as efficient by keeping track not of the most recent position explored, but of the most recent *two* positions explored.

8.1.4. Completely Isolating the Implementation

It is possible in Turbo Pascal to make use of language constructs to help strengthen "the wall." With the kind of ADT modules you have seen previously in this book, it is possible to accidentally violate the wall and not even realize it. For example, suppose that you are implementing a type for storing complex numbers (numbers of the form $a + bi$ where i represents the square root of -1). The ADT specification should include the usual operations for creating and destroying variables, and might include the following additional definitions in the interface part of the module:

```
unit Complex;

interface

type
 Typ = record
    a, b: real;     (* stores (a + b*i) *)
  end;

procedure Create (var C: Typ);

procedure Destroy (var C: Typ);

procedure Change (var C: Typ;
      RealPart, ImagPart: Real);
   (* Changes the variable C to have the given real *)
   (* and imaginary parts.                          *)

function RealPart (var C: Typ): real;
   (* returns the real part of C. *)
```

```
function ImagPart (var C: Typ): real;
   (* returns the imaginary part of C. *)

procedure Assign (var Result: Type;
      Oper: char;
      C1, C2: Typ);
   (* Assigns a value to the variable Result by        *)
   (* applying the given operator (either +, -, *, or /) *)
   (* to the operands C1 and C2 (in that order, as in   *)
   (* C1-C2, not C2-C1).                                 *)
```

Even with the interface clearly defined in this way, you might accidentally make references such as *Number.a* and *Number.b*:

```
writeln (Number.a:5:2, ' + ', Number.b:5:2, ' i');
```

rather than calling the functions *RealPart* and *ImagPart*:

```
writeln (RealPart(Number):5:2, ' + ',
         ImagPart(Number):5:2, ' i');
```

For this implementation, the code will work perfectly, even though it violates the ADT interface. But the implementation might change, as in the following definition that stores a radius and angle instead of a real and imaginary part (i.e., polar coordinates versus Cartesian coordinates):

```
type
 Typ = record
    radius, theta: real;
   end;
```

If such a change is made, the code that makes direct references to fields called *a* and *b* will no longer work. Such bugs are sometimes difficult to locate and eliminate.

It is possible to completely hide the details of a type's implementation through the use of pointers. Turbo Pascal has a predefined type called *Pointer*. Variables of type *Pointer* cannot be dereferenced, which means that the data they point to cannot be accessed directly. Thus, the first step is to change the definition of the complex number type (*Typ*) to be one of these restrictive, generic pointers.

```
type
 Typ = Pointer;
```

The main program can declare variables of type *Typ* and pass them as parameters to the procedures and functions specified in the ADT module's interface, but that's about it. Any attempt to make references like *Number.a* will generate *compiler errors* because *Number* is a generic pointer, not a record with a field called *a*. Even references like *Number^* or *Number^.a* are illegal, because it is illegal to dereference such a variable. Thus, your program will be forced always to follow the ADT interface. If you accidentally screw up, you'll find out when you try to compile the resulting program.

That sounds great from the point of view of the program, because there you want to protect a variable from illegal interference. But if a variable of type *Pointer* is like a safe that can never be opened, what good is it? Fortunately, it is more like a safe with a combination, and as long as you keep the combination hidden in the implementation part of the ADT module, no other code segment will be able to get at the data inside.

The trick is to do something called *typecasting*. Think of making a cast of your face. It could be used to form other substances (e.g., plaster) into the shape of your face. Typecasting is the same idea. You take a variable of one type and "shape" it by using a cast of another type. It would be rather difficult to cast a pebble into the shape of a boulder, because there isn't enough pebble to form a boulder. The other direction is equally troublesome, because what do you do with the leftover boulder when you try to cast it into a pebble's shape? As a result, typecasting can be applied only for structures of *equal size*. One simple case of this occurs when both types are pointers, making them automatically of the same size.

Typecasting is accomplished as follows:

> *<type name> (<variable>)*

For example, given the following definitions:

```
type
 Typ = record
   a, b: real;    (* stores (a + b*i) *)
   end;

 Arry = array [1..2] of real;

var
 TVar: Typ;
 AVar: Arry;
```

you can typecast the variable *TVar* into type *Arry* by refering to *Arry(TVar)*. Similarly, you can typecast the variable *AVar* into type *Typ* by referring to *Typ(AVar)*. Thus, you can make normal references using the normal types:

```
        TVar.a := 12.4;
        TVar.b := 18.9;
        AVar [1] := 22.3;
        AVar [2] := 22.3;
```

or you can typecast the variables into the other form and make the corresponding references:

```
Arry(TVar) [1] := 12.4;
Arry(TVar) [2] := 18.9;
Typ(AVar).a := 22.3;
Typ(AVar).b := 22.3;
```

Here is a short table to summarize some of the references involved:

Variable	Type	Explanation
TVar	Typ	original variable
TVar.a	real	field of original variable
TVar.b	real	field of original variable
Arry(TVar)	Arry	result of typecast
Arry(TVar).a	illegal	typecast variable is an array, not a record
Arry(TVar) [1]	real	array element of typecast variable
Arry(TVar) [2]	real	array element of typecast variable
AVar	Typ	original variable
AVar.a	real	field of original variable
AVar.b	real	field of original variable
Type(AVar)	Typ	result of typecast
Type(AVar) [1]	illegal	typecast variable is a record, not an array
Type(AVar).a	real	field of typecast variable
Type(AVar).b	real	field of typecast variable

To apply this technique to ADT modules, the variables you will be casting into a new shape will all be of type *Typ*, which means they are all of type *Pointer*, the generic pointer type. Because of the size problem, you have to cast it using another pointer type. Let's suppose that it's called *MyTyp*. What should something of type *MyTyp* point to? It should point to whatever underlying structure you want to use for implementing the ADT. Thus, two pointer types are defined, one for the outside world to see (*Typ*), and one for only the implementation part to see (*MyTyp*).

```
Interface Part

type Typ = Pointer

─────────────────────────────

Implementation Part

type MyTyp = ^<intended structure>;
```

The correspondence between the two types is established by casting variables of type *Typ* to match type *MyTyp*. Once cast, such a variable points to something with the intended underlying structure. For example, the original structure was

```
type
  Typ = record
    a, b: real;    (* stores (a + b*i) *)
  end;
```

You have to introduce a new name for this type given that *Typ* now refers to the generic pointer type. How about *RecType*? And how do you define *MyTyp*? It should be a pointer to variables of type *RecType*, the intended underlying structure:

```
type
  MyTyp = ^RecType;

  RecType = record
    a, b: real;    (* stores (a + b*i) *)
  end;
```

Given these definitions, consider some of the references you can make starting with a variable called *C* defined in the main program. The main program knows about type *Typ* only, so it has to be declared to be of that type. But inside the ADT module with the added definitions of *RecType* and *MyTyp*, many references are possible:

Variable	Type	Explanation
C	Typ (pointer)	variable declared in program
C.a	illegal	C is a pointer, not a record
C^	illegal	can't dereference such a variable
C^.a	illegal	can't dereference such a variable
MyTyp(C)	MyTyp	result of casting variable to MyTyp
MyTyp(C).a	illegal	typecaste gives a pointer, not a record
MyTyp(C)^	RecType	dereferenced typecast variable
MyTyp(C)^.a	real	field of dereferenced typecast variable
MyTyp(C)^.b	real	field of dereferenced typecast variable

Let's see how this changes the definition of the original ADT module. For the original interface part with the simple record structure, the following is a valid implementation of the module:

```
implementation

  procedure Create (var C: Typ);
  begin
  end; (* Create *)

  procedure Destroy (var C: Typ);
  begin
```

```
end; (* Destroy *)

procedure Change (var C: Typ;
      RealPart, ImagPart: Real);
begin
 C.a := RealPart;
 C.b := ImagPart;
end; (* Change *)

function RealPart (var C: Typ): real;
begin
 RealPart := C.a;
end; (* RealPart *)

function ImagPart (var C: Typ): real;
begin
 ImagPart := C.b;
end; (* ImagPart *)

procedure Apply (var result: Type;
      oper: char;
      C1, C2: Typ);
begin
 case oper of
  '+':
   Change (result, C1.a + C2.a, C1.b + C2.b);
  '-':
   Change (result, C1.a - C2.a, C1.b - C2.b);
  '*':
   Change (result, C1.a * C2.a - C1.b * C2.b,
        C1.a * C2.b + C1.b * C2.a);
  '/':
   Change (result,
        (C1.a * C2.a + C1.b * C2.b)/
        (sqr(C2.)(sqr(C2.a) - sqr(C2.b)),
        (C1.b * C2.a - C1.a * C2.b)/
        (sqr(C2.)(sqr(C2.a) - sqr(C2.b)));
 end;
end; (* Apply *)

end. (* Complex *)
```

For the most part, every reference to a parameter of type *Typ* has to be typecast and dereferenced. Thus, all the procedures with a parameter called *C* should now make reference to $MyTyp(C)\hat{}$. Procedures *Create* and *Destroy* actually have to perform some work now, given that variables of type *Typ* are pointers. Thus, you must allocate and deallocate space appropriate for storing values of type *RecType*. You will notice that in this case the reference is to $MyTyp(C)$ without the up-arrow for dereferencing, because calls on *new* and *dispose* should be passed the actual pointer variable.

```
unit Complex;

interface

 type
 Typ = pointer;
 (* generic pointer--preserves ''the wall'' *)

 procedure Create (var C: Typ);

 procedure Destroy (var C: Typ);

 procedure Change (var C: Typ;
       RealPart, ImagPart: Real);

 function RealPart (var C: Typ): real;

 function ImagPart (var C: Typ): real;

 procedure Apply (var result: Typ;
        oper: char; C1, C2: Typ);

 type
  MyType = ^RecType;   (* pointer to data *)

  RecType = record   (* actual underlying structure *)
    a, b: real;
    end;

 procedure Create (var C: Typ);
 begin
  new(MyTyp(C));
 end; (* Create *)

 procedure Destroy (var C: Typ);
 begin
  dispose(MyTyp(C));
 end; (* Destroy *)

 procedure Change (var C: Typ;
       RealPart, ImagPart: Real);
 begin
  MyTyp(C)^.a := RealPart;
  MyTyp(C)^.b := ImagPart;
 end; (* Change *)

 function RealPart (var C: Typ): real;
 begin
  RealPart := MyTyp(C)^.a;
 end; (* RealPart *)
```

```
function ImagPart (var C: Typ): real;
begin
 ImagPart := MyTyp(C)^.b;
end; (* ImagPart *)

procedure Apply (var result: Type;
        oper: char;
        C1, C2: Typ);
 var
  a1, a2, b1, b2: real;
begin
 a1 := MyTyp(C1)^.a;
 b1 := MyTyp(C1)^.b;
 a2 := MyTyp(C2)^.a;
 b2 := MyTyp(C2)^.b;
 case oper of
  '+':
   Change (MyTyp(result)^, a1 + a2, b1 + b2);
  '-':
   Change (MyTyp(result)^, a1 - a2, b1 - b2);
  '*':
   Change (MyTyp(result)^, a1 * a2 - b1 * b2,
        a1 * b2 + b1 * a2);
  '/':
   Change (MyTyp(result)^,
        (a1 * a2 + b1 * b2)/(sqr(a2) - sqr(b2)),
        (b1 * a2 - a1 * b2)/(sqr(a2) - sqr(b2)));
 end;
 end; (* Apply *)

 end.
```

The final procedure deserves some special comment. The original has enough references to the fields of parameters *C1* and *C2* that it becomes a grand mess if written using references like *MyTyp(C1)^.a*. Instead, four local variables are used for referring to the two fields included in the variables pointed to by *C1* and *C2*. Notice that the same technique could not be applied to parameter *Result*, because the variable it points to is actually being changed by this procedure, which means that local variables would change only copies of the fields rather than the actual fields. For example, these lines of code would have no affect on variable *Result*:

```
ResA := MyTyp(result)^.a;
ResB := MyTyp(result)^.b;
ResA := 12.4;
ResB := 19.8;
```

while these would change its fields to the values 12.4 and 19.8:

```
MyTyp(result)^.a := 12.4;
MyTyp(result)^.b := 19.8;
```

When this technique is used and the underlying structure is itself a pointer (e.g., a pointer to the head of a linked list), typecasting becomes even simpler because the generic *Typ* variables can be directly cast into the intended type. For example, if the intended underlying structure is as follows:

```
type
  Typ = ^TableRec;

  TableRec = record
    Data: TableElement.Typ;
    Next: Typ;
  end; (* TableRec *)
```

The interface would, as always, define *Typ* to be the generic pointer type:

```
type
  Typ = pointer;
```

and the implementation part would define *MyTyp* as follows:

```
type
  MyTyp = ^TableRec;

  TableRec = record
    Data: TableElement.Typ;
    Next: MyTyp;
  end; (* TableRec *)
```

In this case, references to parameters of type *Typ*, as in two pointers called *First* and *Second*, would be typecast to *MyTyp*, leading to *MyTyp(First)* and *MyTyp(Second)*. For example, to translate this procedure, which uses the original definition of *Typ*:

```
procedure Assign (var First, Second: Typ);
  var
    TEMP1, TEMP2: Typ;
  begin
    if Second = nil then begin
      First := nil;
    end
    else begin
      new(First);
      First^.Data := Second^.Data;
      TEMP1 := First;
      TEMP2 := Second^.Next;
      while TEMP2 <> nil do begin
```

```
          new(TEMP1^.Next);
          TEMP1 := TEMP1^.Next;
          TEMP1^.Data := TEMP2^.Data;
        end; (* While *)
      TEMP1^.Next := nil;
    end; (* If *)
  end; (* Assign *)
```

you simply have to change *First* to *MyTyp(First)*, *Second* to *MyTyp(Second)*, and *Typ* to *MyTyp*. If you forget to make this last change, you will end up with local variables *TEMP1* and *TEMP2* of type *Typ*, requiring you to change all their references to *MyTyp(TEMP1)* and *MyTyp(TEMP2)*. Obviously it's easier to just use *MyTyp* in the first place when defining their type, since they are local variables that you have full control over.

```
    procedure Assign (var First, Second: Typ);
     var
       TEMP1, TEMP2:MyTyp;
    begin
      if MyTyp(Second) = nil then begin
        MyTyp(First) := nil;
      end
      else begin
        new(MyTyp(First));
        MyTyp(First)^.Data := MyTyp(Second)^.Data;
        TEMP1 := MyTyp(First);
        TEMP2 := MyTyp(Second)^.Next;
        while TEMP2 <> nil do begin
          new(TEMP1^.Next);
          TEMP1 := TEMP1^.Next;
          TEMP1^.Data := TEMP2^.Data;
        end; (* While *)
      TEMP1^.Next := nil;
    end; (* If *)
  end; (* Assign *)
```

8.2. LOOP INVARIANTS

The action of a loop can be characterized using a logical assertion known as a *loop invariant*. The idea is that the assertion is true for every execution of the loop, making it a nonvarying or invariant assertion. Such a characterization can be useful for describing a loop, for verifying its correctness and even for generating it in the first place. The most compelling example is the latter case of loop synthesis, so this section uses it as a means of introducing the concept.

Using an invariant, you should think of your loops as fitting the following template:

```
<initialization satisfying invariant>
while <test> do begin
    <solve part of task>.
    <restore invariant>.
end
```

Because the initialization satisifies the invariant and because the invariant is re-stored after each iteration of the loop, you know that it is true just *before* each iteration of the loop. Additionally, because you restore the invariant at the end of the last iteration, you know that it is true after the loop terminates.

```
<initialization satisfying invariant>
while <guard> do begin
    →invariant is true here
    <solve part of task>.
    <restore invariant>.
end
→invariant is true here
```

Through careful selection of the loop invariant, it is possible to generate the loop from the invariant. For example, suppose that you want to write a loop for the *Power* function:

```
function Power(x, n:integer) : integer;
(* pre : n >= 0.                      *)
(* post: Returns x to the nth power. *)
```

The problem is to take two integers x and n and combine them into a single integer representing x^n. Coming up with a workable loop invariant takes a bit of insight, but not an incredible amount. One approach is to use three variables in the invariant:

$$a * b^c = x^n$$

The purpose of the variable a is to accumulate the correct answer so that eventually you can get:

$$a = x^n$$

that would be true when c is 0. Thus, the appropriate test for the loop is ($c <> 0$). In the terminology of invariants, the test is often known as "the guard" in that it guards the exit to the loop, keeping the loop running until the desired condition has been achieved.

The variables b and c are used because they are where we start and, in general, represent the "unprocessed" part of the problem. In other words, it is easy to initialize these variables so that

$$b^c = x^n$$

This can be accomplished simply by setting b to x and c to n. Setting a to 1 at the same time satisfies the invariant automatically.

Thus, using the invariant, both the loop test and the initialization are clear:

```
function Power (x, n: integer): integer;
(* pre : n >= 0.                           *)
(* post: Returns x to the nth power. *)

   var
     a, b, c: integer;
   begin
     a := 1;
     b := x;
     c := n;
     while (c <> 0) do begin
       <solve part of task>.
       <restore invariant>.
       end; (* While *)
     Power := a;
   end; (* Power *)
```

Now all that remains is to write the body of the loop. The precondition guarantees that n is nonnegative, which means that c starts out with a nonnegative value. The loop guard keeps the loop executing until this value has been reduced to 0. The simplest way to make such a value approach 0 is to subtract 1 from it. Thus, to solve part of the task you might say

```
c := c - 1;
```

Then the only question is how to restore the invariant given this new value of c. The new value of c leads to the following:

$$a * b^{(\text{new } c)} = a * b^{(\text{old } c)-1}$$

In order to restore the invariant, we have to throw in another factor of b into a:

```
a := a * b;
```

leading to

$$(\text{new } a) * b^{(\text{new } c)} = ((\text{old } a) * b) * b^{(\text{old } c)-1}$$
$$= (\text{old } a) * b^{(\text{old } c)} = x^n$$

Thus, one correct solution to this problem that satisfies the loop invariant is

```
function Power (x, n: integer): integer;
(* pre : n >= 0.                           *)
(* post: Returns x to the nth power. *)

   var
```

```
      a, b, c: integer;
   begin
   a := 1;
   b := x;
   c := n;
   while (c <> 0) do begin
      c := c - 1;
      a := a * b;
    end; (* While *)
   Power := a;
 end; (* Power *)
```

Although it is somewhat impressive that reasoning about the loop invariant allows you to deduce the details of the code, this loop is a fairly standard approach to the exponentiation problem. A more impressive demonstration of the loop invariant comes from a slightly different approach to the steps:

> *<solve part of task>* .
> *<restore invariant>* .

Suppose that c is an even number. Then another way to make c approach 0 without losing any information about the problem at hand is to say

```
   c := c div 2;
```

This leads to

$$a * b^{(\text{new } c)} = a * b^{(\text{old } c)/2}$$

Thus, to restore the invariant, you have to cancel the division by 2 in the exponent of b. The simplest way to do so is to square b:

```
   b := b * b;
```

leading to

$$a * (\text{new } b)^{(\text{new } c)} = a * ((\text{old } b)^2)^{(\text{old } c)/2} = a * (\text{old } b)^{(\text{old } c)} = x^n$$

You can't be guaranteed to have a value of c that is even, so in fact you need a combination of these two approaches inside the loop:

```
   function Power (x, n: integer): integer;
   (* pre : n >= 0.                          *)
   (* post: Returns x to the nth power. *)
    var
      a, b, c: integer;
   begin
    a := 1;
```

```
b := x;
c := n;
  while (c <> 0) do begin
    if (c mod 2 = 0) then begin
      c := c div 2;
      b := b * b;
    end
    else begin
      c := c - 1;
      a := a * b;
    end; (* If *)
  end; (* While *)
  Power := a;
end; (* Power *)
```

It is not as immediately obvious why this code works. The beauty of the loop invariant approach, however, is that as long as you have no flaw in your logic, you know that the loop is guaranteed to work correctly. If the loop invariant is maintained and the guard properly keeps the loop executing until c becomes 0, then a eventually stores the proper value. And as long as c is reduced toward 0, it should terminate at some point in time.

MODULE DEFINITIONS

I.1. UTILITY MODULES

I.1.1. Chars

```
unit Chars;

interface

procedure Capitalize (var Value: char);
    (* post : if Value was initially a small letter,  *)
    (*       : it is now corresponding capital         *)
    (*       : letter; Otherwise, Value is unchanged   *)
function CapOf (Value: char): char;
    (* post : if Value is a small letter, returns      *)
    (*       : the corresponding capital letter;        *)
    (*       : otherwise returns Value                  *)

procedure WriteChars (var OutFile: text;
    Number: integer;
    Value: char);
    (* pre  : OutFile is open for writing              *)
    (* post : Given number of occurrences of Value     *)
    (*       : written to OutFile                       *)

implementation
```

```
procedure Capitalize (var Value: char);
begin
 if Value in ['a'..'z'] then begin
   Value := chr(ord(Value) - ord('a') + ord('A'));
   end; (* If *)
end; (* Capitalize *)

function CapOf (Value: char): char;
begin
 Capitalize(Value);
 CapOf := Value;
end; (* CapOf *)

procedure WriteChars (var OutFile: text;
      Number: integer;
      Value: char);
 var
  I: integer;
begin
 for I := 1 to Number do begin
   write(OutFile, Value);
   end; (* For *)
end; (* WriteChars *)

end. (* Chars *)
```

I.1.2. Math

```
unit Math;

interface

const
 Pi = 3.14159265358979;
 E  = 2.71828182845904;

function Min (x, y: integer): integer;
   (* post : returns the minimum of x and y *)

function Max (x, y: integer): integer;
   (* post : returns the maximum of x and y *)

function Power (x, n: integer): integer;
   (* pre  : x >= 0                         *)
   (* post : returns x to the nth power *)

procedure SwapInt (var x, y: integer);
   (* post : The values of x and y are exchanged *)

function GCD (x, y: integer): integer;
   (* pre  : (x <> 0) or (y <> 0)                      *)
   (* post : returns the Greatest Common Divisor of x and y *)

function LCM (x, y: integer): integer;
```

```
(* pre  : (x <> 0) or (y <> 0)                              *)
(* post : returns the Least Common Multiple of x and y *)

function Exponent (x, y: real): real;
  (* pre  : x >= 0                          *)
  (* post : returns x to the yth power *)

function Tan (Angle: real): real;
  (* pre  : angle <> k * pi + (pi/2), k = some integer *)
  (* post : returns the tangent of angle              *)

function ArcCos (TheCos: real): real;
  (* pre  : -1 <= TheCos <= +1              *)
  (* post : returns the arccosine of TheCos *)

function ArcSin (TheSin: real): real;
  (* pre  : -1 <= TheSin <= +1              *)
  (* post : returns the arcsine of TheSin *)

function Log (n: real): real;
  (* pre  : n > 0                             *)
  (* post : returns the common log(base 10) of n *)

function Log2 (n: real): real;
  (* pre  : n > 0                             *)
  (* post : returns the log to the base 2 of n *)

implementation

function Min (x, y: integer): integer;
  (* post : returns the minimum of x and y. *)
begin
 if x < y then begin
   Min := x;
  end
 else begin
   Min := y;
  end; (* If *)
end; (* Min *)

function Max (x, y: integer): integer;
  (* post : returns the maximum of x and y. *)
begin
 if x > y then begin
   Max := x;
  end
 else begin
   Max := y;
  end; (* If *)
end; (* Max *)

function Power (x, n: integer): integer;
  (* pre  : n >= 0.                        *)
  (* post : returns x to the nth power. *)
 var
```

```
            PROD, I: integer;
        begin
         PROD := 1;
         for I := 1 to n do begin
           PROD := PROD * x;
          end; (* For *)
         Power := PROD;
        end; (* Power *)

        procedure SwapInt (var x, y: integer);
            (* post : The values of x and y are exchanged. *)
         var
          Z: integer;
        begin
         Z := x;
         x := y;
         y := Z;
        end; (* SwapInt *)

        function GCD (x, y: integer): integer;
            (* pre        : (x <> 0) or (y <> 0).                    *)
            (* post       : returns the Greatest Common Divisor of x *)
            (*            : and y.                                   *)
            (* background : By definition, y = x * (some integer)    *)
            (*            : + (y mod x). By fundamental rule of      *)
            (*            : arithmetic, an integer that divides x and *)
            (*            : y must also divide (y mod x). Thus,      *)
            (*            : GCD(x, y) = GCD(x, (y mod x)).  When     *)
            (*            : x <= y, (y mod x) < y.  Thus, replacing  *)
            (*            : y by (y mod x) with x <= y reduces one of *)
            (*            : the integers. Two integers can't get     *)
            (*            : smaller forever, so eventually one becomes *)
            (*            : 0, meaning the other stores the result.  *)
            (* algorithm  : While x not 0, reduce by setting y to    *)
            (*            : (y mod x) and exchange x and y to maintain *)
            (*            : x <= y. If x > y initially, one extra     *)
            (*            : iteration (to swap). abs(x) in    *)
            (*            : mod to avoid error when (x or y) < 0.     *)
        begin
         while (x <> 0) do begin
           y := abs(y) mod abs(x);
           SwapInt(x, y);
          end; (* While *)
         GCD := y;
        end; (* GCD *)

        function LCM (x, y: integer): integer;
            (* pre  : (x <> 0) or (y <> 0).                      *)
            (* post : returns the Least Common Multiple of x and y. *)
        begin
         LCM := (x * y) div sqr(GCD(x, y));
        end; (* LCM *)

        function Exponent (x, y: real): real;
            (* pre  : y >= 0.                          *)
```

```
      (* post : returns x to the yth power. *)
   begin
    Exponent := exp(ln(x) * y);
   end; (* exponent *)


   function Tan (Angle: real): real;
      (* pre  : Angle <> k * pi + (pi/2), k = some integer. *)
      (* post : returns the tangent of Angle.              *)
   begin
    Tan := sin(Angle) / cos(Angle);
   end; (* Tan *)


   function ArcCos (TheCos: real): real;
      (* pre  : -1 <= TheCos <= +1.           *)
      (* post : returns the arccosine of TheCos. *)
   begin
    if TheCos < 0 then begin
      ArcCos := pi + ArcTan(sqrt(1 - sqr(TheCos)) / TheCos);
     end
    else if TheCos = 0 then begin
      ArcCos := pi / 2;
     end
    else begin
      ArcCos := ArcTan(sqrt(1 - sqr(TheCos)) / TheCos);
     end; (* If *)
   end; (* ArcCos*)


   function ArcSin (TheSin: real): real;
      (* pre  : -1 <= TheSin <= +1.          *)
      (* post : returns the arcsine of TheSin. *)
   begin
    if TheSin = 1 then begin
      ArcSin := pi / 2;
     end
    else if TheSin = -1 then begin
      ArcSin := -pi / 2;
     end
    else begin
      ArcSin := ArcTan(TheSin / sqrt(1 - sqr(TheSin)));
     end; (* If *)
   end; (* ArcSin*)

   function Log (n: real): real;
      (* pre  : n > 0.                         *)
      (* post : returns the common log (base 10) of n. *)
   begin
    Log := ln(n) / ln(10);
   end; (* Log *)


   function Log2 (n: real): real;
      (* pre  : n > 0.                        *)
      (* post : returns the log to the base 2 of n. *)
   begin
    Log2 := ln(n) / ln(2);
```

```
                        end; (* Log2 *)
                    end. (* Math *)
```

I.1.3. CharBuff

```
            unit CharBuff;

        interface

            function Window: char;
                (* post : Returns the character that would be read after *)
                (*      : the next call on ReadChar.                     *)

            function Eoln: boolean;
                (* post : Returns true if input cursor is at end-of-line; *)
                (*      : false otherwise.                                *)

            function Eof: boolean;
                (* post : Returns true if input cursor is at end-of-file; *)
                (*      : false otherwise.                                *)

            procedure ReadChar (var CH:char);
                (* post : If Eoln, CH is set to a space; otherwise, CH is  *)
                (*      : set to the value of the character pointed to by  *)
                (*      : the input cursor and the input cursor is advanced *)
                (*      : to the next character, if any, on the input line. *)

            procedure ReadInt (var Num: integer);
                (* pre  : Input cursor positioned at an integer.          *)
                (* post : Num is set to the value represented by the digit *)
                (*      : sequence (with a possible leading sign) that     *)
                (*      : follows.  If after reading a leading sign        *)
                (*      : character no digit characters are encountered,   *)
                (*      : Num is set to 0.                                 *)

            procedure ReadReal (var Num: real);
                (* pre  : Input cursor positioned at a real.              *)
                (* post : Like ReadInt, but reading a real instead of an  *)
                (*      : integer.                                        *)

            procedure Readln;
                (* post : Input cursor is advanced to the first character *)
                (*      : of the next line, if any.                       *)

        implementation

          type
            FileState = (normal, EndOfLine, EndOfFile, undefined);

          var
            Buffer: char;
            State: FileState;

          procedure FixBuffer;
```

```
begin
 if State = undefined then begin
   Advance;
  end; (* If *)
end; (* FixBuffer *)

function Window: char;
begin
 FixBuffer;
 Window := Buffer;
end; (* Window *)

function Eoln: boolean;
begin
 FixBuffer;
 Eoln := (State = EndOfLine) or (State = EndOfFile);
end; (* Eoln *)

function Eof: boolean;
begin
 Eof := (State = EndOfFile);
 FixBuffer;
end; (* Eof *)

procedure Advance;
begin
 if State = EndOfLine then begin
   State := undefined;
  end
 else if System.eof then begin
   State := EndOfFile;
  end
 else if System.eoln then begin
   State := EndOfLine;
   Buffer := ' ';
   System.readln;
  end
 else begin
   State := normal;
   read(Buffer);
  end; (* If *)
end; (* Advance *)

procedure Readln;
begin
 while not eoln do begin
   Advance;
  end; (* While *)
 Advance;
end; (* Readln *)

procedure ReadInt (var Num: integer);
 var
  NEGATIVE: boolean;
  DIGIT: char;
```

```
                    begin
                     while Window = ' ' do begin
                       Advance;
                       end; (* While *)
                     Num := 0;
                     NEGATIVE := (Window = '-');
                     if Window in ['+', '-'] then begin
                       Advance;
                       end; (* If *)
                     while (Window in ['0'..'9']) do begin
                       ReadChar(DIGIT);
                       Num := Num * 10 + (ord(DIGIT) - ord('0'));
                       end; (* While *)
                     if NEGATIVE then begin
                       Num := -Num;
                       end; (* If *)
                    end; (* ReadInt *)

                    procedure ReadReal (var Num: real);
                     var
                      I: integer;
                      MULTIPLIER: real;
                      DIGIT: char;
                    begin
                     ReadInt(I);
                     Num := I;
                     if Window = '.' then begin
                       Advance;
                       MULTIPLIER := 1.0;
                       while Window in ['0'..'9'] do begin
                         ReadChar(DIGIT);
                         MULTIPLIER := MULTIPLIER * 0.1;
                         Num := Num + MULTIPLIER * (ord(DIGIT) - ord('0'));
                         end; (* while *)
                       end; (* If *)
                    end; (* ReadReal *)

                  begin (* CharBuff *)
                   State := undefined;
                  end. (* CharBuff*)
```

I.1.4. LineBuff

```
                    unit LineBuff;

                    interface

                    procedure SkipSpaces (Value: boolean);
                        (* post : If Value is true, subsequent calls on any of   *)
                        (*      : the input operations will cause any leading     *)
                        (*      : spaces on the current input line to be skipped  *)
                        (*      : before the operation is performed.  If Value is *)
                        (*      : False, subsequent calls will behave normally    *)
                        (*      : without skipping spaces.                        *)
```

```
procedure ReadLine;
   (* post : Next line of input is read into buffer and input *)
   (*      : cursor is positioned at the first character of   *)
   (*      : the line.  MUST be called before any other input *)
   (*      : operations are called.                           *)

function AtEoln: boolean;
   (* post : Returns true if input cursor is at end-of-line; *)
   (*      : false otherwise.                                 *)

function Peek (Ahead: integer): char;
   (* pre  : Ahead >= 1.                                      *)
   (* post : Returns the character that would be read after *)
   (*      : Ahead calls on ReadChar.  If Ahead is 1, it    *)
   (*      : returns the character pointed to by the input  *)
   (*      : cursor.                                         *)

function AtInt: boolean;
   (* post : Returns true if input cursor is positioned at  *)
   (*      : an integer; False otherwise.  Note that if the *)
   (*      : input cursor is positioned at a sequence of    *)
   (*      : spaces followed by an integer, then AtInt      *)
   (*      : returns true only if a call has been made on   *)
   (*      : SkipSpaces and the most recent value passed to *)
   (*      : it was True.                                   *)

function AtReal: boolean;
   (* post : Like AtInt, but looking for a real instead. *)

procedure ReadChar (var Ch: char);
   (* post : If AtEoln, Ch is set to a space; otherwise, Ch *)
   (*      : is set to the value of the character pointed   *)
   (*      : to by the input cursor and the input cursor is *)
   (*      : advanced to the next character, if any, on the *)
   (*      : input line.                                    *)

procedure ReadUnsignedInt (var Num: integer);                *)
   (* post : Any leading spaces on current line are          *)
   (*      : skipped; Num is set to the value represented    *)
   (*      : by the digit sequence that follows.  If the     *)
   (*      : first nonspace is not a digit, Num is set to 0. *)

procedure ReadInt (var Num: integer);
   (* post : Like ReadUnsignedInt, but digit sequence may be *)
   (*      : immediately preceded by a sign character.       *)

procedure ReadReal (var Num: real);
   (* post : Like ReadInt, but reading a real instead of an *)
   (*      : integer.                                       *)

procedure ResetLine;
   (* post : Input cursor is reset to the beginning of the *)
   (*      : current input line.  Note that this does not  *)
   (*      : read another line of input.  This procedure   *)
   (*      : should be used only when you want to process  *)
```

```pascal
   (*         : an input line more than once.                    *)

implementation

uses
  Math;

const
  MaxChars = 200;
  Beep = 7;
  Backspace = 8;
  Delete = 127;

type
  Linearray = array[1..MaxChars] of char;

  BufType = record
    Chars: Linearray;
    Len: integer;
    Cursor: integer;
  end; (* BufType *)

var
  Buf: BufType;
  Skip: boolean;

procedure SkipSpaces (Value: boolean);
begin
  Skip := Value;
end; (* SkipSpaces *)

procedure ProcessChar (var Next: char);
begin
  if (Next = chr(Backspace)) or (Next = chr(Delete)) then begin
    if (Buf.Len = 0) then begin
      write(chr(beep));
    end
    else begin
      Buf.Len := Buf.Len - 1;
    end; (* If *)
  end
  else begin
    Buf.Len := Buf.Len + 1;
    Buf.Chars[Buf.Len] := Next;
  end; (* If *)
end; (* ProcessChar *)

procedure ReadLine;
  var
    NEXT: char;
begin
  Buf.Len := 0;
  while not eoln do begin
    read(NEXT);
    ProcessChar(NEXT);
```

```
    end; (* while *)
 readln;
 Buf.Cursor := 1;
end; (* ReadLine *)

procedure ShiftWindow (Amount: Integer);
begin
 Buf.Cursor := Buf.Cursor + Amount;
end; (* ShiftWindow *)

function AtEoln;(* : boolean*)
 var
  DONE: boolean;
begin
      (* skip leading spaces if and only if skip is true *)
 DONE := not Skip;
 while not DONE do begin
   if Buf.Cursor > Buf.Len then begin
     DONE := true;
    end
   else if (Buf.Chars[Buf.Cursor] <> ' ') then begin
     DONE := true;
    end
   else begin
     Buf.Cursor := Buf.Cursor + 1;
    end; (* If *)
  end; (* While *)
 AtEoln := Buf.Cursor > Buf.Len;
end; (* AtEoln *)

function Peek (Ahead: integer): char;
begin
 ShiftWindow(Ahead - 1);
 if AtEoln then begin
   Peek := ' ';
  end
 else begin
   Peek := Buf.Chars[Buf.Cursor];
  end; (* If *)
 ShiftWindow(1 - Ahead);
end; (* Peek *)

function AtInt: boolean;
begin
 if Peek(1) in ['+', '-'] then begin
   AtInt := Peek(2) in ['0'..'9'];
  end
 else begin
   AtInt := Peek(1) in ['0'..'9'];
  end; (* If *)
end; (* AtInt *)

function AtReal: boolean;
begin
 if AtInt then begin
```

```
    AtReal := true;
  end
 else if Peek(1) in ['+', '-'] then begin
   AtReal := (Peek(2) = '.') and (Peek(3) in ['0'..'9']);
  end
 else begin
   AtReal := (Peek(1) = '.') and (Peek(2) in ['0'..'9']);
  end; (* If *)
end; (* AtReal *)

procedure ReadChar (var Ch: char);
begin
 Ch := Peek(1);
 ShiftWindow(1);
end; (* ReadChar *)

procedure ReadUnsignedInt (var Num: integer);
 var
  DIGIT: char;
begin
 Num := 0;
 while (Peek(1) in ['0'..'9']) do begin
   ReadChar(DIGIT);
   Num := Num * 10 + (ord(DIGIT) - ord('0'));
  end; (* While *)
end; (* ReadUnsignedInt *)

procedure ReadInt (var Num: integer);
 var
  NEGATIVE: boolean;
begin
 NEGATIVE := (Peek(1) = '-');
 if Peek(1) in ['+', '-'] then begin
   ShiftWindow(1);
  end; (* If *)
 ReadUnsignedInt(Num);
 if NEGATIVE then begin
   Num := -Num;
  end; (* If *)
end; (* ReadInt *)

procedure ReadReal (var Num: real);
 var
  I, J: integer;
begin
 ReadInt(I);
 Num := I;
 if Peek(1) = '.' then begin
   ShiftWindow(1);
   J := Buf.Cursor;
   ReadUnsignedInt(I);
   Num := Num + I / Math.Power(10, Buf.Cursor - J);
  end; (* If *)
end; (* ReadReal *)
```

```
                procedure ResetLine;
                begin
                 if Buf.Len > 0 then begin
                   Buf.Cursor := 1;
                  end; (* If *)
                end; (* ResetLine *)

                begin (* LineBuff *)
                 Skip := false;
                end. (* LineBuff *)
```

I.1.5. Peek (Used by Unit *String*)

```
                Unit Peek;

                interface

                 function Window (var InFile: text) : char;
                 (* post : Returns next character from input stream *)

                implementation

                 uses
                  DOS;

                 function Window (var InFile: text) : char;
                 begin
                   if eoln(InFile) then (* nothing *);
                   with TextRec(InFile) do
                     Window := Buffer[BufPos];
                 end; (* Window *)

                end. (* Peek *)
```

I.2. IMPLIED ADTS

I.2.1. Cave

```
                unit Cave;

                interface

                const
                 Size = 5;

                type
                 MarkerType = (Path, DeadEnd);
                           (* Used to specify which kind of marker to place. *)

                 MoveType = (North, South, East, West).
                              (* Used to specify in which direction to move. *)
```

```
procedure Write (var OutFile: text);
   (* pre  : OutFile open for writing; cave initialized. *)
   (* post : Contents of cave written to OutFile showing *)
   (*       : current path.                               *)

function TreasureIsHere: boolean;
   (* pre  : cave initialized; current position is legal.      *)
   (* post : returns true if treasure is at current position; *)
   (*       : false otherwise.                                  *)

function MarkerIsHere: boolean;
   (* pre  : cave initialized; current position is legal.     *)
   (* post : returns true if a marker is at current position; *)
   (*       : false otherwise.                                 *)

procedure PlaceMarker (Marker: MarkerType);
   (* pre  : cave initialized; current position is legal. *)
   (* post : given marker is placed at current position.  *)

function MoveOK (Move: MoveType): boolean;
   (* pre  : cave initialized; current position is legal.   *)
   (* post : returns true if given move is legal (i.e., not *)
   (*       : into a wall or of the edge of the grid); false *)
   (*       : otherwise.                                     *)

function Opposite (Move: MoveType): MoveType;                *)
   (* post : returns the direction opposite the given        *)
   (*       : direction (i.e., south exchanging with north,  *)
   (*       : east with west).                                *)

procedure DoMove (Move: MoveType);
   (* pre  : cave initialized; current position is legal; *)
   (*       : move is legal.                               *)
   (* post : performs the given move, resetting current   *)
   (*       : position.                                    *)

implementation

const
 StartRow = 1;
 StartCol = 1;
 Wall = '*';
 Goal = '$';
 MarkPath = '.';
 MarkDeadEnd = '#';
 Unexplored = ' ';

type
 GridType = array[1..Size, 1..Size] of char;

 CaveType = record
   Grid: GridType;
   Row, Col: integer;
  end; (* CaveType *)
```

```
var
 ACave: CaveType;

procedure WriteWall (var OutFile: text);
 var
  I: integer;
begin
 for I := 1 to Size + 2 do begin
   write(OutFile, Wall);
  end; (* For *)
 writeln(OutFile);
end; (* WriteWall *)

procedure Write (var OutFile: text);
 var
  ROW, COL: integer;
begin
 WriteWall(OutFile);
 for ROW := 1 to SIZE do begin
   write(OutFile, Wall);
   for COL := 1 to Size do begin
     if (ROW = ACave.Row) and (COL = ACave.Col) then begin
      write(OutFile, 'O');
      end
     else begin
      write(OutFile, ACave.Grid[ROW, COL]);
      end; (* If *)
    end; (* For *)
   writeln(OutFile, Wall);
  end; (* For *)
 WriteWall(OutFile);
end; (* Write *)

function TreasureIsHere: boolean;
begin
 with ACave do begin
   TreasureIsHere := Grid[Row, Col] = Goal;
  end; (* With *)
end; (* TreasureIsHere *)

function MarkerIsHere: boolean;
begin
 with ACave do begin
   MarkerIsHere := (Grid[Row, Col] = MarkPath) or
                   (Grid[Row, Col] = MarkDeadEnd);
  end; (* With *)
end; (* MarkerIsHere *)

procedure PlaceMarker (Marker: MarkerType);
begin
 with ACave do begin
   case Marker of
    Path:
     Grid[Row, Col] := MarkPath;
    DeadEnd:
```

```
      Grid[Row, Col] := MarkDeadEnd;
    end; (* Case *)
   end; (* With *)
end; (* PlaceMarker *)

procedure CalcNewCoords (var ACave: CaveType;
      Move: MoveType;
      var NewRow, NewCol: integer);
begin
 NewRow := ACave.Row;
 NewCol := ACave.Col;
 case Move of
  North:
   NewRow := NewRow - 1;
  South:
   NewRow := NewRow + 1;
  East:
   NewCol := NewCol + 1;
  West:
   NewCol := NewCol - 1;
 end; (* Case *)
end; (* CalcNewCoords *)

function MoveOK (Move: MoveType): boolean;
 var
  NEWROW, NEWCOL: integer;
begin
 with ACave do begin
   CalcNewCoords(ACave, Move, NEWROW, NEWCOL);
   if (NEWROW < 1) or (NEWCOL < 1) or (NEWROW > Size) or
      (NEWCOL > Size) then begin
    MoveOK := false;
    end
   else begin
    MoveOK := (Grid[NEWROW, NEWCOL] = Unexplored) or
              (Grid[NEWROW, NEWCOL] = Goal);
   end; (* If *)
  end; (* With *)
end; (* MoveOK *)

function Opposite (Move: MoveType): MoveType;
begin
 case Move of
  North:
   Opposite := South;
  South:
   Opposite := North;
  East:
   Opposite := West;
  West:
   Opposite := East;
 end; (* Case *)
end; (* Opposite *)

procedure DoMove (Move: MoveType);
```

```
    var
      NEWROW, NEWCOL: integer;
    begin
      CalcNewCoords(ACave, Move, NEWROW, NEWCOL);
      ACave.Row := NEWROW;
      ACave.Col := NEWCOL;
    end; (* DoMove *)

    procedure ReadIn (var Grid: GridType);
     var
      ROW, COL: integer;
      INFILE: text;
    begin
     assign(INFILE, 'cave.dat');
     reset(INFILE);
     for ROW := 1 to Size do begin
       for COL := 1 to Size do begin
         if eoln(INFILE) then begin
          Grid[ROW, COL] := Unexplored;
          end
         else begin
          read(INFILE, Grid[ROW, COL]);
          end; (* If *)
        end; (* For *)
       readln(INFILE);
      end; (* For *)
    end; (* ReadIn *)

    begin
     ACave.Row := StartRow;
     ACave.Col := StartCol;
     ReadIn(ACave.Grid);
    end. (* Cave *)
```

I.2.2. Eight Queens

```
    unit Board;

    interface

    const
     NumRows = 8;
     NumCols = 8;

    procedure Write (var OutFile: text);
        (* pre  : OutFile open for writing; board initialized. *)
        (* post : Contents of board written to OutFile showing *)
        (*       : current placement of pieces.                *)

    function Safe (Row, Col: integer): boolean;
        (* pre  : board initialized; 1 <= Row <= NumRows;   *)
        (*       : 1 <= Col <= NumCols.                      *)
        (* post : returns true if a Queen can be placed at   *)
        (*       : position without threatening any Queens in *)
```

```
             (*        : previous rows.                            *)

    procedure Place (Row, Col: integer);
        (* pre  : board initialized; 1 <= Row <= NumRows; *)
        (*       : 1 <= Col <= NumCols.                    *)
        (* post : places a Queen at given position.        *)

    procedure Remove (Row, Col: integer);
        (* pre  : board initialized; 1 <= Row <= NumRows;         *)
        (*       : 1 <= Col <= NumCols.                            *)
        (* post : removes a Queen from given position if present. *)

implementation

const
 UnAssigned = 100;

type
 BoardType = array[1..NumCols] of integer;

var
 Board: BoardType;

procedure WriteDash (var OutFile: text);
 var
  COL: integer;
begin
 for COL := 1 to NumCols do begin
   write(OutFile, '+---');
  end; (* For *)
 writeln(OutFile, '+')
end; (* WriteDash *)

procedure Write (var OutFile: text);
 var
  ROW, COL: integer;
begin
 for ROW := 1 to NumRows do begin
   WriteDash(OutFile);
   for COL := 1 to NumCols do begin
     write(OutFile, '|');
     if Board[COL] = ROW then begin
      write(OutFile, ' Q ');
      end
     else begin
      write(OutFile, '   ');
      end; (* If *)
    end; (* For *)
   writeln(OutFile, '|');
  end; (* For *)
 WriteDash(OutFile);
 writeln(OutFile);
end; (* WriteOut *)

function Safe (Row, Col: integer): boolean;
```

```
            var
             THREATENED: boolean;
             CURRCOL, DIST: integer;
           begin
            THREATENED := false;
            CURRCOL := 0;
            repeat
             CURRCOL := CURRCOL + 1;
             DIST := abs(Col - CURRCOL);
             THREATENED := (Board[CURRCOL] = (Row - DIST)) or
                           (Board[CURRCOL] = Row) or
                           (Board[CURRCOL] = (Row + DIST));
            until (THREATENED) or (CURRCOL = size);
            Safe := not THREATENED;
           end; (* Safe *)

           procedure Place (Row, Col: integer);
           begin
            Board[Col] := Row;
           end; (* Place *)

           procedure Remove (Row, Col: integer);
           begin
            Board[Col] := UnAssigned;
           end; (* Remove *)

           procedure InitBoard (var Board: BoardType);
            var
             COL: integer;
           begin
            for COL := 1 to NumCols do begin
              Board[Col] := UnAssigned;
             end; (* For *)
           end; (* InitBoard *)

           begin
            InitBoard(Board);
           end. (* Board *)
```

I.3. ADTS

I.3.1. Fraction

```
           unit Fraction;

           interface

           type
            Typ = record
              a, b: integer;
              end;

           procedure Initialize (var Fract: Typ;
```

```
              a, b: integer);
      (* pre  : b <> 0                                          *)
      (* post : a/b is reduced appropriately and the result *)
      (*       : is stored in Fract.                             *)

  procedure Assign (var Result: Typ;
        Fractl: Typ;
        Operator: char;
        Fract2: Typ);
      (* pre  : Fractl and Fract have been initialized;           *)
      (*       : Operator in ['+', '-', '*', '/'];                *)
      (*       : not ((Operator = '/') and (Fract2 represents 0)) *)
      (* post : Result is assigned the value obtained by          *)
      (*       : applying the given operator to Fractl/Fract2     *)
      (*       : (e.g., Fractl+Fract2).                           *)

  procedure Write (var OutFile: text;
        var Fract: Typ);
      (* post : value of Fract is written to OutFile. *)

  implementation

  uses
   Math;

      (* The fraction is stored as a record with two integer   *)
      (* fields to store a and b.  Procedure Reduce makes sure *)
      (* that gcd(a,b)=1 and that b > 0.  It is called every   *)
      (* time a fraction takes on a new value.                 *)

  procedure Reduce (var Fract: Typ);
   var
    DIVISOR: integer;
  begin
   if Fract.b < 0 then begin
     DIVISOR := -Math.GCD(Fract.a, Fract.b);
    end
   else begin
     DIVISOR := Math.GCD(Fract.a, Fract.b);
    end; (* If *)
   Fract.a := Fract.a div DIVISOR;
   Fract.b := Fract.b div DIVISOR;
  end; (* Reduce *)

  procedure Initialize (var Fract: Typ;
        a, b: integer);
  begin
   Fract.a := a;
   Fract.b := b;
   Reduce(Fract);
  end; (* Initialize *)

  procedure Assign (var Result: Typ;
        Fractl: Typ;
        Operator: char;
```

```
              Fract2: Typ);
    begin
     case Operator of
      '+':
       Result.a := Fractl.a * Fract2.b + Fract2.a * Fractl.b;
      '-':
       Result.a := Fractl.a * Fract2.b - Fract2.a * Fractl.b;
      '*':
       Result.a := Fractl.a * Fract2.a;
      '/':
       Result.a := Fractl.a * Fract2.b;
      end;
     if Operator = '/' then begin
       Result.b := Fractl.b * Fract2.a;
      end
     else begin
       Result.b := Fractl.b * Fract2.b;
      end; (* If *)
     Reduce(Result);
    end; (* Assign *)

    procedure Write (var OutFile: text;
          var Fract: Typ);
       (* Three primary formats to consider:                    *)
       (*     when Fract.b = 1:            simple integer        *)
       (*     when abs(Fract.a) > Fract.b: (int and int/int)     *)
       (*     otherwise:                   int/int               *)
       (*   Negatives have to be carefully handled in the 2nd and *)
       (*   3d cases                                             *)
    begin
     if (Fract.b = 1) then begin
       System.write(OutFile, Fract.a : 1);
      end
     else if abs(Fract.a) > Fract.b then begin
       if Fract.a < 0 then begin
         System.write('-');
        end; (* If *)
       System.write(OutFile, '(', abs(Fract.a) div Fract.b : 1, '
       and ', abs(Fract.a) mod Fract.b : 1, '/', Fract.b : 1, ')');
      end
     else begin
       System.write(OutFile, Fract.a : 1, '/', Fract.b : 1);
      end; (* If *)
    end; (* Write *)
   end. (* Fraction *)
```

I.3.2. String

```
    unit String;

   interface

    const
     MaxLen = 30;
```

```
          MinChar = 0;
          MaxChar = 127;

          type
           CharList = array[1..MaxLen] of char;

           Typ = record
             Chars: CharList;
             Length: integer;
            end;

           CharSet = set of char;

           string10 = packed array[1..10] of char;

          procedure FixOutput (Width: integer);
              (* post : Subsequent calls on Write will output string   *)
              (*      : values in a fixed column with the given width   *)
              (*      : (padding with spaces after the string value     *)
              (*      : to fill up the column). String values are always *)
              (*      : displayed in their entirety, even if their      *)
              (*      : length exceeds the current column width. Thus,  *)
              (*      : calling this procedure with a width of 0 will    *)
              (*      : generate standard behavior.                      *)

          procedure ConvertToUppercase (Value: boolean);
              (* post : If Value is true, subsequent calls on Read will  *)
              (*      : cause lowercase letters to be converted to their *)
              (*      : uppercase equivalents when read.  For example,   *)
              (*      : if Read would normally have returned 'what FUN I *)
              (*      : had today!', it will now return 'WHAT FUN I HAD  *)
              (*      : TODAY!'. This has NO effect on the definition of *)
              (*      : legal/illegal characters. For example, if legal  *)
              (*      : characters are defined as ['A'..'Z'] and this    *)
              (*      : option is turned on, lowercase letters will      *)
              (*      : still be considered illegal characters (even     *)
              (*      : though IF they were read in, they would be       *)
              (*      : converted to values in the legal range of        *)
              (*      : ['A'..'Z']). If Value is false, subsequent       *)
              (*      : calls on Read do not perform any special         *)
              (*      : conversion on lowercase letters.                 *)

          procedure IgnoreCase (Value: boolean);
              (* post : If Value is true, subsequent calls on Compare    *)
              (*      : will ignore the case of letters when comparing   *)
              (*      : strings (i.e., 'a' and 'A' will be treated the   *)
              (*      : same, 'b' and 'B' will be treated the same,      *)
              (*      : etc.). Thus, Compare would report that the       *)
              (*      : strings 'MICkey' and 'mIcKeY' are equal while    *)
              (*      : this option is on. If Value is false,            *)
              (*      : subsequent calls on Compare will resume          *)
              (*      : distinguishing on the basis of case.             *)

          procedure DefineLegal (NewSet: CharSet);
              (* post : For subsequent calls on Read, legal characters *)
```

```
(*        : are now defined to be NewSet; those not in     *)
(*        : NewSet are now considered illegal.             *)

procedure DefineIllegal (NewSet: CharSet);
   (* post : For subsequent calls on Read, illegal         *)
   (*        : characters are now defined to be NewSet; those *)
   (*        : not in NewSet are now considered legal.     *)

procedure SkipJunk (Value: boolean);
   (* post : If Value is true, subsequent calls on Read will  *)
   (*        : skip any illegal characters (including end-of-  *)
   (*        : line markers) appearing at the front of the   *)
   (*        : input stream before the string-reading operation *)
   (*        : is performed. If Value is false, subsequent  *)
   (*        : calls on Read will behave normally (i.e.,    *)
   (*        : reading only legal characters)              *)

procedure Create (var Str: Typ);
   (* post :    Str is initialized and empty.  MUST be    *)
   (*        :    called before any other ADT operation is *)
   (*        :    applied to Str.                          *)

procedure Destroy (var Str: Typ);
   (* post : Memory allocated for Str is released; *)
   (*        : Str becomes uninitialized           *)

procedure Copy (var Str1, Str2: Typ);
   (* post : value of Str2 has been copied to Str1 *)

procedure Write (var OutFile: text;
      var Str: Typ);
   (* post : value of Str is written to OutFile *)

procedure Read (var InFile: text;
      var Str: Typ);
   (* post : value of Str has been read from InFile *)

function Compare (var Str1, Str2: Typ): char;
   (* post : returns '<' if Str1 < Str2; '=' if Str1 = Str2; *)
   (*        : '>' if Str1 > Str2                          *)
procedure Append10 (var Str: Typ;
      CharConst: string10);
   (* post : CharConst is appended to the end of Str *)

procedure ChangeNth (var Str: Typ;
      n: integer;
      Value: char);
   (* post : Changes nth character of Str to Value *)

function Length (var Str: Typ): integer;
   (* post : returns number of characters in Str *)

procedure DeleteNth (var Str: Typ;
      n: integer);
   (* pre  : 1 <= n <= Length (Str)                       *)
```

```
                         (* post : character at position n is deleted from Str *)

                function Nth (var Str: Typ;
                      n: integer): char;
                   (* pre  : 1 <= n <= Length (Str)                    *)
                   (* post : returns character at position n of Str *)

        implementation

        uses
         Chars, Peek;

        var
         FieldWidth: integer;        (* current field width (0 means     *)
                                     (* none)                            *)
         LegalSet: CharSet;          (* current set of legal characters *)
         ConvertCase: boolean;       (* should case be converted to      *)
                                     (* upper?                           *)
         CaseInsensitive: boolean;   (* should be ignored in compare?    *)
         DoSkipJunk: boolean;        (* did user say to skip junk?       *)

            (* Variable Core *)

        procedure CoreInit;
        begin
                (* nothing *)
        end; (* CoreInit *)

        procedure Create (var Str: Typ);
        begin
         Str.Length := 0;
        end; (* Create *)

        procedure FreeCell (var Str: Typ;
              n: integer);
        begin
         if n = Str.Length then begin
           Str.Length := Str.Length - 1;
           end; (* If *)
        end; (* FreeCell *)

        procedure ChangeNth (var Str: Typ;
              n: integer;
              Value: char);
        begin
         if n = Str.Length + 1 then begin
           Str.Length := Str.Length + 1;
           end; (* If *)
         Str.Chars[n] := Value;
        end; (* ChangeNth *)

        function Length (var Str: Typ): integer;
        begin
         Length := Str.Length;
        end; (* Length *)
```

```
function Nth (var Str: Typ;
       n: integer): char;
begin
 Nth := Str.Chars[n];
end; (* Nth *)


   (* Constant Core *)

procedure Destroy (var Str: Typ);
 var
  I: integer;
begin
 for I := Length(Str) downto 1 do begin
   FreeCell(Str, I);
  end;
end; (* Destroy *)

procedure DeleteNth (var Str: Typ;
       n: integer);
 var
  INDEX: integer;
begin
 for INDEX := n to Length(Str) - 1 do begin
   ChangeNth(Str, INDEX, Nth(Str, INDEX + 1));
  end; (* For *)
 FreeCell(Str, Length(Str));
end; (* DeleteNth *)


procedure Append10 (var Str: Typ;
       CharConst: string10);
 var
  INDEX: integer;
begin
 for INDEX := 1 to 10 do begin
   ChangeNth(Str, Length(Str) + 1, CharConst[INDEX])
  end; (* For *)
end; (* Append10 *)

procedure Copy (var Str1, Str2: Typ);
 var
  I: integer;
begin
 for I := 1 to Length(Str2) do begin
   ChangeNth(Str1, I, Nth(Str2, I));
  end; (* For *)
end; (* Copy *)

procedure Write (var OutFile: text;
       var Str: Typ);
 var
  INDEX: integer;
begin
 for INDEX := 1 to Length(Str) do begin
   System.write(OutFile, Nth(Str, INDEX));
```

```
      end; (* For *)
     Chars.WriteChars(OutFile, FieldWidth - Length(Str), ' ');
    end; (* Write *)

    procedure Read (var InFile: text;
          var Str: Typ);
     var
      NEXT: char;
    begin
     Str.Length := 0;
     while DoSkipJunk and not (Peek.Window(InFile) in LegalSet) and
           not eof(InFile) do begin
       System.read(InFile, NEXT);
      end; (* While *)
     while not eoln(InFile) and (Peek.Window(InFile) in LegalSet)
     do begin
       read(InFile, NEXT);
       if ConvertCase then begin
         Chars.Capitalize(NEXT);
        end;
       ChangeNth(Str, Length(Str) + 1, NEXT);
      end; (* While *)
    end; (* Read *)

    function NthAux (var Str: Typ;
          n: integer): char;
    begin
     if n > Length(Str) then begin
       NthAux := ' ';
      end
     else if CaseInsensitive then begin
       NthAux := Chars.CapOf(Nth(Str, n));
      end
     else begin
       NthAux := Nth(Str, n);
      end; (* If *)
    end; (* NthAux *)

    function Compare (var Str1, Str2: Typ): char;
     var
      I: integer;
    begin
     I := 1;
     while (NthAux(Str1, I) = NthAux(Str2, I)) and (I < MaxLen)
     do begin
       I := I + 1;
      end; (* While *)
     if NthAux(Str1, I) = NthAux(Str2, I) then begin
       compare := '=';
      end
     else if NthAux(Str1, I) < NthAux(Str2, I) then begin
       compare := '<';
      end
     else begin
       compare := '>';
```

```
    end; (* If *)
  end; (* Compare *)

  procedure DefineLegal (NewSet: CharSet);
  begin
   LegalSet := NewSet;
  end; (* DefineLegal *)

  procedure DefineIllegal (NewSet: CharSet);
  begin
   LegalSet := [chr(MinChar)..chr(MaxChar)] - NewSet;
  end; (* DefineIllegal *)

  procedure SkipJunk (Value: boolean);
  begin
   DoSkipJunk := Value;
  end; (* SkipJunk *)

  procedure FixOutput (Width: integer);
  begin
   FieldWidth := Width;
  end; (* FixOutput *)

  procedure ConvertToUppercase (Value: boolean);
  begin
   ConvertCase := Value;
  end; (* ConvertToUppercase *)

  procedure IgnoreCase (Value: boolean);
  begin
   CaseInsensitive := Value;
  end; (* IgnoreCase *)

begin (* String *)
 CoreInit;
 FieldWidth := 0;
 LegalSet := [chr(MinChar)..chr(MaxChar)];
 ConvertCase := false;
 CaseInsensitive := false;
 DoSkipJunk := false;
end. (* String *)
```

I.4. STRUCTURE ADTS

I.4.1. Stack: Array Implementation

```
unit Stack;

interface

 const
  MaxStack = 1000;
```

```
type
 ElementType = integer;

 ElementList = array[1..MaxStack] of ElementType;

 Typ = record
   Elems: ElementList;
   Top: integer;
  end;

procedure Create (var S: Typ);
   (* post : S is initialized and empty *)

procedure Destroy (var S: Typ);
   (* post : Memory allocated for S is released; S is *)
   (*       : uninitialized                           *)

procedure Push (var S: Typ;
     Item: ElementType);
   (* post : Item is added to the top of S *)

procedure Pop (var S: Typ;
     var Item: ElementType);
   (* pre  : not Empty(S).                 *)
   (* post : S has its top element removed. *)
   (*       : Item holds that element.      *)

function Empty (var S: Typ): boolean;
   (* post : True if S is empty, False otherwise *)

implementation

procedure Create (var S: Typ);
begin
 S.Top := 0;
end; (* Create *)

procedure Destroy (var S: Typ);
begin
     (* nothing to do *)
end; (* Destroy *)

procedure Push (var S: Typ;
     Item: ElementType);
begin
 S.Top := S.Top + 1;
 S.Elems[S.Top] := Item;
end; (* Push *)

procedure Pop (var S: Typ;
     var Item: ElementType);
begin
 Item := S.Elems[S.Top];
 S.Top := S.Top - 1;
end; (* Pop *)
```

```
function Empty (var S: Typ): boolean;
begin
 Empty := (S.Top = 0);
 end; (* Empty *)
end. (* Stack *)
```

I.4.2. Stack: Linked List Implementation

```
unit Stack;

interface

type
 Typ = ^StackRec;

 StackRec = record
   Data: TableElement.Typ;
   Next: Typ;
  end; (* StackRec *)

 procedure Create (var S: Typ);
    (* post : S is initialized and empty *)

 procedure Destroy (var S: Typ);
    (* post : Memory allocated for S is released; S is *)
    (*       : uninitialized                           *)

 procedure Push (var S: Typ;
      Item: ElementType);
    (* post : Item is added to the top of S *)

 procedure Pop (var S: Typ;
      var Item: ElementType);
    (* pre  : not Empty(S).                 *)
    (* post : S has its top element removed. *)
    (*       : Item holds that element.      *)

 function Empty (var S: Typ): boolean;
    (* post : True if S is empty, False otherwise *)

implementation

procedure NewNode (var S: Typ;
      Item: TableElement.Typ;
      Link: Typ);
begin
 new(S);
 S^.Data := Item;
 S^.Next := Link;
end; (* NewNode *)

procedure Create (var S: Typ);
begin
```

```
      S := nil;
    end; (* Init *)

    procedure Destroy (var S: Typ);
     var
      TEMP: Typ;
    begin
     while S <> nil do begin
       TEMP := S;
       S := S^.Next;
       dispose(TEMP);
      end; (* While *)
    end; (* Destroy *)

    procedure Push (var S: Typ;
          Item: TableElement.Typ);
     var
      NEWELEMPTR: Typ;
    begin
     NewNode(NEWELEMPTR, Item, S);
     S := NEWELEMPTR;
    end; (* Push *)

    procedure Pop (var S: Typ;
          var Item: TableElement.Typ);
     var
      TEMP: Typ;
    begin
     TEMP := S;
     Item := S^.Data;
     S := S^.Next;
     dispose(TEMP);
    end; (* Pop *)

    function Empty (var S: Typ): boolean;
    begin
     Empty := (S = nil);
    end; (* Empty *)

    end. (* Stack *)
```

I.4.3. Stream

```
    unit Stream;

    interface

     const
      MaxStream = 80;

     type
      ModeType = (Undetermined, Reading, Writing);
      ElementType = integer;
      StreamArray = array[1..MaxStream] of ElementType;
```

```
Typ = record
  Mode: ModeType;
  Data: StreamArray;
  Length: integer;
  CurrPos: integer;
 end; (* Typ *)

procedure Create (var S: Typ);
   (* post : S is initialized and empty.  MUST be called *)
   (*      : before any other ADT operation is applied   *)
   (*      : to S.                                        *)

procedure Destroy (var S: Typ);
   (* post : Memory allocated for S is released; *)
   (*      : S becomes uninitialized             *)

procedure Reset (var S: Typ);
   (*  post : S is in the Reading mode.                   *)
   (*       : Sets the position pointer so that the first *)
   (*       : element in S is the next element returned by *)
   (*       : Read.                                       *)

procedure Rewrite (var S: Typ);
   (*  post : S is in the Writing mode. *)
   (*       : S is empty.               *)

procedure Read (var S: Typ;
      var Item: ElementType);
   (*  pre  : S is in the Reading mode.                   *)
   (*  post : Item returns the value of the element at the *)
   (*       : position indicated by the position pointer.  *)
   (*       : The position pointer references the next item *)
   (*       : in the Stream.                              *)

procedure Write (var S: Typ;
      Item: ElementType);
   (*  pre  : S is in the Writing mode.          *)
   (*  post : Item is appended to the end of S. *)

function AtEnd (var S: Typ): boolean;
   (*  pre  : S is in the Reading mode.                   *)
   (*  post : True if S's position pointer is past the last *)
   (*       : element.                                    *)

implementation

procedure Create (var S: Typ);
begin
 S.Mode := Undetermined;
 S.Length := 0;
end; (* Create *)

procedure Destroy (var S: Typ);
begin
        (* nothing to do *)
```

```
              end; (* Destroy *)

              procedure Reset (var S: Typ);
              begin
               S.Mode := Reading;
               S.CurrPos := 0;
              end; (* Reset *)

              procedure Rewrite (var S: Typ);
              begin
               Destroy(S);
               Create(S);
               S.Mode := Writing;
              end; (* Reset *)

              procedure Read (var S: Typ;
                    var Item: ElementType);
              begin
               S.CurrPos := S.CurrPos + 1;
               Item := S.Data[S.CurrPos];
              end; (* Read *)

              procedure Write (var S: Typ;
                    Item: ElementType);
              begin
               S.Length := S.Length + 1;
               S.Data[S.Length] := Item;
              end; (* Write *)

              function AtEnd (var S: Typ): boolean;
              begin
               AtEnd := S.CurrPos = S.Length;
              end; (* AtEnd *)

              end. (* Stream *)
```

I.4.4. Queue

```
              unit Queue;

              interface

              type
               QueuePtr = ^QueueRec;

               QueueRec = record
                 Data: TableElement.Typ;
                 Next: QueuePtr;
                end; (* QueueRec *)

               Typ = record
                 Head: QueuePtr;
                 Tail: QueuePtr;
                end; (* Typ *)
```

```
procedure Create (var Q: Typ);
  (* post : Q is initialized and empty *)

procedure Destroy (var Q: Typ);
  (* post : Memory allocated for Q is released; Q is *)
  (*      : uninitialized                            *)

procedure Enqueue (var Q: Typ; Item: ElementType);
  (* post : Item is appended at the tail of Q. *)

procedure Pop (var Q: Typ; var Item: ElementType);
  (* pre  : not Empty(Q)                      *)
  (* post : Q has its first element removed. *)
  (*      : Item holds that element.          *)

function Empty (var Q: Typ) : boolean;
  (* post : True if Q is empty, false otherwise *)

implementation

procedure Create (var Q: Typ);
begin
 Q.Head := nil;
 Q.Tail := nil;
end; (* Create  *)

procedure Destroy (var Q: Typ);
 var
  TEMP1, TEMP2: QueuePtr;
begin
 TEMP1 := Q.Head;
 while TEMP1 <> nil do begin
   TEMP2 := TEMP1;
   TEMP1 := TEMP1^.Next;
   dispose(TEMP2);
  end; (* While *)
end; (* Destroy *)

procedure Enqueue (var Q: Typ;
       Item: TableElement.Typ);
 var
  NEWELEMPTR: QueuePtr;
begin
 new(NEWELEMPTR);
 NEWELEMPTR^.Data := Item;
 NEWELEMPTR^.Next := nil;
 if Q.Tail <> nil then begin
   Q.Tail^.Next := NEWELEMPTR;
  end
 else begin
   Q.Head := NEWELEMPTR;
  end; (* If *)
 Q.Tail := NEWELEMPTR;
end; (* Enqueue *)
```

```
            procedure Dequeue (var Q: Typ;
                    var Item: TableElement.Typ);
            begin
             Item := Q.Head^.Data;
             Q.Head := Q.Head^.Next;
             if Q.Head = nil then begin
               Q.Tail := nil;
              end; (* If *)
            end; (* Dequeue *)

            function Empty (var Q: Typ): boolean;
            begin
             Empty := (Q.Head = nil);
            end; (* Empty *)
```

I.4.5. Table: Linked List Implementation

```
            unit Table;

            interface

            type
             TableElement.Typ = <appropriate type for current application>;
             Typ = ^TableRec;

             TableRec = record
               Data: TableElement.Typ;
               Next: Typ;
              end; (* TableRec *)

             procedure Create (var T: Typ);
                (* post : T is initialized and empty.  MUST be called     *)
                (*       : before any other ADT operation is applied to T. *)

             procedure Destroy (var T: Typ);
                (* post : Memory allocated for T is released; *)
                (*       : T becomes uninitialized            *)

             procedure Write (var OutFile: text; var T: Typ);
                (* post : value of T is written to OutFile    *)

             function Empty (var T: Typ) : boolean;
                (* post : True if T is empty, False otherwise *)

             function InTable (var T: Typ; Item: ElementType) : boolean;
                (* post : True if an element of T equals Item, False *)
                (*       : otherwise                                 *)

            procedure Insert (var T: Typ; Item: ElementType);
                (* post : Item is added to T such that T remains sorted. *)

             procedure Delete (var T: Typ; Item: ElementType);
                (* pre  :  InTable(T, Item)                          *)
                (* post :  The first element of T equal to Item is deleted *)
```

```
procedure FindMin (var T: Typ; var Item: ElementType);
  (* pre  : not Empty(T)                              *)
  (* post : Item is set to the element in T whose value is *)
  (*       : minimal.                                  *)

procedure Extract (var T: Typ; Item: ElementType; var NewT: Typ);
  (* post : All elements of T equal to Item (if any) are *)
  (*       : transferred to NewT                       *)

implementation

procedure Create (var T: Typ);
begin
 new(T);
 T^.Next := nil;
end; (* Create *)

procedure Destroy (var T: Typ);
 var
   TEMP: Typ;
begin
 while T <> nil do begin
   TEMP := T^.Next;
   dispose(T);
   T := TEMP;
  end; (* While *)
end; (* Destroy *)

function Empty (var T: Typ): boolean;
begin
 Empty := (T^.Next = nil);
end; (* Empty *)

procedure NewNode (var T: Typ;
       Entry: TableElement.Typ;
       Link: Typ);
begin
 new(T);
 T^.Data := Entry;
 T^.Next := Link;
end; (* NewNode *)

function AtFront (var T: Typ;
       Entry: TableElement.Typ): boolean;
begin
 if T = nil then begin
   AtFront := false;
  end
 else begin
   AtFront := Compare(T^.Data, Entry) = '=';
  end; (* If *)
end; (* AtFront *)
```

```
function GoToNext (T: Typ;
       Entry: TableElement.Typ): boolean;
begin
 if T^.Next = nil then begin
   GoToNext := false;
  end
 else begin
   GoToNext := Compare(T^.Next^.Data, Entry) = '<';
  end; (* If *)
end; (* GoToNext *)

function FindPrevToItem (T: Typ;
       Entry: TableElement.Typ): Typ;
 var
  TEMP: Typ;
begin
 TEMP := T;
 while GoToNext(TEMP, Entry) do begin
   TEMP := TEMP^.Next;
  end; (* While *)
 FindPrevToItem := TEMP;
end; (* FindPrevToItem *)

procedure FindMin (var T: Typ;
       var Item: TableElement.Typ);
begin
 Item := T^.Next^.Data;
end; (* FindMin *)

procedure Write (var T: Typ);
 var
  TEMP: Typ;
begin
 TEMP := T^.Next;
 while TEMP <> nil do begin
   PrintElement(TEMP^.Data);
   TEMP := TEMP^.Next;
  end; (* While *)

end; (* Write *)

procedure InsertFront (var T: Typ;
       Entry: TableElement.Typ);
 var
  NEWELEMPTR: Typ;
begin
 NewNode(NEWELEMPTR, Entry, T);
 T := NEWELEMPTR;
end; (* InsertFront *)

procedure DeleteFront (var T: Typ);
 var
  TEMP: Typ;
```

```
begin
 TEMP := T^.Next;
 dispose(T);
 T := TEMP;
end; (* DeleteFront *)

procedure Insert (var T: Typ;
        Item: TableElement.Typ);
 var
  POSITION: Typ;
begin
 POSITION := FindPrevToItem(T, Item);
 InsertFront(POSITION^.Next, Item);
end; (* Insert *)

procedure Delete (var T: Typ;
        Item: TableElement.Typ);
 var
  POSITION: Typ;
begin
 POSITION := FindPrevToItem(T, Item);
 DeleteFront(POSITION^.Next);
end; (* Delete *)

function InTable (var T: Typ;
        Item: TableElement.Typ): boolean;
 var
  POSITION: Typ;
begin
 POSITION := FindPrevToItem(T, Item);
 InTable := AtFront(POSITION^.Next, Item);
end; (* InTable *)

procedure Extract (var T: Typ;
        Item: TableElement.Typ;
        var NewT: Typ);
 var
  POSITION: Typ;
begin
 Create(NewT);
 POSITION := FindPrevToItem(T, Item);
 while AtFront(POSITION^.Next, Item) do begin
   Insert(NewT, POSITION^.Next^.Data);
   POSITION := POSITION^.Next;
  end; (* While *)
end; (* Extract *)

end. (* Table *)
```

I.4.6. Table: Binary Tree Implementation

```
unit Table;

interface
```

```
type
 Typ = ^TableRec;
 TableRec = record
   Data: TableElement.Typ;
   Left, Right: Typ;
  end; (* TableRec *)

 procedure Create (var T: Typ);
    (* post : T is initialized and empty.  MUST be called     *)
    (*       : before any other ADT operation is applied to T. *)

 procedure Destroy (var T: Typ);
    (* post : Memory allocated for T is released; *)
    (*       : T becomes uninitialized             *)

 procedure Write (var OutFile: text; var T: Typ);
    (* post : value of T is written to OutFile     *)

 function Empty (var T: Typ) : boolean;
    (* post : True if T is empty, False otherwise *)

 function InTable (var T: Typ; Item: ElementType) : boolean;
    (* post : True if an element of T equals Item, False *)
    (*       : otherwise                                  *)

 procedure Insert (var T: Typ; Item: ElementType);
    (* post : Item is added to T such that T remains sorted. *)

 procedure Delete (var T: Typ; Item: ElementType);
    (* pre  :  InTable(T, Item)                                 *)
    (* post :  The first element of T equal to Item is deleted *)

 procedure FindMin (var T: Typ; var Item: ElementType);
    (* pre  : not Empty(T)                                *)
    (* post : Item is set to the element in T whose value is *)
    (*       : minimal                                    *)

 procedure Extract (var T: Typ; Item: ElementType; var NewT: Typ);
    (* post : All elements of T equal to Item (if any) are *)
    (*       : transferred to NewT                          *)

implementation

procedure Create (var T: Typ);
begin
 T := nil;
end; (* Create *)

procedure Destroy (var T: Typ);
begin
 if T <> nil then begin
   Destroy(T^.Left);
   Destroy(T^.Right);
   dispose(T);
```

```
    end; (* If *)
  end; (* Destroy *)

  procedure NewLeaf (var NewElemPtr: Typ;
          Item: TableElement.Typ);
  begin
   new(NewElemPtr);
   NewElemPtr^.Data := Item;
   NewElemPtr^.Left := nil;
   NewElemPtr^.Right := nil;
  end; (* NewLeaf *)

  function IsLeaf (T: Typ): boolean;
  begin
   IsLeaf := (T^.Left = nil) and (T^.Right = nil);
  end; (* IsLeaf *)

  procedure DeleteMax (var Tree: Typ;
          var ItsValue: TableElement.Typ);
   var
    TEMPNODE: Typ;
  begin
   if Tree^.Right <> nil then begin
     DeleteMax(Tree^.Right, ItsValue);
     end
   else begin
     ItsValue := Tree^.Data;
     TEMPNODE := Tree;
     Tree := Tree^.Left;
     dispose(TEMPNODE);
     end; (* If *)
  end; (* DeleteMax *)

  procedure Remove (var BadNode: Typ);
   var
    TEMPNODE: Typ;
    ITSVALUE: TableElement.Typ;
  begin
   if (BadNode^.Left <> nil) and (BadNode^.Right <> nil) then begin
     DeleteMax(BadNode^.Left, ITSVALUE);
     BadNode^.Data := ITSVALUE;
     end
   else begin
     TEMPNODE := BadNode;
     if IsLeaf(BadNode) then begin
       BadNode := nil;
       end
     else if (BadNode^.Left = nil) then begin
       BadNode := BadNode^.Right;
       end
     else if (BadNode^.Right = nil) then begin
       BadNode := BadNode^.Left;
       end;
```

```
      dispose(TEMPNODE);
    end; (* If *)
 end; (* Remove *)

 procedure Delete (var T: Typ;
        Item: TableElement.Typ);
 begin
  if Compare(Item, T^.Data) = '=' then begin
    Remove(T);
    end
  else if Compare(Item, T^.Data) = '<' then begin
    Delete(T^.Left, Item);
    end
  else begin
    Delete(T^.Right, Item);
    end; (* If *)
 end; (* Delete *)

 function Empty (var T: Typ): boolean;
 begin
  Empty := (T = nil);
 end; (* Empty *)

 procedure FindMin (var T: Typ;
        var Item: TableElement.Typ);
 begin
  if T^.Left <> nil then begin
    FindMin(T^.Left, Item);
    end
  else begin
    Item := T^.Data;
    end; (* If *)
 end; (* FindMin *)

 procedure Write (var T: Typ);
 begin
  if T <> nil then begin
    System.write(T^.Left);
    PrintElement(T^.Data);
    System.write(T^.Right);
    end; (* If *)
 end; (* Write *)

 procedure Insert (var T: Typ;
        Item: TableElement.Typ);
 begin
  if T = nil then begin
    NewLeaf(T, Item);
    end
  else if Compare(Item, T^.Data) = '<' then begin
    Insert(T^.Left, Item);
    end
  else begin
    Insert(T^.Right, Item);
```

```
                       end; (* If *)
                  end; (* Insert *)

                  function InTable (var T: Typ;
                         Item: TableElement.Typ): boolean;
                  begin
                   if T = nil then begin
                     InTable := false;
                    end
                   else if Compare(Item, T^.Data) = '=' then begin
                     InTable := true;
                    end
                   else if Compare(Item, T^.Data) = '<' then begin
                     InTable := InTable(T^.Left, Item);
                    end
                   else begin
                     InTable := InTable(T^.Right, Item);
                    end; (* If *)
                  end; (* InTable *)

                  procedure Extract (var T: Typ;
                         Item: TableElement.Typ);

                   procedure Explore (T: Typ);
                   begin
                    if T <> nil then begin
                      if Compare(Item, T^.Data) <> '>' then begin
                       if Compare(Item, T^.Data) = '=' then begin
                        Insert(NewT, T^.Data);
                        end; (* If *)
                       Explore(T^.Left);
                       Explore(T^.Right);
                      end; (* If *)
                    end; (* If *)

                   begin
                    NewT := nil;
                    Explore(T);
                   end; (* Extract *)
                  end. (* Table *)
```

I.4.7. Deque

```
                  unit Deque;

                  interface

                  type
                   TableElement.Typ = integer;

                   DequePtr = ^DequeRec;

                   DequeRec = record
```

```
   Data: TableElement.Typ;
   Next, Previous: DequePtr;
  end; (* DequeRec *)

 Typ = record
   Head: DequePtr;
   Tail: DequePtr;
  end; (* Typ *)

 procedure Create (var D: Typ);
    (* post : D is initialized and empty *)

 procedure Destroy (var D: Typ);
    (* post : Memory allocated for D is released; D is *)
    (*       : uninitialized                           *)

 procedure PutFront (var D: Typ; Item: ElementType);
    (* post : D has Item appended to its front. *)

 procedure PutBack (var D: Typ; Item: ElementType);
    (* post : D has Item appended to its back. *)

 procedure GetFront (var D: Typ; var Item: ElementType);
    (* pre  : not Empty(D)                             *)
    (* post : The front element of D has been removed. *)
    (*       : Item holds that element.                *)

 procedure GetBack (var D: Typ; var Item· E .ementType);
    (* pre  : not Empty(D)                             *)
    (* post : The back element of D has been removed.  *)
    (*       : Item holds that element.                *)

 function Empty (var D: Typ) : boolean;
    (* post : True if D is empty, false otherwise *)

implementation

procedure Create (var D: Typ);
begin
 D.Head := nil;
 D.Tail := nil;
end; (* Create *)

procedure Destroy (var D: Typ);
 var
  TEMP1, TEMP2: DequePtr;
begin
 TEMP1 := D.Head;
 while TEMP1 <> nil do begin
   TEMP2 := TEMP1;
   TEMP1 := TEMP1^.Next;
   dispose(TEMP2);
```

```
   end; (* While *)
end; (* Destroy *)

procedure NewNode (var D: DequePtr;
      Entry: TableElement.Typ;
      Front, Back: DequePtr);
begin
 new(D);
 D^.Data := Entry;
 D^.Previous := Front;
 D^.Next := Back;
end; (* NewNode *)

procedure PutFront (var D: Typ;
      Item: TableElement.Typ);
 var
   NEWELEMPTR: DequePtr;
begin
 NewNode(NEWELEMPTR, Item, nil, D.Head);
 if D.Head <> nil then begin
   D.Head^.Previous := NEWELEMPTR;
   end
 else begin
   D.Tail := NEWELEMPTR;
   end; (* If *)
 D.Head := NEWELEMPTR;
end; (* PutFront *)

procedure PutBack (var D: Typ;
      Item: TableElement.Typ);
 var
   NEWELEMPTR: DequePtr;
begin
 NewNode(NEWELEMPTR, Item, D.Tail, nil);
 if D.Tail <> nil then begin
   D.Tail^.Next := NEWELEMPTR;
   end
 else begin
   D.Head := NEWELEMPTR;
   end; (* If *)
 D.Tail := NEWELEMPTR;
end; (* PutBack *)

procedure GetFront (var D: Typ;
      var Item: TableElement.Typ);
begin
 Item := D.Head^.Data;
 D.Head := D.Head^.Next;
 if D.Head = nil then begin
   D.Tail := nil;
   end
 else begin
   D.Head^.Previous := nil;
```

```
      end; (* If *)
   end; (* GetFront *)

   procedure GetBack (var D: Typ;
          var Item: TableElement.Typ);
   begin
    Item := D.Tail^.Data;
    D.Tail := D.Tail^.Previous;
    if D.Tail = nil then begin
      D.Head := nil;
     end
    else begin
      D.Tail^.Next := nil;
     end; (* If *)
   end; (* GetBack *)

   function Empty (var D: Typ): boolean;
   begin
    Empty := (D.Head = nil);
   end; (* Empty *)
   end. (* Deqeue *)
```

I.4.8. Graphs

```
   unit GraphADT;

   uses
    StreamADT;

   const
    NoConnection = 0;
    MaxNodes = 40;

   type
    ConnectArray = array[1..MaxNodes] of integer;
    NodeRec = record
      LastConnection: integer;
      MarkVal: integer;
      Connections: ConnectArray;
     end; (* NodeRec *)
    NodeArray = array[1..MaxNodes] of NodeRec;
    Typ = record
      NumNodes: integer;
      Nodes: NodeArray;
     end; (* Typ *)

   procedure Create (var G: Typ);
      (* post : G is initialized and empty *)

   procedure Destroy (var G: Typ);
      (* post : Memory allocated for G is released; G is *)
      (*       : uninitialized.                          *)
```

```
procedure AddEdge (var G: GraphTyp;
    FromNode, ToNode: integer);
  (* post : There is an edge from FromNode to ToNode in G. *)

procedure AddWeightedEdge (var G: Typ;
    FromNode, ToNode: integer;
    Weight: integer);
  (* post : There is an edge with weight Weight from *)
  (*      : FromNode to ToNode in G.                 *)

procedure RemoveEdge (var G: Typ;
    FromNode, ToNode: integer);
  (* pre  : There is an edge from FromNode to ToNode in G. *)
  (* post : There is not an edge from FromNode to ToNode   *)
  (*      : in G.                                          *)

function GetWeight (var G: Typ;
    FromNode, ToNode: integer): integer;
  (* pre  : There is an edge from FromNode to ToNode in G. *)
  (* post : Returns the weight of the edge from FromNode   *)
  (*        and ToNode in G.                               *)

function ConnectionExists (var G: Typ;
    FromNode, ToNode: integer): boolean;
  (* post : Returns TRUE if there is an edge from FromNode *)
  (*      : to ToNode in G.                                *)

function NumNodesWithEdges (var G: Typ): integer;
  (* post : Returns the number of nodes in G that are *)
  (*      : connected to other nodes by edges.        *)

procedure ZeroAllMarks (var G: Typ);
  (* post : The marks of all the nodes in G are set to zero. *)

procedure SetMark (var G: Typ;
    Node: integer;
    Value: integer);
  (* post : The mark of node Node in G is set to Value. *)

function GetMark (var G: Typ;
    Node: integer): integer;
  (* pre  : The mark of node Node in G has been set. *)
  (* post : Returns the mark of node Node in G.      *)

procedure Neighbors (var G: Typ;
    var S: StreamTyp;
    Node: integer);
  (* pre  : S is initialized.                              *)
  (* post : S contains the node numbers of Node's neighbors *)
  (*      : S is in the Reading mode;                      *)
  (*      : S's position pointer references its first      *)
  (*      : element.                                       *)

implementation
```

```pascal
procedure Create (var G: Typ);
 var
  I, J: integer;
begin
 G.NumNodes := 0;
 for I := 1 to MaxNodes do begin
   G.Nodes[I].LastConnection := 0;
   G.Nodes[I].MarkVal := 0;
   for J := 1 to MaxNodes do begin
     G.Nodes[I].Connections[J] := NoConnection;
    end; (* For *)
  end; (* For *)
end; (* Create *)

procedure Destroy (var G: Typ);
begin
end; (* Destroy *)

function Max (First, Second: integer): integer;
begin
 if First > Second then begin
   Max := First;
  end
 else begin
   Max := Second;
  end; (* If *)
end; (* Max *)

procedure AddWeightedEdge (var G: Typ;
    FromNode, ToNode: integer;
    Weight: integer);
begin
 G.NumNodes := Max(G.NumNodes, FromNode);
 G.NumNodes := Max(G.NumNodes, ToNode);
 with G.Nodes[FromNode] do begin
   Connections[ToNode] := Weight;
   LastConnection := Max(LastConnection, ToNode);
  end; (* With *)
end; (* AddWeightedEdge *)

procedure AddEdge (var G: Typ;
    FromNode, ToNode: integer);
begin
 AddWeightedEdge(G, FromNode, ToNode, 1);
end; (* AddEdge *)

procedure RemoveEdge(var G: Typ;
    FromNode, ToNode: integer);
begin
 G.Nodes[FromNode].Connections[ToNode] := NoConnection;
end; (* RemoveEdge *)

function GetWeight(var G: Typ;
    FromNode, ToNode: integer): integer;
```

```
begin
 GetWeight := G.Nodes[FromNode].Connections[ToNode];
end; (* GetWeight *)

function ConnectionExists (var G: Typ;
    FromNode, ToNode: integer): boolean;
begin
 ConnectionExists := G.Nodes[FromNode].Connections[ToNode]
                      <> NoConnection;
end; (* ConnectionExists *)

function NumNodesWithEdges (var G: Typ): integer;
begin
 NumNodesWithEdges := G.NumNodes;
end; (* NumNodesWithEdges *)

procedure ZeroAllMarks (var G: Typ);
 var
  I: integer;
begin
 for I := 1 to MaxNodes do begin
   G.Nodes[I].MarkVal := 0;
  end; (* For *)
end; (* ZeroAllMarks *)

procedure SetMark (var G: Typ;
    Node: integer;
    Value: integer);
begin
 G.Nodes[Node].MarkVal := Value;
end; (* SetMark *)

function GetMark (var G: Typ;
    Node: integer): integer;
begin
 GetMark := G.Nodes[Node].MarkVal;
end; (* GetMark *)

procedure Neighbors (var G: Typ;
      var S: Stream.Typ;
      Node: integer);
 var
  I: integer;
begin
 Stream.Rewrite(S);
 for I := 1 to G.Nodes[Node].LastConnection do begin
   if ConnectionExists(G, Node, I) then begin
     Stream.Write(S, I);
    end; (* If *)
  end; (* For *)
 Stream.Reset(S);
end; (* Neighbors *)

end. (* GraphADT *)
```

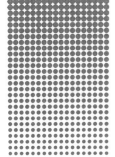

II

ANSWERS TO PROBLEMS

CHAPTER 1

Self-Check Exercises
Section 1.2

1. The local variables are considered inside the black box because they can be accessed only by the execution block of the procedure or function. If Pascal scope rules were changed to allow other parts of the program to manipulate these local variables, then they would become part of the interface rather than a local detail.

2.
```
function ln(num:real) : real;
        (* pre  : num > 0.0.                                      *)
        (* post : returns an approximation to the natural log *)
        (*      : of num.                                         *)
```

Section 1.3

1. When the interface part of the module being defined makes reference to definitions in the module being used, then the *uses* clause should be in the interface part. This situation might arise, for example, when the module being defined makes reference to a type defined in the module being used. If all references to the module being used are in the implementation part of the module being defined, the *uses* clause should be kept in the implementation part to keep the interface as simple as possible.

2. Direct references to the variable *TheSum* will prove more efficient than the indirection of accessing function *Sum*. This would generally be considered secondary, however, to the protection and flexibility provided by the function. It provides protection in that variable *TheSum* can be examined only outside the module, not altered. It provides flexibility in that if you later decide that obtaining the sum involves more than just looking up the value of *TheSum*, the use of the function allows you to rewrite the module without having to rewrite the high-level code.

CHAPTER 2

Self Check Exercises
Section 2.2

1. Without a call on *Create*, the variable is completely uninitialized. There is no way for the module to examine such a variable to discover that it needs to be created, because all of its fields are undefined.

2. If the implementation of the ADT involves a complete data structure, then simple assignment will always work. But when the implementation instead stores references to data rather than the data itself (as in the second implementation of strings), then simple assignment will merely cause the two variables to refer to the same storage, not to create a new copy of the data.

Section 2.3

1. The specification for *FindMin* says that it finds the first table element of minimal value. It is important that this also be the value that *Delete* removes, in case you want to use these two procedures in unison.

2. You would need to replace the clause

```
Compare := =;
```

with

```
Compare := String.Compare(x.Name, y.Name);
```

CHAPTER 3

Self Check Exercises
Section 3.2

```
1. procedure Inform (N: integer;
        Message: MsgType);
```

```
begin
 if N = 1 then begin
   Give Message to person;
 end
 else if N > 0 then begin
   choose two people to tell;
   Give Message to first person;
   Inform((N div 2 - 1), Message);
   Give Message to second person;
   Inform((N div 2) - 1, Message);
   if odd(N) then begin
     Give Message to person;
   end; (* If *)
 end; (* If *)
end; (* Inform *)
```

```
2. 40      30
   30      10
   10
```

This function computes the greatest common divisor of its two parameters.

Section 3.3

```
1. function Power (X, N: integer): integer;
   begin
    if N = 0 then begin
      Power := 1;
    end
    else begin
      Power := X * Power(X, N - 1);
    end; (* If *)
   end; (* Power *)
```

```
2. function Power(X, N:integer): integer;
   begin
    if N = 0 then begin
      Power := 1;
    end
    else if odd(N) then begin
      Power := X * Power(X, N - 1);
    end
    else begin
      Power := sqr(Power(X, N div 2));
    end; (* If *)
   end; (* Power *)
```

3. 11111111

4. It won't work because every recursive call must reduce the size of the problem. In the case of $n = 2$, though, one of the recursive calls does not reduce the size of the problem (it again tries to solve a problem of size 2).

Section 3.4

```
1. procedure Solve (Col: integer);
     var
       ROW: integer;
   begin
     if Col > Queens.NumCols then begin
       Queens.Write(output);
     end
     else begin
       for ROW := 1 to Queens.NumCols do begin
         if Queens.Safe(ROW, Col) then begin
           Queens.Place(ROW, Col);
           Solve(Col + 1);
           Queens.Remove(ROW, Col);
         end; (* If *)
       end; (* For *)
     end; (* If *)
   end; (* Solve *)
```

Section 3.6

```
1. function Fib (N: integer): integer;
     var
       NUM, LAST, TEMP, I: integer;
   begin
     LAST := 1;
     NUM := 1;
     for I := 2 to N do begin
       TEMP := NUM;
       NUM := LAST + NUM;
       LAST := TEMP;
     end; (* For *)
     Fib := NUM;
   end; (* Fib *)
```

```
2. function FibCalls (N: integer): integer;
   begin
     if N <= 2 then begin
       FibCalls := 1;
     end
     else begin
       FibCalls := 1 + FibCalls(N - 1) + FibCalls(N - 2);
     end; (* If *)
   end; (* FibCalls *)
```

3. Since the nth Fibonacci number is approximated by c^n, $c^n = c^{n-1} + c^{n-2}$. Dividing by c^{n-2} yields $c^2 = c + 1 \rightarrow c = \sqrt{5} + \frac{1}{2}$.

Programming Exercises

```
1. function NumDigits (Num: integer): integer;
   begin
```

```
      if Num div 10 = 0 then begin
        NumDigits := 1;
       end
      else begin
        NumDigits := NumDigits(Num div 10) + 1;
       end; (* If *)
    end; (* NumDigits *)
```

3.
```
procedure Binary (Num: integer);
  begin
   if Num div 2 = 0 then begin
     write(Num : 1);
    end
   else begin
     Binary(Num div 2);
     write(Num mod 2 : 1);
    end; (* If *)
  end; (* Binary *)
```

5.
```
procedure ReadFirstNonSpace (var Infile: text;
        var CH: char);
  begin
   repeat
    read(Infile, CH);
   until CH <> ' ';
  end; (* ReadFirstNonSpace *)

procedure ReadNum (var Infile: text;
        StartChar: char;
        var Num: integer);
  begin
   Num := ord(StartChar) - ord('0');
   repeat
    read(Infile, StartChar);
    if StartChar in ['0'..'9'] then begin
      Num := Num * 10 + (ord(StartChar) - ord('0'));
     end; (* If *)
   until not (StartChar in ['0'..'9']);
  end; (* ReadNum *)

procedure Eval (var Infile: text;
        var Result: integer);
  var
   CH: char;
   OP1, OP2: integer;
  begin
   ReadFirstNonSpace(Infile, CH);
   if CH in ['0'..'9'] then begin
     ReadNum(Infile, CH, Result);
    end
   else begin
     Eval(Infile, OP1);
```

```
Eval(Infile, OP2);
case CH of
  '+':
    Result := OP1 + OP2;
  '-':
    Result := OP1 - OP2;
  '/':
    Result := OP1 div OP2;
  '*':
    Result := OP1 * OP2;
  end; (* Case *)
 end; (* If *)
end; (* Eval *)
```

CHAPTER 4

Self Check Exercises
Section 4.2

1. An advantage of dynamic variable allocation is that the number of variables need not be known at compile-time. On the other hand, arrays yield immediate access to each element.

2. `true`
   `false`
   `true`
   `true`
   `true`
   `true`
   `false`
   `false`

Section 4.3

1. Problems arise because you will need to add the items to the end of the list rather than the front. This is both slower (since you must traverse the list each time) and more complicated, because you must stop the traversal at the last element, which is a little tricky. You can solve the speed problem by maintaining pointers to both ends of the list, but that just makes the code more complex.

2.
                                         2   6   12

                                         2   0   10

                                         0   4   10

                                         4   0   10

Section 4.4

1. This procedure will work because *Head* is passed to *NewNode* as both a *var* and a *value* parameter. Thus, when the new element is allocated and *Head* is set to point to it, the old value of *Head* is preserved.

2. This procedure inserts *value* at the end of the list pointed to by *Head*.

Section 4.5

1. This procedure writes out the contents of a file of integers in reverse order. The problem is the loop test S < > nil. This test assumes a particular implementation of the Stack, and thus violates the integrity of the abstraction.

Section 4.7

1. You would have to treat the case where you are to insert before the first element as a special case. This includes inserting into an empty list. The following code solves the problem:

```
function GoToNext (T: Typ;
        Item: ElementType);
begin
 if T^.Next = nil then begin
   GoToNext := false;
   end
 else begin
   GoToNext := Item > T^.Next^.Data;
   end; (* If *)
end; (* GoToNext *)

procedure Insert (var T: Typ;
        Item: ElementType);
 var
  POSITION: Typ;
begin
 if T = nil then begin
   InsertFront(T, Item);
   end
 else if Item < T^.Data then begin
   InsertFront(T, Item);
   end
 else begin
   POSITION := T;
   while GoToNext(POSITION, Item) do begin
     POSITION := POSITION^.Next;
    end; (* While *)
   InsertFront(POSITION^.Next, Item);
  end; (* If *)
end; (* Insert *)
```

Section 4.8

1. When solving this problem iteratively, you use a temporary pointer to traverse the list while looking for the desired position. This pointer must stop at the record before that position because you will need to modify that record's *Next* field, which serves to link in the next record in the list. When solving the problem recursively, however, you can pass the actual *Next* fields as *var* parameters into the next recursive call. Thus, by changing the pointer in the current recursive call you are automatically also changing the link from the previous record.

Programming Exercises

```
1. procedure Reverse (var Infile, Outfile: text);

    type
     ListPtr = ^ListRec;

     ListRec = record
       Data: char;
       AtEOLN: boolean;
       Next: ListPtr;
      end; (* ListRec *)

    var
     HEAD, TEMP: ListPtr;
     CH: char;

   begin
    new(HEAD);
    HEAD^.AtEOLN := true;
    HEAD^.Next := nil;
    while not eof(Infile) do begin
      while not eoln(Infile) do begin
        read(Infile, CH);
        new(TEMP);
        TEMP^.Data := CH;
        TEMP^.AtEOLN := false;
        TEMP^.Next := HEAD;
        HEAD := TEMP;
       end; (* While *)
      readln(Infile);
      new(TEMP);
      TEMP^.AtEOLN := true;
      TEMP^.Next := HEAD;
      HEAD := TEMP;
     end; (* While *)
    while HEAD <> nil do begin
      while not HEAD^.AtEOLN do begin
        write(Outfile, HEAD^.Data);
```

```
            HEAD := HEAD^.Next;
          end; (* While *)
        writeln(Outfile);
        HEAD := HEAD^.Next;
      end; (* While *)
  end; (* Reverse *)
```

3. ```
procedure PrintQueue (var Q: Queue);
   var
    TEMP: Queue.Typ;
    ITEM: ElementType;
  begin (* PrintQueue *)
  Queue.Create(TEMP);
  while not Queue.Empty(Q) do begin
    Queue.Dequeue(Q, ITEM);
    Queue.Enqueue(TEMP, ITEM);
    PrintElement(ITEM);
    end; (* With *)
  end; (* While *)
  while not Queue.Empty(TEMP) do begin
    Queue.Dequeue(TEMP, ITEM);
    Queue.Enqueue(Q, ITEM);
   end; (* With *)
  end; (* While *)
  Queue.Destroy(TEMP);
  end; (* PrintQueue *)
```

5. ```
procedure DeleteAll (var Head: ListPtr;
         Target: char);
  begin
   if Head <> nil then begin
     if Head^.Data = Target then begin
       DeleteAll(Head^.Next, Target);
       TEMP := Head;
       Head := Head^.Next;
       dispose(TEMP);
      end
     else begin
       DeleteAll(Head^.Next, Target);
      end; (* If *)
    end; (* If *)
  end; (* DeleteAll *)
```

7. ```
function NumNodes (Head: ListPtr): integer;
  begin
   if Head = nil then begin
     NumNodes := 0;
    end
   else begin
     NumNodes := 1 + NumNodes(Head^.Next);
    end; (* If *)
  end; (* NumNodes *)
```
```

9.
```
function DirectlyContains (ListA, ListB: ListPtr): boolean;
begin
 if (ListA = nil) then begin
   DirectlyContains := true;
   end
 else begin
   DirectlyContains := (ListA^.Data = ListB^.Data) and
                        (DirectlyContains(ListA^.ListB^.Next));
   end; (* If *)
end; (* DirectlyContains *)

function Contains (ListA, ListB: ListPtr): boolean;
begin
 if (ListA = nil) then begin
   Contains := true;
   end
 else if (ListB = nil) then begin
   Contains := false;
   end
 else if (ListA^.Data = ListB^.Data) then begin
   Contains := DirectlyContains(ListA^.Next, ListB^.Next) or
               Contains(ListA, ListB^.Next);
   end
 else begin
   Contains := Contains(ListA, ListB^.Next);
   end; (* If *)
end; (* Contains *)
```

11.
```
procedure Reverse (var List: ListPtr);
   var
     NEWLIST, TEMP: ListPtr;
   begin
   NEWLIST := nil;
   while List <> nil do begin
     TEMP := List;
     List := List^.Next;
     TEMP^.Next := NEWLIST;
     NEWLIST := TEMP;
     end; (* While *)
   List := NEWLIST;
   end; (* Reverse *)
```

CHAPTER 5

Self Check Exercises
Section 5.2

1. 1, 2, 3, 6
2. 4, 5, 7, 8

3. 1
4. 4, 5, 6
5. 3
6. 3
7. 2, 3

Section 5.3

1. 4
2. 6, 7, 8
3.
```
procedure BuildATree (var Root: TreePtr);
begin
  NewLeaf(Root, 1);
  NewLeaf(Root^.Left, 2);
  NewLeaf(Root^.Left^.Left, 4);
  NewLeaf(Root^.Left^.Right, 5);
  NewLeaf(Root^.Right, 3);
  NewLeaf(Root^.Right^.Left, 6);
  NewLeaf(Root^.Right^.Left^.Left, 7);
  NewLeaf(Root^.Right^.Left^.Right, 8);
end; (* BuildATree *)
```

Section 5.4

1.
```
procedure RightToLeft (aNode: TreePtr);
begin
  if aNode <> nil then begin
    RightToLeft(aNode^.Right);
    writeln(aNode^.Data);
    RightToLeft(aNode^.Left);
  end; (* If *)
end; (* RightToLeft *)
```

2. (a) 1, 2, 4, 5, 3, 6, 7, 8
   (b) 4, 2, 5, 1, 7, 6, 8, 3
   (c) 4, 5, 2, 7, 8, 6, 3, 1

Section 5.5

1.
```
function Sum (aNode: TreePtr): integer;
begin
  if aNode = nil then begin
    Sum := 0;
  end
  else begin
    Sum := aNode^.Data + Sum(aNode^.Left) + Sum(aNode^.Right);
  end; (* If *)
end; (* Sum *)
```

```
2. function Shortest (aNode: TreePtr): integer;
   begin
     if aNode = nil then begin
       Shortest := -1;
     end
     else begin
       Shortest := Min(Shortest(aNode^.Left),
                       Shortest(aNode^.Right)) + 1;
     end; (* If *)
   end; (* Shortest *)
```

Section 5.7

1.

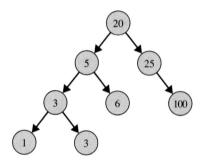

Preorder: 20, 5, 3, 1, 3, 6, 25, 100

Inorder: 1, 3, 3, 5, 6, 20, 25, 100

Postorder: 1, 3, 3, 6, 5, 100, 25, 20

```
2. procedure Descending (Tree: TreePtr);
   begin
     if Tree <> nil then begin
       Descending(Tree^.Right);
       writeln(Tree^.Data);
       Descending(Tree^.Left);
     end; (* If *)
   end; (* Descending *)
```

Section 5.8

1. You could have used the leftmost node of the desired node's right subtree because it must also be a leaf, and must come immediately after the desired node. Thus, it is easy to delete and can be moved into the desired node's position while maintaining the binary search tree's ordering.

Programming Exercises

```
1. function NumLeft (Tree: TreePtr): integer;
   begin
    if Tree = nil then begin
      NumLeft := 0;
     end
    else if Tree^.Left = nil then begin
      NumLeft := NumLeft(Tree^.Right);
     end
    else begin
      NumLeft := 1 + NumLeft(Tree^.Left) + NumLeft(Tree^.Right);
     end; (* If *)
   end; (* NumLeft *)


3. procedure Mirror (TreeIn: TreePtr;
          var TreeOut: TreePtr);
   begin
    if TreeIn = nil then begin
      TreeOut := nil
     end
    else begin
      new(TreeOut);
      TreeOut^.Data := TreeIn^.Data;
      Mirror(TreeIn^.Left, TreeOut^.Right);
      Mirror(TreeIn^.Right, TreeOut^.Left);
     end; (* If *)
   end; (* Mirror *)


5. function CompletelyBalanced (Atree: TreePtr): boolean;
     var
       FUNCTEMP: boolean;
   begin
    if Atree = nil then begin
      FuncTemp := true;
     end
    else begin
      FuncTemp := CompleteNode(Atree^);
      if FuncTemp then begin
        FuncTemp := (Height(Atree^.Right) = Height(Atree^.Left));
        if FuncTemp then begin
        FuncTemp := CompletelyBalanced(Atree^.Left);
        if FuncTemp then begin
        FuncTemp := CompletelyBalanced(Atree^.Right),
       end;
      end; (* If *)
     CompletelyBalanced := FuncTemp;
   end; (* CompletelyBalanced *)
```

7. program ConstructTree;

```
const
 MaxTraverse = 20;

type
 TravArray = array[1..MaxTraverse] of char;
 TravType = record
   Data: TravArray;
   Len: integer;
  end; (* TravType *)

 TreePtr = ^TreeRec;
 TreeRec = record
   Data: char;
   Left, Right: TreePtr;
  end; (* TreeRec *)


var
 PreT, InT, PostT: TravType;
 Tree: TreePtr;

procedure ReadTraversal (var Trav: TravType);
begin
 Trav.Len := 0;
 while not eoln do begin
   Trav.Len := Trav.Len + 1;
   read(Trav.Data[Trav.Len]);
  end; (* While *)
 readln;
end; (* ReadTraversal *)

function FindIndex (var InT: TravType;
      CH: char): integer;
 var
 I: integer;
begin
 I := 1;
 while InT.Data[I] <> CH do begin
   I := I + 1;
  end; (* While *)
 FindIndex := I;
end; (* FindIndex *)

procedure BuildTree (var Tree: TreePtr;
      PreT, InT: TravType);
 var
  PrePos: integer;

 procedure DoBuild (var Tree: TreePtr;
      InStart, InFinish: integer;
      var PrePos: integer);
  var
   Index: integer;
  begin
```

```
    if InStart <= InFinish then begin
      PrePos := PrePos + 1;
      new(Tree);
      Tree^.Data := PreT.Data[PrePos];
      Index := FindIndex(InT, Tree^.Data);
      DoBuild(Tree^.Left, InStart, Index - 1, PrePos);
      DoBuild(Tree^.Right, Index + 1, InFinish, PrePos);
    end
  else begin
    Tree := nil;
  end; (* If *)
 end; (* DoBuild *)

begin
 PrePos := 0;
 DoBuild(Tree, 1, InT.Len, PrePos);
end; (* BuildTree *)


procedure PrintPost (Tree: TreePtr);
begin
 if Tree <> nil then begin
   PrintPost(Tree^.Left);
   PrintPost(Tree^.Right);
   write(Tree^.Data);
  end; (* If *)
end; (* PrintPost *)

begin
 ReadTraversal(PreT);
 ReadTraversal(InT);
 BuildTree(Tree, PreT, InT);
 PrintPost(Tree);
end. (* Main *)
```

9. (a)

1) Expression: T

2) Expression: (T∨F)

3) Expression: ((~F)∧T)

4) Expression: ((~F)∨(F∧T))

(b)
```
procedure Parse (var Infile: text;
        var Root: TreePtr);
var
  CH: char;
begin
 new(Root);
 if Infile^ <> '(' then begin
   read(Infile, Root^.Data);
   Root^.Left := nil;
   Root^.Right := nil;
   end
 else begin
   read(Infile, CH);
   if Infile^ <> '~' then begin
     Parse(Infile, Root^.Left);
     end
   else begin
     Root^.Left := nil;
     end; (* If *)
   read(Infile, Root^.Data);
   Parse(Infile, Root^.Right);
   read(Infile, CH);
   end; (* If *)
end; (* Parse *)
```

(c)
```
procedure PrintExpression (var Outfile: text;
        Root: TreePtr);
begin
 if Root <> nil then begin
   if Root^.Data in ['T', 'F'] then begin
     write(Outfile, Root^.Data);
     end
   else begin
     write(Outfile, '(');
     if Root^.Data <> '~' then begin
       PrintExpression(Outfile, Root^.Left);
       end; (* If *)
     write(Outfile, Root^.Data);
     PrintExpression(Outfile, Root^.Right);
     write(Outfile, ')');
     end; (* If *)
   end; (* If *)
end; (* PrintExpression *)
```

(d)
```
function Eval (Root: TreePtr): boolean;
begin
 if (Root^.Left = nil) and (Root^.Right = nil) then begin
   Eval := Root^.Data = 'T';
   end
 else begin
   case Root^.Data of
    '^':
     Eval := Eval(Root^.Left) and Eval(Root^.Right);
    'V':
```

```
              Eval := Eval(Root^.Left) or  Eval(Root^.Right);
            '~':
              Eval := not Eval(Root^.Right);
          end; (* Case *)
        end; (* If *)
      end; (* Eval *)
```

CHAPTER 6

Self Check Exercises
Section 6.2

1. Some other factors that influence running time:
   (a) the particular input to the program
   (b) the quality of code generated by the compiler
   (c) speed of the instructions on the machine used to execute the program
   Some reasons to ignore growth rate:
   (a) If the program is to be run only a few times, then the cost of development will dominate all costs.
   (b) If the program is to be run only on "small" inputs, then some constant overhead factors may dominate the running time.
   (c) Efficient algorithms may require too much space.
   (d) Complicated but efficient algorithms may be too costly to maintain.

2. (a) Parameter (n): Number of elements on the list. Complexity Class: O(n).
   (b) Parameter (n): Number of elements in the tree. Complexity Class: O(n).
   (c) Parameter (n): Number of elements in the list Complexity Class: O(n).
   (d) Parameter (n): Number of elements in the tree. Complexity Class: O(log n) (assuming a balanced tree).
   (e) Parameter (n): Number of stars to output. Complexity Class: O(n).

Section 6.3

1. If the data aren't sorted, then you can't make any assumptions about the position of the desired number relative to a number in the array. You thus lose the ability to eliminate half of the remaining elements on each iteration of the loop.

2. (a) Since the 8 is the middle element, it is found immediately.

(b)

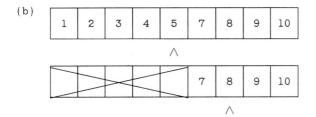

(c)

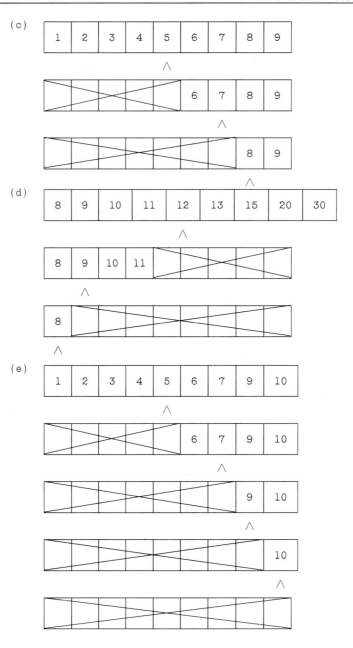

(d)

(e)

Section 6.4

1. $O(n \log n)$

2. $O(n)$

3. (a) $T(1) = c_1$
   $$T(n) = T(n/3) + c_2$$
   (b) $T(n) = T(n/3) + c_2$
   $$= T(n/9) + 2c_2$$
   $$= T(n/27) + 3c_2$$
   $$= T(n/3^i) + ic_2$$

   We want $n/3^i = 1$, so choose $i = \log_3 n$

   $$T(n) = T(1) + (\log_3 n)c_2$$
   $$= c_1 + (\log_3 n)c_2$$

   (c) $O(\log n)$

4. (a)
   $$T(1) = c_1$$
   $$T(n) = T(n-1) + c_2 n$$

   (b)
   $$T(n) = T(n-1) + c_2 n$$
   $$= T(n-2) + 2c_2 n - c_2$$
   $$= T(n-3) + 3c_2 n - 3c_2$$
   $$= T(n-4) + 4c_2 n - 6c_2$$
   $$= T(n-i) + ic_2 n - (i^2 - i)/2c_2$$

   We want $n - i = 1$ so choose $i = n - 1$

   $$T(n) = T(1) + (n-1)c_2 n - (n^2 - 3n + 2)/2c_2$$
   $$= c_1 + n^2 c_2 - nc_2 - (n^2 - 3n + 2)/2c_2$$

   (c) $O(n^2)$

Section 6.5

1. (a) (5, 13, 8, 1, 4, 6)
   (1, 13, 8, 5, 4, 6)
   (1, 4, 8, 5, 13, 6)
   (1, 4, 5, 8, 13, 6)
   (1, 4, 5, 6, 13, 8)
   (1, 4, 5, 6, 8, 13)

(b)
```
                          (5,  13,  8,  1,  4,  6)
                        /       /  \           \
                      (5,  13,  8)      (1,  4,  6)
                     /    /    \      /    /    \
                   (5,  13)   (8)  (1,  4)        (6)
                  /      \      / /       \           /
                (5)      (13)  / (1)        (4)      /
                  \      /   /      \      /        /
                 (5,  13)   /       (1,  4)        /
                     \     /            \         /
                    (5,  8,  13)          (1,  4,  6)
                        \                    /
                      (1,  4,  5,  6,  8,  13)
```

(c)
```
                          (5,  13,  8,  1,  4,  6)
                        /     /          \       \
                      (1,  4)    5      (8,  13,  6)
                     /      \          /       \
                   ()    1  (4)      (6)    8  (13)
                        / \   / \          / \
                      () 4 ()() 6 ()    () 13 ()
                        \  /  \  /         \    /
                        (4)   (6)          (13)
                         /       \          /
                  (1,  4)          (6,  8,  13)
                      \                    /
                    (1,  4,  5,  6,  8,  13)
```

2. The speed increase occurs because the current method requires that each call on *Merge* allocate space for this temporary every time *Merge* is called. Accessing this array nonlocally would eliminate this costly overhead associated with each call on *Merge*.

3. In this case, one recursive call sorts an empty list, while the other sorts a list of size $n - 1$, and we get the following recurrence relation:

$$T(0) = c_1$$
$$T(n) = T(0) + T(n - 1) + c_2 n = T(n - 1) + c_2 n + c_1$$

Solving this you get:

$$
\begin{aligned}
T(n) &= T(n - 1) + c_2 n + c_1 \\
&= T(n - 2) + (2n - 1)c_2 + 2c_1 \\
&= T(n - 3) + (3n - 3)c_2 + 3c_1 \\
&= T(n - 4) + (4n - 6)c_2 + 4c_1 \\
&= T(n - i) + [in - (i(i - 1)/2)]c_2 + ic_1
\end{aligned}
$$

Since you want $T(n)$ in terms of $T(0)$, set $i = n \rightarrow$

$$T(n) = T(0) + [(n)(n) - [(n)(n-1)/2]]c_2 + (n)c_1$$
$$= (n+1)c_1 + [n^2 - (n^2+n)/2]c_2$$
$$= (n+1)c_1 + [(n^2-n)/2]c_2$$

which is $O(n^2)$.

4. Partitioning is $O(n)$ because it traverses the list exactly once, and thus the growth rate of its running time is proportional to the number of elements in the list.

Section 6.6

1.

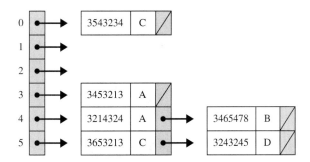

2. The problems with the strategy of just scanning for the next free element is that items will tend to clump together. A collision causes a new element to be occupied, thereby increasing the likelihood of more collisions. Further, if the data are related and the hash function tends to clump related data together, this problem will compound itself. Other rehash schemes involve scanning a number of elements ahead rather than scanning consecutive elements, which presumably will result in less clumping. In actuality, though, this leads to the same clumping problem. More complicated methods involve using "random," but reproducible, numbers to compute the next index.

3. The only limit on the number of items that can be stored using open hashing is the amount of space allocated by the system for dynamic variable allocation, which is generally quite large. For closed hashing, though, the number of elements that can be stored is equal to the number of elements in the array.

Programming Exercises

1. ```
procedure Merge (var First, Second, Sorted: ListPtr);
begin
```
```

```
          if First = nil then begin
            Sorted := Second;
            Second := nil;
           end
          else if Second = nil then begin
            Sorted := First;
            First := nil;
           end
          else begin
             if First^.Data < Second^.Data then begin
               Sorted := First;
               First := First^.Next;
              end
             else begin
               Sorted := Second;
               Second := Second^.Next;
              end; (* If *)
             Merge(First, Second, Sorted^.Next);
           end; (* If *)
      end; (* Merge *)


      procedure GetSubLists (var List, List1, List2: ListPtr);
      begin
       List1 := List;
       List2 := List;
       while (List2 <> nil) do begin
          List2 := List2^.Next;
          if List2 <> nil then begin
            List2 := List2^.Next;
            if List2 <> nil then begin
              List1 := List1^.Next;
             end; (* If *)
           end; (* If *)
        end; (* While *)


       List2 := List1^.Next;
       List1^.Next := nil;
       List1 := List;
       List := nil;
      end; (* GetSubLists *)


      procedure Mergesort (var List: ListPtr);
       var
        LIST1, LIST2: ListPtr;
      begin
       if List <> nil then begin
          if List^.Next <> nil then begin
            GetSubLists(List, LIST1, LIST2);
            Mergesort(LIST1);
            Mergesort(LIST2);
            Merge(LIST1, LIST2, List);
           end; (* If *)
```

```
      end; (* If *)
   end; (* Mergesort *)



3. procedure Partition (var FullQueue, QLessEq, QGreater: Queue.Typ;
         Pivot: integer);
   var
    NUM: integer;
   begin
    Queue.Create(QLessEq);
    Queue.Create(QGreater);
    while not Queue.Empty(FullQueue) do begin
      Queue.Dequeue(FullQueue, NUM);
      if NUM <= Pivot then begin
        Queue.Enqueue(QLessEq, NUM);
       end
      else begin
        Queue.Enqueue(QGreater, NUM);
       end; (* If *)
     end; (* While *)
   end; (* Partition *)

   procedure CopyTo (var FromQ, ToQ: Queue.Typ);
    var
     NUM: integer;
   begin
    while not Queue.Empty(FromQ) do begin
      Queue.Dequeue(FromQ, NUM);
      Queue.Enqueue(ToQ, NUM);
     end; (* While *)
   end; (* CopyTo *)

   procedure Combine (var FullQueue, QLessEq, QGreater: Queue.Typ;
         Pivot: integer);
   begin
    CopyTo(QLessEq, FullQueue);
    Queue.Enqueue(FullQueue, Pivot);
    CopyTo(QGreater, FullQueue);
   end; (* Combine *)


   procedure Quicksort (var Q: Queue.Typ);
    var
     QLESSEQ, QGREATER: Queue.Typ;
     PIVOT: integer;
   begin
    if not Queue.Empty(Q) then begin
      Queue.Dequeue(Q, PIVOT);
      Partition(Q, QLESSEQ, QGREATER, PIVOT);
      Quicksort(QLESSEQ);
      Quicksort(QGREATER);
      Combine(Q, QLESSEQ, QGREATER, PIVOT);
     end; (* If *)
   end; (* Quicksort *)
```

CHAPTER 7

Self Check Exercises
Section 7.1

1. One method would be to number each of the weights, yielding a "weight #1", "weight #2", etc. You would then add a parameter to the *AddWeightedEdge* and *GetWeight* routines specifying the weight to which you are referring. You would also add a *RemoveWeight* operation that would allow you to remove one of the weights without removing the entire edge.

2. Rather than just storing an integer for each connection, you would instead use a boolean to determine whether or not there is a connection, along with an integer weight value. This yields the following data structure:

```
const
 MaxNodes = 40;

type
 ConnectRec = record
   IsConnection: boolean;
   Weight: integer;
  end; (* ConnectRec *)
 ConnectArray = array[1..MaxNodes] of ConnectRec;
 NodeRec = record
   LastConnection: integer;
   MarkVal: integer;
   Connections: ConnectArray;
  end; (* NodeRec *)
 NodeArray = array[1..MaxNodes] of NodeRec;
 Typ = record
   NumNodes: integer;
   Nodes: NodeArray;
  end; (* Typ *)
```

Section 7.2

1. The recursive version processes each node's neighbors in the order returned by the *Graph.Neighbors* routine. The Stack version adds these nodes to a Stack, and thereby reverses their order.

2. It must be local because each recursive call represents a node in the graph. Since each node has its own list of neighbors, making this variable local to the procedure allows each node to maintain its neighbor list while other calls are being processed.

3. The problem is that vector multiplication involves summing up values, and negative weights lead to the possibility that a sum will be zero, which in the array implementation of the Graph ADT would remove the edge.

4. First, the minimal cost-spanning tree must span the entire graph, and this method of selecting the edges for the spanning tree would not, in a directed graph, ensure that every node was reachable. In an undirected graph, this

method will not necessarily yield the minimal value, since it doesn't take into account that edges are two-way, and it may thus lead to redundant edges.

Programming Exercises

1.
```
procedure ArchiveGraph (var Outfile: text;
        var G: Graph.Typ);
  var
   I, J: integer;
  begin
   for I := 1 to Graph.NumNodesWithEdges(G) do begin
     for J := 1 to Graph.NumNodesWithEdges(G) do begin
       if Graph.ConnectionExists(G, I, J) then begin
         writeln(Outfile, I, J,
                 Graph.GetWeight(G, I, J));
       end; (* If *)
     end; (* For *)
   end; (* For *)
  end; (* ArchiveGraph *)

procedure RestoreGraph (var Infile: text;
        var G: Graph.Typ);
  var
   NODE1, NODE2, WEIGHT: integer;
  begin
   while not eof(Infile) do begin
     readln(Infile, NODE1, NODE2, WEIGHT);
     Graph.AddWeightedEdge(G, NODE1, NODE2, WEIGHT);
   end; (* While *)
  end; (* RestoreGraph *)
```

3. Replace the call on *Graph.Neighbors* in the *PrintChildren* with a call on *DepthFirstTrav*. Everything else can remain the same.

APPENDIX

III

PROGRAMMING STYLE

Although a program that doesn't work properly is not very useful, a program whose code is unreadable if often just as useless. This is because most programs are either *long*, in which case the programmer will need to be able to understand the code, or they are used, modified, and maintained by others, in which case a poorly written program will soon become a discarded program. For this reason, it is important that your programs are both well-structured and presented using clear and readable style. The following are some specific items that combine to create a program's style:

1. A *consistent* use of capitalization to make clear the different parts of your program, such as keywords, local variables, constants, parameters, and so on. In this text standard Pascal identifiers are put in lowercase, important user-defined identifiers, such as global constants, types, and variables, and procedure and function names, have their first letter capitalized (along with the first letter of every word in multiword identifiers), and local variables are fully capitalized.

2. A *consistent* indentation scheme to show the levels of control.

3. Good use of constants (as a rule of thumb, any number besides −1, 0, and 1 should be declared as a constant).

4. Use of meaningful identifier names.

5. Generous use of "white space" to separate important parts of the program (such as procedures).

6. Well-written comments that make clear the important parts of the code.

   (a) Program, procedure, and function headings.

(b) Important variables and constants.

(c) Complicated code.

Further, once you have decided on your style of presentation, you should make sure you consistently apply that style, both within a program and across programs. Being consistent makes it likely that both you and maintainers of your code will be able to easily read your programs.

Below is the indentation scheme used in this book.

ITERATIVE CONSTRUCTIONS

```
for -------- do begin
   ----;
   ----;
   ----;
 end; (* For *)

while -------- do begin
   ----;
   ----;
   ----;
 end; (* While *)

repeat
   ----;
   ----;
   ----;
 until ------;
```

CONDITIONAL CONSTRUCTIONS

• One-way conditions

```
if ------- then begin
   ----;
   ----;
   ----;
 end; (* If *)
```

• Two-way conditions

```
if ------- then begin
   ----;
   ----;
   ----;
  end
```

```
else begin
  ----;
  ----;
  ----;
 end; (* If *)
```

- Multi-way conditions

```
if ------- then begin
  ----;
  ----;
  ----;
 end
else if ------- then begin
  ----;
  ----;
  ----;
 end
else if ------- then begin
  ----;
  ----;
  ----;
 end
else begin
  ----;
  ----;
  ----;
end; (* If *)

case ------- of
 [label]:
  ----;
 [label]:
  ----;
 [label]:
  ----;
end; (* Case *)
```

MISCELLANEOUS CONSTRUCTIONS

```
with ------- do begin
  ----;
  ----;
  ----;
 end; (* With *)
```

PROCEDURE, FUNCTION, AND PROGRAM CONSTRUCTIONS

The form of each of these is the same, substituting *function* or *procedure* for *program* below.

```
program --- (---);

const
----;
----;
----;
----;

type
----;
----;
----;
----;

var
----;
----;
----;
----;
begin
----;
----;
----;
end. (* name of this thing. *)
```

Notice that we always put in the *begins* and *ends*. This has two advantages. First, it often occurs that a construct that you originally thought would not need a *begin-end* block eventually will need one. By always putting them in, you avoid having to reindent large amounts of code later. Second, placement of semicolons becomes easy. You always put a semicolon at the end of a line, unless that line ends with a *begin*.

INDEX